Building Early Modern Edinburgh

Building Early Modern Edinburgh

A Social History of Craftwork and Incorporation

Aaron Allen

EDINBURGH
University Press

Edinburgh University Press is one of the leading university presses in the UK. We publish academic books and journals in our selected subject areas across the humanities and social sciences, combining cutting-edge scholarship with high editorial and production values to produce academic works of lasting importance. For more information visit our website: edinburghuniversitypress.com

Edinburgh University Press Ltd
The Tun – Holyrood Road
12 (2f) Jackson's Entry
Edinburgh EH8 8PJ

First published in hardback by Edinburgh University Press 2018

Typeset in 10.5/13 Sabon by
Servis Filmsetting Ltd, Stockport, Cheshire,
and printed and bound by CPI Group (UK) Ltd, Croydon, CR0 4YY

A CIP record for this book is available from the British Library

ISBN 978 1 4744 4238 1 (hardback)
ISBN 978 1 4744 4239 8 (paperback)
ISBN 978 1 4744 4240 4 (webready PDF)
ISBN 978 1 4744 4241 1 (epub)

Contents

Tables

Illustrations

Abbreviations

DSL	Dictionary of the Scots Language, available online at: http://www.dsl.ac.uk/
ECA	Edinburgh City Archives
Edin. Burgs	*Roll of Edinburgh Burgesses and Guild-Brethren*, 2 vols: 1406–1700; 1701–1760, ed. C. B. B. Watson (SRS, 1929; 1930)
Edin. Recs	*Extracts From the Records of the Burgh of Edinburgh*, 13 vols, eds J. D. Marwick et al. (SBRS & Edinburgh, 1869–1967)
ELCALHS	East Lothian Council Archive and Local History Service, John Gray Centre
ER	*The Exchequer Rolls of Scotland*, 23 vols, eds J. Stuart et al. (Edinburgh, 1878–1908)
General Report, 1835	Greenshields, J. B., *General Report of the Commissioners Appointed to Inquire into the State of Municipal Incorporations in Scotland* (London: His Majesty's Stationery Office, 1835)
Knox, *History*	John Knox, *History of the Reformation in Scotland*, 2 vols., ed. W.C. Dickinson (Edinburgh, 1949)
Mill, 'Inventory'	ECA, SL12/236, A. J. Mill, 'Rough Inventory of Records Belonging to the Wrights and Masons of Edinburgh' (1923)
Mill Recs	ECA, Mill Records, A1-A46 and B1-B6 (Mary's Chapel Papers, 1475–1678). 'A': Charters and Documents, and 'B': Minute Books. See also Mill, 'Inventory' for details of A and B groups.
Minute Books	ECA, SL34/1/1-14, Minute Books 1669–1755 and 1842–1910 and Acc.622/1-8 & 73, Minute Books 1755–1842 and 1910–47
MWA	*Accounts of the Masters of Works*, 2 vols, eds H. M. Paton et al. (Edinburgh, 1957–82)
NLS	National Library of Scotland
RMS	*Registrum Magni Sigilli Regum Scotorum (Register*

	of the Great Seal of Scotland), 11 vols, eds J. M. Thomson et al. (Edinburgh, 1882–1984)
RPC	*Register of the Privy Council of Scotland*, 38 vols, eds J. H. Burton et al. (Edinburgh, 1877–2009)
RPS	*The Records of the Parliaments of Scotland to 1707*, K. M. Brown et al. eds (St Andrews, 2007–15), http://www.rps.ac.uk
RSS	*Registrum Secreti Sigilli Regum Scotorum* (*Register of the Privy Seal of Scotland*), 8 vols, eds M. Livingstone et al. (Edinburgh, 1908–82)
SBRS	Scottish Burgh Records Society
Scots Peerage	J. Balfour Paul (ed.), *The Scots Peerage*, 9 vols (Edinburgh, 1904–14)
SHS	Scottish History Society
SRS	Scottish Record Society
TA	*Accounts of the (Lord High) Treasurer of Scotland*, 13 vols, eds T. Dickson et al. (Edinburgh, 1877–1978)

Foreword to the History of the United Incorporations of St Mary's Chapel of Edinburgh

Little did I think when elected to the Incorporations in 1972 that I would be asked to perform this pleasant task by our author Dr Aaron Allen. First a few words about us. We were formed as an organisation on 15 October 1475 by Seal of Cause, and consisted solely of Masons and Wrights although other trades were added later, with the objective being to provide a controlled standard of service and execution of work, together with welfare to members and their families and aid to the Convenery of Trades of Edinburgh. Laws were formulated and revised from time to time, a major revision taking place on 18 September 1778, with others following, particularly in 1923, 1957 and 2001. These of course had to be ratified by the Court of Session.

The Incorporations expanded greatly in the early nineteenth century when 105 new tradesmen were admitted, and this would have been required to aid in the construction of the New Town. Their coffers too would have increased and the power exercised allowed their Deacon (Chairman) when Convener of Trades to be an unelected member of the City Council. They had become a very powerful and rich body.

Over the last century the original objectives have virtually ceased, the number of members much reduced, but recently there has been a revival of interest in the history and pageantry of the City. The Incorporations have rightly been able to join in this, under the leadership of recent Deacon Conveners. My family have been involved for at least 200 years when my great grandfather was Deacon, followed by his sons towards the end of the nineteenth century, who both became Deacon Conveners. An uncle and cousins followed later with myself in 1972 and my son as a member in 1996. Possibly a grandson will follow.

I considered it would be a good idea to explore the history of the United Incorporations and to commit it to paper or some other medium. Accordingly, I mooted the idea in 2009 and it was agreed that a report and a cost estimate for such a work would be produced. This information was available in 2012 and here I must record my indebtedness, as must all of us, to Professor Michael Lynch, lately professor of Scottish History at Edinburgh University, who set us on the correct path with his sage advice.

On 11 May 2015 a report was submitted to the AGM of the Incorporations and it was agreed without exception that the history should proceed and funds were set aside to cover the cost. At the same time I was authorised to proceed with the arrangements. Professor Lynch had suggested Dr Aaron Allen as a suitably skilled researcher and this was agreed through the Department of Development and Alumni and Professor Cameron, now Head of the School of History, Classics and Archaeology at Edinburgh University.

It is usual in a foreword to comment on those who have been involved and it gives me the greatest pleasure to do so now. First to thank Professor Lynch, who set us on the right road, and to Professor Cameron, who kept us there. We must not forget James Jones of Development and Alumni, who set things up, and his successor Emma Lacroix, who brought everything to fruition. Our thanks are due to them for their diligence and understanding of our requirements.

Work has proceeded over the last three years with the draft chapters submitted to me on schedule. Dr Allen has shown the greatest interest in this history and in so doing has kept me informed monthly of progress. We are indebted to Dr Allen and our thanks are recorded here. His efforts are commended to you as another chapter recording the history of our great City.

H. Bruce Field
Deacon of Masons (2002–16)
Golspie
March 2017

Preface
The Mary's Chapel Project

When in 1999 I first visited Edinburgh, I was immediately impressed by the stone architecture. Coming from a forested area in theUpper Peninsula of Michigan, the vernacular tradition I was used to relied predominantly on timber. Seeing the elegant Georgian tenements, or the seventeenth-century ashlar frontages of Mylne's Court and Gladstone's Land, left an abiding impression of a stone-built capital; one in which even the architecture reminded the visitor of the nation's accomplished and lasting history. Indeed, this impression had been vindicated four years earlier in 1995, when UNESCO bestowed 'World Heritage Site' status upon Edinburgh, recognising the value of the surviving stone monuments to the wider global community, and the importance of preserving them for future generations. The buildings of the Old Town are indeed precious, with examples of fabric from at least the twelfth century surviving today. But what about the builders of this impressive townscape? One way of looking at early modern Edinburgh is to see two specific groups: the consumers and the producers. The diverse inhabitants of all types and ranks were the consumers of the buildings, but as for the builders – it was their ingenuity, creativity and skill that produced the urban fabric UNESCO recognised as being so very important to the coming generations; yet so little work has been done on this important group.

While several of the buildings or parts of buildings from the medieval and early modern period survive, the great majority have either been replaced or updated with 'modern' façades. It is therefore a very interesting problem trying to reconstruct the lost cityscape of the early modern capital. Similarly, the builders are naturally all gone, yet the sources are fairly strong for resurrecting both buildings and builders. This study, while concerned in part with both buildings and builders, will instead focus on a particular institution which had an impact on both – the Incorporation of Mary's Chapel.

Despite increasing scholarly interest in Edinburgh's role as a European capital city, there is still much work to be done on the socio-economic institutions of this important royal burgh. Indeed, most of the recent work touching on the builders of the city has focussed more on the architects than on the corporate and municipal structures which governed their work. This book seeks to redress this imbalance by exploring the Incorporation of Mary's Chapel, which was the legal body set up in 1475 to oversee the workers of wood and stone.

There are numerous people I would like to thank for their support for this project. Firstly, I am grateful to Deacon Bruce Field and the Incorporation of Mary's Chapel who gave me the opportunity to undertake this research. It was Deacon Field who originally thought of the project, and it was only through the Incorporation's provision of funding through Development and Alumni at the University of Edinburgh that the Mary's Chapel Project was able to proceed. This began with an archives scoping exercise in 2014, which produced both a published article in *Scottish Archives*, and a forthcoming article in a special edition of *Architectural Heritage* on Anna Jean Mill and what at the time were the missing Mary's Chapel records.[1] It also led to the production of this book from 2015 to 2017. I have enjoyed every minute of the research, and I am grateful for their support. I do hope that my endeavours have produced something worthy of their institution.

At the University of Edinburgh, I would like to thank Professor Ewen Cameron, who patiently supervised my research fellowship and gave feedback on my writing, despite the considerable demands on his time in his role as Head of the School of History, Classics and Archaeology. I've benefitted greatly from his feedback, and I am grateful to him. Mr James Jones and Ms Emma Lacroix of Development and Alumni were most helpful in facilitating the project, and Edinburgh University kindly allowed me to change the terms of my existing teaching fellowship to accommodate time for the Mary's Chapel Project.

It is my understanding that it was Professor Emeritus Michael Lynch who first suggested that I should undertake the research on Mary's Chapel. Since completing my PhD research under the guidance of both Professor Lynch and Dr Pat Dennison, they have been a constant source of support and encouragement, and I owe them both so very much. Many of the topics covered in this study of Mary's Chapel are due to the interests they sparked in me as a postgraduate student, and I am truly blessed to have studied with them.

I also owe a great debt to numerous colleagues at the University of Edinburgh with whom I had many helpful and enjoyable conversations about craftwork. These include Professor Stana Nenadic, Dr Keren Protheroe, Professor Richard Rodger, Professor Martin Chick, Professor Steve Boardman, Dr Julian Goodare, Dr Trevor Griffiths, Professor Nuala Zahedieh, Professor Louise Jackson, Dr Cordelia Beattie, Dr Alasdair Raffe, Dr Felix Boecking, Dr Gayle Davis, Dr Zubin Mistry, Dr Paul

Kosmetatos, Professor Adam Fox, Dr Donncha O'Rourke, Dr Ben Russell, Dr Thomas Ahnert, Dr David Rosenthal and Dr Tanja Romankiewicz. Again, I am very blessed to work alongside them, and my work has benefitted greatly from our conversations.

Likewise, I have benefitted from conversations with colleagues at other institutions. I had the opportunity to give a paper from this book at the University of Dundee, where Dr Chris Storrs, Dr Alan MacDonald, Dr Alan Kennedy, Dr Pat Whatley and Professor Graeme Morton all made me feel most welcome with a very helpful discussion of the findings. Indeed, Dr MacDonald not only gave helpful feedback, but also kept me from disaster by spotting a mistake in my tables – two weeks before the submission of the typescript to the publishers. Dr Tawny Paul shared valuable transcriptions of petitions, and discussed the wider context of craftwork with me. Dr Cathryn Spence, Professor David Stevenson and Sue Mowat all discussed the project with me and offered helpful advice at several points. Henry Fothringham shared his encyclopaedic knowledge of Edinburgh's incorporated trades, as well as several articles he'd written and data on craft deacons. His transcriptions of the convenery minutes were absolutely indispensable, and I owe him a huge debt.

Dr Michael Pearce has been especially helpful, by sharing notes on Perth Wrights' minutes, and guiding me through the rather difficult jargon of sixteenth-century furniture. We are also currently working on a complete transcription of the five 'missing' minute books in amongst the Mill records found in the Edinburgh City Archives.[2] I have greatly enjoyed our conversations, which have made a strong contribution to the pages that follow.

The staff of the Edinburgh City Archives, including the former Edinburgh City Archivist Richard Hunter, as well as the current staff, Henry Sullivan, Brenda Connoboy, Peter Clapham, Vikki Kerr, and Jennifer Hogg, have been absolutely fantastic in their help and patience with my enquiries. Their repository holds untold treasures, and the city should be very proud of its archives staff. I am indebted to them.

Numerous specialists helped me to understand the wider building industry and the technical details associated with the building trades. The masons of Land Engineering gave myself and several colleagues a tour of the scaffold during the restoration work on McEwen Hall, while the firm Remus helpfully explained the processes and tools associated with upholstery. Many other tradesmen patiently answered questions on how their tools work, or what knowledge one would need to be able to undertake their jobs. Many even allowed me to 'have a go'. This gave valuable opportunities to cut and hole slates, hew stone, and generate more scrap wood than I would like to admit! Mr Peter Swinson explained aspects of health and safety in the building industry today, and Dr Stephen Jackson of the National Museum of Scotland offered guidance on furniture and suggested valuable sources for the project. Lewis Young, Ian Robertson, and Alan Dickson all helped me understand various aspects of the relationship between Freemasonry and stonemasonry.

There are also many people outside of Edinburgh who have shown an interest in the project. Thanks are given to Mrs Nancy Besonen from my home town in Michigan for writing an article for the *L'Anse Sentinel* on the Mary's Chapel Project when I uncovered the lost Mill records.[3] Thanks are also given to Allison Cunningham and Caroline Sutherland of Ayrshire Archives for their help in accessing the minutes of the Ayr Squaremen. Ms Laura Field and Dr Catriona Ellis both helped with data collection for the masons and glassinwrights. Also, Dr David Motadel, Dr Paul Horsler, and the helpful staff at the London School of Economics and Political Science Library, went out of their way to assist in finding a rare newspaper clipping on the 1764 journeymen strikes in Edinburgh. This made a huge contribution to the final chapter, and I am grateful for their help.

Finally, and perhaps most importantly, those closest to me have made this project possible, and I cannot thank them enough. My God blessed me with the opportunity, while my family on both sides of the Atlantic encouraged me in this endeavour. In particular, my wife Joanna and sons, Jack and Theo, were a constant support. They patiently put up with my ranting about how sieves were made, and even humoured me with conversations about craft altars and endogamous marriage patterns. My sons even helped me take up woodworking, so that I could better understand what the men and women who worked in the building trades knew. I am grateful to all of them, and this project could not have happened without their support.

NOTES

1. Allen, A., 'Finding the Builders: Sources Lost and Extant for Edinburgh's Incorporation of Mary's Chapel', in *Scottish Archives: The Journal of the Scottish Records Association*, 20 (2014); and Allen, A., 'The Missing Records of the Edinburgh Building Trades: Mill's 'Rough Inventory' and the Incorporation of Mary's Chapel', in *Architectural Heritage* (Forthcoming: 2018). The latter will be a special edition of papers from the 2015 conference at the University of Edinburgh: 'The Architecture of Scotland in its European Setting: 1660–1750'.
2. ECA, Mill Recs, B1–B5.
3. Besonen, N., 'Allen Helps Unearth Treasure Trove in Scotland', in *L'Anse Sentinel*, (L'Anse, Michigan, 16 March 2016), 7.

To the memory of
Rev. William E. Allen,
who taught me to say:

'I will fetch my knowledge from afar,
and will ascribe righteousness
to my Maker.' Job 36:3

Introduction
Incorporation and the Corporate Framework

For as we have many members in one body,
and all members have not one office, So we
being many, are one body in Christ, and
every one, one another's members.

1599 Geneva Bible, Romans 12: 4–5

This book is intended to be a social history of an important institution of the Scottish capital – the Edinburgh 'Incorporation of Mary's Chapel'. This composite body of ten different arts sought to control the building trades in the town from its foundation in 1475 until the abolition of 'exclusive privileges of work' in 1846. Despite the vicissitudes of nineteenth-century reforms, the Incorporation still survives today and continues to contribute to the culture and heritage of the UNESCO World Heritage Site which it helped to build.

As an incorporated trade, or 'craft guild' to use the modern shorthand found in the wider European historiography, the crafts held a considerable amount of power in Edinburgh, though as we shall see there were numerous challenges to their claim of exclusive rights. Practically, the Incorporation represented only a certain rank of master craftsman. This excluded the great majority of unfree servants, journeymen and labourers who worked for them, when allowed, as well as the many wives, widows and daughters who also laboured beside them. Although the overall population of the building trades was therefore far larger than the privileged oligarchy of masters which sought to control them, this will not be a book about the builder in general. Instead it will focus on the corporate entity that attempted to control both the labour market and the building sites within the jurisdiction of their royal burgh and its suburbs. These legal privileges were always contested, and by the seventeenth century were increasingly difficult to enforce. Still, the Incorporation continued to hold influence in burgh affairs long after its trade-regulatory privileges were removed.

This remarkable survival is strikingly counterintuitive when one considers the composite nature of this group of trades; a feature of Scottish corporatism which is markedly different from that of many other cities in early modern Europe. The Incorporation of Mary's Chapel was not composed of a single trade, but instead it incorporated ten distinct and highly-unequal arts, which vied for control of the Incorporation. Because of their composite nature, one could argue that the Incorporation of Mary's Chapel had greater need for unity. If divided, they were less able to protect their members' privileged position in the complex society of a growing European capital. This prompts the central question of this study: as a composite craft, faced with competition from within and without, how did the Incorporation build and maintain unity amongst its members?

As will be demonstrated in the following chapters, to achieve this they focussed on building a suitable identity. They avoided conflict by taking on a corporate name which did not show favouritism to any one of the ten arts. 'Mary's Chapel' was not 'Masons' or 'Wrights'. They also began referring to themselves in their minutes as 'the House', as they sought to model themselves on two other composite institutions: the family and the wider household. These were the very building blocks of a stable, godly society, despite the inherent challenges of bringing together different individuals with potentially-conflicting agendas into one corporate unit. By looking to the household, they found a model which included both the privileged kinship group, along with outsiders allowed to be co-resident. To the master, mistress and children were added the servants, while to the masons and wrights were added not only the other eight trades, but also the journeymen, apprentices and tolerated stallangers.

Of course, there were also many who remained outside the House. Municipal authorities and influential customers complicated the questions of autonomy and control, while demographic growth within and without the town increased the number of unfree challengers in the labour market. The very idea that the Incorporation was a household implied legitimacy for the few within, and illegitimacy for those without, but as any observer would surely have noticed, the family unit rarely survived intact. Death, remarriage, growth to adulthood and the leaving of the parental household all pointed to the complicated nature of the household, raising questions about just how stable it really was as an institution. Likewise, the Incorporation was also complicated, and building unity was therefore a central strategy for its survival. By using untouched, recently-rediscovered archival materials to look at this 'House' which sought to control the building trades, it is hoped that this monograph will make a contribution to our understanding of the complicated institution of composite corporatism. To begin, we must first consider the context of corporate work.

CONTEXT OF CORPORATISM

Guilds

Guilds were associations of people which came together to pursue some common purpose. They were 'friendly societies' with religious, economic, and political overtones, and a means for the imposition of organisation and order upon medieval and early modern society.[1] Though sources for the early history of guilds in Europe are often difficult to find, by the later medieval period we increasingly see legal status granted to these groups, with a corresponding growth in the frequency of guild statutes.[2] This is all a crucial part of a wider system of social organisation which historians refer to as 'corporatism', implying the coalescing of groups in the pursuit of common rights and privileges, to the explicit exclusion of outsiders.[3] As Farr eloquently summarises:

> Confraternities and guilds of merchants and craftsmen predated the corporate regime, but corporate theory of the fourteenth century joined hands with demographic and economic forces to formalize a political and juridical system that would last into the nineteenth century.[4]

Hence corporatism provides the context for the craft guild which was so common across the continent of Europe; a legal entity with claims to exclusive privileges and fraternal security.

Corporatism in the form of the craft guild was indeed common, though it was not necessarily unvaried. Despite their variations, the aspect of corporatism that universally translates is the idea of fraternity, or brotherhood. In England and in the English colonies they were usually called 'companies', while in France they were '*corps*'. Both terms clearly imply solidarity. Naturally there were limits to how unified such groups really were, and membership was, of course, restricted. Still, the phenomenon of the corporate body of crafts mirrored the wider corporate body of the burgh itself; an urban society metaphorically explained as being the body of Christ: the *Corpus Christianum*.[5] Such images of unity were not always the reality.

In Scotland the craft guild was not called a 'guild', but instead an 'incorporated trade', as the term guild was specifically reserved for the predominantly-merchant body of importers and exporters. Indeed, for the first century of corporatism in Scotland, the stereotypical theme in the historiography tends to be conflict between the merchants of the guilds and the craftsmen of the incorporated trades, rightly or wrongly.[6] Hence, 'craft guild' is indeed a convenient shorthand for the historian, though technically it is inaccurate in a Scottish context. In Edinburgh, the incorporation for the building trades was first called the 'Incorporation of Masons and Wrights', and later the 'Incorporation of Mary's Chapel'.[7]

Composite Corporatism

Terminology and structure varied across Europe's regional examples of corporatism, from nation to nation, and city to city as well. Scotland, whose largest settlement, Edinburgh, had only about 20 to 25,000 people in 1635,[8] did not usually have large enough markets to sustain large, autonomous crafts. In addition to this, political access, the threats to privileges and religious observance all encouraged the banding together of similar crafts. Hence the Scottish incorporated trade was most often a composite group of crafts, often having their types of tools and materials in common. For example, many burghs had incorporations of 'hammermen', which included the various metalworking trades, such as founders and blacksmiths. Because they all worked in metal and used hammers, they were incorporated together. In the capital, only the occasional craft grew strong enough to break away from their composite incorporation. The usual model was for roughly similar trades to band together, unlike the numerous companies of London,[9] or corporations of Paris,[10] which both represented much larger markets for the goods and services provided by their crafts. That said, there were exceptions to the size of the market determining corporate structure, as illustrated by the metalworkers and woodworkers of Amsterdam. This city represented a very large market indeed, yet both of these groups of trades were organised as composite craft guilds, just like those in the much smaller settlement of Edinburgh. Indeed, the Amsterdam Guild of St Joseph had ten different woodwork trades, just like Edinburgh's ten trades in the Incorporation of Mary's Chapel, so clearly market size cannot be the only factor.[11] Clearly more work is needed on the phenomenon of the composite corporatism, and this study will hopefully push forward this discourse.

With noted exceptions, due to complex combinations of factors, the composite nature of craft organisation often translated to all but the largest of Europe's urban settlements, where the market economy could sustain relatively homogenous groups of craftsmen large enough and affluent enough to form their own craft guild. Though London usually had separate companies for the various trades,[12] in Edinburgh, very few crafts had their own individual incorporation. The metalworkers of London, such as the Goldsmiths, Pewterers, Blacksmiths, Armourers and Cutlers,[13] were all distinct companies, but in Edinburgh they were all combined into the Incorporation of Hammermen – with the important exception of the elite craft of the Goldsmiths, who broke away from the other metalworkers by the 1520s.[14] The building trades of the two capitals follow a similar pattern, with London having individual companies of Carpenters, Plumbers, and Painters, to name but a few,[15] while in Edinburgh the one Incorporation of Mary's Chapel included ten separate crafts in one corporate body with two deacons.[16]

In Delft in 1611, the Guild of St Lucas included, 'all those earning their living here by the art of painting, be it with fine brushes or otherwise, in oil or watercolours; glassmakers; glass-sellers; faienciers; tapestry-makers; embroiderers; engravers; sculptors working in wood, stone or other substance; scabbard-makers; art-printers; booksellers; sellers of prints and paintings, of whatever kind they may be.'[17] Admittedly, these lean more towards the decorative arts, but there are still parallels with the Edinburgh Incorporation of Mary's Chapel, which included painters, glaziers and upholsterers.

In the phenomenon of the Scottish composite incorporation we see both interesting parallels and divergence between the corporatism of the capital and that of other burghs. Smaller burghs might see the builders joined with other crafts, as with the Kelso Hammermen taking in a maker of wheels, boxes and windows in 1759.[18] In most burghs, the workers in stone and wood were incorporated together at some point. Haddington's Incorporation of Wrights and Masons also included coopers, slaters, and 'others' in 1530.[19] Ayr's Incorporation of Squaremen likewise included multiple trades, as did numerous other examples across Scotland.[20] Dundee's building trades had attempted to unite in both the sixteenth and seventeenth centuries, though it was not until 1741 that they were allowed to incorporate.[21] Perth's building trades not only incorporated, but even included nonrelated trades, such as bookbinders and surgeons.[22]

On the other hand, two of Scotland's larger burghs took a very different approach to organisation of the building trades. Glasgow's building trades were originally incorporated together with the Masons in 1551, though by 1600 the Coopers and Wrights had each been given individual seals of cause, or charters of incorporation, suggesting separation rather than combination.[23] Glasgow's building trades, unlike those of the larger capital, appear to have rejected composite corporatism. Though it is difficult to imagine that they would not have been forced to work together on the building site, the records of the Glasgow convenery of trades demonstrate that relations between the groups were not always cordial.[24] In a similar fashion, Aberdeen's 1532 seal of cause included only the 'Couparis, Wrichts, and Measones', while the 1541 version listed six crafts: masons, wrights, carvers, coopers, slaters and painters, though apparently they also later split.[25] Why the building trades of the larger capital managed to stay together when those of Aberdeen and Glasgow separated is not apparent, but burgh politics and size of markets must factor heavily in the various decisions which brought this situation about. Allowing more incorporations might have meant allowing more craft councillors, diluting the control of the existing burgh oligarchies. The greater economic opportunities of a growing burgh such as Glasgow must have encouraged specialisation and separation of crafts, as seen in larger European cities. How far these applied to Scottish corporatism in general must be left for another study though. Suffice it to say here that composite corporatism, or the joining of similar trades into a single corporate body, was very common in Scotland.

This was for a range of reasons. Occasionally it was the markets that encouraged banding together. Whether sharing a workplace, such as the building site, or sharing access to materials, with the politics of access to limited wood supplies in a heavily-deforested country, competition could make for a compelling argument for incorporation. At times, it was fashion, as with the architectural styles which required so many different trades to be fully realised. Other times it was technology which brought crafts together, as seen by the tools used to symbolise certain incorporations. Hence the symbolic crowned hammer of the 'hammermen' brought together a diverse range of metalworkers, while the builders' square and dividers often acted as a focal point for the building trades (Figure I.1).

The choice of craft symbol is always very interesting, whether looking at the Edinburgh Incorporation of Mary's Chapel, with their use of the square and compass for the Wrights, and compass with three towers for the Masons,[26] or looking at the more humble Elgin Incorporation of Cordiners, with their characteristic half-moon 'shaping knife' under a crown. In a period when the language of allegory was so very important to the way society communicated, the choice of symbols to represent the corporate body has much to tell us about the aspirations, self-image and skills of the craftsmen they represent. What is interesting here, is that the tools the building trades chose are at once both humble and technologically sophisticated.

The Masons and Wrights could have chosen the hewing axe, so crucial to taking purchased raw materials down to usable stock, or they could have chosen the plane, which gave them usable surfaces on their workpieces.

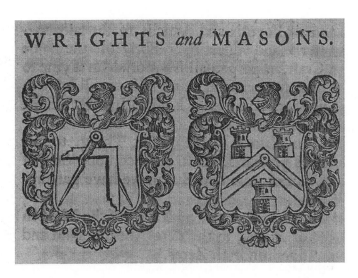

Figure I.1 Craft shields from 1753 showing the arms of the 'Wrights and Masons'
From Maitland's *History*, 301. Note the order of the crafts, as well as the use of the square and dividers. By kind permission of the University of Edinburgh, Special Collections.

Braces, bits, chisels and mallets were all crucial to craftwork, some for cutting, some for transferring the energy of their own muscles to the tools with which they did the work; a distinct element of the pre-modern and pre-industrial craft technology. Yet, the Edinburgh Masons and Wrights chose for themselves and their eight allied trades the simple square and dividers. Why? Moreover, why did other incorporations in smaller burghs follow suit? Glasgow, Aberdeen and Dundee, all used the square and dividers to symbolise their building trades, and in some burghs the trades even adopted the humble tools into their incorporation's name, such as the Ayr 'Squaremen'.[27]

These tools had clear allegorical significance, and acted as unifiers for the individual tradesmen who made up the incorporations. In geometric terms, both compass and dividers bring two separate lines together, in the same way that the Incorporation brought such different groups of craftsmen together. As symbols, they proclaimed publicly the trustworthiness of the building trades, and the soundness of their work and skill. Though not all of the ten member trades of Mary's Chapel used the square, it was in all of their interests to be seen as giving the proverbial 'square deal'. The compass device was even more important, as it firmly stated exactitude and precision, while at the same time reflecting the corporate nature of the trades; this was one incorporation encompassing ten different crafts, and those who had the skills and connections to be members *must* be more trustworthy than those who were not. Of course image often differs from reality, and freedom of the Incorporation was never a meritocracy. Still, it was in the Incorporation's interest to project an image of unity and reliability; to suggest to their customers that along with their legal status and privileges came a monopoly on skill and knowledge, and hence they chose the square and compass to emblazon their 'armorial ensigns'.

For the privileged few, these various factors acted as unifiers, encouraging composite corporatism. While one might expect specialisation to act against composite unity, occasionally it too could act as a unifier, especially when the individual, specialist trade fitted a niche within the wider market which was not already covered by the larger trades within the composite body. For example, although the Incorporation of Mary's Chapel usually tried to exclude unfreemen who might wish to undertake woodwork within the capital, some woodworkers were so specialist in their products that they were simply not seen as a threat to those making timber-framed houses, furniture, or barrels. Hence bowers were incorporated from fairly early on, and 'panton-heal makers', who made the wooden soles for pattens, were allowed in on licence.[28] The Haddington Incorporation granted a similar licence to Ferquhard Anderson to 'mak tirleiss (trellises) mak or mend quhells for spining or spindells to quhells & siclyk thingis' – for a yearly payment of course.[29] Any wright could make a patten or a spinning wheel, but for most tradesmen, there were other products which held their attention.

So, while specialisation occasionally brought crafts apart, as in Glasgow, it could also be a mechanism for bringing unfreemen into the corporate fold. Of course this is the interesting paradox of corporatism. It was at once characterised by both unity and exclusivity, by banding together for common purpose, and by shutting out through special privileges. This corporate structure is the primary context for the Incorporation of Mary's Chapel and therefore of this book. However, corporatism must also have its contexts, and in this case it is naturally feudalism. Corporate privileges stemmed from the authority of the monarch, theoretically vested in the royal-burgh community as tenants-in-chief under no one but the crown. The reality was more complex, with the interests of the three estates complicating the issue of authority through their interference in municipal affairs.

Possibly more important, however, is the impact of feudalism on social relationships, as it implied a certain rigidity within the hierarchical feudal pyramid. The incorporations were indeed feudal, as they held their privileges from the town, which in turn held privileges from the crown. Within the incorporations there was again a hierarchical structure, with deacons, boxmasters, quartermasters, and an officer (Figure I.2) to enforce the will of 'the House'. Even the moniker, 'the House', implies a form of paternal

Figure I.2 'St Mary's Chapel, Officer'
Edinburgh, mid-nineteenth century. ECA, Howie Print 75. By kind permission of City of Edinburgh Council.

hierarchy, a subject which will be explored in the next chapter. But though the trades were indeed hierarchical, and did indeed hold their privileges corporately and from the crown, we should not be so foolish as to assume that this implies unity. As with Cain and Abel, the brothers of Mary's Chapel did not always see eye to eye.

Process of Incorporation

The Two Freedoms: Burgessship and Mastership

The context of corporatism might have resonance across Europe and other parts of the world, but there were subtleties of the Scottish incorporated trade which make comparisons with external examples both difficult and rewarding. In fact, the Edinburgh incorporated trades were not always that similar to those of other Scottish burghs, though a fair bit of copying of the Edinburgh model did take place. For example, while many burghs had only seven or eight incorporated trades, Edinburgh had fourteen.[30] This number was not matched until the seventeenth century, when Glasgow incorporated its fourteenth trade – a foreshadowing of the ambitions that would take the small ecclesiastical burgh to 'Second City of the Empire'. Although Glasgow may have ensured that it too had a convenery of fourteen deacons, it would be wrong to assume that the corporate bodies of the two burghs – or of any two burghs – were wholly identical. Moreover, any two trades within a burgh were often quite distinct. Still, there are some aspects of Scottish corporatism which can be generalised, and the most crucial of these was the need for freedom which, at least in theory, was required to practise a trade.

In 1570 the Edinburgh town council noted that, 'the cheif libertie and fredome of ane fre burgh of royaltie consistes in twa thingis, the ane in using of merchandice, the other in using of craftes.'[31] Merchant commerce and craft production were indeed important aspects of the privileges of the royal burghs, though it is important to underline how limited these privileges were within the populace of any given royal burgh. To enjoy these privileges, one first had to be a freeman, or 'burgess', of the town. It has been suggested that in 1635 only about 30 per cent of householders within the capital were actually burgesses, highlighting how exclusive access was to the rights of trade and manufacture.[32] Although there were other routes, such as paying a form of toll, or 'stallanger fee', allowing temporary access to markets, or simply breaking the law and trading clandestinely as an 'unfreeman', the most important and sought-after route to access was the purchase of freedom from the dean of guild.

Of course the issue of freedom was not quite as simple as this either. First of all, one had to have the monetary resources to be able to afford freedom. Secondly, one had to have access through a connection to the existing oligarchy, either through familial connections, marriage, having served an apprenticeship with a freeman, or through some form of 'gratis' grant of freedom from the council. Purchase without this connection was theoretically possible, for an exorbitant price.[33]

Confusingly, this freedom of the town, or burgesship, was only one of the necessary freedoms for undertaking craftwork. Along with the purchase of burgesship, the craftsman also needed to purchase freedom of the incorporation which regulated their particular craft. Some craftwork remained unincorporated, such as that of the maltsters, but for the incorporated trades one needed both freedom of the town and freedom of the craft. Unfortunately for would-be entrants, becoming a freeman was a very expensive business.

Aside from the cost in time, for example, dedicating the prescribed seven years to an apprenticeship, as well as the usual additional time working for wages as a journeyman, the costs of both burgesship, paid to the dean of guild, and 'upset', paid to the Incorporation, could be quite prohibitive. One had to have considerable funds in order to be allowed into the privileged circle of freemen. In 1564, for example, a former apprentice of a freeman needed £5 for burgesship, while an unfreeman with no connection to the burgess community needed £20.[34] Similar prices can be seen throughout the early modern period, with freemen's sons always having a distinct advantage.[35] By 1647 the prices were raised substantially, with 'strangers', or unfreemen, being expected to pay £160 together with £10 for arms, 'by and attour thair vpsett'.[36] The high prices served to not only perpetuate the oligarchy, giving precedence to those who were connected, but also to help regulate competition within the privileged circle of freemen, ensuring that not too many with connections were allowed in all at once.

Intriguingly, the 1475 seal of cause for the Masons and Wrights doesn't actually mention the need for burgesship. Others do, however. The seal of cause for the Surgeons explicitly states that an incoming craftsman must be made burgess before becoming a master of their Incorporation.[37] Perhaps it was simply assumed to be the norm, and therefore overlooked for the building trades. The Coopers' 1489 seal of cause does not state the need for burgesship either, though it does imply the need for freedom of the town by discussing how unfreemen did not share in civic burdens:

> outlandisfolkis ... hafand nother stob nor stake within this towne, nor yit walkis nor wardis nor yit beris sic portable chargis with tham as extentis and

vtheris quhen thai occur . . . hurtis and scaithis the saidis masteris in thair fredomes and priuilegis contrar to all gud reull ordour and polecy within burgh
. . .[38]

Clearly the need for freedom of the town pertained to the Incorporation,
even if the council did not mention it in the original seal of cause. It was
certainly stated as a requirement a century later, when in 1574 the plough-
wright Adam Whitelaw was accepted as a freeman.[39]

Perhaps the lack of burgesship requirements in the seal of cause was an
oversight; perhaps it was an intentional 'loophole' to ensure ease of finding
labour for the building site. There was a clause to ensure control, through
the inspection of 'sufficiency' of work; a term which often appears in the
early records when denying mastership.[40] Whether intentionally left out
or simply an oversight, the issue of the missing burgesship clause presents
an interesting problem. By 1517 the Incorporation was appealing to the
Archbishop of St Andrews to ratify and reinforce their claim to exclusive
privileges, as he was senior to the Dean of St Giles, the town's collegiate
kirk.[41] Clearly they were intent on enforcing the need for freedom of the
craft.

As inflationary pressures mounted, tensions within the burgh often
boiled over, and at various times craft privileges were ratified, taken away
and reinstated.[42] Through the early sixteenth century there were various
troubles with the merchant establishment, and James V granted an edict
in 1529 in favour of craftsmen,[43] though parliament in 1540 made an act
against the building trades of the whole kingdom due to their charging
exorbitant prices.[44] Perhaps this was due to the inflationary pressures of the
'Price Revolution', which no doubt drove up building costs in the sixteenth
century. The 1540 act stated that anyone with a building to erect could
choose either free or unfree craftsmen as they found most expedient, and
that freemen were not to try and stop the unfree from working.[45] Though
privileges were apparently restored in 1556 when the queen regent reaffirmed craft privileges, by the 1570s the town council was still citing the
1540 act against craftsmen.[46] These pressures on the crafts were eventually
eased in 1583 with the new burgh constitution, or 'sett'. By decreet arbitral
of 1583 the merchants and crafts came to an agreement over privileges and
council representation, and one of the items in the parliamentary ratification stated that 'na maner of persoun be sufferit to use merchandice or
occupie the handie wark of ane frie craft within this burgh or yit to exerceis the libertie and privilege of the said burgh without he be burges and
frieman of the samine.'[47] From 1583 it was written into the burgh sett that
a freeman of the Incorporation also needed to be a freeman of the town.

The Incorporation still struggled in their attempts to ensure compliance, though occasionally it was the trades themselves which turned a blind eye to craftsmen who took freedom of trade without purchasing burgessship.[48] There were still numerous examples of their need to defend the exclusion of unfreemen, but from 1583 they were at least guaranteed council representation, and were therefore intertwined with the burgh establishment. This no doubt helped, though by the eighteenth century the enforcement of both burgh and craft freedoms was breaking down.[49]

In addition to this first freedom of burgessship, the second freedom of mastership within the Incorporation was also expected. This usually seems to have entailed a monetary payment for 'upset', or setting up as a master, as well as the provision of a banquet. In 1554 an upset payment of 10 shillings is recorded, whilst in 1579 several payments for both upset and banquet are recorded as being £4 6s 3d – for freemen's sons.[50] Although it is tempting to read the inflationary effects of the 'Price Revolution' into this disparity in upset costs, the data is simply too sparse to draw firm conclusions. Indeed, many of the listed payments were 'in part', making it unclear just what the final cost was.

Whilst the term 'burgess' is quite straightforward, the term 'master' can occasionally be misleading. Many histories of labour use the word 'master' without explanation, leading occasionally to confusion. In the same way that Scottish usage of 'merchant' could imply anything from a major importer and exporter down to a petty retailer, the term 'master' could also have several meanings. In a purely economic sense, it could mean 'employer' or 'boss', as with those described by parliament in 1661 as being 'masters' over servants and apprentices in manufactories.[51] Alternatively, 'master' in a corporate sense implied both a level of skill and a legal status; a 'freeman' of a legally incorporated trade, such as those annually chosen to serve as quartermasters for the Incorporation of Mary's Chapel.[52] Both types could be in positions of power over other workers, but the master of the Incorporation had specific privileges and entitlements through the legal framework of corporatism, enshrined in charters or 'seals of cause'. A domestic servant might serve his or her 'master', but this was a purely economic relationship, while a journeyman who hoped to become a 'master' instead longed for the legal privileges of membership in a recognised body of skilled craftsmen. As corporate privileges were always contested, there were always challenges to this system, and unfreemen often took illegal servants, usurping the status of 'master'. They may have been over their servants in an economic sense, but they were still not legally entitled to be their masters. In this book, the word master will always denote a freeman of the Incorporation.

Equally problematic, was that masters of the building trades were often paid wages, in effect making them employees just like unfree labourers. In the secondary literature on the building trades in late-medieval and early modern Europe, there have been several important studies which have focussed on issues surrounding wages and cost of living.[53] The wage differential between masters, journeymen and labourers theoretically reflects the range of skills on the building site, though the complexities of engaging labour for a whole project indicate a more nuanced division between these groups. Knoop and Jones, in their study of Scottish masons, looked at the differing systems of direct labour and contract work, which were alternative ways of engaging builders. The former saw an 'in-house' appointee, such as a master mason or a master of works, who would deal with sourcing labour, while the latter saw labour sourced by the craftsman who obtained the contract.[54] Of course the wages paid to these labourers varied depending on a range of factors, including their status, the time of year, and the state of the economy.[55] One must also add to these the pressures of demographic change, and the corresponding impact on the labour market. Though a freeman would no doubt have fared better than a servant or a labourer through the 'Price Revolution' of the sixteenth century,[56] they too would have had to weather the vagaries of the labour market with an income made up of wages and payments in kind.

Despite problems of terminology and the complexities of employment schemes, which both cloud our understanding of the place of the freeman within the building trades, perhaps more problematic is the fact that the rules were often ignored. A freeman of the Incorporation apparently needed to be a burgess, yet there were examples of those who did not become burgesses until after their admission to the Incorporation. Gilbert Clewcht held the office of boxmaster within the Incorporation on 12 November 1553,[57] but he apparently was not actually a burgess until the following February.[58]

Others worked their whole life in the town without ever becoming a burgess. When James Stevinson's testament dative and inventory were prepared, he was simply described as 'wright indweller in Edinburgh'.[59] Indeed, the numbers of unfreemen working in the building trades must have been quite substantial, though they are impossible to guage. In 1558 when the town prepared a muster roll of fencible men between the ages of sixteen and sixty, there were supposed to be lists given in of numbers of freemen masters and servants, such as journeymen and eligible apprentices.[60] While most of the crafts gave detailed numbers, the building trades did not, despite being warned under pain of warding of the deacon of masons.[61] What happened is not clear, though the numbers for the masons and wrights were never included. The building trades have always held a high demand for labourers, and it is not hard to imagine that the failure to submit numbers was due to the Incorporation not fully knowing who was employed at any given point. Perhaps the challenges of quantifying a fluid labour population were accepted by the council as an excuse for non-submission? Clearly there were challenges to keeping track of free and unfree; of burgess masters and servant journeymen.

Although it was usually in the interest of the freemen to limit entry into their privileged group, ensuring that there was enough work to sustain their members, often there was reason to bring unfreemen in, usually through toleration as journeymen, servants, or some other label for labourers, but occasionally as accepted freemen. The rather unpleasant fracas between two painters is illustrative here. Walter Binning and David Workman were both painters in the capital, though only the former was a freeman of the Incorporation.[62]

The council records give some important details of this dispute, which happened just before Christmas of 1553. Several freemen of the Incorporation aided Walter Binning in an attack and attempted imprisonment of Workman, who was an unfree painter working for Mr James Watson. Interestingly, his employment was with the tolerance and licence of George Durie, the Abbot of Dunfermline.[63]

It is recorded that just before 'the Feist of Yule', implying winter work, 'the maist pairt of the paintouris craftismen of this burgh' were away in Hamilton, doing work for the Governor, James Hamilton. As the painters were apparently all away, possibly under compulsion of the regent,[64] Mr James Watson decided to hire an unfree painter to 'cum to this burgh for perfiting and ending of the syd wallis of his said hous'. While David Workman was painting Watson's house, Walter Binning found out and came back to Edinburgh with John Cunningham, deacon of the wrights, David Graham, a mason, and several 'complicis'. They entered Watson's house and confiscated Workman's 'haill warklomis', or tools, and were in the process of forcing him to come with them, when Watson returned home and confronted the tradesmen. There was apparently a scuffle in which Watson was wounded, but it ended only with threats to come back and 'strike up' the doors of this house to remove the unfree painter.

Watson made a complaint to the council, who reviewed the case. Upon considering Workman's testimony, the tradesmen were found to be in the wrong, but were given eight days to make amends; a decidedly light punishment, which points to the delicate nature of the case. Though the use of force by the freemen was wrong, and all parties had been working under the licence of the Abbot, there was still the rather uncomfortable fact that Workman was simply not a freeman. This, of course, did not stop the council from employing him to paint the interior of the Tolbooth in the 1580s.[65]

While David Workman was not a burgess, or 'free' of the town, until February 1585–6, Walter Binning was not listed in the burgess rolls either. In the 1583 burgesship entry for his apprentice, Richard Binning, the text lists Walter Binning as 'glaisinwrycht' only; not as a 'glassinwrycht burgess' as would be the usual format for such entries.[66] Moreover, Walter is not listed in the burgess rolls himself, suggesting that he was free of the Incorporation, but was not free of the town. As an apparent freeman of the Incorporation, it is more likely that he was accidentally omitted, as there are numerous cases of the council accepting claims of children's rights to burgesship when their parents were accidentally not on the roll.[67] Perhaps Binning's is such a case, as he was clearly established with the Incorporation of Masons and Wrights. Workman, on the other hand, was not free of the Incorporation, despite his licence from the Abbot of Dunfermline. Hence, the dispute.

What is important about this case is what it shows us about the freedom to work. Two freedoms were theoretically needed – burgesship to be free of the town and mastership to be free of the Incorporation. As the population rose in the sixteenth century it became increasingly difficult to monitor these rules, and therefore unfreemen working within the town was a constant problem. Of course it was in no one's interest to have conflict, and the talents of both painters were well-recognised. In and after March 1553–4, Binning appears twice in the dean of guild's accounts for painting eighteen panels – presumably of glass – and several 'armis' in the choir of St Giles.[68] If not a burgess of the town, he was certainly seen as capable and employable by the council. He was later employed for painting 'the mannikin and the beirrar of the townis armes' between Yule of 1554 and February 1554–5.[69] Further kirk work of 'paynting of Sanct Geill' took place in 1555; the very saint of the good town itself.[70] This type of task would hardly be given to someone not trusted by the council. Further kirk work came in March of 1556–7,[71] and in 1558 he was painting 'the tryumphe' made for the the marriage of Mary, Queen of Scots.[72] In Spring of 1560 he painted certain pillars in the kirk green,[73] and in 1561 was given canvas for preparing 'triumphis and fairssis' at the trons, the Tolbooth, the Market Cross, and the Netherbow Port.[74] Clearly the freeman of the Incorporation, Binning, was trusted by the dean of guild, despite his apparent lack of burgesship.

By 1580, David Workman was accepted into the Incorporation as a free master,[75] though it was not until 1586 that he received burgesship.[76] Both painters were very slow to purchase burgesship in a century noted for its inflationary burdens, and both painters were still given painting contracts by the council. Both men were eventually incorporated into the Masons and Wrights, though Workman was not accepted until much later in his career. Clearly the requisite freedoms of burgesship and mastership did not always have a bearing on who worked. Perhaps these examples of ignoring the rules reflect the increasing complexity of administering a growing urban populace; perhaps they show the occasionally-competing interests of the town and Incorporation.

For the building trades in particular, it would appear that the rigidity of the corporate framework seems to have been only loosely observed, especially in the 1500s. Was corporatism entrenched in the 1600s, only to be eroded into the 1700s? Whether this was the case or not, the context of corporate privileges and regulations, whether observed in breech or as the reality, set the backdrop to the development of the Incorporation of Mary's Chapel and therefore must be used as the yardstick – or ellwand – to which our understanding of the building trades is measured. As we shall see, rigidity and flexibility were both tools wielded by the incorporated tradesmen as they sought to control their work and the House that offered them a privileged place in society.

Formation and Recording of the Incorporation of Mary's Chapel

Within the contexts of corporate privilege and feudalism, the craftsmen and women[77] of the capital's building trades began to coalesce into the legal entity that they would become in 1475 – the Incorporation of Masons and Wrights, and later in the seventeenth century, the Incorporation of Mary's Chapel. While questions of 'why' will be addressed throughout the book, it is perhaps useful to outline *how* this happened here; a brief narrative to further contextualise the coming chapters.

Scottish craft organisation of some loose form clearly predates the first known seal of cause, which would appear to have been that granted to the Edinburgh Incorporation of Hatmakers.[78] Such documents were called seals of cause because of the application of the wax seals of the issuing authorities.[79] This was apparently not the first genre of craft charters used in the kingdom of Scotland, as earlier examples of legal recognition and authority being bestowed on a group of craftsmen can be found in grants of altars. Both the Cordiners and the Skinners had such religious charters granted to them in 1449 and 1450 respectively, though their seals of cause did not come until 1479 and 1474.[80] By contrast, the Masons and Wrights received both of these charters – the grant of an altar and the seal of cause – on the same day in 1475, perhaps reflecting a more refined corporate structure by the later 1400s, as well as the legal distinctions between con-fraternities and incorporated trades.[81]

While religious aspects of incorporation were clearly a unifying force, the trade-related functions were also important. From 1424, at the apparent instigation of James I, parliament decreed that, 'In each town of the realm in each sundry craft used therein there be chosen a wise man of their craft ... who shall be held deacon or maister man over the layff ...'[82] While there was disagreement over the office of deacon and the powers involved, this would become not only a crucial element of the Scottish incorporated trades, but also of burgh councils throughout the kingdom. The decrees about deacons, such as the 1457 statute which instituted the office for the Edinburgh goldsmiths, suggest a considerable level of organisation prior to when the official seals of cause were actually granted.[83]

On 15 October 1475, both a grant of an altar and a seal of cause were issued to the Masons and Wrights of Edinburgh, giving them official legal status as an incorporated trade. In one day two charters gave them both a religious focus of an altar dedicated to Sts John the Baptist and Evangelist, and the right to deacons, with its implications for a degree of self-regulation. While these were far from autonomy, they still recognised the skills and value of the building trades to the wider burgh community, and allowed them to both participate in public life as a corporate body and to regulate certain technical aspects of their work. Price fixing was theo-retically still in the hands of the council, and deacons were elected from council-approved 'leets', or lists, but incorporation was still a position of honour and trust within the capital.[84]

Between their charter of incorporation in 1475 and their final loss of privileges in 1846, the Masons and Wrights grew to include not only the builders who worked in wood and stone, but also various allied trades who worked in these mediums. In 1489 the coopers were incorporated with the Masons and Wrights,[85] and through the sixteenth and seventeenth centu-ries other trades were brought in. Inclusion in the Incorporation meant access to certain privileges, which were jealously defended.

Interestingly, most histories that discuss the Incorporation tend to focus on a few key dates to explain the building trades. Whilst 1475 and 1489 are most often mentioned, a 1517 ratification by the Archbishop of St Andrews, a 1633 confirmation by the town council, and a 1635 confirma-tion by Charles I usually figure in their story, demonstrating the need for confirmation of their privileges in the face of constant challenge to their exclusive entitlements. Also usually included is the date of 1618, which was previously thought to be the date when the Incorporation came to own St Mary's Chapel in Niddry's Wynd, though an inventory of writs in the National Library of Scotland (NLS) suggests that it was actually 1601.[86] Still, 1618 is perhaps as important as 1475 in the way historians have discussed the Incorporation, as it symbolises the formation of a new identity; an identity focussed on a corporately-owned property rather than the occupations of the two senior crafts. Indeed, this identity would survive long after their right to exclude unfreemen from work had been formally abolished in 1846.

These two aspects of history and privilege seem to have gone hand-in-hand. When in the later eighteenth century the Incorporation found itself struggling to exclude unfreemen from working in the town, it would appear that they had a form printed to make it easier to pursue the law-breakers in the courts. This 'summons of declarator' not only gave the legal justification for demanding their attendance before the Lords of Council and Session, 'in his Majesty's name and authority', but it also laid out the history of the Incorporation, relying on the precedent of the centuries to justify their chartered privileges.[87] As liberalism was becoming the domi-nant ideal, with its free-market implications, the corporate rights of an exclusive minority were harder to defend, so the Incorporation appealed to a sense of respect for history. Hence the talismanic dates of 1475 and 1633 were ready and waiting on the pre-printed forms. Names were then written into the blank spaces on the forms, demanding their compliance with the increasingly out-of-date laws. As shall be seen, it was a losing battle, but what this says about the way the Incorporation viewed their past is most instructive.

The free craftsmen were not the only ones to take an interest in their history. Naturally, the Incorporation of Mary's Chapel has also figured in numerous histories of the capital itself, both recognising and reinforcing their position as part of the burgh establishment. Although there have been many such histories written, four in particular give insight into the place of the Incorporation in the historiography of the Scottish capital. From the 1700s we see a clear indication that historians who have looked at the Incorporation have sought to consult official records, many of which survive today. Interestingly, the ways in which these records have been used to view the history of the building trades are far from uniform.

William Maitland's 1753 account of the Masons and Wrights in his *History of Edinburgh* is very detailed in certain aspects, suggesting that he was well informed about their specific history.[88] That said, his general view of the Scottish incorporated trade leaves something to be desired. After listing the dominant incorporations, he discussed several others under the heading 'Inferior Trades or Crafts', which is all quite plau-sible.[89] What is problematic, is that several trades which were actually amalgamated within various incorporations are randomly listed in his work, with bowers, coopers and glaziers noted as being part of the Masons or Wrights, but mixed in with various Hammermen trades, and under the heading of 'Barbers'.[90] Similarly, the painters, plumbers, sieve-wrights, slaters and upholsters are noted as being part of the 'Company of Masons and Wrights', but are all mixed in with various Hammermen trades, and under the section entitled 'Litsters or Dyers', making for a very confusing account of what he describes as forty-two 'Arts and Mysteries or Companies of Trades in *Edinburgh*'.[91] His flawed understanding of Edinburgh's corporate structures are therefore explained using an English model: the 'incorporated trade' becomes the 'company', and the fourteen trades are deconstructed into forty-two 'Arts and Mysteries',[92] bringing the capital of North Britain firmly in line with his own experiences of London – a much larger market with fewer examples of composite corporatism.

In the details of the Masons and Wrights, however, Maitland shows considerable knowledge. He correctly notes the dates of their seals of cause, and mentions their ratifications by Archbishop Andrew Forman, James V and Charles I. He notes a decree of the Court of Session in 1703 which regulated the internal structure of the crafts incorporated with the Masons and Wrights. Indeed, he even seems familiar with the origins of the chapel from which their actual name derived.[93] Though his understanding of the wider Scottish model of craft organisation might be slightly flawed, his grasp of the historical details shows a genuine attempt to understand the building trades of Edinburgh. Was this information given to him by the Incorporation themselves?

By contrast, Hugo Arnot, writing in the 1770s, focussed on the role of the Incorporated Trades in civic life, listing each in order of precedence and explaining in the very least how they related to the town council.[94] All fourteen entries are short biographies, usually mentioning seals of cause or some form of relationship with the council. Some are more detailed than others; while the Hammermen are noted for their ownership of a hall, the single sentence about the Furriers states only that they owe their existence to the council.[95] Arnot did slightly better with the 'Wrights and Masons'. Aside from 'double representation in the town-council', their fifteenth-century pedigree is given, as well as a vague statement about royal confirmations. Perhaps more interesting, is that Arnot notes Mary's Chapel: 'This community has, in Niddry's Wynd, a modern hall, for holding their meetings. It is called *Mary's Chapel*, having been originally a chapel dedicated to the Blessed Virgin.' It's medieval, Catholic origins are casually brushed over, while the skill of the builders in updating façades to the latest classical fashions is celebrated in the Palladian *modernity* of the hall – high praise indeed.

Perhaps a more thorough approach was taken by James Colston, whose 1891 *The Incorporated Trades of Edinburgh* dedicated an entire chapter to the Incorporation of Mary's Chapel.[96] This began with a general potted history of the foundation and growth of the Incorporation, covering the key dates of the seals of cause and ratifications, and following previous examples, detailing the 1703 Court of Session decree. Half of the chapter is given over to recounting the 1475 and 1489 seals of cause, but Colston makes no distinction between the grant of the altar and the first seal of cause itself. The published council records also give the text of these documents together, having been granted on the same day, though consultation of the original charters, which were only recently rediscovered, demonstrates that they were indeed separate documents rather than a single 'seal of cause'.[97] The last five pages discuss sundry topics, including weapons and the 1558 muster; craft prayers and oaths; the widows' funds; the nineteenth-century laws of the Incorporation; and the chapel which gave the name of 'Mary's Chapel' to the body of craftsmen.[98]

Other histories have included material on the Incorporation, such as the two recent articles by the author,[99] or the excellent, but unpublished, PhD thesis of Sebastian Pryke,[100] but perhaps the most important modern study has been Lewis's book on the building of Edinburgh's New Town.[101] Though this is not a study of the Incorporation itself, it gives an in-depth account of the building trades in general at a time when Incorporation authority and influence was waning. Unfreemen, such as journeymen, figure heavily, demonstrating how far the shift away from corporate privileges had gone by the mid-eighteenth century.

Individual trades which are part of the Incorporation have naturally figured in several studies, though perhaps the most work has been done on the masons, due wholly to the social phenomenon of freemasonry. Freemasons, or 'lodges', were originally workers in stone. The term 'lodge' was taken from the temporary shelters on the building sites used by the workmen.[102] Inside, work was done, meals were taken and sleep was had by itinerant masons. Hence, the lodge became a form of house for the workers, and interestingly, 'lodge' became the word for describing the body of freemasons, just as 'house' became that of the overall Incorporation of Mary's Chapel.

As demonstrated by the 'Schaw Statutes' of 1598, Freemasonry developed out of a desire to control the labour market for stonework during a period of demographic expansion and monetary inflation in the later 1500s.[103] More people meant more labour, which drove down the value and the cost of their work. The labour market apparently became flooded with semi-skilled masons, or 'cowans', which the free masons, or those who had the right to work as free masters of the trade, sought to either exclude from the building site, or at least control. The arguments behind this control were predicated on skill. It was argued that a fully-trained mason was able to not only build walls, as any cowan could do, but also to carve the stones and undermine existing walls for repairs.[104]

From early on the crafts had been tasked with reviewing the skill of potential entrants. The 1475 seal of cause recommended a court of four masters to examine the 'sufficiency' of those who wished to join.[105] This, of course, was achieved through the institution of the essay. With the population of the capital more than doubling in the century after 1540,[106] this must have become quite a challenge. A new system was needed, and in the 1590s the masons looked not to a burgh-based system, but instead to a national one for the whole 'realme'.[107] Although this was not wholly successful, it did have an interesting social and economic impact on the building trades, as witnessed by the numerous works on the history of freemasonry which also discuss the Incorporation of Mary's Chapel.

Though much has been written on the wider topic of freemasonry, several key works should be mentioned here. Masonic historians, such as Knoop and Jones, working in the early twentieth century, and Harry Carr, who was active mid-twentieth century, have made notable contributions.[108] While their works are important, their wider genre of masonic history has often been treated with distrust.[109] More recent work by a non-masonic historian, David Stevenson, has done much to bridge the gap between academic history and the work of freemasons with an interest in the development of their lodges. Aside from his two excellent studies of origins and extent of freemasonry as a social movement, Stevenson has also published an important article on the apprenticeship system, tying lodges and incorporations firmly into the socio-economic context developed by Knoop and Jones half a century earlier.[110] All of these works shed important light on one of the key trades of the Incorporation of Mary's Chapel, despite their focus on the parallel institution of the Lodge of Mary's Chapel.

The overlap between the Lodge and the Incorporation is, at times, confusing. In strictest terms, the Incorporation's authority did not extend beyond the burgh boundaries, while the tradesmen often travelled farther afield for seasonal work. Clearly the two institutions must have been complementary at times. Some historians, as with Knoop and Jones, have argued that the Incorporation attempted to control the Lodge, hinting at the potential conflict of interests between the ten incorporated crafts within the Incorporation.[111] There is evidence that the Lodge could function as a committee of the Incorporation, in that it was a specifically mason-related meeting. For example, in 1705, when there were complaints about journeymen taking work from master masons, the Lodge wrote of 'this citie' and 'this brough' rather than the lodge, shire or area, suggesting a natural overlap with the Incorporation's legal jurisdiction.[112]

Sebastian Pryke, citing Harry Carr, stated that the Edinburgh Lodge of Freemasons, 'was like a shadow to the Incorporation, and neither body was ever mentioned by the other in their respective minutes.'[113] This may have been true for the earlier period, though the Incorporation records do discuss the use of Mary's Chapel for meetings of the Lodge in the later 1700s.[114] Still, the point stands that while membership lists for the two bodies might have been very similar, especially for the masons, the two groups were indeed distinct institutions.

One is left with an impression that from 1598 the two bodies overlapped quite a bit, becoming closer as non-masons began to join the Lodge from the mid-1600s. As their membership became more diverse, bringing in 'non-operatives', or non-stoneworkers, including gentlemen, other trades from the Incorporation also became represented within both bodies.[115] From 1721 we have the first non-freemason deacon of the masons of the Incorporation; a glazier named Wardrope, who was admitted to the Lodge under protest.[116] Clearly the two bodies were still quite close by this period, though their memberships did not overlap completely.

By the mid-eighteenth century it would appear that the Freemasons were increasingly diverse – and increasingly separate from the Incorporation of Mary's Chapel.[117] In 1741, for example, the Incorporation of Hammermen discussed letting part of their hall, the Magdalene Chapel, to 'some Free and accepted Masons'.[118] Late eighteenth-century freemasonry was certainly no longer dependent on working in stone, just as working in stone in Edinburgh was no longer dependent on being a freeman of the Incorporation. The rigidities of the older systems simply did not fit with the liberal views of the age.

In terms of the historiography of the various trades which made up the Incorporation of Mary's Chapel, the masons were clearly the best covered, due to the previously-mentioned connections with freemasonry. That said, several of the other trades have also received a modest degree of attention. Pryke's thesis on the Edinburgh furniture trade has shed much light on the wrights' involvement in furnishing the interiors of buildings.[119] Other important studies, such as Apted and Hannabuss's biographical dictionary of Scottish painters, have included valuable research on the capital while pursuing their topic for the entire nation.[120] Charles Whitelaw's treatise on arms producers included the bowers,[121] and Jill Turnbull's study of

Scottish glass has much to say about the glassinwrights.[122] These ambitious and important national studies have all helped to shape our understanding of the Edinburgh Incorporation of Mary's Chapel, and though none of these have focussed solely on the Incorporation, this present work owes much to them, as fortunately they all overlapped with some aspect of the building trades.

Still, there has not yet been a full study of the Incorporation of Mary's Chapel, despite the fact that the Scottish capital is today a World Heritage Site. It is hoped that this present book will go some way to filling the need for a full study of the Incorporation which sought to control the builders of the Scottish capital from 1475 to 1846, and which continues today in its charitable functions. Hence, this introductory chapter has sought to explore the context in which the Incorporation developed, from the phenomenon of the craft guild, whether composite or otherwise, to the feudalistic structures of society; from the narrative of incorporation to the ways in which historians have viewed the process of incorporating the building trades in Edinburgh. From here the first and second chapters will look at the internal relationships within 'the House', both between craft and craft in a composite incorporation, and beyond the privileged free craftsmen to their wider households, looking to wives, widows, servants and apprentices. Chapter 3 will examine identity formation through relations with the kirk, exploring themes of eternal security, earthly status and the material provision of shelter before and after the Reformation. Chapter 4 will consider relations between the Incorporation and the burgh, considering regulation and autonomy; prices and customers; the importance of place; and the battle to control unfree competition. Finally, the concluding fifth chapter will explore the decline and abolition of corporate privileges, with the transition to more liberal ideas and economic thought.

Throughout these chapters, an inherent problem of composite corporatism will be explored: the problem of unity. A unified House had legitimacy, which was crucial for maintaining status and privilege. How did the often-divided Incorporation manage the competing interests of ten individual arts within a single corporate body? How did they build unity? As shall be seen, they used the best models that were available to them, or the family and the household. Considering the clear value of the World Heritage Site these trades built, it is doubtful that such a short look at the Incorporation can fully do justice to the topic. Hopefully it will persuade others to look more closely at both the Incorporation of Mary's Chapel and the wider context of composite corporatism.

NOTES

1. Torrie (Dennison), E. P. D., *The Guild Court Book of Dunfermline, 1433–1597* (Edinburgh: Scottish Record Society, 1986), xiv, and Farr, J. R., *Artisans in Europe, 1300–1914* (Cambridge: Cambridge University Press, 2000), 20–1.

2. Farr, *Artisans*, 24–5, citing in particular the work of Bernard Chevalier, 'Corporations, Conflits Politiques et Paix Sociale en France aux XIVe et XVe Siècles', in *Revue Historique*, 268 (1982), 17–44.

3. As Farr states, 'the corporate regime gained definition *by* the principle of exclusion.' Ibid., 29.

4. Ibid., 24.

5. Lynch, M., *Edinburgh and the Reformation* (Edinburgh: Edinburgh University Press, 1981), 54, and Dennison, E. P., 'The Myth of the Medieval Burgh Community', in Harris, B. and MacDonald, A. (eds), *Scotland: The Making and Unmaking of the Nation, c.1100–1707*, Vol. 3 (Dundee: Dundee University Press, 2006), 137.

6. For more on the debate about how opposed merchants and craftsmen were in early modern Scottish towns, see Lynch, *Edinburgh and the Reformation*, Chapter 4, 49–66. See also Chapter 4 of this book, looking specifically at the relationship from the perspective of the Incorporation.

7. Throughout this book, the terms, 'Incorporation', 'Masons and Wrights', 'Mary's Chapel', or 'the House', will be used when referring to the body that regulated the Edinburgh building trades, as they themselves used these terms at different times. Therefore, I have attempted to use the terminology that most closely reflects the primary sources.

8. Lynch, *Edinburgh and the Reformation*, 11.

9. Rappaport, S., *Worlds Within Worlds: Structures of Life in Sixteenth-Century London* (Cambridge: Cambridge University Press, 2002), 92, and Unwin, G., *The Gilds & Companies of London* (London: George Allen & Unwin Ltd, 1938), 370–1.

10. Trout, A., *City of the Seine: Paris in the Time of Richelieu and Louis XLV, 1614–1715* (New York: St Martin's Press, 1996), 198–9, and Fitzsimmons, M. P., *From Artisan to Worker: Guilds, the French State, and the Organization of Labour, 1776–1821* (Cambridge: Cambridge University Press, 2010), 7–10.

11. Prak, M., 'Corporate Politics in the Low Countries: Guilds as Institutions, 14th to 18th Centuries', in Prak, M., Lis, C., Lucassen, J., and Soly, H. (eds), *Craft Guilds in the Early Modern Low Countries* (Aldershot: Ashgate, 2006), 100–1.

12. Unwin, *Gilds & Companies of London*, 370–1.

13. Ibid., 370–1.

14. Dalgleish, G., and Maxwell, S., *The Lovable Craft, 1687–1987* (Edinburgh: Royal Museum of Scotland, 1987), 4, and Munro, J. and Fothringham, H. S.

(eds) *Edinburgh Goldsmiths' Minutes, 1525–1700* (Edinburgh: Scottish Record Society, 2006).

15. Unwin, *Gilds & Companies of London*, 370–1.

16. This is made even more complex with the advent of Freemasonry in 1598, though this attempt at national organisation does not appear to have had an interest in breaking ties with the local organisation of incorporations in the burghs. The Masons in Edinburgh remained both a Lodge and, separately, a part of the Incorporation of Mary's Chapel; two parallel and apparently complementary organisations with very different jurisdictions.

17. Montias, J. M., *Artists and Artisans in Delft: A Socio-Economic Study of the Seventeenth Century* (Princeton: Princeton University Press, 1982), 75.

18. Moffat, A., *Kelsae: A History of Kelso from Earliest Times* (Edinburgh: Birlinn, 2006), 107. In Aberdeen in the 1800s painters and glaziers were also in their Incorporation of Hammermen. See: Anonymous, 'Hammermen Trade of Old Aberdeen: Extracts From the Minutes', in *Aberdeen Journal Notes and Queries*, Vol. 2, No. 73 (1909), 258–60.

19. NRS, GD98/11/10/2, Extract act of the Burgh Court of Haddington as to payment by the craftsmen of their weekly penny for augmentation of God's service at St. John's altar in the parish kirk of Haddington, 30 June 1530.

20. Ayrshire Archives, B6/24/1, 'Minute Book of the Wrights and Squaremen of the Burgh of Air. 1556, Apr. 7–1724, Oct. 10', f3r: 'wrichtis masonnis glassinwrytis cooprs and the aitis of the said bur^t of air'.

21. Smith, A. M., *The Three United Trades of Dundee: Masons, Wrights & Slaters* (Dundee: Abertay Historical Society, 1987), 30 and 45, and Warden, A. J., *Burgh Laws of Dundee* (London: Longmans, Green & Co., 1872), 574–604.

22. Carnie, R. H., 'Perth Booksellers and Bookbinders in the Records of the Wright Calling, 1538–1864', in *The Bibliotheck*, 1:4 (1958), 24–39 and NLS, Ms.19288, 'Perth Wrights' Minutes', f5v, 16 April 1621. I am grateful to Dr Michael Pearce for kindly sharing his notes on this manuscript source with me.

23. The coopers appear to have left in 1569, the wrights in 1600. Cruikshank, J., *Sketch of the Incorporation of Masons; and the Lodge of Glasgow St John* (Glasgow: W. M. Ferguson, 1879), 3–6; Original 1551 seal of cause held by Glasgow City Archives, GB243/T-TH12; Hughan, W. J., *The Wrights of Glasgow* (London: George Kenning, 1899), 3; and Mair, C., *History of the Incorporation of Coopers of Glasgow* (Glasgow: Angels' Share, 2004), 16.

24. Lumsden, H., *The Records of the Trades House of Glasgow, A.D. 1605–1678* (Glasgow: Trades House of Glasgow, 1910), 9 and 27–8.

25. Bain, E., *Merchant and Craft Guilds: A History of the Aberdeen Incorporated Trades* (Aberdeen: J. & J. P. Edmond & Spark, 1887), 236 and 238–9.

26. This device was in use by the mid-eighteenth century, as described by Pennecuik and illustrated by Maitland. Pennecuik, A., *An Historical Account of the Blue Blanket: or Crafts-Men's Banner* (Edinburgh: David Bower,

1722), 40, and Maitland, W., *The History of Edinburgh from its Foundation to the Present Time* (Edinburgh: Hamilton, Balfour and Neill, 1753), 301. See also, Fothringham, H. S., *Heraldry of the Incorporated Trades of Edinburgh* (Edinburgh: Convenery of the Trades of Edinburgh, 2013).

27. Hughan, *Wrights of Glasgow*, 3; Bain, *Merchant and Craft Guilds*, 236; Smith, *Three United Trades of Dundee*, 34 and 70; and Ayrshire Archives, B6/24/1, 'Minute Book of the Wrights and Squaremen of the Burgh of Air. 1556, Apr. 7–1724, Oct. 10'.

28. See for example the suburban panton-heal maker, John Elder, who was allowed to make patten-heals, shoe lasts and golf clubs in Calton. ECA, SL34/1/1, 1 February 1676.

29. East Lothian Council Archive and Local History Service (ELCALHS), John Gray Centre, HAD/13/2/4, Minute Book of the Wrights and Masons 1616–1751, 25 June 1636, 'Libertie grantit to ferquhard andersone to work'.

30. There was a degree of fluidity, with a few lesser incorporations forming and falling away over the early modern period, but the number of officially-recognised incorporated trades in Edinburgh was fourteen. Examples of the 'lesser' incorporations include the Incorporation of Candlemakers and the Incorporation of Silk and Ribbon Weavers. For more on these two trades, see Allen, A., 'Production and the Missing Artefacts: Candles, Oil and the Material Culture of Urban Lighting in Early Modern Scotland', in *Review of Scottish Culture*, 23 (2011), and *Edin. Recs*, 1689–1701, 11.

31. *Edin. Recs*, 1557–1571, 273.

32. These figures do not tell us about the non-householders. Still, the limited nature of access is apparent. Lynch, *Edinburgh and the Reformation*, 10.

33. For more on the routes to burgesship and changing costs, see Allen, A., *The Locksmith Craft in Early Modern Edinburgh* (Edinburgh: Society of Antiquaries of Scotland, 2007), 29–30 and 44 (Table 2.5).

34. *Edin. Burgs*, 3.

35. See Allen, *Locksmith Craft*, 44 (Table 2.5), and Marwick, J. D., *Edinburgh Guilds and Crafts* (Edinburgh: Scottish Burgh Record Society, 1909), 30.

36. Marwick, *Edinburgh Guilds and Crafts*, 170.

37. Colston, J., *The Incorporated Trades of Edinburgh* (Edinburgh: Colston & Co., 1891), 2.

38. *Edin. Recs*, 1403–1528, 57–8.

39. ECA, Mill Recs, B5, 11 December 1574. Along with a limited list of items he was allowed to work on, such as ploughs, sleds, barrows, etc., he was also required to 'produce his ticket', meaning his burgess ticket.

40. See for example, Mill, 'Inventory', 15 (undated, 1555), 18 (20 February 1574–5) and 19 (15 June 1575).

41. Mill, 'Inventory', 3. In the 1517 response he commanded the curates to warn the various building trades to pay their apprenticeship and entry fees. See Appendix 2.

42. For further details of this process, see Lamond, R., 'The Scottish Craft Guild

as a Religious Fraternity', in *The Scottish Historical Review*, 16:63 (1919), 200–11, and Grant, I. F., *The Social and Economic Development of Scotland Before 1603* (Edinburgh: Oliver and Boyd, 1930), 425–35.

43. Smith, J., *The Hammermen of Edinburgh and Their Altar in St Giles Church* (Edinburgh: William J. Hay, 1906), lxxxi.

44. Anentis conductioune of craftismen: *RPS*, 1540/12/84. Date accessed: 12 February 2016.

45. Ibid.

46. See Knoop, D. and Jones, G. P., *The Scottish Mason and the Mason Word* (Manchester: Manchester University Press, 1939), 51–2, and *Edin. Recs*, 1573–1589, 58, for details of a 1577 case where the council sustained the right of unfree builders to work in the town.

47. 'Ratificatioun of the decreit arbitrale betuix the merchandis and craftismen of Edinburgh': RPS, 1584/5/100 (last accessed 11 February 2016).

48. *Edin. Recs*, 1655–1665, xxxix and 290.

49. Anonymous, *The Scots Magazine*, 52: May (Edinburgh: Murray and Cochrane, 1790), 255.

50. 1554: Mill, 'Inventory', 15, 6 June 1554 and ECA, Mill Recs, B1, f16r, 6 June 1554; 1579: ECA, Mill Recs, B1, undated entry following 2 May 1579: 'Patrik meyne boxmasteris ressait 1579'.

51. *RPS*, 1661/1/344 (last accessed 14 May 2015).

52. See for example, the Incorporation's first volume of minutes: ECA, SL34/1/1.

53. See for example, the important 'Phelps Brown & Hopkins Index' discussed in Phelps Brown, E. H. and Hopkins, S. V., 'Seven Centuries of Building Wages', and Phelps Brown, E. H. and Hopkins, S. V., 'Seven Centuries of the Prices of Consumables, Compared with Builders' Wage-Rates', both in Carus-Wilson, E. M. (ed.), *Essays in Economic History*, Vol. 2 (London: Edward Arnold Ltd, 1966), 168–96, and also a critique of their index in Woodward, D., 'Wage Rates and Living Standards in Pre-Industrial England', in *Past & Present*, 91 (1981), 28–46. A European perspective is given in Braudel, F. P. and Spooner, F., 'Prices in Europe from 1450 to 1750', in Rich, E. E. and Wilson, C. H. (eds), *The Cambridge Economic History of Europe from the Decline of the Roman Empire, Volume 4: The Economy of Expanding Europe in the Sixteenth and Seventeenth Centuries* (Cambridge: Cambridge University Press, 1967), 374–486. For Scottish prices and builders' wages, see Gibson, A. J. S. and Smout, T. C., *Prices, Food and Wages in Scotland, 1550–1780* (Cambridge: Cambridge University Press, 1995), Chapters 1, 8 and 9, and Gray, R. Q., *The Labour Aristocracy in Victorian Edinburgh* (Oxford: Clarendon Press, 1976), Chapter 4.

54. Knoop and Jones, *Scottish Mason*, 9–15.

55. Ibid., 32 and 37–8.

56. Lythe suggests that the 'top-grade craftsmen of Edinburgh seem to have enjoyed threefold increase in money wages' between 1560 and the early 1600s. Lythe, S. G. E., *The Economy of Scotland in its European Setting,*

1550–1625 (Edinburgh: Oliver and Boyd, 1960), 30. This would seem to be validated by the Gibson and Smout's data on weekly income and household expenditure for masons and labourers. Gibson and Smout, *Prices, Food and Wages*, Figure 9.3, 361.

57. Mill, 'Inventory', 14.

58. 'Clewch, Gilbert, burgess, lathamus, fabric of the church; dewtie given to Mr. Jhonn Prestoun, baillie, be right of office 28 Feb. 1553–4.' By 1561 he was also made a guild brother, with the provision that he move from the Canongate into Edinburgh. *Edin. Burgs*, 112.

59. NRS, CC8/8/63, James Stevinson, 9/6/1647.

60. See Lynch, *Edinburgh and the Reformation*, 9–10 and 23, citing 'Ms Co. Recs., ii, fos. 126v–131r, 132r–137v'; Grant, *Social and Economic Development of Scotland*, 412–13; and *Edin. Recs*, 1557–1571, 23–5.

61. *Edin. Recs*, 1557–1571, 24.

62. For more on their careers and the dispute, see Apted, M. R. and Hannabuss, S. (eds), *Painters in Scotland 1301–1700: A Biographical Dictionary* (Edinburgh: Edina Press Ltd, 1978), 4, 28–9 and 107. For possible familial connections between the Edinburgh Binnings and the Flemish Benings, see McRoberts, D., 'Notes on Scoto-Flemish Artistic Contacts', in *Innes Review*, 10:1 (1959), 91–6.

63. Durie was related to the Beatons on his mother's side. The following account of the dispute is from *Edin. Recs*, 1528–1557, 194–5.

64. Apted and Hannabuss, *Painters in Scotland*, 4.

65. *Edin. Recs*, 1573–1589, 226 (1581) and 461 (1585–6).

66. *Edin. Burgs*, 57: 'Binnie (Binning, Bunning), Ryt., B., glaisinwrycht and messenger, as p. to Walter Bynning, glaisinwrycht 7 Aug. 1583'. Note the lack of the abbreviation 'B.' after the trade of the apprentice's master, which normally appears in such burgesship entries.

67. Marwick, *Edinburgh Guilds and Crafts*, 149–50.

68. Adam, R. (ed.), *Edinburgh Records: The Burgh Accounts*, vol. 2 (Edinburgh, 1899), 26 and 28.

69. Ibid., 38.

70. Ibid., 43.

71. Ibid., 73, '. . . for painting of twa trene pillaris'.

72. *Edin. Recs*, 1557–1571, 26.

73. This is not the whitewashed interior one would expect in the reformed kirk. Adam, *Burgh Accounts*, 94: '. . . for painting grene of the xxiij pillaris and the loft . . .'

74. *Edin. Recs*, 1557–1571, 121.

75. Mill, 'Inventory', 21.

76. Interestingly, this was for, 'good service to be done to the good town'. *Edin. Burgs*, 537.

77. A 1508 'alienation' of an annual rent was listed by Mill as being '. . . in name and behalf of all the brethren and sisters of the Craft . . .', though whether

this means female workers or wives and daughters of masters is difficult to determine. Mill, 'Inventory', 1.

78. Bain, *Merchant and Craft Guilds*, 39. Lamond states that the first seal of cause was to the Edinburgh Incorporation of Skinners, in 1474, though the Hatmakers' seal of cause predates it by just under ten months. Lamond, 'Scottish Craft Gild as a Religious Fraternity', 204, and *Edin. Recs*, 1403–1528, 26 and 28.

79. Mill's partial transcription of a 1517 letter from the Archbishop of St Andrews states that the 1475 charter for the Masons and Wrights was issued 'under the seal of common cause'. Mill, 'Inventory', 3.

80. Colston, *Incorporated Trades of Edinburgh*, 93, and Maitland, *History of Edinburgh*, 305.

81. See Chapter 3 for more on the differences between confraternities and incorporations, though it should be said that more work is needed on this subject, both for Scotland and for the wider European historiography. The text of the two 1475 charters given to the Masons and Wrights can be found in *Edin. Recs*, 1403–1528, 30–2, and in the first appendix of this book.

82. As quoted by Lamond, 'Scottish Craft Gild as a Religious Fraternity', 200.

83. The Goldsmiths did not receive a seal of cause until 1483, when they were incorporated into the wider incorporation of metalworkers, the Hammermen. For more on the 1457 statute, see Lamond, 'Scottish Craft Gild as a Religious Fraternity', 201 and 204.

84. It would appear that it was not always the council which set the price of labour. Compare Fraser, W. H., *Conflict and Class: Scottish Workers, 1700–1838* (Edinburgh: John Donald, 1988), 17, and the 1671 'Act Anent Journeymens Wages', in ECA, SL34/1/1, 22. For leeting of deacons, see for example the 'admmission of Ro^t Milne to be deacon' entry for 11 April 1674 in ECA, SL34/1/1, 34.

85. See Appendix 1 for text.

86. NLS, Acc.7257, Rolled MS Inventory of Writs, numbers 14–17. See Appendix 6 for text. See also NLS, Acc.8617, Bundle 1, Legal Papers and Accounts, 1601–80 for the 1601 contract from James Chalmers.

87. NLS, Acc.7056: Boxes 1 and 2 (copies in both), 1787 Summons of Declarator. The Incorporation also included a short account of their history on the first page (endpaper, verso) of one of their scroll, or rough-working, minute books, showing that their clerk had apparently been tasked with going through the extant records. ECA, Acc.622/13: Scroll Minutes 1815–1822.

88. Maitland, *History of Edinburgh*, 301.

89. Ibid., 311.

90. Ibid., 314.

91. Ibid., 317.

92. Ibid., 317.

93. Ibid., 301.

94. Arnot, H., *The History of Edinburgh, from the Earliest Accounts to the Year*

1780 (Edinburgh: Thomas Turnbull, 1816), 404–9. The order Arnot gives for the fourteen incorporations is: 1: Surgeons; 2: Goldsmiths; 3: Skinners; 4: Furriers; 5: Hammermen; 6: Wrights; 7: Masons; 8: Tailors; 9: Baxters; 10: Fleshers; 11: Cordiners; 12: Weavers; 13: Walkers; and 14: Bonnetmakers.

95. Ibid., 407.

96. Colston, *The Incorporated Trades of Edinburgh*, 65–75.

97. *Edin. Recs*, 1403–1528, 30–2; ECA, Mill Recs, A1, 1475 Grant of Altar and A2, 1475 Seal of Cause; and Mill, 'Inventory', 1.

98. Colston, *The Incorporated Trades of Edinburgh*, 71–5.

99. Allen, A., 'Finding the Builders: Sources Lost and Extant for Edinburgh's Incorporation of Mary's Chapel', in *Scottish Archives: The Journal of the Scottish Records Association*, 20 (2014), 90–106, and Allen, A., 'The Missing Records of the Edinburgh Building Trades: Mill's 'Rough Inventory' and the Incorporation of Mary's Chapel', in *Architectural Heritage* (Forthcoming: 2018).

100. Pryke, S., 'The Eighteenth Century Furniture Trade in Edinburgh: A Study Based on Documentary Sources', Unpublished University of St Andrews PhD Thesis (1995), 11–35.

101. Lewis, A., *The Builders of Edinburgh New Town, 1767–1795* (Reading: Spire Books Ltd, 2014).

102. Stevenson, D., *The Origins of Freemasonry* (Cambridge: Cambridge University Press, 2005), 15, 16, and 36–7. See Plate 4 of this book for an illustration of such a lodge.

103. Stevenson, *Origins of Freemasonry*, 68 and 71. For the 'Shaw Statutes' of 1598, which are clearly preoccupied with the organisation of workers, as well as the first minute of the Lodge minutes, which deals with the employment of a 'cowan', see Carr, H. (ed.), *The Minutes of the Lodge of Edinburgh, Mary's Chapel, No. 1, 1598–1738* (London: Quatuor Coronati Lodge, 1962), 36–9 and 42.

104. Smith, *Three United Trades of Dundee*, 49.

105. *Edin. Recs*, 1403–1528, 31–2.

106. The greatest rise apparently came after the plague outbreak of 1584. Lynch, *Edinburgh and the Reformation*, 3 and 10–11. See also Lynch, M., *Scotland: A New History* (London: Pimlico, 2000), 171, which suggests that the population doubled between 1550 and 1625, and tripled by 1650.

107. Stevenson, *Origins of Freemasonry*, 61–2 and 68, and Carr, *Minutes of the Lodge of Edinburgh*, 36, where the Shaw Statutes were set down at Edinburgh on 28 December 1598, 'to be obseruit be all the maister maissounis within this realme . . .'

108. Knoop and Jones, *Scottish Mason*; Carr, H., *The Mason and the Burgh* (London: Quatuor Coronati Lodge, 1954); and Carr, *Minutes of the Lodge of Edinburgh*.

109. Stevenson, *Origins of Freemasonry*, xi and 2–3.

110. Stevenson, D., *The First Freemasons: Scotland's Early Lodges and their*

Members (Aberdeen: Aberdeen University Press, 1989); Stevenson, *Origins of Freemasonry*; and Stevenson, D., 'Apprenticeship: Scottish Stonemasons' Indentures, 1573–1740', in *Scottish Archives: The Journal of the Scottish Records Association*, 17 (2011).

111. Knoop and Jones, *Scottish Mason*, 66–8.
112. Carr, *Minutes of the Lodge of Edinburgh*, 226: 'Att Maryes Chapell the 27 dece[r] 1705: The q[ch] Day y[e] deacon of the massons and his breathering taking to y[r] Consideration that y[r] are se[ver]al of y[e] masters of this house that toleratt jurnmen to work up an down this Citie Contrair to y[r] oath of admission and particulary deacon Nisbet who tolerat Thomas Patersone . . . any such person . . . to be punished acording to y[r] fault or priveledge of this brough'.
113. Pryke, Thesis, 46.
114. For example: ECA, Acc.622/4, Minute book, 1796–1807, 16–17, 6 February 1797: Convener Braidwood informs the Incorporation that arbiters in a case with a Mr Reid had found that he had claim to the convening room, 'except when occupied by the Incorporations or the Masons Lodge of Saint Mary's Chapel'. ECA, Acc.622/31, Rental Book, 1783–7, 79: A rental list of 1785 states that the 'Lodge of free Masons' paid £5 for a year's rent of Mary's Chapel in Niddry's Wynd.
115. Pryke, Thesis, 47. For more on non-operatives, as opposed to 'operative', stone-working masons, see Stevenson, *Origins of Freemasonry*, 180–2, 192.
116. Carr, *Minutes of the Lodge of Edinburgh*, 272–3.
117. Pryke, Thesis, 47.
118. ECA, ED008/1/7, Incorporation of Hammermen Minute Book, 67, 7 February 1741: 'propos[a]lls to lett a part of the Chappell to the Freemasons': 'A Proposall being made to the house by some Free and accepted Masons in Edinburgh for taking from the house a Lease of the Backpart of the Chappell in order to make a Masons Lodge of The house judges it would be for the Interest of the hammermen that part of the Chappell was sett off and therefor remitts to the Deacon and Theasurer and ane Committee consisting of the persons following viz Deacon Wilson Deacon Gifford D. Boswell D. Simpson and William Corse to Commune with the Gentlemen that desired the proposal might be made and to sett that part of the Chappell to them to the best Advantage . . .'
119. Pryke, Thesis.
120. Apted and Hannabuss, *Painters in Scotland*.
121. Whitelaw, C. E., *Scottish Arms Makers* (London: Arms and Armour Press, 1977).
122. Turnbull, J., *The Scottish Glass Industry, 1610–1750: 'To Serve the Whole Nation with Glass'* (Edinburgh: Society of Antiquaries of Scotland, 2001).

1

Headship and Inclusion

Now, freedome being that which all men naturally covet, thir pershuars ambition swells no hyer than to be declared freemen, and not slaves, to be capable of the deaconrie, not to be deacons; and since in all their common evidents, they are designed *confratri* (for *confratres*), let their animosities be this day buried, and all ordained, by your Lordships decreet, to live togither like bretheren in unity.

Sir John Lauder of Fountianhall[1]

In the context of corporatism, with its emphasis on protectionism and privilege, it is highly interesting that the clerks of the Incorporation used the term 'the House' when making reference to the corporate body that employed them.[2] Though their official public name would change from 'Incorporation of Masons and Wrights' to 'Incorporation of Mary's Chapel' in the seventeenth century,[3] their private name used within their minutes and accounts was most often 'the House'; not 'the Chapel'.[4] So why did they choose 'the House'? What was it about the household that they identified with?

As noted by Ewen and Nugent in their introduction to the important collection of essays, *Finding the Family in Medieval and Early Modern Scotland*:

Many quasi-family institutions used the language of the family, and both the immediate locality of one's community, as well as the broader political, social, economic and religious communities looked to family relationships for organizational principles.[5]

This is certainly true of the Incorporation of Mary's Chapel. Farr, writing on European corporatism in general, noted that, 'A well-ordered society, as theorists never tired of proclaiming, was based upon the well-ordered family, which was supposedly regulated and disciplined by the father, the male head of household.'[6] In part, this is observed in the corporate regime's, 'concern for subordination and discipline of inferiors'.[7] As we shall see, 'inferiors' is a term which needs careful consideration, as it was not only the young journeyman or the younger apprentice who fitted this term, but also those free masters who were not part of the increasingly-defined craft aristocracy. In Mary's Chapel there were those senior crafts which led the Incorporation, and the other trades that sought inclusion over the seventeenth century; a drawn-out argument over the deaconhood which highlights uncomfortable issues of precedence and rank.

This early modern preoccupation with status was predicated on a need for order, and the chief building block for order was the household. It is therefore no wonder that the Incorporation modelled themselves on the family unit; a point illustrated by the fact that the masters within 'the House' were referred to as 'brethren'. Here we see a form of a family unit, but not one based on kinship alone. While ties to the established members were indeed important, a wider range of factors might have brought one into this privileged group of craftsmen.

The use of the term 'House' was not just to denote a specific community within the wider urban community of the capital. It was also a claim of privileged exclusivity, which was, of course, in keeping with early modern pretensions to rank. Flandrin has used eighteenth-century English and French dictionary entries to demonstrate that both 'family' and 'house' were characteristic of the elite, as with the common usage of 'House of Stewart', or 'House of Tudor' today.[8] By applying the term to the Incorporation, a claim to superiority was being made. As a general trend of aping the elite, later commentators would make astute observations on this type of affectation, as illustrated by the Chevalier de Jaucourt in his *Encyclopédie*:

> It is vanity that has imagined the word *house*, in order to mark even more blatantly the distinctions effected by fortune and chance. Pride has therefore decreed in our language, as in past times among the Romans, that the titles, the great dignities and the great appointments continuously held by people of the same name should form what one calls the *houses* of the people of quality, whereas one describes as *families* those of citizens who, clearly distinguished from the dregs of the populace, perpetuate themselves in an Estate, and transmit their line from father to son in honourable occupations, in useful employments, in well-matched alliances, a proper upbringing, and agreeable and cultivated manners . . .[9]

Whether a claim to prideful exclusivity, or an attempt to instil a sense of unity amongst the brethren in an aspiring godly society, it was 'the House' which was chosen as an identifier for the Incorporation, though as we shall see, it was neither exclusive nor unified at many points in its long history.

Following on from exclusivity, we must briefly consider those who were excluded, and here we return to the concept of the 'stranger' mentioned in the Introduction. The meaning of this term is, of course, broad. It could refer to the hated unfreeman. A craftsman could have been born in Edinburgh, but without the freedom to work, he was an unrecognised stranger. Alternatively, a stranger could be someone from abroad. When economic troubles bring uncertainty to the labour market, it is sadly a common response for workers to blame foreigners, though, as Robert Tittler points out, the 'usual rivalry between native and foreign workmen' often included both violent conflict and inclusive mixing.[10] Edinburgh's builders certainly demonstrated resentment of foreigners, though surprisingly they also demonstrated a very inclusive attitude to some foreign craftsmen.

In 1684 when an unfreeman wished to gain admission to the Incorporation, he foolishly boasted that his work was, 'as good as any come from France or England', implying that the work of the usual Edinburgh craftsmanship was not quite at this level.[11] Needless to say, he was found lacking and was discharged from working in the capital. Whether or not Scottish craftsmanship was on a par with that of other countries is beside the point. There was a perceived difference in quality between domestic and imported goods, which one would expect would inflame tensions between foreign and local craftsmen.

The Incorporation of Mary's Chapel, though, proved to be remarkably welcoming to foreign craftsmen. Aside from a sincere admiration of the artistic and architectural styles of the continent, as emphasised by the adoption of Palladian style for the eighteenth-century façade of their own convening hall, Mary's Chapel (Figure 1.1), or the Netherlandish influences on Scottish vernacular architecture with the famous 'crow-step' gables, the Incorporation also welcomed craftsmen from other countries with apparently-open arms. The Mansion family were from France, and one of their number, Andro, was most likely brought in by James V as part of a group of French craftsmen, which one would expect to alienate him from the Scottish craftsmen.[12] Mansion's nationality was apparently no bar to both joining the Incorporation and even serving as one of the arbitrators in an internal craft dispute.[13] Instead of resenting the Frenchman as a stranger, he was respected as a figure of authority in craft affairs. Indeed, other Frenchmen were also mentioned in the Incorporation's papers, such as 'gilliam ye franche payntir', emphasising a remarkable openness to foreign talent rather than a closed-shop mentality, at least in the early Incorporation.[14]

This last point is of particular significance in light of the use of 'the

Figure 1.1 'A View of St Mary's Chapel'

From Maitland's, *History*, 167. By kind permission of City of Edinburgh Council Libraries.

House' as an identifier. While the masters were self-consciously referred to as 'brethren', the membership of the House was not always closed to outsiders, or 'outland men',[15] who were often allowed to be co-resident. As we shall see in these first two chapters, the use of the term 'House' meant both the family and the wider household, whether kin or not. Of course 'family' and 'household' are not wholly the same, and not everyone under the House was considered a brother; nor, for that matter, were all brothers equal. Considering the context, we should not expect equality within the House. As Farr also rightly observed, 'the corporate regime gained definition *by* the principle of exclusion', and in composite corporatism exclusion was not only of outsiders.[16]

So, this interesting, but occasionally problematic, combination of the concepts of family and household leaves us with a few questions about 'the House'. If the Incorporation was indeed akin to a house, who exactly was in the house, and why? Within this house, who were the brethren? Was it just the master craftsmen periodically listed as freemen in the Incorporation's minute books? Or should the family element of 'the House' be viewed more broadly? Clearly it was more complicated than just the freemen, just as the household in early modern Edinburgh was more complicated than just the nuclear family of husband, wife and children.

Here we must look at another important concept for the early modern period – the concept of privilege. Although this is a very broad concept in any period, for the corporate framework it was at least governed by law, though various courts, from that of the Incorporation's twelve masters to the arbitration of the monarch himself, all had their own versions of how the law should interpret these privileges. One aspect of privilege in particular tied in with the Incorporation identifying itself as a household, and that was the 'Law of Primogeniture'. Sanderson, speaking of the family in general in early modern Scotland, noted that:

> Provision for all the family had to take account not only of limited resources but also of the law of primogeniture. This determined that where there were several children the inheritance would automatically go to the oldest surviving son, and the others would have to fend for themselves or rely on his help and generosity.[17]

This particular law fitted well with the corporate framework, which was fundamentally based on the protectionist and privileged policies of an established oligarchy of craftsmen. Though there were upholsterers and bowers who were free of the Incorporation, it was the eldest sons – the masons and wrights – who held the inheritance for much of their history. This included access to the office of deacon and even the very name of the corporate body – the 'Incorporation of Masons and Wrights'. Over time this privileged status was harder to defend, and by the seventeenth century a new name, the 'Incorporation of Mary's Chapel', would replace the previous title's connotations of privilege, just as restricted access to the 'deaconheid' was relaxed.[18]

So, the use of terms 'House' and 'brethren' imply both order and unity. They imply control of a household, where some individuals were accepted in, though the great majority were excluded for the benefit of the privileged few. In the context of composite corporatism, there was real need to build unity amongst these brethren – brethren who did not always agree on what was best for the House, or who should make the paternal decisions. These first two chapters will explore why the Incorporation identified with the household as an organisational ideal. If they were really brothers within a house, which of the brothers controlled that house? Who was included within the house? As the next chapter will explain, the house included more than just the brethren, but first of all, this chapter will explore the inclusion and exclusion of those brethren in terms of the headship of the House. Indeed, it was not just the brethren who were included, as there was also a second tier of craftsmen allowed in, giving greater definition to the aristocracy which ruled the House.

HEADSHIP AND CONTROL OF THE HOUSE

Inclusion amongst the members of the Incorporation had substantial socio-economic and political benefits, but not all members, let alone all con-nected to the House, were equally privileged. From early on we can see the formation of an aristocracy within the House, as the senior trades sought to differentiate themselves from the other trades which joined the Incorporation. Indeed, control of the 'House' mirrored the familial privi-leges and obligations of the husband and father in the many households of early-modern society, so differentiation amongst the various crafts allowed consolidation of control.

In 1475, when the building trades were first incorporated by the council, there were only two trades mentioned in the seal of cause: the masons and the wrights.[19] Fourteen years later, a second seal of cause was granted to the coopers, who were 'conformit to . . . and bundin with tham'.[20] By 1517, when the Archbishop of St Andrews confirmed the Incorporation's privileges, the list of incorporated trades had grown to include masons, car-penters, coopers, glassinwrights, bowers, slaters, and 'dykers', who appar-ently built walls only.[21] The earliest known pre-Reformation minute books of 1553–60 mention various trades in amongst the notes on meetings:[22]

masons, wrights, coopers, bowers, slaters, sawers,[23] wallers,[24] a 'pionar', or pioneer,[25] a 'spargenor', or plasterer,[26] painters, and glassinwrights. After the Reformation we also find 'plewcht wrychts', or plough-wrights,[27] and roughlayers, who like wallers apparently stacked rather than shaped stones.[28] Most of these were mentioned in relation to payments, often quarterly, but occasionally for their upset payment upon becoming freemen.

What is most striking about this group of sixteenth-century trades is the diversity compared to the precise, regular lists of the ten trades in the seventeenth century. It is not that there weren't lists before, as lists of both random craftsmen making quarterly payments and lists of craftsmen organised by individual trades, such as 'masons', or 'sawars', figure heavily in the earlier minutes.[29] It is also not that there weren't other trades involved in the seventeenth century, when we find regular, ordered lists, or 'rolls', of the ten trades. As the periodic entries of stallangers prove, there were other types of craftsmen besides the official ten trades of Mary's Chapel.

For some reason, possibly administrative simplicity, the Incorporation settled on ten trades by 1670, if not before. From at least that point, they were always listed in a set order: masons, wrights, coopers, bowers, glaziers, painters, slaters, plumbers, sievewrights and upholsterers.[30] From 1670 we see a crystallisation of the order and makeup of the lists of the ten trades incorporated within Mary's Chapel.[31] The sequence and composition of these lists are consistent into the modern period, suggesting a less-fluid organisation than the Incorporation of the sixteenth century, though one or two of the smaller trades do appear to have died out by the later period.

The established order of the ten trades was used by Roderick Chalmers when he repainted the chimney piece for the Incorporation's meeting hall at Mary's Chapel in 1720 (Plate 1). The masons and wrights are at the centre, with the remaining eight trades flanking them from left to right, working outwards towards the least-senior arts at the very edges. In this way, the two senior trades took pride of place, with the right-hand place always given to the apparently more-senior trade: masons, on the right-hand side of the wrights; coopers on the right-hand side of the bowers; etc., moving from the most-senior at the centre, to the least-senior on the periphery. Chalmers exhibited these ten trades' work in front of one of the more prestigious buildings on which they worked – the royal palace of Holyrood. Here we see not only the ten arts of the House, but a representation of their individual skills and products. More importantly, we see a key example of their combined efforts in a royal building of national importance, symbolising the potential which could be achieved by a unified Incorporation. As will be seen later, agreeing on the chimney piece was problematic enough, let alone achieving true unity amongst the brethren of the House.

STALLANGERS

While the seventeenth century saw what appears to have been a more crys-tallised, uniform structure of ten official arts within the Incorporation, there were also other trades which sought admission to the House, though not all were accepted as freemen under the ten trades. Just as an Edinburgh house-hold included both blood relations and those co-resident, the House incor-porated other trades beyond the ten official arts represented in Chalmers' chimney piece. For a fee, a second tier of tolerated craftsmen known as 'stallangers' were allowed in the House. As the name would imply, these craftsmen were licensed – usually for a limited time – to produce specific wares to be sold at market stalls. A fair variety of crafts were represented here, though the common factor tended to be specialisation.

The term 'wright', as with 'merchant', was often general in meaning, applying to both a builder of houses and a builder of furniture (eg: both joiner and carpenter).[32] The seventeenth century, however, appears to have seen increased specialisation of aspects of Edinburgh's occupational struc-ture.[33] In Mary's Chapel we see such specialised trades being brought in through toleration, but occasionally being allowed to become fully-accepted, official trades. Examples can be seen in the wheelwrights, turners and sawers. Theoretically, any wright could make a wheel, turn a spindle piece or saw out boards for their work, if they chose to invest the time and precious resources into the specialist tools, such as lathes or saws.[34] By at least the seventeenth century, though, there were craftsmen in Edinburgh who specialised in these tasks. Indeed, the very fact that tradesmen such as the burgess 'turner and brushmaker', William Schaw were willing and able to specialise gave them a way into the House, even if only as tolerated stallangers.[35]

Such a division of labour had to first serve the needs of the Incorporation, as it was their privileges which were technically being encroached upon. Hence a 1671 'Act anent turners & sawers pryces for their work' specified not only that the Incorporation would 'rectify' their prices, but that the turners and sawers were '. . . bound to serve the brethren of wrights before any other within burgh in all tyme coming.'[36] If there was not enough autonomy over prices for freemen, there was apparently even less for stal-langers. Still, they were allowed in to serve the needs of the House's freemen; were able to employ servants and journeymen; and apparently had a degree of freedom as to which freemen they sold their products and labour.[37]

The capital was not alone in allowing such practices. Similar tolera-tion was granted within the building trades at Haddington, as long as the wooden wares applied only to a niche market and did not interfere with the work of the freemen wrights.[38] Indeed the issue of interference was taken quite seriously, and numbers of stallangers were usually kept low. Prior to 1700, only three turners were listed as having purchased burgesship in Edinburgh, and only five more before 1760.[39] In the winter of 1672 the Incorporation's minutes include an, 'Act Anent the turners of Edinburgh in ther favors', which responded to a complaint by the turners that they were overrun by new admissions.[40] They asked that no more would be allowed in, save those who were sons of burgesses or apprenticed to one of their number. Interestingly, the Incorporation agreed, despite the fact that they were not a free craft of Mary's Chapel. These stallangers often supplied parts and labour to the freemen, and allowing a surplus of labour would theoretically have driven costs down, to the advantage of the freemen, yet protectionism and the principle of protecting the market share of those within the House appears to have been prioritised.

In terms of the admission of stallangers, there were many ways in which they might have been brought into the House. Occasionally it was through the necessity of their work, as suggested by the fact that John Eason, wheel-wright, was not only made stallanger, but was granted this status for life.[41] Examples from other incorporations or burghs demonstrate that stallanger status was usually limited to a year or two, as some craftsmen would try to avoid the expensive upset costs of freedom and simply continue to work as a stallanger.[42] For Eason the privilege was granted for life for only £40, demonstrating his usefulness within the House.[43]

At other times, admission to stallanger status was due to a recommendation from the town council. It would appear that this was not always welcomed. In 1712 the dean of guild and council noted in the council minutes that they were going to admit Stephen Forrest as a burgess, 'dispensing with the dues in respect of his singular art in Basketmaking . . .'[44] The council also noted that they had 'recommended him to the Incorporation of wrights and masons for the like favour . . .',[45] though interestingly he doesn't seem to have been entered in the burgess rolls until 1736, suggesting that there was some problem with his entry.[46] Intriguingly, there does not appear to have been any mention of Forrest in the Incorporation's minutes. Did they take exception to the council's interference?

Unfortunately the basketmaker's case is less than clear, though other cases of council recommendation are more straightforward. When the council remitted Ralph Eguttor,[47] a musical instrument maker who had petitioned them, the Incorporation put his entry to a vote and agreed to admit him as a freeman and to allow him to take an apprentice. Perhaps this was due to the £130 he offered, or perhaps it was the prestige of his particular art.[48]

Whether through necessity, or through council patronage, many arts approached the Incorporation for the right to work within their 'House'. Many of these worked only as tolerated stallangers, though occasionally this foot in the corporate door lead to something more permanent. For example, the sievewright craft was originally allowed in only as a tolerated group, but by the seventeenth century they were one of the ten official arts listed in the rolls. In 1568, John Cunningham was given 'licence and tolerance' to make sieves and riddles. These were common household and agricultural implements, used for separating and cleaning, as with newly threshed grain, which might have chaff or stones.[49] Indeed, they were also used on the building site for preparing mortar, so it is understandable why the Incorporation would grant him first tolerance, and, shortly after, freedom, to make his sieves and sell them on the market day with the coopers' wares.[50] While the sievewrights were never numerous, they eventually became accepted as an official art within the Incorporation, though by the mid-eighteenth century the rolls began to list no names under the heading of their trade, suggesting an early decline.[51]

Plumbers, on the other hand, became even more important in the modern era. Like the sievewrights, it would appear that plumbers were a tolerated group before they became one of the ten arts of the Incorporation, again demonstrating how some trades managed to prove their value to both burgh and Incorporation. While they are listed as one of the ten arts in the rolls from 1670, a Court of Session ruling over political access found that they did not enter the Incorporation until after 1646.[52] Indeed, Edinburgh did not admit a plumber to burgesship until the 1640s, despite the antiquity of their craft.[53]

What is perhaps more interesting, is the fact that plumbers came into the building trades rather than the metalwork trades. Plumbers, as their name would suggest, worked with lead.[54] Plumbers did indeed work with a metal, but due to the use of this material for water management, the trade was incorporated with the builders rather than the metalworkers. Eventually this brought about a dispute with the metalworkers of the Incorporation of Hammermen, as the skill set and methods used for plumbery involved both casting and the making of hollow-wares, such as pipes and cisterns.[55] Indeed, it is telling that the dispute, when it came, was due to a plumber having been trained by a pewterer, which was one of the more influential of the metalworking trades.

The plumber art itself was not new in Scotland, but was actually of some antiquity due to the traditional use of lead sheeting for covering roofs of some expensive buildings.[56] The seventeenth century saw an apparent upsurge in the occupation, as water management took on greater importance in urban building, with more sophisticated and elaborate systems.[57] In terms of architectural applications, Curtis has suggested an increased use of lead down-pipes with the onset of Classicism in the seventeenth-century.[58] The usual essay of a plumber was related to water,[59] as illustrated in Chalmers' 1720 depiction of a plumber making a cistern (see Plate 1). Cisterns helped ensure efficient and tidy removal of waste water, providing overflow space for times of particularly heavy rain. Dirty water overflowing the gutters and spilling onto the streets was unseemly, and perhaps the phenomenon of plumbers being incorporated into Mary's Chapel in the seventeenth century is indicative of the wider architectural changes as Edinburgh moved from the timber-built medieval burgh to the elegant stone-built capital.[60] Clearly parallels should be drawn with Borsay's 'English Urban Renaissance' of the post-Restoration period. [61]

Indeed, as part of what might be considered a wider urban renaissance, many towns across Europe modernised the provision of their water supply in the early modern period. The plumbers' abilities in water management gave them the skill set to move water from external springs across uneven terrain, or to build mechanical pumps to draw water out of the ground.[62] Plumbers and plumbery were clearly quite important aspects of the building site by the end of the seventeenth century, which is precisely why the Incorporation of Mary's Chapel found themselves in a dispute with the Incorporation of Hammermen. Both of these incorporations used 'the House' to describe themselves, and here we see a conflict between houses; a conflict over privilege which reflects the socio-economic divisions within the burgh community of the post-Restoration capital.

The controversy arose not over the product or service, but instead over the materials and methods, as lead was cast by both plumbers and pewterers. Traditionally, the building trades had relied on the Hammermen to supply architectural hardware, such as locks, nails and wall anchors,[63] or to sharpen their tools, but by the later seventeenth century relations were somewhat troubled. Conflict with the Hammermen had arisen over the furnishing of blacksmiths' and locksmiths' work for buildings, and in April of 1676 the masons and wrights were told by the Convenery of Edinburgh's fourteen trades not to 'medle with any other mans trade', suggesting they were finding alternative sources.[64] Perhaps this spurred the Incorporation of Mary's Chapel on in their pursuit of the apprentice plumber?

Hence, in May of 1676 Patrick Skirvine, plumber, put in a bill for the Incorporation of Mary's Chapel against the Incorporation of Hammermen for admitting one George Whyt, who had apparently been apprenticed to a pewterer, but was given an essay 'to be ane ffreeman plummer'.[65] The crucial point was that his essay for the pewterer craft in the Incorporation of Hammermen was to be a lead cistern, which was usually the work of the plumbers in Mary's Chapel. The Convenery declared that the essay should be expunged, as it was not customary, and a pewterer's essay should be assigned in its place, though the troubles did not end here.[66]

In September of the same year, Whyt was employed by Robert Young to 'take away excresset water and to convey the same to his brewhouse'.[67] He began work, so the deacon of wrights and other members of Mary's Chapel broke down his work bench, took materials and threatened and injured him 'as if he had bein no frieman'.[68] The Convenery found a way through this rather delicate situation, and ruled that a freeman plumber of Mary's Chapel should finish the work.[69]

Whilst this whole episode says little for unity amongst the Edinburgh incorporated trades, it does point to some of the challenges faced by craftsmen in the context of corporatism. Plumber work was quite old in some senses, but new aspects of the work took on greater importance, and the regulation and oversight of these new elements had to be carefully negotiated to maintain order both within the wider burgh community and between the two 'houses' which sought to control lead work.

Conflict was not only between houses, but also within the 'House' of Mary's Chapel, and not all crafts made the transition from tolerated stallangers to one of the ten internal arts. Generally stallangers were accepted in manageable numbers, as long as they were firmly under the authority of such municipal institutions as the incorporated trades. The stallangers of the Incorporation of Mary's Chapel certainly fitted this description, though occasionally there was conflict over this toleration, as not all members of the House necessarily shared a view as to the benefits of allowing them such favourable access to their markets.

Some stallangers were too far outside of Incorporation control, as with the many suburban stallangers. While suburbs had long been a problem for the Edinburgh incorporated trades, they also brought certain opportunities, and by the mid-seventeenth century Edinburgh had a degree of control over suburban workers.[70] As the building trades often took work outside the burgh, they were already used to a more-permeable jurisdiction, though masters living and working outside the town walls was a very different thing to unfreemen selling their wares on the capital's doorstep.[71]

Through licensing, a certain number of unfree 'stallangers' were permitted. The Incorporation apparently had no problem with John Bartleman, wheelwright in the neighbouring regality burgh of Canongate, setting up as a stallanger in Edinburgh. He paid the boxmaster £40 and was allowed to work his trade.[72] On the other hand, they did have a problem with James Anderson, a plasterer's servant in South Leith, when the Leith craftsmen admitted him as a stallanger.[73] It was one thing for Mary's Chapel to take stallangers in the suburbs, but a very different proposal for suburban crafts to 'intrude' upon their privileges and take stallangers of their own.[74] Both trades were necessary, but both tradesmen were not necessarily under the Incorporation's authority.

While stallangers could be a tolerated group under the protection of the Incorporation, not all who sought to rent their freedom were allowed to practise their trade. Some were simply too similar to work already being done within the ten trades of Mary's Chapel, adding to the existing competition in the markets. Interestingly, not all members of the House agreed on who should or should not be allowed to pay stallanger fees and work in the town or its liberties, though there were certain authorities outside of the House from which help could be sought. In the late summer of 1676 an unfree painter had approached Mary's Chapel about setting up as a stallanger, which the free painters naturally took exception to. The masons and wrights overruled the painters and the other seven trades, and allowed the unfree painter's enrolment as a stallanger, so in September of 1676 the eight junior crafts of Mary's Chapel appealed to the Convenery of Trades to pass an act, 'for preventing of all such attempts be any unffriemen of the saids airts in all tyme coming' for both Mary's Chapel and for the crafts in Leith.[75] The key factor here was that the would-be stallanger was working in a trade which was already an accepted art within the Incorporation. The painters were already present in the House, and they jealously guarded their privileges, which the more senior members of the House were quite happy to let out for a fee.

The Convenery, leaving the deacons of the masons and wrights out for the sake of fair arbitration, put the issue to a committee, as this touched on all corporate privileges across the trades of the capital. Eventually it was decided to 'put a stop to all invasiones or incroachmeents' by declaring that for all of the fourteen trades of Edinburgh no one was to be admitted either a freeman, unless they were an apprentice, a freeman's son, or were married to a freeman's daughter, or a stallanger, unless they had been approved of unanimously by the 'special consent and assent of the haill maisters of that airt of whilk the said persone seeks to be admitted'.[76] The two deacons of Mary's Chapel could only protest and take the usual instruments for their records.

Enforcing such rigid rules was naturally problematic,[77] and the very same day on which the Convenery ruled about stallangers meeting unanimous approval of their respective trade, the ruling was called upon for another case, again in regards to the Incorporation of Mary's Chapel.[78] This instance seems to have been much more heated, as certain bowers were upset about the admission of John Elder, pantonheel maker in Calton, to work in St Ninian's Row.[79] Partly, this might have been due to the fairly recent case of John Hay, pantonheel maker in St Ninian's Row, who the Incorporation had discharged from work until he explained certain unspecified abuses to the House.[80] It appears that they were happy to come down on Hay, though two years later Elder was blithely admitted to work in the same suburb without consent of the bowers.[81] The chief problems with Elder's admission were firstly the products he was licensed to make, and secondly, that it came during a time of particular difficulties between the trades in the House, as will be discussed shortly. Elder was to make pantonheels, shoe lasts and golf clubs as stallanger in Calton, and was apparently allowed to set up a second shop in Edinburgh itself.[82] The making of shoe lasts was apparently part of the bowers' art, and therefore this stallanger was encroaching, both upon their work and upon their market within the municipal boundaries.[83] The Convenery ruled with the bowers, ordaining that Elder should be put in jail for not bothering to explain himself to the fourteen trades, and that the deacons of the masons and wrights should each pay a fine of 10 merks.[84]

These two cases of the painter and the pantonheel maker illustrate important points about stallangers and their relations within the House. First of all, as some products might have been common between different trades, as with bowers and pantonheel makers both producing lasts, all freemen within the House did not necessarily sympathise with their brethren over rights of production, though corporate structures were broadly inclined to uphold existing privileges. Secondly, the parallels between headship of a household and accountability to municipal or societal authority, which demonstrates a limit to the autonomy of the individual, has much to say about the limits of corporate power, as illustrated by the overruling of the deacons who, at least in theory, controlled the House.

So, a substantial divide between masters and stallangers often went hand in hand with a need for their services. Some were denied access to protect the interests of the freemen, while others appear to have simply been semi-skilled, in that they were more labourers than fully-qualified craftsmen. One example of this from 1568 demonstrates the differences between the trades such as dykers, wallers and roughlayers, from fully-trained masons:

> The quhilk day William Hendirsoune is becummit fre to wirk wallis dyks and simple houses with clay sand and lyme allanerlie and oblissis him nocht to wirk nor lay na hewyng nor brocheing wirk bot ye samyn yat he hes enterit in to undir ye pane of tynsale of his sylver yat he hes gevin quhilk is iii li deliverit to jhone mellross boxmaister.[85]

Hendirsoune was more than competent to build simple, vernacular habitation, but he was not permitted to turn his hand to more elaborate, decorative work such as carved ashlar pieces.[86]

Similar hierarchies are visible in the other trades, as with the 1575 case of Johne Quhytelaw. Having been set an essay for freedom as a wright, he seems to have refused the test, but through the benevolence, favour and good will of the Incorporation, was allowed to work in the town on a strictly limited number of products.[87] He was deemed sufficient in certain types of furniture, but without a full essay, his privileges were limited. As with the cases above, the tolerated stallanger was very much a second-class citizen, to use the phrase, though it would be wrong to assume that all of the ten accepted arts were equal in standing within the House. Here, the office of deacon is instructive, as the headship of the House highlights how very divided it could be.

THE FIGHT OVER THE 'DEACONHEID'

As with many early modern households, headship of the Incorporation was a patrimony to be inherited through the law of primogeniture. Masons and wrights had always held sway, though these eldest sons did not go unchallenged for the control of the House.[88] Indeed, the brothers often fought over a range of both petty and occasionally more serious issues.[89] Sometimes these disputes were over work, as in 1580 between the bowers and the wrights over the making of spears,[90] or in 1631 when the masons and slaters disagreed over which craft should rightly be able to mend chimney heads.[91] A much more divisive argument was had over the headship and control of the House, as the eight 'younger sons' took issue with their lack of access to the office of deacon.

It would appear that the masons and wrights both had a deacon from at least the sealing of their foundation charter in 1475, as the document refers to 'the dekynnis and overmen of the craftis'.[92] Both crafts were to choose four '. . . personis of the best and worthiest of the twa craftis . . . twa masonis and twa wrychtis, that sall be sworne, quhilkis sall serche and se all wirkis at the craftismen wirkis, and that it be lelely and treulie done to all biggaris . . .', highlighting the shared leadership by the masons and wrights over the 'biggaris'.[93] These 'oversmen' were to aid the two deacons in, 'reuling governyng of the saidis twa craftis, and honour and worschipe of the towne, and for treuth and lawte of the saidis craftis proffitable baith for the wirkaris and to all biggaris'.[94]

Here we see the beginnings of a crucial dilemma in composite corporatism. Two crafts were indeed incorporated, but reference was made not only to the masons and wrights, but all of the 'workers and biggers' of the building trades. A fundamental logic was given shape here, that a deacon of masons could oversee all stoneworkers, both labourers and fully-skilled freemen. Likewise, a deacon of wrights could oversee all woodworkers, and fourteen years later this was borne out when the coopers were incorporated under the 'dekyin and kirk maisters of the Wrichtis'.[95] They were bound with them, and from this point forward, they were always under the deacon of wrights – but never deacons themselves.

As other trades joined what would come to be called 'the House', headship was obstinately retained by the two senior trades; a deacon of the masons and a deacon of the wrights. By the seventeenth century, however, the legitimacy of this practice was questioned by the other eight trades, and by the 1670s huge divisions were visible in both the Incorporation and the wider burgh society. In response to the danger of fire, municipal regulations encouraged the use of stone over wood, which no doubt encouraged division between the masons and wrights.[96] Economic crises, such as the severe harvest failure of 1674,[97] proved challenging, and the privileges of royal burghs over their competitors were being eroded.[98] These wider uncertainties seem to have had an impact on Edinburgh, breeding division both in the House and in the capital. Within the Incorporation, there seems to have been a lack of confidence in the leadership. As the craftsmen as a whole had sought political representation on the Edinburgh council in the sixteenth century,[99] the non-masons and non-wrights sought and eventually won representation in their own House, prompting questions about just how brotherly relations within Mary's Chapel really were.

Although 1665 is a crucial date in the controversy over the 'deacon-heid',[100] being the first step in the events of the 1670s, some sources point to earlier examples of the tension between the senior and junior brethren of the House.[101] In 1665, John Milne, mason, protested to the council that the leet they'd returned to the Incorporation for their annual elections included, 'persones who ar not of our craft'.[102] An earlier incident in 1610, involving the coopers, had apparently been dealt with by dismissing their brother craft as a mere pendicle of the Incorporation, though the Convenery had ruled in the coopers' favour, stating emphatically that they were 'ane pairt of thair bodye'.[103] The language and image of a single body aside, little appears to have changed in practice, as the two senior trades continued to monopolise the headship of the House. By 1675, however, the disputes between brothers took on a much harsher edge.[104]

The issue of access to the deaconry was taken quite seriously by all sides, as it was seen to 'prejudge' the liberties and privileges of the Incorporation.[105] The eight junior crafts clearly had less sway in their

House, while the two senior crafts feared losing their influence. For the masons, there was the added complication of their deacon also being an important official in the parallel Freemasonic institution of the Lodge of Mary's Chapel.[106] If a slater or a glazier became deacon of the masons, then they would preside over the freemasons of the Incorporation as well, complicating their hierarchical organisation. Since 1475 a very clear aristocracy had developed within the increasingly-composite Incorporation, and the two senior crafts of masons and wrights had no intention of giving up their control of the House.[107]

But in 1665 and again in 1673, the town council aggravated the tensions between the masons and wrights and their brethren by adding craftsmen from the other trades to the election leets for the two deacons.[108] Both parties – the masons and wrights on one hand, and the other eight trades on the other – raised 'declarators' at the Lords of Council & Session, being unable to solve the dispute with more traditional urban authorities. The crux of the issue rested on the status of the other eight trades, as it was undisputed that the masons and wrights were incorporated from 1475. It was found that by 1583, when the burgh received a new 'sett', or constitution,[109] there were clearly bowers, slaters, coopers, painters and glaziers in the Incorporation, but the sievewrights, plumbers and upholsterers could not be proven to have been admitted by 1583.[110] Though the status of the last three was uncertain, the first seven trades were clearly deemed equal.

The Lords of Session shifted their focus onto the last three trades, as they had apparently been incorporated after 1646, 'long after the Sett'.[111] It was agreed that the Sett had not forbidden the 'assuming of new trades', and these were not, by precedent of the Hammermen taking a coppersmith as a deacon, denied equal privileges to the rest of the Incorporation.[112] Therefore, the three new trades should have been equal to the seven older trades, and therefore as able as the masons and wrights to hold the office of deacon.

Other factors were also considered, such as sufficiency of work. Could a plumber accurately judge the work of a wright or mason?[113] Here the precedent of all masters voting on 'Essays and sufficienciencies of the Masters which are entered to every Trade' was raised, highlighting that a plumber was no less able to judge the work of a wright than a wright was able to judge the work of a plumber.[114]

Honour was considered, as early-modern society was highly status-conscious. Considering the humble nature of the three last 'petty trades', the masons and wrights mused to Stair that:

it were a great detriment to the Government of the Town, that persons of so mean Imployment might be capable to be Deacons, and so capable of the

Government of the Town . . . and consequently cannot be thought to be admitted to the highest capacity of that Incorporation . . .[115]

Appealing to the Lords' sense of rank did not work, however, as perhaps they were already wary of further divisions in the capital.

Stair made reference to the current 'Division and Faction in the Town',[116] and by May of 1677 this concern was borne out with the brutal suppression of a craft riot. This incident would give a small section of Edinburgh's Holyrood Park the new place name of 'Murder Acre', where tensions between merchant and craft youth led to loss of life.[117] Yet, the complexities of these burgh tensions are the key point, as the masons and wrights were allegedly allied to the merchants. Fountainhall made reference not to merchants versus craftsmen, but 'the present agreement betuen the merchants, and wrights, and maissons, against thir other trades', emphasising the fact that these tensions were about a retrenchment of the aristocracy.[118]

The Lords of Session did not share the opinion of the aristocracy of Mary's Chapel, and they instead ruled in favour of the other eight trades. It was declared that they had equal privileges with the masons and wrights, regardless of when the particular trade was incorporated.[119] Therefore, all ten trades were legally 'capable to be Deacons', though the tensions, and the monopolisation of control, did not go away so easily.[120]

With the issue of deaconry underlying, other fissures appeared in the relationship between the brethren of the House, including arguments over the admission of new freemen. Intriguingly, the factions which seem to have arisen were not always along craft lines, demonstrating a range of opinion amongst the individual ten arts. Whilst the minutes are fairly quiet about these disputes, the intervention of the Convenery sheds valuable light on them.

In May of 1676 a dispute between the bowers and the wrights went before the Convenery. The deacon of the wrights, John Herries, had admitted one Samuel Hay to a wright's essay,[121] as he had done an apprenticeship with a wright, but soon after this was changed to a bower's essay.[122] Both wrights and bowers worked with similar materials, tools and techniques, but they were clearly separate crafts. When the bowers complained to the Convenery of the town's fourteen craft deacons, it was ruled that 'both airts cannot subsist in one persone'.[123] The essay could not be changed to that of another craft, clearly illustrating both a divide between the work of the ten trades and the tendency of the two senior trades to control the other eight. An earlier case from 1615 also revealed this, when the deacon of the wrights, 'upone plane malice without onie ressoun', admitted a freeman bower without consent of the bower craft, 'diminising and usurping . . . thair liberties'.[124]

The same day the Convenery heard another complaint regarding disputed admissions to Mary's Chapel, but here the divisions cut across craft lines with both factions containing craftsmen of the same trades. The deacons of masons and wrights had put in a complaint against their boxmaster, Andrew Sheirer, who was also a mason, and against a group of wrights who had stood up and left during a meeting.[125] Further controversy arose from the admission of a cooper, James Bald, and from 'expressiones irreverend', highlighting how divided the House was at this point.

Relations continued to be rocky through to September of 1676. The Convenery received further petitions from the eight junior arts complaining about the two senior trades' decisions. They had admitted stallangers and suburban craftsmen to the annoyance of the other trades, and despite the recent ruling of the Court of Session, the Incorporation continued to be a divided House.[126]

While the records do not always give us the full picture, the occasional glimpse can be found, and it is clear that divisions continued to rumble on after the 1676 ruling of the Lords of Session. Indeed, by 1690 relations had reached a crisis point, with the two deacons themselves falling out, and the Convenery calling for the door of their meeting house at Mary's Chapel in Niddry's Wynd to be closed up.[127] Within a month a plan was in place for the Convenery to act as arbitrators between the crafts, and a new decreet arbitral was subscribed, 'for setling of brotherly love, amity and concord among them'.[128] A range of issues were dealt with, from disputes over widows and procedures for assigning essays, to boxmasters holding corporate funds and expenses of the deacons when attending the magistrates.[129]

Perhaps most importantly, the 1690 decreet arbitral dealt with the order of precedence. In 1475 the masons had been listed first in the seal of cause, while in 1583, the burgh sett gave the wrights before the masons.[130] Both versions had been used in the Incorporation's records, though the rolls always began with the masons first.[131] Clearly rank had been an issue, and might have been the crucial factor in the falling out of the two deacons. After the arbitration of the Convenery in 1690, they were to take turns presiding over meetings, though lists were to carry the former order of precedence.

Though this should have been the end of their disputes, the problems were clearly not resolved. A further decreet arbitral was required in 1703, taking the dispute back to the Court of Session as in the 1670s.[132] In an attempt to clear up the issue of the deaconry, the ten arts were reorganised into two 'denominations':

... the bowers, glasiers plummers and upholsterers to be joyned with the measones under the denominatione of the deaconrie of the measones ... the coupers
painters sclaitters and sevewrights to be joyned with the wrights under the
denominatione of the deaconrie of the wrights ...[133]

Leets were to be voted upon by the whole 'united Incorporatione consisting
of all the ten trades', and all members were declared capable of both voting
and being elected.[134] Lastly, the bureaucracy was refined, with stipulation that of the eight quartermasters, who were elected to help govern the
Incorporation, two should be wrights; two should be from the other crafts
in the wrights' denomination; two should be masons; and two should be
from the other crafts in the masons' denomination.[135]

Precedence, however, continued to be a problem, as emphasised by the
Chalmers' painting of the ten trades. This painting was a replacement of a
very similar one done by James Norrie, which was itself a replacement.[136]
Norrie's painting was to be a chimney piece for display in the convening
hall of Mary's Chapel, but when Norrie did the work he changed the order
of the tradesmen, sparking a row over order of precedence.[137]

This somewhat farcical episode began with several wrights and a slater
who, 'in a clandestine manner', broke into the convening hall and altered
the chimney piece, though they later confessed and apologised.[138] The
deacon of the masons still put in a complaint, as they too disliked the order
of the new chimney piece, which apparently had the masons to the left-hand
side of the wrights, giving precedence and greater honour to the wrights
on the right-hand side.[139] Although the masons pointed to the traditional
order of the rolls, where the masons always came first,[140] the wrights
pointed to the 1583 decreet arbitral, before suggesting that the offending
painting be divided up and displayed on opposite sides of the room to
avoid the issue making 'divisions or animosities'.[141] Other trades, including
the coupers and bowers, also complained about the order.[142] Finally it was
decided to simply make a new one along the lines of the original, which
presumably is the Chalmers' painting which survives in the collections at
the Trades Maiden Hospital (Plate 1).[143]

Despite intervention from the magistrates, the Convenery and even
the Court of Session, still the Incorporation proved to be a House divided.
The issue of headship tested brotherly accord, but this was, of course, not
unique to the Edinburgh building trades.[144] Of course, there had always
been the potential for discord, as seen by the numerous examples of dis-
obedience to deacons.[145] Still, the later seventeenth century appears to
demonstrate an acute level of division, making the survival of the 'United
Incorporation of Mary's Chapel' to the present day all the more remarkable. So why, exactly, did they come together in the first place?

WHY JOIN?

As we've seen, admission to the House was certainly not a guarantee of autonomy or equality, and while some trades were well established, control of the House was not a given, even for the two most senior trades. This leaves us with this important question about these ten accepted arts and sundry tolerated stallangers: why did they join?

For one of the eight crafts that joined the masons and wrights after 1475, we have the text of a charter to help explain their motives. The coopers' 1489 seal of cause referred to three specific problems which were to be addressed by incorporation. First of all, there was the 'keping of gud reull ordinance and statutis', implying expectations about what a legal framework would do for this particular community of woodworkers.[146] Secondly, it specified the upholding of 'diuine seruice and augmentatioun thairof at Sanct Jhonis altar', highlighting the fraternal, Christian focus of their body.[147] Lastly, it discusses the growing problem of the suburban worker, or the 'outlandisfolkis . . . hafand nother stob nor stake within this towne . . . nor yit beand sufficient in thair labour and werkmenschip'.[148] The reasons for the coopers joining were complex, including legal status, religious observance and economic protectionism. Unfortunately, the other trades did not leave such clear statements of intent, though a few factors can be identified from the surviving documentation.

One reason to join together was to be able to regulate access to precious raw materials. Scotland was not a wood-rich country, with much of its timber coming from abroad. Indeed, the Scandinavian supply chain was so well established that the Norwegians refer to the period around the early seventeenth century as the 'Scottish Period', and the timber trade as the '*Skottehandelen*', or 'Scottish Trade', emphasising the importance of Scotland as a consumer of their timber.[149] If access to the larger pieces of timber or more-scarce varieties, such as oak, was problematic, then it made sense to work together to manage access. Robert Tarule has pointed out that white oak was crucial to several occupations, as it was easy to work, making for more-easily joined pieces.[150] Wrights prized it for their furniture, but coopers absolutely needed it for their casks, which had to hold liquid. To achieve this, straight, uniform and tight-fitting surfaces needed to be produced, and inferior wood was of little use.

Not all of the ten arts in Mary's Chapel needed access to the same materials, as a bower had no need to use glass, and a glazier had little use for yew. Still, it was still a useful device to have a corporate network to ensure supply saw as little disruption as possible. Hence, there are numerous acts of the Incorporation which were intended to facilitate the acquisition of materials. One example is the 1670 'Act Anent buying of timber', where it was decreed that all brethren who made bargains on timber had to offer it to the Incorporation at cost value before attempting to retail the wood.[151]

Production, as well as raw materials, might also have been a factor, as regulation of competition was a crucial aspect of the Incorporation. Joining not only gave access to markets, as with the 1568 case of the sieve-wright who was granted tolerance to have his sieves displayed next to the coopers' work in the market,[152] but it also gave protection against others who sought to sell the same products. While the first sievewright we know of was effectively a stallanger first, but soon after a freeman, by the eighteenth century they were one of the ten established arts, and they turned to their brethren in the House when unfreemen were attempting to sell sieves on the High Street.[153]

As with competition being a reason to gain access, occasionally the lack of competition was a reason to grant access, as specialisation often proved excellent leverage for getting a foot in the door. Sievemakers got in by specialising in a product which was important to the consumers, but not as important to the producers. Other niche products had a similar effect in facilitating entry to the Incorporation. Glaziers were increasingly necessary for the production of genteel architecture, but were not enough of a threat to the other trades for them to be excluded like certain labourers.[154] Upholsterers likewise found a niche market by specialising in furnishing the interiors of buildings and adding value to furniture.[155] For the other trades who made the buildings and the furniture, this was a complementary art rather than a source of competition.[156]

Aside from materials and markets as drivers of unification, with the building trades we cannot set aside the contexts of the Renaissance and classicism and, in particular, the Vitruvian ideal. Vitruvius was a Roman architect and engineer in the first century BC who wrote an important treatise on architecture known as *De Architectura*, or *The Ten Books on Architecture*, as English translations have it.[157] His books were highly influential during the Renaissance, and it is quite telling that architects such as Palladio were involved in illustrating sixteenth-century editions of Vitruvius's work.[158]

Indeed, Vitruvius helped shape the idea of the Renaissance architect as a well-rounded, man of parts. The first chapter of Book I, which is on the education of an architect, begins with the exhortation:

> The architect should be equipped with knowledge of many branches of study and varied kinds of learning, for it is by his judgement that all work done by the other arts is put to test. This knowledge is the child of practice and theory.[159]

He continued to elaborate on the variety of skills he foresaw the architect needing:

> Let him be educated, skilful with the pencil, instructed in geometry, know much history, have followed the philosophers with attention, understand music, have some knowledge of medicine, know the opinions of the jurists, and be acquainted with astronomy and the theory of the heavens.[160]

His justification for this was that the educated man would leave more lasting remembrance in his treatises, and the man who could draw could more easily communicate 'the work which he purposes'.[161] An understanding of optics was needed for lighting; arithmetic for calculating costs and measurements; and geometry for symmetry. Moreover, geometry was necessary as it taught the use of rule and compasses, 'by which especially we acquire readiness in making plans for buildings in their grounds, and rightly apply the square, the level, and the plummet.'[162] Through his argument for a broad education, we see not just a single art of architecture, but the incorporation of numerous arts into one capable and useful body; the Vitruvian ideal.

This, of course, chimes with so much of what we know about the mason-architects of early modern Scotland, from the importance placed on symbolic tools, to the composite nature of their organisation. As Stevenson has so aptly observed, '. . . the Vitruvian definition of the architect was conveniently wide, so it could be used to justify involvement in a variety of trades.'[163] Indeed, as Vitruvius had ten books, covering such diverse topics as brick, lime, stone, timber, painting, water management and machinery,[164] the Incorporation of Mary's Chapel also had ten arts, along remarkably similar lines.[165]

The House certainly embodied Vitruvius's 'many branches of study',[166] and there is strong evidence that their understanding of their skill was influenced by the Vitruvian ideal. For example, following the death of the important mason, John Mylne, in 1667, an inscription above Mary's Chapel in Niddry's Wynd reportedly included the following:

> Rare man he was, who could unite in one
> Highest and lowest occupation.
> To sit with Statesmen, Councillors to Kings
> To work with Tradesmen, in Mechanick things.
> May all Brethren, Myln's steps strive to trace
> Till one, withall, this house may fill his place.[167]

As with the Vitruvian architect, the House was to be all encompassing; it had to be sufficiently skilful, and – crucially – it had to be united, as with all skills being in one body.

Clearly the Vitruvian ideal influenced the craftsmen of Mary's Chapel. Still, as seen in the discussion above about the brethren and their struggles, the Incorporation was far from ideal when it came to corporate unity. Certain attempts were made to seek amity and concord, through common symbols to which the craftsmen could unite, or through feasting and socialising. Perhaps the family that eats together does indeed stay together, as the House survived as the 'United Incorporations of Mary's Chapel'. Despite the formation of a clear aristocracy, and a reaction to their monopolisation of the headship, the divided House managed to remain a standing House, demonstrating the skilfulness and hard work of the builders.

NOTES

1. Lauder of Fountainhall, Sir John, *Historical Notices of Scottish Affairs*, vol. 1, 1661–1683 (Edinburgh: T. Constable, 1848), 97.
2. This was certainly in use by 1670, if not earlier. ECA, SL34/1/1, 13, 22nd July 1670. See throughout: ECA, SL34/1/1–14; ECA, Acc.622/1-8; and ECA, Mill, 'Inventory', 13A, 1678.
3. See Chapter 3.
4. It is worth noting that the Incorporation of Hammermen also referred to themselves as 'the House'. Allen, A., *The Locksmith Craft in Early Modern Edinburgh* (Edinburgh: Society of Antiquaries of Scotland, 2007), 12.
5. Ewen, E. and Nugent, J., 'Introduction: Where is the Family in Medieval and Early Modern Scotland?', in Ewen, E. and Nugent, J. (eds), *Finding the Family in Medieval and Early Modern Scotland* (Aldershot: Ashgate, 2008), 6.
6. Farr, J., *Artisans in Europe, 1300–1914* (Cambridge: Cambridge University Press, 2000), 33.
7. Ibid., 26.
8. Flandrin, *Families in Former Times*, 7.
9. Chevalier de Jaucourt, as quoted in Ibid., 6–7.
10. Tittler, R., *Portraits, Painters, and Publics in Provincial England, 1540–1640* (Oxford: Oxford University Press, 2012), 112.
11. ECA, SL 34/1/1, 159, 25 September 1684.
12. Dunbar, J. G., *The Stirling Heads* (Edinburgh: Her Majesty's Stationery Office, 1975), 23.
13. ECA, Mill Recs, B1, f6v, f12v and f13v.
14. Ibid., B3, f6r, 28 May 1559.
15. See for example, ECA, Mill Recs, B1, f5v.
16. Farr, *Artisans in Europe*, 29.
17. Sanderson, M. H. B., *A Kindly Place? Living in Sixteenth-Century Scotland* (East Linton: Tuckwell Press, 2002), 49.

18. See Chapter 3 for more on the change of name, and see below for more on the dispute over access to the office of deacon.

19. ECA, Mill Recs, A2, and *Edin. Recs*, 1403–1528, 31–2. See Appendix 1 for text.

20. The whereabouts of the original are at present unknown. *Edin. Recs*, 1403–1528, 57–8. See Appendix 1 for text.

21. ECA, Mill Recs, A8, and Mill, 'Inventory', 3. See Appendix 2.

22. The following lists are interspersed throughout the three earliest extant minute books prior to the Reformation (Ibid., B1–B3), though the less common examples will be cited below.

23. Ibid., B1, f8r: This example is a payment of 12 d to Gawyne Broun, 'sawar', and his marrow, or partner, though other sawyers also are listed.

24. Ibid., B1, f14r: Andro Gordoun, waller, who made a quarter payment, or f16r: Alexander Bryce, 'admittet as fre man to be ane wallar alannerly'.

25. Ibid., B1, f10r and f15r: John Forrest, 'pionar'. For more on the work of pioneers, which is best described as digging, see *MWA*, 1529–1615, xl.

26. ECA, Mill Recs, B3, f5v: James Blakwod, spargenor, who paid his upset in 1559. See also Mill Recs, B5, f52v, and ECA, SL34/1/1, 3 (at back of volume), compts.

27. ECA, Mill Recs, B5, f4v: 1574 admission of Adame Quhytelaw, 'freman as plewchwrycht'. For more on plough-wrights' work in Edinburgh and Scotland in general, see Andrew Gray's, *The Plough-Wright's Assistant; or, A Practical Treatise on Various Implements Employed in Agriculture* (Edinburgh: Archibald Constable & Co., 1808).

28. ECA, Mill Recs, B4, f3v, and B5, f52v. For more on 'wallers' and 'layers', see Knoop, D. and Jones, G. P., *The Scottish Mason and the Mason Word* (Manchester: Manchester University Press, 1939), 30–1, and Salzman, L. F., *Building in England Down to 1540: A Documentary History* (Oxford: Clarendon Press, 1997), 30–1.

29. For example, the 1555 minutes give separate lists of the trades incorporated just like the seventeenth century equivalents, though the headings vary from minute book to minute book prior to 1669. The 1555 minutes include lists of: masons, wrights, bowers, coopers, glassinwrights, slaters and sawers (ECA, Mill Recs, B2, f3v-f5r), whilst the 1568–9 minutes include lists for: masons, wrights, coopers, roughlayers, bowers, glassinwrights and slaters (ECA, Mill Recs, B4, f2v-f4r). With a few differences in makeup and order, it would appear that the consistency of the later seventeenth-century was not present in the sixteenth century.

30. The minutes from 1583 to 1669 are still missing, and were not included in the find of the missing 'Mill Records' in the ECA. The first such list of the ten trades in the order given above is actually dated 1670. ECA, SL34/1/1, 1–2, 16–17, 20–1, 26–7, etc. The order continues to be used in subsequent volumes' lists. This order is also given in the minutes of the Convenery of Trades. Munro, J. and Fothringham, H. S. (eds), *Act Book of the Convenery*

of *Deacons of the Trades of Edinburgh 1577–1755*, vol. 1 (Edinburgh: Scottish Record Society, 2011), 341. Edinburgh was, of course, not the only burgh with a composite body of building trades. For example, Aberdeen's 1541 seal of cause lists 6 crafts: '. . . measons, wrights, carvers, coupers, sclaters, painters . . .' and makes reference to the plural 'deacons', though their trades apparently split at a later date. Bain, E., *Merchant and Craft Guilds A History of the Aberdeen Incorporated Trades* (Aberdeen: J. & J. P. Edmond & Spark, 1887), 236, 238–9, and 241.

31. This might have been used earlier, but the minutes from 1583 to 1669 are missing at present.

32. For more on the variety of wood-working trades which came under the term 'wright', see Anonymous, *A Poem Inscribed to the Members of St. Mary's Chapel. Upon the Most Honourable, Ancient, and Excellent Art of Wright-Craft. By a Brother of the Craft.* (Edinburgh: David Gray, 1757), 3–5: 'This Name is like the Trunk of some great Tree, From which we many goodly Branches see . . .'

33. See for example previous work on the metalwork trades in Allen, A., *The Locksmith Craft in Early Modern Edinburgh* (Edinburgh: Society of Antiquaries of Scotland, 2007), 15 and 24–5, and Allen, A., 'Production and the Missing Artefacts: Candles, Oil and the Material Culture of Urban Lighting in Early Modern Scotland', in *Review of Scottish Culture*, 23 (2011), 32–3 and 41–4.

34. This statement is admittedly controversial. George Sturt, writing of his own experiences as a wheelwright in late-nineteenth- and early-twentieth-century Farnham, Surrey, noted with glee how an estate carpenter employed at Farnham Castle built a wagon in his workshop – only to find out that it could not turn sharply enough to make it out of the workshop door. Sturt, G. *The Wheelwright's Shop* (Cambridge: Cambridge University Press, 1958), 69–74.

35. 'Petition for William Schaw Turner craveing that he may have liberty to work within the Incorporations privilidges In turning wheells &c granted': 'There was lykewayes a petition given in by William Schaw turner & brush maker burges of Edr Craveing to be allowed & authorized not only to make all sorts of timber work for brushes whither squared or turned But also all other turned work such as Lint wheells or others he should have occasion to doe within the privilidges of this house upon pay of ffourty pound scots money which he offerd being the ordinary upsett what is payed by other wheellwrights and Turners Which petition being Considered by the house They after full debate thereannent By plurality of voices granted & hereby grants the desire of the said petition provideing the petitioner not only cause book all his journeymen & servants in this Incorporation books & pay the same deues therefor as their own journeymen are in use to doe But also that he make no sort of square wright work except what relates to the art of brush & Lint wheell making allenerly.' ECA, SL34/1/4, 97, 25 April 1719.

36. ECA, SL34/1/1, 22, 16 December 1671.

37. For stallangers employing others, see the petition of Willliam Schaw, turner and brushmaker, quoted above. ECA, SL34/1/4, 97, 25 April 1719.

38. 'The samen day the saids deacones & friemen hes gevin Libertie & licence to Ferquhard Andersone indwellar in the said burh [of Haddington] to mak tirleiss [trellises] mak or mend quhells for spining or spindells to quhells & siclyk thingis in tymecuming for payment yerlie of xxvi s viij d money to be payit at the four quarter dayes in the forme & numbers Jon Grahame works & payis therfor providing the same wark be nowayes prejudiciall to the craft of wrytcraft . . .' East Lothian Council Archive and Local History Service (ELCALHS), John Gray Centre, HAD/13/2/4, Minute Book of the Wrights and Masons 1616–1751, 25 June 1636.

39. *Edin. Burgs*, 1406–1700, 179, 311 and 481, and 1701–1760, 39, 53, 98, 154 and 219. William Schaw is not among these, as he took burgessship as a brushmaker. Ibid., 183.

40. 'The which day Alexr Nisbett deacon of the masons Robert Ellott deacon of the wrights Robert Bill boxmaster with the Masters & brethren Conveened for the tym anent ane suplication given in be the turners of Edr wherin they Complane that they ar overrun be putting in of many persons of turner Craft be vertew of mairie Chappells authoritie upon them to ther great hurt therfor they desyred the deacons & brethren not to suffer any to Come in except those who had right be pairents burgessship or prentiship or when they ar few in Number and not able to serv the leidges whereupon the deacons & brethren granted ther request' ECA, SL 34/1/1, 23, 3 February 1673.

41. 'Admission John Easson wheill wright Recept 40 lib . . . The quhilk day the deacons Maisters and remanent brethren & confrarie Admitted John Easson wheilwright In and to the priveledges of this burgh concerning his said craft as ane stallanger during all the dayes of his lyftyme and payd to the Boxmaister ffourtie pundis scots wt the clerk & officers dews' ECA, SL34/1/1, 9, 30 April 1670.

42. '. . . and gif he beis sufficient in his craft, and not of powar to mak his expenssis hastely vpoun his fredome, he sall bruk the priuiledge of a stallanger for ane yeir and na langar . . .' Smith, J., *The Hammermen of Edinburgh and Their Altar in St Giles Church* (Edinburgh: William J. Hay, 1906), 183. For general burgh laws limiting the time allowed to be a stallanger to one or two years, see for example: *Edin. Recs*, 1403–1528, 36 and 41, and Renwick, R., *Extracts from the Records of the Burgh of Peebles, 1652–1714* (Glasgow: SBRS, 1910), 63.

43. ECA, SL34/1/1, 9, 30 April 1670.

44. *Edin. Recs*, 1701–1718, 238.

45. Ibid., 238.

46. *Edin. Burgs*, 72, where both the council minute of 1712 and the actual entry of 1736 are cited.

47. For some reason this does not appear to be in the published council records. *Edin. Recs*, 1689–1701 and 1701–1718.

48. ECA, SL34/1/4, 9 November 1709. It would appear that he was a freeman, though his name does not appear in the rolls of masters for subsequent years.

49. For details on the use, construction and materials of pre-modern sieves and riddles, two excellent studies from Ireland are: Lucas, A. T., 'Making Wooden Sieves', in *The Journal of the Royal Society of Antiquaries of Ireland*, 81:2 (1951), and Lucas, A. T., 'Further Notes on Making Wooden Sieves', in *The Journal of the Royal Society of Antiquaries of Ireland*, 84:1 (1954). Note the similarities between the Irish sieves and the one depicted by Chalmers in Plate 1.

50. 'The quhilk day Archibald Gray and Jhone Cunynghame dekyns hes gevin licence and tollirance to Jhone Stevinsone seif makir with consent of walter balcaskye everie man of ye coupers for ye tyme for to place and lay his seiffs and riddills one ye mercat day besyde ye cowpers wirk in ye burgh of Edinburgh and offirs him to pay therfor his oulklie pennye quarterlie ay and quhill he be fre and gif he be worthie therfor he sall pay als mickle for his fredome as ony uther siclike of his occupatioun hes done of befor . . . The sext of februare forsaid ye said Jhone Stevinsone is admittet fre & sworne to be leill & trew to all ye bredir without onye payment taken bot allanerlie to pay hes dewitie in tyme to cum as quarterlie compts or ony uther siclike thingis as becummis him to do befoir Archibald Gray Jhone Cunynghame and Robert Ewyn notare' ECA, Mill Recs, B4, f5v, 3rd February 1568.

51. They were listed ninth in the rolls from at least 1670. ECA, SL34/1/1, 1–2, etc. For their apparent decline, see for example the roll for 1739 in ECA, SL34/1/6, 363, 1739 List of Freemen.

52. Dalrymple of Stair, Sir James, *The Decisions of the Lords of Council & Session, In the Most Important Cases Debate Before Them; From July 1671 to July 1681 . . . Part Second* (Edinburgh, 1687), 405.

53. *Edin. Burgs*, 152 (Thomas Dods, 1644), and 453 (Alexander Skirven, 1642 (sic) as servant to Thomas Dods). See also *Edin. Recs*, 1626–1641, 87, where Thomas Dods is engaged to care for the wells and pumps for the town.

54. This is from the Latin, *plumbum*.

55. Munro and Fothringham, *Act Book of the Convenery*, Vol. 1, 341.

56. See for example, Weaver, L., 'Some Architectural Leadwork. Article VII – Scottish Lead Spires', in *The Burlington Magazine for Connoisseurs*, Vol. 9, No. 41 (Aug., 1906), 304–12.

57. Curtis, R., 'Lead', in Jenkins, M. (ed.), *Building Scotland: Celebrating Scotland's Traditional Building Materials* (Edinburgh: John Donald, 2010), 122.

58. Ibid., 122.

59. Alexander Thom, plumber, was admitted to an essay in 1676 of, 'ane eln of sheet lead mad & brunt in a pyp of four inches of diameter . . .' ECA, SL34/1/1, 40, 25th May 1676. Patrick Campbell, also a plumber, had an essay in 1717 of, 'ane cistern, & two mandrall lengths of Lead pipes brunt to gether in ane joynt'. ECA, SL34/1/4, 80, 2 February 1717.

60. Campbell, I. and Stewart, M., 'The Evolution of the Medieval and Renaissance City', in Edwards, B. and Jenkins, P. (eds), *Edinburgh: The Making of a Capital City* (Edinburgh: Edinburgh University Press, 2005), 32.

61. Borsay, P., *The English Urban Renaissance: Culture and Society in the Provincial Town 1660–1770* (Oxford: Clarendon Press, 1991).

62. For examples: Regensburg piped in spring water from Dechbetten and Prüll in 1548 and 1642. Historischen Museum Regensburg, *Regensburg: Wasser und Stadt* (Regensburg: Museen der Stadt Regensburg, 1997), 5, 10 and 14; In 1582, a German named Peter Morris helped London to pipe Thames water from an 'artificial forcier' at London Bridge up a steeple and from there to Leadenhall. Stow, J., *A Survey of London Written in the Year 1598* (Stroud: The History Press, 2005), 172; Belfast brought in piped water in 1678. Gillespie, R., 'Landlords and Merchants: Belfast 1600–1750', in Clarke, H. B., (ed.) *Irish Cities* (Dublin: Mercier Press, 1995), 24; and Edinburgh replaced its open wells with closed pump mechanisms in 1631, and then with piped water from Comiston in 1672. For more on this drawn-out process, see *Edin. Recs*, 1604–1626, 172; *Edin. Recs*, 1626–1641, 87; and Lewis, D., *Edinburgh Water Supply A Sketch of its History Past and Present* (Edinburgh, 1908), 3–4.

63. See for example, Allen, *Locksmith Craft*, Chapter 5: 'The Locksmith's Work'.

64. Munro and Fothringham, *Act Book of the Convenery*, vol. 1, 320.

65. Ibid., 321.

66. Ibid., 322. Although the leaden essay for a pewterer might not have been customary, there was a precedent of pewterers working in lead, as with the work done by a pewterer in 1558 for the Queen's marriage, 'for making pypis to the out passage of wyne' at the Mercat Cross. Mill, A. J., *Mediaeval Plays in Scotland* (Edinburgh: William Blackwood & Sons Ltd, 1927), 183–4.

67. Munro and Fothringham, *Act Book of the Convenery*, Vol. 1, 350–1.

68. Ibid., 350–1.

69. Ibid., vol. 1, 351, and vol. 2, 7–8.

70. Allen, A., 'Conquering the Suburbs: Politics and Work in Early Modern Edinburgh', in *Journal of Urban History*, 37:3 (2011), 423–43.

71. That is not to say that burgess masters of the Incorporation were allowed to live and work where they pleased. While there were many examples of freemen living outside the town walls, there were also examples of the municipal and craft authorities attempting to crack down on the perceived abuse and force the freemen to move back into the town. One example of this was the Incorporation refusing to defend one of their sievemakers against a Leith brewer who was selling sieves and riddles in a shop on the High Street, until the sievemaker moved his house and shop back into the town. ECA, SL34/1/4, 98, 6 June 1719.

72. ECA, SL34/1/3, 8 March 1709.

73. ECA, SL34/1/1, 97, 28 May 1681.

74. It is highly likely that different suburbs would have had different levels of success in this, as unlike South Leith, Canongate was a burgh of regality, and had its own suburbs before Edinburgh bought superiority over them. Allen, 'Conquering the Suburbs', 429–30 and 434–5. The word 'intrude' is used in the Incorporation's minutes in relation to the admission of James Anderson. ECA, SL34/1/1, 97, 28 May 1681.

75. Munro and Fothringham, *Act Book of the Convenery*, Vol. 1, 327.

76. Ibid., Vol. 1, 328.

77. For example, the granting of gratis burgesship to soldiers complicated this issue. *Edin. Burgs*, 9.

78. Munro and Fothringham, *Act Book of the Convenery*, Vol. 1, 331–3.

79. A panton, or patten, was a wooden overshoe for protecting one's normal shoes from the ubiquitous muck of the urban environment. A pantonheel was apparently the wooden part of this type of shoe, which according to the Edinburgh council in 1562, was the work of the cordiners: 'The pair of mulis, pantonis, brotekynnis, and all vther wark pertenyng to the cordiner craft . . .' *Edin. Recs*, 1557–1571, 155. Clearly this suburban craft was intended to supply wooden parts for a crucial leather-work trade. A 1646 testament of one George Smyth, 'Heilmaker', suggests that birch was a common wood used for these heels, as he held forty 'peices of birk' worth £6 in amongst other tools, materials and household goods. NRS, CC8/8/61, 744. For more on pantons, see Fitch, C., and Davis, D. H., *The History of the Worshipful Company of Pattenmakers of the City of London* (London: Worshipful Company of Pattenmakers, 1962). For more on 'Calton' and 'St Ninian's Row', see Harris, S., *The Place Names of Edinburgh: Their Origins and History* (Edinburgh: Steve Savage, 2002), 136–7 and 507. The exact relationship between the two places is unclear, though St Ninian's Row was apparently adjacent to Calton, but in Low Calton, which appears to have been outside the barony of Calton. Both are depicted on early maps, the details of which are available in Harris on the pages given above. These can be accessed via the National Library of Scotland's digital collection of maps, available at: https://maps.nls.uk/towns/.

80. ECA, SL34/1/1, 31, 28 June 1673.

81. Ibid., 38, 1 February 1676.

82. He was admitted, '. . . to his freedom in st Ninians Raw for makeing of pantonheills lasts and Gouff Clubs allenarly . . .' ECA, SL34/1/1, 38, 1st February 1676. The complaint by the bowers to the Convenery gives further details. Munro and Fothringham, *Act Book of the Convenery*, Vol. 1, 331–3.

83. Munro and Fothringham, *Act Book of the Convenery*, Vol. 1, 332.

84. Ibid., 333.

85. ECA, Mill Recs, B4, f4v, 6 August 1568.

86. This minute of 1568 anticipates the Lodge of Freemasons' later regulations against 'cowans', who similarly were semi-skilled dykers. See Carr, H. (ed.), *The Minutes of the Lodge of Edinburgh, Mary's Chapel, No. 1, 1598–1738*

(London: Quatuor Coronati Lodge, 1962), 36–9 and 42, and Smith, A. M., *The Three United Trades of Dundee: Masons, Wrights & Slaters* (Dundee: Abertay Historical Society, 1987), 49.

87. ECA, Mill Recs, B5, f6r, 1 May 1575: '. . . Johne quhytelaw wrycht band and obleist him self of his awin fre motive will voluntarilie uncompellit or coactit Nocht to wirk ony uyer wark in tyme coming bot . . . Lattrounis (lecterns), cofferis chairis and stules and that in his awin buith and of his awin tymber and sall wark na warkis within this burgh in ony housses yereof except under past maister of the wrycht craft for wages . . .'
88. I'm grateful to Deacon Bruce Field for explaining the seniority of the masons' deacon in craft affairs, and for sharing one of the Incorporation's copies of their printed 2001 *Laws*, where Section 4 states that the deacons 'shall preside alternately at all Meetings of the Incorporations'. United Incorporations of St Mary's Chapel, *Laws of the United Incorporations of St Mary's Chapel* (Dingwall: UISMC, 2001), 1.
89. See for example: NLS, Acc.7332, Box 2, Group 2: 'Complaints' of members and related memoranda 1666–7.
90. 22 February 1580: 'The quhilk day the haill bowaris submittit theme selffis to the judgement of the dekynnis anent the contraversie betuix thame and the wrytis for making of lang rydeing and ganging speiris and Williame Stevinstoun dekyn of the wrytis tuke his submissioun to his brethrenis advisment upoun the quhilk bowaris submissioun Gilbert Prymros dekyn of the chirurgianis for him self and remanent dekynnis tuke ane act [*signed*] A Gibsone Notarius'. Munro and Fothringham, *Act Book of the Convenery*, Vol. 1, 15.
91. Ibid., 137.
92. See Appendix 1. *Edin. Recs*, 1403–1528, 31–2.
93. Ibid., 31–2.
94. Ibid., 31–2.
95. Ibid., 57–8.
96. For more on this, see Rodger, R., 'The Evolution of Scottish Town Planning', in Gordon, G. and Dicks, B., *Scottish Urban History* (Aberdeen: Aberdeen University Press, 1983), 77–8.
97. Lynch, M., *Scotland: A New History* (London: Pimlico, 2000), 309.
98. Dennison, E. P., 'Urban Society and Economy', in Harris, B. and MacDonald, A. R. (eds), *Scotland: The Making and Unmaking of the Nation, c.1100–1707*, vol. 2 (Dundee: Dundee University Press, 2006), 145.
99. See Chapter 4.
100. Deaconhead, or headship of the Incorporation.
101. Carr, in relation to Deacon John Corse and non-masons appearing on council leets, or lists of acceptable candidates for office, cryptically mentions the year 1648, though details of what exactly happened, or of his sources, were not included, though he does cite a later volume of the council minutes. Carr, H., *The Mason and the Burgh* (London: Quatuor Coronati Lodge, 1954), 68.

102. *Edin. Recs*, 1655–1665, 377.
103. Munro and Fothringham, *Act Book of the Convenery*, Vol. 1, 80–2.
104. The 1675–6 dispute over the deaconry is best explained by two detailed accounts from senators of the College of Justice who helped arbitrate in the case: Dalrymple of Stair, Sir James, *The Decisions of the Lords of Council & Session, In the Most Important Cases Debate Before Them; From July 1671 to July 1681 ... Part Second* (Edinburgh, 1687), 382–5 and 405–6, and Lauder of Fountainhall, *Historical Notices*, 93–7.
105. *Edin. Recs*, 1655–1665, 377.
106. Carr, *Minutes of the Lodge of Edinburgh*, 273.
107. One commentator noted that the, 'composite structure of Scottish craft guilds, which allowed a craft aristocracy to emerge relatively quickly within each guild, is important, for it points to a revision of the accepted nature of the urban hierarchy in fifteenth-century Scottish towns.' Lynch, M., 'Towns and Townspeople in Fifteenth-Century Scotland', in Thomson, A. F. (ed.), *Towns and Townspeople in the Fifteenth Century* (Gloucester: Alan Sutton, 1988), 183. Clearly this revision is applicable to the seventeenth-century as well.
108. Dalrymple of Stair, *Decisions*, 383.
109. Fountainhall describes the decreet arbitral of 1583 as being 'like the Toune's *Magna Carta*'. Lauder of Fountainhall, *Historical Notices*, 94. See Chapter 4 for more on this.
110. Ibid., 93–7.
111. Dalrymple of Stair, *Decisions*, 405.
112. Lauder of Fountainhall, *Historical Notices*, 96–7.
113. Dalrymple of Stair, *Decisions*, 384.
114. Ibid., 384.
115. Ibid., 405.
116. Ibid., 384.
117. Lauder of Fountainhall, *Historical Notices*, 151–61.
118. Ibid., 96.
119. Ibid., 97.
120. Dalrymple of Stair, *Decisions*, 406.
121. ECA, SL34/1/1, 39, 25 March 1676: 'ane ovall table with ane ovall frame 4 wings to be hung with Irin work'.
122. Munro and Fothringham, *Act Book of the Convenery*, Vol. 1, 322.
123. Ibid., 323. There are some interesting examples in the Incorporation of past practice contradicting this, as with the sixteenth-century 'painter and glazier', or the seventeenth-century 'wright and upholsterer', but these were apparently not considered by the Convenery. Indeed, the council employed Patrick Crunyeane as 'stone cutter (or mason) and carpenter of the Town's common work'. Carr, *Mason and the Burgh*, 68.
124. Munro and Fothringham, *Act Book of the Convenery*, Vol. 1, 92–3.
125. Ibid., Vol. 1, 323.
126. Ibid., Vol. 1, 327–9 and 331–3.

127. Ibid., Vol. 2, 113–14. Their clerk was also discharged from attending meetings until the controversy was cleared up.
128. Ibid., Vol. 2, 117 (quotation) and 114–20.
129. Ibid., Vol. 2, 113 and 119; 118; 119; and 119 respectively.
130. *Edin. Recs*, 1403–1528, 31, and 1573–1589, 266.
131. For example: ECA, Mill Recs, B2, f6r, 12 September 1555, as opposed to the order of the rolls post-1670.
132. For the text of the decreet as recorded by the council, see Appendix 8. *Edin. Recs*, 1701–1718, 59–60.
133. Ibid., 59.
134. Ibid., 59–60. This aspect of who was permitted to vote was also a problem in other incorporated trades, as it led to the perpetuation of craft oligarchies. The Edinburgh Goldmsiths' minutes record a meeting of the fourteen craft deacons to discuss a particular controversy in which some crafts' deacons made the lists to be handed in to council, whereas others were made by vote of the whole incorporation. Munro, J. and Fothringham, H. S. (eds) *Edinburgh Goldsmiths' Minutes, 1525–1700* (Edinburgh: Scottish Record Society, 2006), 278–9. Interestingly, the issue cropped up again in Mary's Chapel's 1703 decreet arbitral.
135. Appendix 8 and *Edin. Recs*, 1701–1718, 59–60.
136. Macmillan, D., *Scottish Art, 1460–1990* (Edinburgh: Mainstream Publishing, 1990), 84–5, and Wahrman, D., *Mr. Collier's Letter Racks: A Tale of Art & Illusion at the Threshold of the Modern Information Age* (Oxford: Oxford University Press, 2012), 171–3.
137. See Appendix 9 and ECA, SL34/1/4, 87–8, 22 November 1718; 88–9, 29 November 1718; 100, 2 August 1719; and 106, 3 February 1720.
138. ECA, SL34/1/4, 87–8, 22 November 1718 and 88–9, 29 November 1718.
139. Ibid., 88–9, 29 November 1718.
140. '. . . He contended that the same could not now be altered without the plaine violatione of the rights & privilidges of the Incorporation of the measons, whose right of being first called in the rolls of this house is expressly reserved to them By the Decreet arbitral following upon the submission betwixt the masons & wrights & eight airts . . .' ECA, SL34/1/4, 88, 29 November 1718.
141. For full text, see Appendix 9. '. . . altho any right or privilidge that the masons had of being first called in the rolls of this In Corporatione be thereby reserved to them The wrights privilidge of being first mentioned in the Sett of the good toun of Edr & called in the Councill rolls thereof Is by that Decreet arbitral also reserved to them . . .' ECA, SL34/1/4, 88–9, 29 November 1718.
142. Ibid., 100, 2 August 1719.
143. Ibid., 106, 3 February 1720. Chalmers was paid £100 for this painting in 1721. See Appendix 9 for excerpts from the minutes and accompts. Ibid., Unpaginated 1721 Discharge.
144. The Haddington Wrights and Masons minutes included an ordinance that freemen of the crafts were only to take their grievances to the deacons and

freemen and not any other authority. East Lothian Council Archive and Local History Service (ELCALHS), John Gray Centre, HAD/13/2/4, Minute Book of the Wrights and Masons 1616–1751, 11 January 1632: 'act anent persutes befor ye deaconis'.

145. Take, for example, the 1553 minute of the Edinburgh Masons and Wrights: 'And if ony fre maister of the hail craufts nor if this present crauft disobeys ye ordinats of ye dekynnis & the maisteris & will nocht ansuer to yer ordinants & gud rewell that every maister swa doand sall pay for every falt iiij s & sall pay ye officiar feis on yer awyn expensis gif ony officiar beis requirit yerto for poynding of thaym' ECA, Mill Recs, B1, f4v, 11th February 1553–4.

146. See Appendix 1. *Edin. Recs*, 1403–1528, 57–8.

147. Ibid. See also Chapter 3.

148. Ibid. See also Chapter 4.

149. Newland, K., 'The Acquisition and Use of Norwegian Timber in Seventeenth-Century Scotland', in *Vernacular Architecture*, 42 (2011), 72; Lorvik, M., 'Mutual Intelligibility of Timber Trade Terminology in the North Sea Countries During the Time of the 'Scottish Trade'', in *Nordic Journal of English Studies* 2:2 (2003), 225; and Lillehammer, A., 'The Scottish-Norwegian Timber Trade in the Stavanger Area in the Sixteenth and Seventeenth Centuries', in Smout, T. C. (ed.), *Scotland and Europe, 1200–1850* (Edinburgh: John Donald, 1986), 97.

150. Tarule, R., *The Artisan of Ipswich: Craftsmanship and Community in Colonial New England* (Baltimore: Johns Hopkins University Press, 2004), 50–1.

151. 'Act Anent buying of timber: The quhilk day George Herries present deacon of the wrights with the old deacons masters and remanent brethren of the wrightcraft being conveined Statuts and ordaines that in all tyme coming No brother within the Incorporatione sall be Acepted to buy any bargans of timber and to retail the same without first ane offer be maid to the deacon being for the tyme and the said Incorporatione according to the trew value yerof And if any brother sall be found to contraveine this act Thir presents sall make him lyable to the censor of the hous ~~~John Hamilton Clk' ECA, SL34/1/1, 13, 22 July 1670.

152. ECA, Mill Recs, B4, f5v, 3 February 1568.

153. See above for details of this brewer who usurped the sievewrights' trade. ECA, SL34/1/4, 98, 6 June 1719.

154. Turnbull, J., *The Scottish Glass Industry, 1610–1750* (Edinburgh: Society of Antiquaries of Scotland, 2001), 52–6, and Murdoch, R., 'Glass', in Jenkins, M. (ed.), *Building Scotland: Celebrating Scotland's Traditional Building Materials* (Edinburgh: John Donald, 2010), 128–30.

155. The word 'uphold', from which we get 'upholder', or 'upholsterer', apparently refers to repairs in our context, implying the addition of soft furnishings to existing furniture. Walton, K. M., 'The Worshipful Company

of Upholders of the City of London', in *Furniture History*, 9 (1973), 41. One early-twentieth-century historian claimed that the upholstering of chairs began in the reign of James VI, though the author who made this claim gave no sources. Warrack, J., *Domestic Life in Scotland, 1488–1688* (New York: E. P. Dutton and Company, 1921), 118. It would appear that there was an upholsterer working in Edinburgh by 1540, as the Chamberlain of St Andrews' discharge for that year includes a payment of £3 9s for beds: 'William Ybdy, upholsterer, for the furnishing of two small beds (*pro garnizatura duorum parvorum lectorum*), as per precept, Edinburgh, Nov. 29, 1540, 3l. 9s.' Hannay, R. K. (ed.), *Rentale Sancti Adnree: Being the Chamberlain and Granitar Accounts of the Archbishopric in the Time of Cardinal Betoun, 1538–1546* (Edinburgh: Scottish History Society, 1913), 108. Indeed, the addition of soft cushioning to furniture was only one part of the work of the upholsterer, who really focussed on the furnishing of the interiors made by the other building trades. Habib, V., 'Eighteenth-Century Upholsterers in the Edinburgh Old Town', in *Scottish Archives: The Journal of the Scottish Records Association*, 11 (2005), 68.

156. There was an episode of competition with the saddler craft of the Incorporation of Hammermen, who in 1685 were allowed to 'stuff and cover' the chairs made by the wrights. Munro and Fothringham, *Act Book of the Convenery*, Vol. 2, 74. While the majority of the seventeenth-century minute books for Mary's Chapel are missing, the burgess rolls suggest that the first 'upholsterer-wright' was Gilbert Bell in 1663, who was the son of a leather worker and freeman of the Incorporation of Mary's Chapel by 1670. *Edin. Burgs*, 53 and ECA, SL34/1/1, 1–2, 1670 roll of freemen.

157. Vitruvius and Morgan, M. H. (translator), *The Ten Books on Architecture* (New York: Dover, 1960).

158. Ackerman, J. S., *Palladio* (London: Penguin, 1991), 27.

159. Vitruvius, *Ten Books on Architecture*, 5.

160. Ibid., 5–6.

161. Ibid., 6.

162. Ibid., 6.

163. Stevenson, D., *The Origins of Freemasonry* (Cambridge: Cambridge University Press, 2005), 108. For more on the significant cultural shift of architecture moving from being dismissed as a mere mechanical art to being seen as prestigious marriage of theory and practice, see ibid., 108–16.

164. Vitruvius, *Ten Books on Architecture*, 42, 45, 49, 58, 210, 244, and 283.

165. It is, perhaps noteworthy here that Amsterdam also had ten woodworking trades, though how much of this is coincidence is difficult to say. Was this Vitruvian influence? Prak, M., 'Corporate Politics in the Low Countries: Guilds as Institutions, 14th to 18th Centuries', in Prak, M., Lis, C., Lucassen, J., and Soly, H. (eds), *Craft Guilds in the Early Modern Low Countries* (Aldershot: Ashgate, 2006), 100–1.

166. Vitruvius, *Ten Books on Architecture*, 5.
167. Stevenson, *Origins of Freemasonry*, 116, and Mylne, R. S., *The Master Masons to the Crown of Scotland and their Works* (Edinburgh: Scott & Ferguson and Burness & Company, 1893), 158–9.

2

Family, Household and Obligation

The last chapter began to unpick the Incorporation's chosen identifier of 'the House', which was the usual manner in which the Incorporation referred to themselves in their minute books. Moving on from the issues surrounding inclusion and the headship of the House, this chapter will explore the rest of the household beyond the brethren. The craftsmen needed their wider households for a range of reasons, but they also carried obligations to those households, just as they carried obligations to the House itself. These obligations were primarily to provide stability and security, but as will be demonstrated, the brethren of the House relied on the wives, children and servants within their households to be able to meet these obligations. Just as the building trades of Edinburgh were far greater than just the privileged freemen of the craft aristocracy, so too the Incorporation was more than just the master craftsmen.

The importance of the term 'the House' is that it implied both an attempt at social control and a desire for an ordered, godly society in Edinburgh. Farr has argued that the European craft guild as an institution was 'a device designed to organize and order society'.[1] This was true not only politically and economically, but also socially. Stone, in his study of the family in early modern England, observed that without a standing police force, the household was a crucial element of social control, as it 'helped keep in check potentially the most unruly element in any society, the floating mass of young unmarried males'.[2] Craft guilds, through apprenticeships and the employment of young journeymen, had many of these young males to keep in check, and therefore there was a social imperative on the careful regulation of the corporate body. The House had to be kept in good order not just for their own sake, but for the common well of the whole of burgh society. When the Incorporation of Mary's Chapel chose 'the House', they fully intended to model their corporate institution on the very building block of the well-ordered early-modern society – the godly household.[3]

Aside from wanting to be *seen* as a godly household, upright in character and integral to burgh society, the craftsmen also *needed* their individual households, as the evidence suggests that all co-residents within a given household made some form of contribution to the household economy. While there were indeed more mouths to feed, there were also more backs to help shoulder the load. In marriage a craftsman gained a business partner, and in parenthood, a future addition to the household labour force. By taking in apprentices and then journeymen, there were certainly costs involved, but there were also more hands to make the work lighter, though this involved a considerable investment in time before they were able to contribute effectively. Allowing people to join a household held both advantages and disadvantages, but as with the biblical model of Adam and Eve, the craft economy relied on helpers.

So, just as the House incorporated more than just one craft, the household in early-modern Edinburgh included a range of individuals. The essence of this fundamental fact was even enshrined in taxation. With the poll tax of the later seventeenth-century, it was decreed that all 'masters of Families and households' were to go on 20 August 1694 at ten o'clock in the morning to their parish church to,

> give up their names, qualities, degrees and value of their estates with a full and true list under the hand of ther whole servands, prentices and residents within their families to the effect the resptective poles may be stated and set down by the saids magistrats.[4]

Responsibility of the head of house was not just for blood relations alone, but for all who were co-resident. Indeed, the mixed household of several bloodlines was much more common in early modern Europe, as most workers tended to live with their masters.[5]

While this made sense economically, due to the cost of setting up an independent household, it also prompted social concerns in terms of regulating the behaviour of young men without blood connections to the nuclear family unit. Farr, in his study of European corporate structures, discusses a 'concern for subordination and discipline of inferiors'.[6] This preoccupation with status was often predicated on order, and the chief building block of order in the early modern period was the household. It is therefore no wonder that the Incorporation modelled themselves on the family unit; a point illustrated by the adoption of the descriptors, 'the House' and 'brethren', when speaking of their incorporated trade.

Farr, writing on European corporatism in general, noted that, 'A well-ordered society, as theorists never tired of proclaiming, was based upon the well-ordered family, which was supposedly regulated and disciplined by the father, the male head of household.'[7] This raises an important point, as 'family' and 'household' are not wholly synonymous. Family might be predicated on kinship, but it also might include others who were co-resident, bringing it more in line with the concept of the household. When the Incorporation chose the term 'the House' to describe themselves, they were explaining the complexities of their corporate community, as it was modelled on the hierarchical family unit, as shown in the last chapter. This was a complex social grouping based on both familial kinship and non-familial co-residence.[8] In the same way that the Incorporation held more crafts than just the masons and wrights, the household held more than just blood relations, making the label of 'the House' wholly apt for a composite incorporated trade.

Needless to say, not everyone in the House was equal. As we have seen, the 'brethren' alone were far from equal, though for the early modern period we should not expect equality within the House. As Farr also rightly observed, 'the corporate regime gained definition *by* the principle of exclusion.'[9] This exclusion pertained to the privileged position of freemen over unfreemen, but it also extended to the standing of the craft aristocracy within the House. Moreover, exclusion has parallels with the relationship between master and household, as authority within the craft household theoretically rested firmly with the male husband or father, bringing into sharp focus the parallels between fatherhood and deaconhood. There are, however, limits to the usefulness of this model for understanding the craft household in early modern Edinburgh.

While the brethren managed to secure greater political access through the office of deacon, the 'sisters of the craft' were in a far less-powerful position.[10] Still, there can be no doubt that they were integral to both the individual craft households and to the wider House. Widows often carried on the businesses of their deceased husbands, and craft daughters trans-ferred standing to would-be freemen, though their contributions as skilled or semi-skilled individuals to the work environment is often difficult to discern. As with craft sons, they too posed certain obligations, and though primogeniture might have given advantages to the eldest sons, as with the two senior trades of masons and wrights, still there is little doubt that the common good was usually sought for the whole House, regardless of trade, age, or gender.

Hence, this chapter will explore the makeup of the House beyond the headship of the deacons, masters and brethren. The masters of the House had a duty of care to those within their households, so it is important to consider some of the factors which brought individuals into the craft household and therefore into the House. Whether someone was in the house because of kinship, or simply co-resident, the interactions between

master and wife, master and child, or master and servant were all predicated on obligation. Marriage, education, craft training and work were
four crucial institutions which connected the masters to their wider households. Patterns of both craftsmen's marriages and those of their daughters
will be looked at, as will education of the youth and training of craft
children and apprentices. Inheritance of trade from fathers to sons will be
looked at for craft children, as will the prospects of moving beyond this
training into the privileged ranks of the masters. The topics of status and
gender in work will be considered, whether for the co-resident journeymen,
or the 'sisters of the craft'. Let us begin with those immediately under the
masters, by focussing on the 'sisters of the craft'.

MISTRESSES OF THE HOUSE: CRAFT MARRIAGES

In a patriarchal society, it is not really surprising that the craftsmen controlled the House, mirroring the role of the father to that of the mother
and children. But as with fatherhood, the headship of a household was
much easier when undertaken with the help of a partner, and both the
metaphorical 'House' and the individual craft households relied upon the
contributions of wives and daughters. Unfortunately, the records available
for the study of corporatism do not always lend themselves to the study
of the women in the craft households. Hence, there has not been enough
attention paid to the crucial role of women in craft affairs.

Although women are often hidden from history in the surviving sources,
there are some excellent examples which give us valuable insight. So, what
can we know about the wives and daughters of the Incorporation, and
what does this suggest about the formation of composite unity? One way
to approach this question is to consider the marriage patterns of the craftsmen, as this gives a small, but important, window into the experiences of
the craftsman's wives and daughters. First, let us consider the institution of
marriage in Edinburgh, as there can be little doubt of its importance in the
early modern Scottish capital.

Why Marriage Mattered

When looking beyond the House to the wider burgh society, we get a sense
of just how much marriage mattered. For example, there is evidence that
marriage implied responsibility in early-modern Edinburgh. When James
Brown, a bookbinder, became a burgess, it was stipulated in his entry that
John Ewyne, glassingwright, would provide surety for his taxation and
participation in the town watch *until* he was married.[11] From that point

forward the young bookbinder was apparently deemed responsible enough to be trusted with burgh duties and obligations, linking marriage with both honour and obligations to the common weal.

Clearly marriage did matter, but why? There was, no doubt, an emotional bond on a personal level, though approaching this with the sources available is difficult at best. In terms of religious belief, marriage was patterned on the biblical example of Adam and Eve, and helped to reinforce the teaching of the kirk. Socially, the marriage bond promoted stability, as it helped provide security for daughters in a patriarchal society, and security and status for sons in a partnership that was likely to be 'the most lasting and least soluble' social bond formed by the craftsmen.[12] Possibly more importantly, it was an economic bond that brought women into the masculine environment of the Incorporation – both the environment of the 'House', making them 'sisters of the craft', but also, occasionally, the environment of the work site.

To emphasise this last point, we must consider the nature of occupations in the early modern period. Livelihoods were rarely gained by a single activity. Most individuals would have had both their primary occupation, but also numerous secondary occupations, carried on by either themselves, their family members, or a combination of the two. A good example of the need for this is the tendency for work in the building trades to be seasonal.[13] Slaters normally worked at considerable heights, especially in Edinburgh, which was known for the height of its buildings in the early modern period. Ice and snow on a slate roof increased the normally-high danger of falls from a height, which are still the primary cause of death in the Scottish building industry today.[14] It is therefore little surprise that one slater in Cruden, Aberdeenshire, gave his apprentice time off from Martinmas (11 November) 1733 to Candlemas (2 February) 1734, as he apparently did not see himself having work for him over these winter months.[15] Of course not all winter work for slaters involved slating. One slater in Edinburgh submitted a bill to the Incorporation for removing snow from one of their roofs in New Assembly Close, demonstrating just one of several by-employments for those used to working at a height.[16]

Though it is not possible to gauge just how slow winter work was, nor how pervasive this problem of seasonality was across the ten trades within the House, the need for supplementary income seems quite logical. Some contracts were quite large, and took years, while others were smaller repairs, so the work of the family business most likely would have been a patchwork of different jobs at different times. Hence, secondary occupations to make ends meet would have been a sensible strategy for providing for one's house. Evidence of the secondary occupations is not always forthcoming, though there are numerous examples which provide insight. The slater George Schanks, who was a burgess and a brother of the guild, also kept a tavern.[17] John Reid, whose 1562 burgess entry listed his occupation as 'wright and maltman', clearly had an interest in brewing,[18] while William Hutcheson's 1685 entry gave 'wright and stentmaster'.[19] Some secondary occupations were obviously complementary, as with the coopers who also brewed or dealt in wine,[20] or the cooper who was also apparently a litstar, or dyer.[21] Especially with multiple occupations, it would make sense for the whole family to contribute.

Unfortunately, if it is difficult to find evidence of secondary occupations and by-employments for craftsmen, it is even more so for the women of the House. There is certainly evidence for craftsmen's widows spinning.[22] This was traditionally a domestic by-employment, and there is no reason to think that this was not pursued by the younger wives of working craftsmen (Plate 2). Whether via traditional domestic production, or through participation in their husbands' craftwork, the crucial point is that the 'sisters of the craft' made important contributions to the domestic economy of their households.

For whatever reason the partnership of marriage was entered into, the women of the House were not just involved in their own separate livelihoods, or feeding their own resources from secondary occupations and by-employments into the family coffers, but instead they were an integral part of a partnership. There was, no doubt, a spectrum of involvement, and the partnerships were far from equal, but the evidence suggests that many craftsmen's wives were heavily involved in their husband's businesses.

A fair amount of work has been done on this topic for other countries, such as England,[23] but for Scotland there is much work yet to be done.[24] The main problem with uncovering the role and level of involvement of craft wives in their husbands' businesses is the nature of the records, which tend to record only the most necessary information. The master is always mentioned, and occasionally the labour force, but specifics are not always forthcoming. There are tantalising exceptions, such as the 1761 complaint that deacon Dewar's servant, John Smeal, had been 'inticed & seduced by Deacon Veitch or his spouse to fee with them'.[25] The occasional glimpse of the involvement of wives in a craft partnership aside, the usual focus of the records tends to be on the transaction rather than on those involved in helping the master in the execution of the work, so finding the role of women in this male-dominated environment is usually difficult.

One place to start, though, is with the labour force, as when the master died they were often retained by the business. In fact, provision was often made for widows continuing their late husbands' businesses by 'keeping' their husbands' journeymen, pointing at the very least to a previously-established ability to oversee their work and manage the actual business. Still, this was toleration on the part of the House rather than an encouraged practice. In 1680 a complaint was given in to the House by John Yetts, upholsterer, regarding a journeyman abusing this custom. One David Aikman was taking work,

> under precept of being journeyman to the relict of Jon Young wright wherefore and in effect that it was informed that the benefite of his work was applyet to his owin use and that he was offering to take prenteisses to himself and that he was ane maried man keeping ane familie and working in his owin hous[26]

While the upholsterer making the complaint had no problem with Young's relict continuing his business, he did take exception to the journeyman working as a freeman, making his own business decisions in his own house and supporting his own household.

The following year a licence was given to the relict of John Young, wright, for keeping journeymen for her own use. The licence stipulated that she was to have no 'copartnership' with them, and that she was not to 'pack and peel' with them.[27] Again, carrying on her husband's business was fully approved, though setting up an unfreeman in a master's place, or acting as a merchant in import and export, were both seen as abuses of the House's benevolence. The toleration was based on charity rather than financial sense for growing the business.

What is important in these two examples, though, is that the keeping of journeymen by the widows of the House was clearly a tolerated custom. While this was not quite the same as being able to work of their own accord, even this was a grudging recognition of both their ability and their involvement in the work of the House's craftsmen. They were not to be co-partners with their journeymen, but in certain circumstances they were allowed to be in charge.

Custom and the implications for ability aside, a possibly more-convincing piece of evidence for the integral nature of craft wives working with their husbands in the family businesses is found in the will for the deceased wright, Walter Denniestone. When Denniestone died in 1631, his inventory and testament was 'ffaythfulie maid & given up' by his 'relict spouse'.[28] It was his wife who calculated that the thirty-eight deals, at 5s 3d the piece, were worth £10 2s and 8d, or that a hundred 'queinsbrug knappels' were worth £10. It was also his wife who knew the difference between chairs that were 'outred' and those which were not, or that two 'mort kists', or coffins, were worth £3. Indeed, her ability to distinguish between small rough spars, corbels of oak, and clefts of small wainscot, let alone to compute their market value, demonstrates more than a working knowledge of her late husband's trade. Clearly Denniestone's wife had been an integral part of the family business.

Marriage, as an institution, clearly did matter to the House. It mattered to the individual craft families for a range of reasons, many of which are difficult to find evidence for. It also mattered to the House, corporately. As mentioned earlier, marriage had implications for responsibility, and this cut both ways, as the House incurred responsibilities for the marriages of its members. Hence, incorporated trades often denied widows access to corporate privileges if they remarried,[29] or maintained that apprentices not be allowed to marry.[30] Though the social implications of marriage were important, as they theoretically promoted unity, the economic aspects appear most often in the records. Clearly it is too cynical to think that craft marriages were all about economics, but the Incorporation's concern for its substantial obligations made the economic side of the marriage partnership more overt in its minutes and accompts. So, what can we learn about marriages of the brothers and sisters of the craft?

Matches in a Composite Craft

Unfortunately, we simply do not have sources for studying *all* of the marriages of those in the Incorporation, though the Edinburgh burgess rolls give us an interesting sample to look at.[31] When a craftsman became a burgess, they were entered into the council's roll of burgesses and guild brethren. Although burgesship did not necessarily mean freedom of the Incorporation, the patterns visible for the burgesses will still serve as a rough approximation of the free masters of the House.[32] As burgesship brought access to closely-guarded burgh privileges, this source usually included a record of what right they had to become a burgess. For some this was through 'right of wife', having married the daughter of a freeman.

By looking at the burgesses of the trades in Mary's Chapel who were listed in the rolls as having attained their burgesship through right of wife, we get a glimpse of the marriage patterns for a very specific subsection of the House's brethren. Though not a view of the whole House, it is still a coherent group. To illustrate the limited size of this sample, we know that at least 585 wrights took burgesship in Edinburgh from 1406 to 1760, though only 108 of these were through marriage, or 'right of wife'. Hence, our sample of wrights' marriages is at best only 18 per cent of the actual free craftsmen.[33] Still, to the best of our knowledge, it does represent those who *married into* this privileged group. While others were the sons of freemen, or did an apprenticeship with a freeman, our sample sought freedom of the town through marriage, so the data presented in Table 2.1 still has much to say about craft and corporate endogamy.

Endogamy is the practice of marrying within one's own group. Marriage was not simply about choosing a partner and reproducing; it also allowed individuals and family units to pursue strategies for the elevation of their standing and status, whether socially, politically or economically.[34] Therefore, endogamous marriage could be a double-edged sword. It cemented ties between craft families of the same trade, but it also cut off other avenues of advancement.[35] A journeyman cooper marrying his master's daughter made him a son-in-law to a freeman, even if he could never be a freeman's son. But by marrying the daughter of another cooper, he was closing off the possibility of marrying the daughter of a social superior, such as a merchant, lawyer or minor laird.

Of course marrying within one's own social stratum did not always mean marrying humbly. Indeed, such a match could also be quite beneficial for achieving upward social mobility, as demonstrated by the case of the wright, John Forrester.[36] Forrester became a burgess in 1642 by right of his wife, Catheren Mawer, who was the daughter of William Mawer, a burgess tailor. When his father-in-law became a brother of the guild in 1645, an affiliation much more prestigious than simple burgesship,[37] Forrester followed suit, again by right of his wife. Here we see a wright who attained not only freedom of the city, but also freedom of the guild, with its privileges of importation and exportation, all through marrying another craftsman's daughter. As one's fortunes rose, so did those of the other. Hence, we must be careful to avoid suppositions about endogamous marriages, as marrying within one's group did not necessarily deter social mobility.

In the growing historiography of artisanal marriage patterns, there is a general view that endogamous marriage within guilds was not the normal pattern.[38] The sample from Mary's Chapel has something to add to this, as it highlights another facet to the complicated question of artisanal endogamy. Much of the historiography looks at individual trades, but what about marriage patterns in the context of *composite* corporatism? Is endogamous marriage any more common when one is not only cementing ties within trades, but also ties across trades in an Incorporation of ten different arts? Although only a small percentage of the actual marriages are visible, Table 2.1 and Table 2.2 make some interesting, if tentative, suggestions about craft and corporate endogamy in the marriages of the House. Beginning with craftsmen's marriages, as can be seen in Table 2.1, those taking burgessip through the right of their wife tended to marry within their social strata, and showed a reasonably high tendency towards endogamy in terms of the similarity between their trade and that of their fathers-in-law. Totals for the whole Incorporation show that out of 214 sampled marriages, all of which were to a burgess's daughter, 50 per cent of these were endogamous marriages to the daughter of a burgess of the same trade, while only 4 per cent were to the daughter of another one of the other nine arts in the Incorporation. Here we see different levels of endogamy. While 60 per cent of masons married another mason's daughter, only 4 per cent of masons married the daughter of one of the other nine trades within the Incorporation. Similarly, 55 per cent of glaziers married another glaziers' daughter, while only 9 per cent found a partner from the daughters of the other Mary's Chapel trades.

Of the endogamous matches in our sample of 'right of wife' marriages, the slaters, coopers and masons showed the greatest tendency to look to their own trade for finding a master's daughter to marry. Others looked farther afield. The bowers, plumbers, sievewrights and upholsterers all chose partners whose fathers had trades which were different to their own, though with such small numbers of recorded marriages for these arts, their statistics are far from conclusive.

Marriages outside of the Incorporation, but within one's social stratum, as with a painter marrying the daughter of a surgeon,[39] or a mason marrying the daughter of a stabler,[40] tended to be less common than endogamous matches, but were still considerable at 25 per cent. For the purposes of this study, merchants are considered a stratum above, based on the struggle for parity with the merchants in burgh politics in the 1500s.[41] Here, marriages to the daughter of a merchant were only 14 per cent of the whole sample, highlighting the greater emphasis on craft matches over those with merchants. Some trades showed a greater tendency towards such merchant matches, as with the wrights at 21 per cent. Marriages with professional families accounted for only 1 per cent of the sample, while 6 per cent of the marriages did not list the occupation of the father of the bride.

Hence we see that of the craftsmen obtaining freedom by marrying a burgess's daughter, 54 per cent chose daughters from within the House,[42] while 25 per cent married outside the House, but within their social stratum. This could be argued to suggest a reasonably high percentage of endogamy, though it also raises an interesting point about endogamous marriage, in that the precise definition of the label is not wholly clear in an Edinburgh context. Endogamy could be qualified as exclusively referring to marrying within one's own trade, or it could be used for marriages within the composite incorporation as a whole. It might even refer to one's social stratum, including all craft families, but excluding those of merchants, professions or those of higher status yet.

The marriage patterns of this small sample of craftsmen are informative, but perhaps by considering a different approach to marriage, as with the known marriages of the *daughters* of freemen, we will enhance our view of the wider Incorporation's matches. While the previous table looked at the marriages of those craftsmen of the Mary's Chapel trades who took burgesship through the right of their wives, the sample in Table 2.2 looks at marriage from the perspective of the daughters themselves. Where marriage was endogamous, it will appear in both tables, once from the point of view of the husband, and once from the perspective of the wife, which explains why some of the figures in these two tables are similar.

As mentioned above, in cases of burgesship through right of wife the trade of both the incoming burgess and that of their father-in-law is usually recorded. By taking a count of the various types of occupation of those who married the *daughter* of a burgess from one of the ten arts of Mary's Chapel, a rough indication is visible of marriage patterns for this particular group of 'sisters of the craft'. Again, burgesship did not necessarily mean freedom of the Incorporation, but the patterns visible from the burgess rolls will serve as a rough approximation, but only for the sample of 'right of wife' marriages.

Again, there is a relatively high percentage of endogamous marriages for craft daughters, with 48 per cent marrying men from their fathers' craft, and 4 per cent marrying men from another trade within the wider House. For marriages to other craftsmen, or similar unincorporated occupations, such as stablers or gardeners, the figure is 22 per cent, whilst marriages to the next social strata, merchants and professionals, were 17 per cent and 4 per cent respectively. This might suggest that the daughters of craftsmen were slightly more likely to marry above their social group than their fathers or brothers.

Looking at Table 2.2 by individual trade, endogamous marriage in the same trade tended to be highest for the daughters of slaters, coopers and masons, though not quite as high as with the craftsmen in Table 2.1. Though the painters showed reasonably high endogamous tendencies, with 44 per cent of their sampled daughters marrying another painter, a third of their admittedly-small sample married men who had some profession, such as education, ministry or law. The smaller trades proved elusive in the sample, with no plumbers', sievewrights' or upholsterers' daughters being recorded as marrying incoming burgesses.

The data presented in Tables 2.1 and 2.2 is not a complete view of the marriages of the House, though as a sample of those seeking freedom of the burgh through right of their wife, or of those wives passing their fathers' freedom on to their husbands, the tables make some interesting

Table 2.1 Marriages of Mary's Chapel's Craftsmen

	Masons	Wrights	Coopers	Bowers	Glaziers	Painters	Slaters	Plumbers	Sievewrights	Upholsterers	Incorporation totals
To daughter of the same craft	30 (60%)	51 (47%)	11 (61%)	0 (0%)	6 (55%)	4 (57%)	5 (63%)	0 (0%)	0 (0%)	0 (0%)	107 (50%)
To daughter of another Mary's Chapel craft	2 (4%)	2 (2%)	0 (0%)	0 (0%)	1 (9%)	1 (14%)	1 (13%)	0 (0%)	0 (0%)	1 (50%)	8 (4%)
To another craftsman's daughter	11 (22%)	28 (26%)	3 (17%)	4 (57%)	2 (18%)	1 (14%)	2 (25%)	2 (100%)	1 (100%)	0 (0%)	54 (25%)
To a merchant's daughter	3 (6%)	23 (21%)	1 (6%)	0 (0%)	1 (9%)	1 (14%)	0 (0%)	0 (0%)	0 (0%)	1 (50%)	30 (14%)
To a daughter from the professions	1 (2%)	2 (2%)	0 (0%)	0 (0%)	0 (0%)	0 (0%)	0 (0%)	0 (0%)	0 (0%)	0 (0%)	3 (1%)
Father's trade not given	3 (6%)	2 (2%)	3 (17%)	3 (43%)	1 (9%)	0 (0%)	0 (0%)	0 (0%)	0 (0%)	0 (0%)	12 (6%)
Total of recorded marriages	50	108	18	7	11	7	8	2	1	2	214

Figures indicate the number of marriages (and percentage) of craftsmen of the primary Mary's Chapel crafts (in order of precedence) taking partners from the six groups given in the left-hand column, along with total numbers of marriages recorded for each occupational group. The percentages are rounded (to the nearest 1). Data taken from *Edin. Burgs*, 1406–1760.

Table 2.2 Marriages of Daughters of Mary's Chapel's Trades

	Masons' daughters	Wrights' daughters	Coopers' daughters	Bowers' daughters	Glaziers' daughters	Painters' Daughters	Slaters' daughters	Plumbers' daughters	Sievewrights' daughters	Upholsterers' daughters	Incorporation totals
To husband of the same craft	30 (51%)	51 (47%)	11 (52%)	0 (0%)	6 (38%)	4 (44%)	5 (56%)	0 (0%)	0 (0%)	0 (0%)	107 (48%)
To another Mary's Chapel craft	2 (3%)	5 (5%)	0 (0%)	0 (0%)	1 (6%)	0 (0%)	0 (0%)	0 (0%)	0 (0%)	0 (0%)	8 (4%)
To another craftsman	9 (15%)	28 (26%)	7 (33%)	0 (0%)	2 (13%)	1 (11%)	2 (22%)	0 (0%)	0 (0%)	0 (0%)	49 (22%)
To a merchant	11 (19%)	18 (17%)	2 (10%)	1 (100%)	4 (25%)	1 (11%)	2 (22%)	0 (0%)	0 (0%)	0 (0%)	39 (17%)
To a husband with a profession	1 (2%)	5 (5%)	0 (0%)	0 (0%)	1 (6%)	3 (33%)	0 (0%)	0 (0%)	0 (0%)	0 (0%)	10 (4%)
No trade given	6 (10%)	2 (2%)	1 (5%)	0 (0%)	2 (13%)	0 (0%)	0 (0%)	0 (0%)	0 (0%)	0 (0%)	11 (5%)
Total of recorded marriages	59	109	21	1	16	9	9	0	0	0	224

Figures indicate number of marriages (and percentage) of daughters of the ten Mary's Chapel crafts taking partners from the six groups given in the left-hand column, along with total numbers of marriages recorded for each occupational group. The percentages are rounded (to the nearest 1) for clarity. Data taken from *Edin. Burgs*, 1406–1760.

suggestions. How representative they are of the experiences of the rest of the House's men and women is not clear, but they still give us a small but valuable window into craft marriages. From these a few tentative hypotheses might be put forward. First of all, it is clear that the experience and aims of marriage were not identical across the ten trades, suggesting that the prospects of a wright or a wright's daughter were not the same as those of a cooper or a cooper's daughter. Did this exacerbate the tensions outlined in the preceding chapter on headship?

Secondly, it is very clear that endogamous marriage appears in roughly half of the sampled marriages, demonstrating a tendency for the House to look within the House for partners. To add nuance to this, endogamous marriage for the sample from Mary's Chapel really meant marrying within one's own trade, rather than across the ten trades of the House. In the wrights, marriages within their trade can be seen in 47 per cent of the two samples, and the wrights tended to be on the lower end of the endogamy scale. For masons, coopers and slaters the figures were higher, and those of the glaziers and painters were roughly comparable.

If craft endogamy was fairly common for members of a single art or trade, at roughly 50 per cent, *corporate* endogamy, or marriage within the rest of the Incorporation, was strikingly low, at 4 per cent for crafts-men's choice of wives, and 4 per cent for daughters' choice of husbands – if indeed they had a choice in the matter. Cross-trade marriages did happen, as when Robert Clephane, wright, married Hellen Forrest, daughter of Thomas Forrest, glazier in 1722, but these were far from the usual pattern.[43] Perhaps these cross-trade marriages were intended to solidify business partnerships, as a glazier would clearly have business with a wright when undertaking contracts, but the rarity of these cross-trade marriages does undermine the idea of a unified House. Indeed, the sample of marriages suggests not brethren in unity, but instead a House divided.

EDUCATION: CRAFT CHILDREN AND DEPENDENTS

Marriage patterns might demonstrate a compartmentalised, divided House, but the records of the Incorporation suggest that the craftsmen agreed on the importance of education and learning. Indeed, corporate and individual resources were used fairly liberally for the education of those within the House, whether the immediate children of the family, or those co-resident, such as apprentices, journeymen and servants. Education covers several aspects. The obvious example would be the apprenticeships through which craft techniques and technology were passed down. These were important, and they will be considered separately below, but there were other aspects of education beyond craftwork that were also valued by the Incorporation.

General Education

As heads of household, craft masters were responsible for the complete education of those under their care. This included religious instruction and church attendance. Interestingly, this responsibility can be seen to have been mirrored by the House as well. When James Herriot, glazier, died in the 1730s, the Incorporation was petitioned for a plaid and a copy of the Bible for his daughter, Elizabeth Herriot.[44] While Herriot could clearly no longer provide for the material needs of his daughter, he also could not attend to the religious instruction of the girl, and the House was called upon to help fill both of these roles.

The Incorporation also undertook provision of general education. The phenomenon of corporatism in Europe overlapped with the Renaissance, the Reformation, and the Enlightenment, making for an intellectual context that increasingly valued knowledge and learning. For the members of Mary's Chapel, the value of education is apparent, as anyone working in wood needs to understand measurement, and therefore have at least basic numeracy. Anyone planning a building, which was clearly much more complex, also needed a sophisticated understanding of geometry. For the builders especially, learning mattered.

An excellent illustration of the necessity of education can be found on James Craig's cartographic proposal for the New Town (Figure 2.1). James Craig was not only a 'mason-turned-architect', but also a would-be town planner.[45] When Craig's 1768 plan for the New Town was printed, the central cartouche was illustrated with the tools of his mason trade, which were fundamental symbols of his merit for the task at hand.[46] One might understandably see an order of precedence in the layout of the various items in the cartouche's border, with its characteristic rococo asymmetrical shape, foliage and implements. Towards the back, on the far right, just before sections of a column, waiting to be erected, lies the mason's mell, hammer and chisels. Before these, moving left towards the centre, lies a plumbline, rule, square, and dividers, but in the foreground, and at the centre of this cartouche, which carries an excerpt from the poet Thomson's *Liberty Part V*, lies a globe and several books, speaking to the centrality of both knowledge and learning to the endeavours of the builders who would bring his plan into reality. The products of the mason were indeed important, as were his tools, but pride of place went to knowledge, demonstrating the fully-rounded Vitruvian architect.

Figure 2.1 Detail from Cartouche of James Craig's Plan of the New Town
NLS, EMS.s.647, Craig, J., *To His Sacred Majesty George III . . . this Plan of the new streets and squares, intended for his ancient capital of North-Britain . . .* (Edinburgh, 1768). Courtesy of the National Library of Scotland.

While the design of buildings would soon be professionalised and would eventually be taught at universities rather than in the shop to apprentices, access to the knowledge of the building trades was increasingly available to the general public.[47] How far this intellectual context pervaded Scottish society is beyond the scope of this study, but for the free and unfree of the building trades there is substantial evidence of education being valued. It has, for example, been shown that literacy rates in Scotland were quite high, and an ability to read and write would no doubt have been useful in sustaining any business in the capital. Of course literacy was not universal, and the records and papers of the Incorporation do occasionally mention a craftsman's hand being guided by their clerk.[48] Still, it is clear that education made a difference in the lives and business practices of the members of the House.

Further evidence of the value ascribed to education within the House can be seen in the clear interest in craft-related literature. In the medieval period the usual method of transfer of craft knowledge was through formal, indentured apprenticeship, but by the eighteenth century printing had allowed dissemination through published works on building techniques, pattern books and price books, which were available to both builder and customer.[49] One Edinburgh author of a treatise on Palladian design, George Jameson, held classes for journeyman in his house, emphasising the capital's culture of knowledge sharing and dissemination.[50] Even the genre of poetry was taken up by the craftsmen, as illustrated by the anonymous 1757 publication of *A Poem Inscribed to the Members of St. Mary's Chapel. Upon the Most Honourable, Ancient, and Excellent Art of Wright-Craft*.[51] Not only was the House engaging with literature, but they were involved in its production. Indeed, Houston's work on literacy rates has suggested that illiteracy in Lowland Scotland was much less common for wrights than for other trades, such as baxters, weavers, shoemakers or fleshers.[52] Clearly, learning mattered, and interestingly, the House was heavily involved in its provision.

A great boost to the culture of valued learning in Scotland came with the Reformation, when the reformers emphasised the necessity of education and literacy skills in the spreading of reformed theology.[53] From at least 1562 the idea of a school in every parish was included in Protestant teaching.[54] To a considerable degree, the establishment of schools became a national priority, and legislation to increase provision was produced in 1633 and 1696.[55] The Education Act of 1696 called again for a school for every parish in Scotland, but full coverage and adequate provision was simply not an easy target to meet. There was certainly help from the private sector, though, as numerous 'dame' and 'adventure' schools added to the parish provision.[56] The Incorporation of Mary's Chapel, as with the other incorporated trades in the capital, found themselves in a position to help with this extra provision, emphasising the important role the House played in educating burgh society.

It is known that schools were provided in Edinburgh by the Incorporation of Skinners and the Incorporation of Hammermen.[57] The Incorporation of Mary's Chapel likewise was involved in the support of schoolmasters in the seventeenth century, though details are somewhat hazy. An inventory of the writs included in the Incorporation's papers mentions William Draphane, schoolmaster, while the research of Durkan and Reid-Baxter found that Robert Lindsay, Edward Draffin, William Draffin and John Penman were schoolmasters connected with St Mary's Chapel in Niddry's Wynd.[58] As minutes for the early seventeenth century are missing, little can be known about these men, though a minute from 1719 shows that this tradition continued into the eighteenth century.[59]

Aside from provision of their own schoolmasters, the House also supported the town's 'hospitals', which in this context were orphanages for the care and education of burgesses' children. One important example of this was Heriot's Hospital. George Heriot was a wealthy Edinburgh goldsmith who died in 1624 without an heir. He left a considerable sum of money to the town council for the creation of a 'hospital for orphans', which was to be based on the London example of Christ's Hospital, founded by Edward VI in 1552.[60] Scholars at the hospital, who were 'Poor Fatherless orphans

Burgess Bairns of Honest decent and their Mother unable to maintain them being in a weak condition',[61] were instructed in reading and writing Scots; working with accounts; Latin rudiments; and, of course, the Presbyterian catechism.[62] Hence literacy, numeracy and religion were the main focus.

Although Heriot's bequest was indeed a noble work, space at the hospital was limited, so few of the 'bairns', or children, of the House would have received a place in the institution. Lockhart's research into the occupational background of the scholars' parents has shown that 870 children from the Incorporation of Mary's Chapel attended Heriot's.[63] Of these, only 172 were from the eighteenth century, whilst 594 were from the nineteenth century, demonstrating increased provision and increased consumption over the course of the hospital's history. Still, there was more need, as this one hospital only cared for sons.

The turn of the eighteenth century saw improvements, as additional provision of education for girls was implemented. One of the new hospitals from this period was specifically for the daughters of craftsmen who could no longer take care of them. When in the 1690s the Merchant Company of Edinburgh initiated plans to build a hospital 'for the maintenance and education of poor maidens by charitable benefactions',[64] the craftsmen were invited by the town council to join with the merchants. The crafts decided to invest in their own hospital, and by 1704 the Edinburgh Convenery of Trades recorded their unanimous assent:

> It being put to the vote whither or not there shall be a Hospitall erected by the Trades of this burgh, towards the mantinance of the daughters of decayed tradsmen, and others who shall be presented by the contributors to so pious a work, the samen was carried in the affirmative without a contrair vote.[65]

Property was purchased near Horse Wynd, to the south of the Cowgate, and a house was prepared to serve as the hospital, with a governess, a schoolmistress and servants being engaged.[66] With parliamentary and private backing, the hospital soon had a constitution and a 'court', or board of governors, including the deacons of the trades.[67] Part of their work in managing the hospital's affairs and assets included decisions about which children were to be admitted.

Young girls who entered the Trades Maiden Hospital (Figure 2.2) were to be 'brought up in the fear of God', by being taught reformed Christianity.[68] They were also to be taught reading, writing, arithmetic, and music, as well as certain domestic skills, such as how to make stockings, lace, 'coloured and white seam', spinning, carding, washing and dressing of linen, dressing of meat, housecleaning, needlework, and 'ordinary household thrift'.[69] Clearly the intention was to provide them with the skills to be good wives,

Figure 2.2 'Trades Maiden Hospital, Winter Dress [female]'
Edinburgh, mid-nineteenth century. ECA, Howie Print 59. By kind permission of City
of Edinburgh Council.

though intriguingly, neither the matron nor the schoolmistress was allowed to be married.[70] It is noteworthy, however, that reading, writing and arithmetic would have made the girls most useful for the running of a business. Were such factors taken into account when choosing a marital partner?

While this no doubt helped with the burden of provision for the daughters of 'decayed craftsmen', there were practical limitations to how many girls the hospital could accommodate. Indeed Colston records that in the nineteenth century the Incorporation of Mary's Chapel was only allowed four of the fifty presentations to the hospital.[71] The Trades Maiden Hospital would have helped, and provision for girls was certainly progressive, but neither Heriot's Hospital nor the Trades Maiden Hospital were final answers to the pressing obligations of providing for the 'poor bairns' of the House.

Craft Training: From Father to Son?

After basic education at one of the various forms of school in the town, specialist training in craft knowledge was the next potential step for the teenaged children of the House who had ambitions for working within one of the ten arts of Mary's Chapel. For those whose fathers were in the Incorporation, this might mean following in their footsteps and training with their fathers, though for others it might mean entering into indentures for an apprenticeship.[72] Apprenticeships often took the children out of their biological parents' households and put them into the household of their masters, which potentially both disrupted the family units and solidified inter-household social bonds. Hence, one of the roles of an overarching corporate structure, such as the House, was to facilitate and govern these extra-household relationships.

Indeed, certain obligations were enshrined in the day-to-day practices of the incorporated trade. Masters may have theoretically controlled the labour of their apprentices, which was one of the benefits to taking on and training those who were effectively low- to non-skilled staff, but they were also responsible for their upkeep, education and general well-being.[73] The taking of apprentices was therefore a substantial investment of time and resources. In the initial years of the indentures they were of little value to the business, and added to the mouths that needed feeding. Through training, though, they later became much more useful on the worksite, and eventually brought in more money to the masters' coffers.[74]

As the interests of the two parties – master and apprentice – were not wholly equal throughout the period of their training, a legal contract was customary to formalise the relationship and protect both parties.[75]

Indeed, these contracts were reinforced by various pieces of legislation against enticing away apprentices from their masters.[76] Although this was enshrined in the Incorporation's 1475 seal of cause,[77] it apparently did not stop the practice, as such legislation was often reissued, as when the wrights, fleshers and cordiners had been recruiting the apprentices and servants of bonnetmakers in the sixteenth century.[78] Complaints about the poaching were made to the town, and the legislation was reiterated, but the practice remained a problem.

And a problem it was. To entice an apprentice away from his master was to undermine a social contract as well as a legal one. To do so was to chip away at the wider social fabric, and hence it undermined the burgh community as a whole. If there were problems between master and apprentice, it was expected that they be worked out in-house. For the apprentices of the incorporated trades, this often meant within the wider House, as their incorporation was their immediate and proper court of appeal. When Walter Galloway had a 'difference' with his master, the wright William Galloway, elder, 'the house Referred the same to Deacon Sandilands, John Nasmith & Thomas Kylle'.[79] As with any household, disputes could be dealt with by appealing to the arbitration of the wider family, so long as one submitted to that arbitration and did not simply break the bonds and leave the House.

Apprentices often posed challenges for both their masters and for the wider House, as they were usually teenagers. While a definitive age for beginning apprenticeships is not easily found, Stevenson makes the point that a seven-year apprenticeship from the age of 14 would lead to completion at 21.[80] The 1475 seal of cause stipulated apprenticeships of no less than seven years,[81] and Carr's work suggests that this was usually adhered to.[82] There were, of course, exceptions, and Stevenson gives examples of both shorter and longer terms, ranging from five to eight years.[83] While these do not show a precise age, they still broadly cover the teenage years. Indeed, in the early 1690s when reviewing the Incorporation's pension giving, two children were taken off the list because they were 15 years of age. Instead they were to be 'put to Trades'.[84] In apprenticeships, the responsibility for raising teenage children therefore fell to the master and his wife rather than the biological parents, demonstrating the important role that the House was playing in the structure of the wider urban society.

Of course not all apprentices being trained by members of the House were the same age, nor were they all from the same background. William Edgar, wright, was made burgess and guildbrother on 23 March 1726, by right of his father, John Edgar 'of Wedderlie', who was also a burgess and guildbrother. William appears to have been the second son, as one 'John of

Watherly' was also made burgess and guildbrother by right of their father in 1736, suggesting that the first son inherited the lands and title, while the younger son was set up with a promising trade and prestigious membership in the guild.[85] Not all craftsmen would have had such a start, being connected from the beginning to both the landed interest and the capital's guildry. There were obviously very different circumstances for each youth beginning their training with a craft.

Some apprentices came from afar, and some came from the immediate community in which they hoped to work; some left a household to join that of their master, while others were fortunate enough to train with their biological father or a close relative. In a patriarchal society one might expect that there had been less worry about provision for the sons of craftsmen, though their futures were far from settled by virtue of their gender. Not all craftsmen's sons followed in their fathers' footsteps. An eighteenth-century glazier, James Forrest, had one son who became a bookbinder while the other became a writer, or lawyer.[86] In 1614, the son of a cooper showed considerable social mobility in becoming burgess and guild brother as the Bishop of Galloway.[87] Some craftsmen did have sons who followed in their fathers' footsteps, but this was far from universal.

Naturally, many histories of crafts and craftwork comment on the likelihood of sons to follow in their fathers' footsteps, but there does not seem to have been a stereotypical model. Friedrichs, in his study of early modern Nördlingen, found that about three-fifths of his sample of men followed their fathers' occupations.[88] Rappaport, looking at London, also found a figure of three-fifths following their fathers' trades, though the samples were taken in different ways.[89] Dolan, specifically discussing weavers and leatherworkers in sixteenth-century Aix, found that the former often passed their occupation from father to son, while the latter did not.[90] Farr recounts numerous examples from across central and northern Europe of percentages of sons following their fathers' trades, ranging from as high as 87 per cent for Augsburg smiths, to 0 per cent for Bruges barrelmakers. The overall figure for York from 1375 to 1500 was 51 per cent, with individual trades varying from 16 to 78 per cent.[91] The huge variation in these figures points to problems in comparing samples with such wide geographic and cultural disparity, not to mention the lack of uniformity in the ways in which the data was collected. Hence, despite an interesting group of studies, there is no set model for craftwork and father-to-son transferral of status and skill.

In Edinburgh, the sources for looking at father-to-son connections within the Incorporation are not as forthcoming as one would like. While burgess-ship was not the same as freedom of the Incorporation, data from the imperfect Edinburgh *Burgess Rolls* will serve as a suitable substitute, as in theory one needed burgesship to join an incorporated trade.[92] Examples of this rule being broken have already been discussed, but the variation between the two lists will not take away from the valuable insight that the burgess figures give us about father-to-son transferral in the population of freemen.[93]

The status of 'heir' to a burgess brought opportunities not necessarily present for those who became freemen by marriage or apprenticeship. Here the examples of the coopers and the wrights are illustrative. As mentioned above, to become a burgess one took one of several routes, such as by 'right of wife', through marrying a freeman's daughter; by apprenticeship; or by some act of council, bypassing the normal regulations. Although these were all common routes, one would expect that in order to sustain and perpetuate an oligarchic circle of privileged insiders the route of 'right of father' would have to be the most common. This route was reserved for either heir or second son of a previous burgess.[94]

Burgesship, or freedom of the town, was heavily weighted in favour of those already connected to the privileged group,[95] but the greatest privilege went to the eldest sons of burgesses. The council noted the expected prices for access to this freedom in March of 1507, with eldest sons as heirs paying only 6s 8d, but second sons paying 13s 4d, and daughters likewise having 'the privilege of the secund son'.[96] Unfreemen, however, were to pay £3. While there was movement in the price of burgesship for unfreemen throughout the sixteenth and seventeenth centuries,[97] the prices for burgesses' bairns were confirmed and apparently enshrined in the new burgh sett from the 1583 decreet arbitral: '. . . the privelege alwayes of the bairnis of burgessis and gild brether nocht beand prejugeit heirby, quha sall pay the awld and accustomat dewtie to the dene of gild allanerlie.'[98] Clearly those taking burgesship would have done so through right of father wherever possible, as the cost differential was simply too great.

This means that of the burgess coopers and wrights, for example, we will most likely have a fairly complete picture of how many entrants had fathers who were *freemen*, as this was a decided advantage. Unfortunately, we cannot say with the same certainty what proportion of entrants took on the same *trade* as their father before them. Some sons might have had precisely the same trade, but if they were born and raised in another part of Scotland, their fathers probably would not have been freemen of the capital, so their sons would have entered through some other route, such as serving apprenticeships or marrying a freeman's daughter. Their father's trades would therefore not be listed in our source, meaning we will not get a complete view of father-to-son transferral.

We can, however, see the proportions of entrants that used 'right of father' to follow in their fathers' footsteps, both in terms of gaining burgesship and in choosing an occupation, as the father's trade was usually given for such entries in the burgess rolls. As a sample, this is flawed, as it only records the privileged few whose fathers were already burgesses. Accepting this flaw, our view of the object itself is hazy, but the perspective it gives on what is missing is extraordinary.

Of these privileged entrants to burgesship, our examples of the coopers' sons and the wrights' sons suggest that the Incorporation was far from a self-perpetuating oligarchy. By carefully searching the first two volumes of the published burgess rolls for all entries of these craftsmen we can see that there were 118 burgess entries for all coopers and 585 entries for all wrights. Of the 118 burgess entries for coopers, only 24 were by 'right of father', or roughly 20 per cent, which clearly represents the establishment's sons.[99] Of these 24 privileged sons, only 14 were listed as having followed in their fathers' footsteps to take up the family trade of coopering. So, sons of burgess coopers represent only 12 per cent of the whole body of burgess coopers, demonstrating that the transferral of burgesship from cooper father to cooper son was far from the usual practice. This was not a self-perpetuating group, but a remarkably inclusive one.

Similar findings can be seen with the wrights. Of the 585 burgess entries for wrights, only 124 were by 'right of father', and of these 124, only 51 were the sons of burgess wrights, giving percentages fairly similar to those of the coopers. Of the 585 burgess wright entries, 21 per cent were sons of burgesses and 9 per cent were sons of burgess wrights. So of the two example trades of wrights and coopers, roughly 20 per cent of entrants were the sons of free burgesses and only about 10 per cent had followed in their fathers' footsteps. Based on burgesship, it is highly likely that 'new blood' was an important feature of the Incorporation, as very few of the freemen were allowed in because their fathers were already members. It was simply untenable to *only* allow freemen's sons into the freedom of the House, and the great majority either married into the 'family' or served as indentured apprentices.[100] This, of course, says nothing of the overall labour market where both free and unfree worked.

Just as not all craftsmen's sons followed in their fathers' footsteps, not all the House's orphans stayed within the House. Many were not given a choice in the matter. In 1680 Jonet Thomsone, relict of umquhile David Anderson, slater, gave in a bill, 'craveing that his eldest chylde might be putt to ane calling . . .'[101] The House agreed, and allowed him to be bound to any person of any art within the Incorporation, though interestingly no mention is made of considering a calling outside the building trades. On the other hand, when James Braidie's child was put to a trade in 1687, he was given his choice, and decided upon the weaver trade.[102] When the

House put one of their orphans to a trade, they did not always demand that the trade be within the House, most likely due to particular circumstances. Braidie's child was already living with a weaver, so the apprenticeship seemed appropriate, but for other cases the judgement was different. Given the right circumstances, favouring those within the Incorporation took priority, but otherwise, expediency was the rule of the day.

This, of course, translates to most areas of the Incorporation's provision, as individual experiences often differed. For example, Andrew Paterson, wright, received burgess-ship as apprentice to James Scott, but within seven years he had married well, to Isobell, the daughter of a merchant guild brother, and through this connection was able to obtain guild-brethrenship.[103] Whereas the master, Scott, only obtained freedom of the town and freedom of the Incorporation, his apprentice went on to also become a brother of the guild. The opportunities afforded to the brothers and sisters of the crafts were simply not equal.[104]

In part, this helps to explain why rules were often bent or ignored. A good example of this was the requisite booking of apprentices, which did not always happen. By not declaring your apprentices one saved money on the 'prentice silver' owed to the House, and got around regulations about numbers of apprentices.[105] This not only affected the Incorporation, though, as the council occasionally complained about masters omitting to book their apprentices with the Dean of Guild. In 1675 the bower John Monro sought his freedom of the town from the Dean of Guild, only to find out that his deceased master, Hew Monro, had not booked him. Fortunately for the bower, the council found his request reasonable, and decided that he should not suffer for his master's neglect.[106] Such cases were apparently quite common, as the council lamented in their minutes a generation before in 1656.[107] For some, the rule was outdated and restrictive, highlighting the gradual breakdown of corporatism.

Indeed, it has been suggested that apprenticeship itself was in decline by this period, and previous work on the masons might support this idea.[108] Looking at the bookings in the Incorporation's accompts, in 1670 there were 29 apprentices booked, whilst in 1770 there were only 15.[109] More work is needed on this aspect of Scottish corporatism, but for our purposes here, it does raise important questions about one particular form of provision from the House – that of work. As corporatism began to decline, was there a perception that membership of the House was less able to ensure stable employment? Was the Incorporation seen as more of a hindrance to work than the best route to a reliable income? Here, the stage beyond apprenticeship is crucial, as it was the journeymen who were either allowed in or kept out of the inner circle of privileged freemen of the House. Of course, they were not the only group whose access to work was restricted, so following on from the journeymen we will look at provision of work for the women of the crafts.

ACCESS TO WORK: THE HOUSE BEYOND THE HEADSHIP

There was no guarantee of admission to the status of freeman just because an upholsterer or a glazier had served an apprenticeship with a master of the Incorporation. Many factors came into play in deciding who was allowed in and who was not, let alone who was allowed to work *for* a freeman and who was not. Having trained with a freeman set one in good stead, as did marrying the daughter of a freeman, or being a free-man's son, but at the end of the day, if the market could not sustain more masters vying for the available work, then the House would become more conservative with its admissions. Hence, many apprentices who became journeymen found themselves unable to progress to mastership.[110] Indeed, the Incorporation's papers give ample evidence of elderly journeymen who spent their whole careers as unfree wage labourers.[111] This is, of course, of the utmost importance, as one's status so often came into play in deciding who had the right to work and who did not.[112]

Journeymen and Feed Servants

Those co-resident within the House were very much subordinate to their masters, with the law reinforcing the masters' position of authority.[113] This posed challenges for the journeymen, due to the nature of their status. Journeymen were quite simply waged labour, with 'journey' coming not from tendencies to migrate, but instead from the French, *journée*, which implied a day's labour. Journeymen were therefore the employees, firmly under the masters. As Farr has observed, journeymen were, 'liminal figures, in some ways part of the guild order, but simultaneously excluded from the respectable ranks of masters'.[114] Hence when they disagreed with their masters over control of their labour, it was perceived not as a purely economic issue, but instead as a threat to the broader social order.[115]

　　One record of the relationship between master and 'feed man', so called because of their fee, or wages, is found in the Incorporation's minutes for the 1550s:

> The quhilk day Adam Robertson wrycht granntit opinly in presens of Johne Owchiltre dekin & in presens of all ye breder that he was & is feit servand to Patrik Schang wrycht for ye space of thre ʒeirs nixt ye first of witsonday last by past ffor thre merkis ye first ʒeir, iiij merkis ye nixt ʒeir & four merkis ye

third ȝeir to gidder with meit drynk bedding endurying the said ȝeirs upoun ye quhilks ye said Patrik askit ane act[116]

Not only did the relationship need to be declared openly to the Incorporation, which highlights just how few similar entries are to be found, but in it we find rare evidence of the nature of the relationship. Robertson was contractually – and publicly – bound to serve Schang for three years, with a pay rise after the first year. On top of his fee, he also was to receive food, drink and bedding, highlighting that he was co-resident in his master's household. Though this was not a bad living,[117] with no rent to pay and food apparently provided, it did come at a cost in terms of autonomy.

The 'feit servand' Adam Robertson never became a burgess,[118] and while his name is included in a list of servants in 1559, he does not appear again in the few surviving minutes, suggesting that he did not join the ranks of masters either.[119] It would appear that he simply remained a journeyman. While perhaps his relationships with both his master and the House did not change after his three years were finished, over the early modern period the wider association of journeymen and masters did change. Although the law often protected the privileges of the masters, it also strove to protect the needs of the wider community, and over the eighteenth century journeymen found that they could use the courts to fight their masters over some aspects of labour, such as the number of hours worked.[120]

More importantly, the social bonds between master and journeyman were changing, with what has been argued to be a widening gap between employer and employee.[121] Generally speaking, the traditional model of payment in wages, food, drink and board, 'gave way to a more strictly cash relationship', which in turn eroded the paternalistic links between the master and his co-resident servant.[122] How widespread this was for the journeymen of Mary's Chapel is difficult to say, as there is less evidence about residency patterns than one would like.[123] Fraser's work on Scottish journeyman might well be applicable, though more work is needed on this important group, both within the capital and within the wider nation.

Residency patterns for the House's journeymen are difficult to establish with certainty, though other aspects of their work are clearer. While in theory journeymen were fully trained, being beyond the apprenticeship stage, and more skilled than just labourers, they were still not perceived as being fully qualified; an aspect used to keep them firmly in their place and to control the work they undertook. One example from 1568 demonstrates the differences between subordinate craftsmen and their more privileged masters. In that year, William Hendirsoune was granted limited freedom to work on walls, dykes and simple houses with clay, sand and lime only.[124] He was judged competent to build basic earthen houses, but was forbidden to work with hewn stone or decorative carving.[125] But was this due to a lack of skill, or was it simply a way to control competition?

Similarly, Johne Quhytelaw was allowed to sit an essay for freedom of the Incorporation as a fully-qualified wright in 1575. When he declined to make the essay, the Incorporation responded by simply limiting his work to a set range of furniture types, such as lecterns, coffers, chairs and stools.[126] Clearly Quhytelaw was skilled enough to make these pieces of furniture, but without the full essay, his work was restricted.

Farr, looking at the European building trades in general, points out the increased specialisation of the numerous crafts needed to produce a building.[127] In the examples of Hendirsoune and Quhytelaw we see a form of *forced* specialisation. Though becoming a waller or a furniture maker was indeed work within the building trades, in these particular cases the work was actually used by the Incorporation to control the craftsmen's labour, and to exclude those who were not approved of.

This, however, implies that the entire House agreed on this approval, which was clearly far from the case. Some masters took too many journeymen, just as others forgot to book their servants and pay the requisite booking fees.[128] Likewise, the various acts against journeymen breaking their contracts by deserting masters' service also reveal that at least some fellow craftsmen were quite happy to employ the deserters, given the opportunity.[129] Clearly there was a degree of collusion with the journeymen, emphasising that the headship of the House was not always of a single mind. Similar problems appear in the minutes of other incorporations in other burghs, demonstrating that it was not only the Edinburgh trades which struggled over issues of labour, and not only the Edinburgh masters who occasionally colluded with their journeymen.[130]

As the population grew, it became harder to keep track of labour, and journeymen began to grow more autonomous throughout the eighteenth century, establishing their own societies independent of the House.[131] As Stevenson has shown, the masons, with their 'parallel hierarchies of public incorporation and secret lodge', give interesting insights into this process.[132] By the later seventeenth century, the journeymen masons had been thoroughly excluded from the running of both the Lodge and the Incorporation, heightening resentment of their status and leading them to feel that the headship of the House – or houses, to include the Lodge – no longer had their interests at heart.[133] The journeymen masons withdrew and in 1708 formed their own society for their own 'distressed poor'.[134] The focus of this, and of other journeymen societies, was their common charity box, mimicking the provision of the incorporated trades, and further loosening the former bonds of master over servant.[135]

At first, it would appear that the masters were in favour of the 'mutual support' element of the journeymen societies, but when they started holding their own initiation ceremonies the tone changed. The dispute went before the Court of Session, and was eventually settled by arbitration in 1715.[136] The masons of the Lodge were clearly opposed to an independent body of journeymen, but elements of the Incorporation would appear to have felt less threatened by the societies, as indicated by the minute of its official blessing with the 'Act of the Incorporation In favours of such of the journeymen wrights as have joyned in the society':

> The same Day Thomas Herron wright & present overseer of the Society of the Journeymen Wrights box Represented to the house that not withstanding of all the paines & care that had been taken for advanceing & bringing the said Journeymen wrights their stock or box for relieveing their poor distresst bretheren relicts & Orphants their necessities to some good accompt Yet a great many of their bretheren Jouneymen both old residenters in toun & others that came dayly to work therein Delay & refuse to joyne in the said society by paying in their small entry money of half a croun & six pence per quarter pretending they may joyne in that society at any time they think fit, And probably not till they be objects of Charitie themselves . . .[137]

Despite imposing an overseer, the journeymen societies still removed an element of control from the headship of the House, but it also meant fewer 'mouths to feed', so to speak.[138]

Sisters of the Craft

In terms of access to work, journeymen were not the only disputed group within the House, as the 'sisters of the craft' had always had a role to play in the building trades. This reference to 'sisters', from a 1508 charter relating to annual rents of the Incorporation's altar, made it quite clear that women were very much part of the corporate body, but it is still not clear if this implied the right to work as free craftworkers, or simply that they enjoyed the benefits of the altar.[139] Indeed, very similar phrasing can be found in a fifteenth-century charter of the London Carpenters, so perhaps the phrase was simply legal jargon rather than an intentional statement about gender and work.[140] Either way, they were clearly part of the House, and it was in this capacity that widows enjoyed the right to continue their late husbands' businesses. This was confirmed by the convenery in 1690, in their decreet arbitral for the dispute within Mary's Chapel:

Item wee ordaine the relicts of all friemen to have power and libertie to exercise that airt and craft wherof ther husbands were friemen, so long as they continue unmarried and does nothing prejudiciall to the rules and statuts of the incorporation.[141]

By allowing them to continue, the House was providing work, though upon remarrying, the widows were deemed to no longer need this support. Though work can be seen as a form of charitable provision, this is not to say that the 'sisters' were without skill. Examples beyond the House help to confirm that women in the building trades were quite capable, and their work was highly valued.

One such example comes from the records of the royal building works, which were recorded in the *Accounts of the Masters of Works*. While they were probably not in the Incorporation, several women were involved in the provision of building materials to the craftsmen. 'Besse the nutrice' in Abbey Close furnished shells for masons' mortar.[142] Archebald Dauling's 'wife in Leith' sold oak timbers for scaffolding and flooring, sawn deals, and roofing slates by the thousands,[143] while Katrine Maling provided puncheons for scaffolding.[144] Others provided fodder for the horses that hauled materials, highlighting the important transportation networks that kept the building industry going.[145]

Later accounts for the seventeenth century show women in more hands-on roles, such as bringing loads of lyme and sand to the building works at Dumbarton,[146] or the cart loads of hewn stonework brought by Effie McDull from the quarry at Inverleith Craigs to Edinburgh Castle.[147] McDull is of particular interest, as the drink-silver payments are recorded as being to *her* men, implying McDull's oversight of the workmen. Whether 'sisters of the craft' or not, these women provide a glimpse of the overall context of the early modern building industry, and it is certainly likely that the brethren of the Incorporation would have done business with these women.

Occasionally the town council would hire female craftworkers. The dean of guild accounts list several, such as the 1778 payment by the city chamberlain to 'Widow Duncan, Cooper' who supplied the town with two puncheons, having apparently outsourced the hoops for the casks.[148] 'Widow Cowan, Wright' was recorded in the Dean of Guild's tradesmen accounts for work from 1776–7 of 'taking down & putting up seats, with wood & nails' and for mending seats and tables in the New North Church.[149] Both of these examples demonstrate craftswomen bringing their own skills to bear on public contracts. They sourced their own materials, as indicated by the additional discharge to Widow Duncan for 'hoops for the Casks', implying that she purchased specialist parts for use on her or her workers' puncheons. Whether with the help of employees, or by themselves, they supplied the labour, but how equal they were to their male counterparts is difficult to say.

The discharge for Widow Cowan's work came to £3 7s 10d, though the imprecise nature of the tabulation makes it hard to compare with other tradesmen. The same page of the accounts that records Widow Cowan's wright-work also includes the previous day's discharge of 17s 8d for sundry work to Francis Brodie, a freeman of Mary's Chapel and father of the infamous deacon.[150] Included in Brodie's entry was a payment of 2s 6d for 'Mending seat in N North Church, with dale & nails'.[151] Widow Cowan's work in the same church of 'a days work mending seats, with wood & nails' brought her 3s. Was Brodie's work also contained to a single day, and how many seats were mended? How many tradesmen were in the employ of either Brodie or Cowan? Unfortunately, we have little to go on to draw meaningful comparisons between the established freeman of the Incorporation and the tolerated widow working for the town. Still, we do see clearly a female wright making a living 'with wood & nails'.

Royal and town works clearly brought women into the building trades, but this does not imply acceptance by the Incorporation. Indeed, one case of a craftswoman who was made a burgess by the town and who had a contract with a freeman of the Incorporation suggests that the House only allowed female workers in extraordinary circumstances. Mrs Sara Dalrymple was very much a craftswoman, who was not only a successful employer of journeymen furniture makers, but also an expert herself in the arts of japanning, veneering and 'perspective work'.[152] It was due to this particular skill set, which was not commonly available in Scotland, that the town council made her a burgess in 1709:

> The Councill granted liberty and licence to Sarah Dalrymple, daughter to Charles Dalrymple of Waterside, to use her trade of japanning as a burges of this City all the days of her lifetime and her continuing unmarried providing alwayes she imploy the freemen of this City for the timber work . . .[153]

As long as she did not marry, and only used freemen, her status was thus ensured, though this did not include recognition from the Incorporation; a point which would cause problems for her in the future.

Despite her burgeship, no mention was made of Dalrymple in the minutes of the Incorporation until 1720, implying a rather cool reception for the burgess japanner.[154] Though details are sparse, a 1717 inventory of her shop and workhouse refer to her as 'Mrs Sara Dalrymple', possibly suggesting that she had married.[155] A note on the inventory stipulated that her servants were allowed to finish the pieces already in progress, between the January date of the inventory and 15 May.[156] It would appear that her right to work was being questioned.

Three years later Mrs Dalrymple signed a contract to work with a freeman wright, Gilbert Couper.[157] In the contract, Couper bound himself to patronise Dalrymple of 'all manner of Finneired & Japanned Work' that she could make in the space of one year. He agreed to hire any servants that she wanted 'for her working her said Work'. Ownership of the servants was to be his, though apparently payment of their wages, as well as direction over the work to be done, was down to Mrs Dalrymple. Couper was to oversee deliveries to customers, as he was to own 'the said Work to be done or Wrought by his men'. Finally, Couper stated that he would defend Dalrymple 'to ye utmost of his power against the Incorporation of the Wrights of Edinburgh', so long as she refunded him any legal expenses. It would appear that their venture failed, as this contract survives in the Incorporation's papers, with the signatures at the bottom emphatically crossed out.

That same year, a complaint was made to the House about Couper's relationship with the burgess japanner. The clerk recorded the Incorporation's demand that he 'produce any Contract or agreement', which it would appear he did.[158] Dalrymple then petitioned the Incorporation to allow her to keep working, 'haveing with great industry pains and expenses acqueired the airt of Jappanning & perspective worke (the latter never befor practised in Scotland)'.[159] While a committee was set to consider the request, and a considerable sum of 300 merks 'for the use of the poor' was offered by Dalrymple to sweeten the deal,[160] the Incorporation did not look favourably on a woman from outside the House working in joinery and veneering. They did, however, agree to allow her to keep working japanned work, so long as she employed only 'freemen of this incorporationes to prepare the wood she Jappanns upon'.[161] Hence, Mrs Dalrymple was allowed to carry on one part of her trade.

This was not necessarily the letter of the law. Though her 1709 liberty and licence stated that she was only allowed to work in japanning, it also stipulated that she must remain unmarried and must employ only freemen. By 1717 it would appear that she was married, and by 1720 she contracted herself to employ unfree servants. The fact that they allowed her to continue in just one of her three stated skills of japanning, veneering and perspective work, has been interpreted as being down to the fact that she could produce goods 'unobtainable in Edinburgh'.[162] Though veneering and perspective work were too close to the normal work of the wrights, her ability to add value to furniture through the application of japanning ensured her survival in the Edinburgh furniture market, though the House was adamant that they, and not her, would define the parameters of her work.

Conclusion

The craft economy was clearly so very much more than single 'small master' craftsmen working alone in their booths and shops, but it was also much more than just about craft production. Social factors were intertwined with the economic unit of the craft household, bringing both privileges and obligations. Clearly provision of work was not shared equally across the House. Instead, the Incorporation attempted to reserve work for the privileged few, to ensure that the freemen had enough income to support both themselves and their household. This meant restricting many within those households, and not just those unfreemen from beyond the House. Hence, the craft economy was carefully balanced between restrictive, protectionist policies, and the needs of those associated with its members. Occasionally, outside authorities, such as the crown or the town, interfered with corporate jurisdictions, which offered the unprivileged certain opportunities. At times the House reacted defensively, obstinately fighting expensive legal battles, though at other times they were willing to allow certain exceptions, as with Mrs Dalrymple's japanning, or the journeymen wrights joining the journeymen's society. Access to work was one of the benefits the House was able to provide, but it was often contested and usually controversial.

As Scotland was changing, so was its capital. The population was growing, stone buildings were replacing those of wood, and certain aspects of the makeup of the House were beginning to change. As argued by Fraser, cash payments were replacing payments in room and board in the relationship between the master of the household and the feed man.[163] This tied in with the wider erosion of corporatism, as corporate privileges became increasingly difficult to defend. Thus began the process of the journeymen leaving the House, though other aspects of traditional provision remained. As will be seen in the final chapter, new ideas about work were changing the increasingly-outdated corporate structures, though before this we must turn our attention to the relationships between craft and kirk and craft and burgh, as the Christian and urban contexts were crucial for the rise and eventual fall of the privileged incorporated trades.

NOTES

1. Farr, J., *Artisans in Europe, 1300–1914* (Cambridge: Cambridge University Press, 2000), 20.
2. Stone, L., *The Family, Sex and Marriage in England, 1500–1800* (London: Penguin, 1990), 28.
3. For more on the family and the house as cornerstones of early-modern Scottish

society, see Ewen, E. and Nugent, J., 'Introduction: Where is the Family in Medieval and Early Modern Scotland?', and Falconer, J. R. D., 'A Family Affair: Households, Misbehaving and the Community in Sixteenth-Century Aberdeen', both in Ewen, E. and Nugent, J. (eds), *Finding the Family in Medieval and Early Modern Scotland* (Aldershot: Ashgate, 2008), 8, 140 and 149.

4. *Edin. Recs*, 1689–1701, 15 August 1694, as quoted in Dingwall, H. M., *Late Seventeenth-Century Edinburgh: A Demographic Study* (Aldershot: Scolar Press, 1994), 22.

5. Farr, *Artisans in Europe*, 24.

6. Ibid., 26.

7. Ibid., 33.

8. Flandrin, J., *Families in Former Times: Kinship, Household and Sexuality* (Cambridge: Cambridge University Press, 1979), 4–5.

9. Farr, *Artisans in Europe*, 29.

10. This term 'sisters of the craft' comes from a 1508 'alienation by Walter Maiʒone, mason (lathanius), burgess of Edinburgh, of an annual rent of 40 s. in favour of James Scury, mason, John Duncan, wright (carpentario) and Master James Gibson, Chaplain, in name and behalf of all the brethren and sisters of the Craft and their successors . . .' Mill, 'Inventory', A4, 8 May 1508.

11. 'Brown, James, B[urgess], buikbyndere, as s[on] to Walter B., tailyeour; Jhonn Ewyne, glasinwricht, souerty for extents, watches, airmour quhele mairit (till married) 25 Oct. 1588'. *Edin. Burgs*, 1406–1700, 75.

12. Farr, *Artisans in Europe*, 245.

13. For examples of winter work, see Salzman, L. F., *Building in England Down to 1540: A Documentary History* (Oxford: Clarendon Press, 1997), 59, 448–9, 549. For variation in summer and winter wage rates in Scotland, highlighting the slow-down of winter work, see Knoop, D. and Jones, G. P., *The Scottish Mason and the Mason Word* (Manchester: Manchester University Press, 1939), 32 and 39.

14. I'm grateful to Mr Peter Swinson, general health and safety consultant whose clients included Tailor Wimpy, for providing this information on the Scottish building industry in the early-twenty-first century. According to the Health and Safety Executive's website, falls from a height accounted for 34 of the 72 worker deaths in construction in 2007–08, or 47 per cent. Health and Safety Executive, 'Falls and Trips in Construction', available at: www.hse.gov.uk/Co nstruction/campaigns/fallstrips/index.htm (last accessed 7 September 2016).

15. Whether this was a blessing of time 'to his oun disposal', or a curse of unemployment, is not clear, but the implications for his master's business are apparent. Baptie, D., 'Apprentices in the North East of Scotland', in *Scottish Archives: The Journal of the Scottish Records Association*, 9 (2003), 38–9.

16. NLS, Acc.7056, Box 2, 1795–6 Bill of Jo Ritchie, slater for £12 6s for snow removal and repairs.

17. *Edin. Burgs*, 1406–1700, 446–7. In May of 1648 he was imprisoned in the

tolbooth and had his tavern door closed up due to a drunken rant against the provost and bailies.

18. Ibid., 1406–1700, 417.
19. Ibid., 1406–1700, 266. 'Stent' was a form of tax.
20. Ibid., 1701–1760, 36, 86 and 169.
21. Ibid., 1406–1700, 379.
22. For example, NLS, Acc.7332, Box 2, Group 12, Petitions, 1757–8, Item 18, Barbara Campbell.
23. An excellent example of this is the work of Donald Woodward, who looks at the role of women in the building trades of Northern England in his chapter on labour. Woodward, D., *Men at Work: Labourers and Building Craftsmen in the Towns of Northern England, 1450–1750* (Cambridge: Cambridge University Press, 2002), 108–15. For the topic of women and work in Euopre more generally, see Hanawalt, B. A. (ed.), *Women and Work in Preindustrial Europe* (Bloomington: Indiana University Press, 1986), and Farr, *Artisans in Europe*, 33–41 and 107–13.
24. A noteworthy, if brief, exception to this is the short section on the status of women in the furniture trades, and the subsequent commentary on Sara Dalrymple in the unpublished doctoral thesis of Sebastian Pryke, 'The Eighteenth Century Furniture Trade in Edinburgh: A Study Based on Documentary Sources' (University of St Andrews PhD Thesis, 1995), 9–10, 17–18 and 290. Importantly, Pryke has demonstrated that some wives helped with their husbands' accounts.
25. ECA, Acc.622/1, 220, 14 November 1761.
26. ECA, SL34/1/1, 91, 24 June 1680.
27. Ibid., 104, 31 December 1681. 'Packing and peeling' referred to packaging goods for transportation and unpacking them for distribution; in other words, the handling of merchandise. See DSL, 'Pak': '1. *tr.* To pack (goods, merchandise) in a package, bale . . .'; and 'Pele': '5. To unpack or unwrap (bulk goods); to separate into smaller packages for retailing . . .'
28. NRS, CC8/8/55, 533–5, 15 October 1631. I'm grateful to Dr Michael Pearce for sharing his transcription of this testament with me.
29. For example, see the 1690 decreet arbitral reaffirming Edinburgh's widows' rights to work: 'Item wee ordaine the relicts of all friemen to have power and libertie to exercise that airt and craft wherof ther husbands were friemen, so long as they continue unmarried and does nothing prejudiciall to the rules and statuts of the incorporation.' Munro, J. and Fothringham, H. S. (eds), *Act Book of the Convenery of Deacons of the Trades of Edinburgh 1577–1755*, vol. 2 (Edinburgh: Scottish Record Society, 2011), 119. The Perth Glovers stipulated as late as 1905 that 'widows of all members are entitled to [an annuity of £30], but it shall be forfeited on their entering into another marriage.' Wilson, G., *Annals of the Glover Incorporation 1300 to 1905* (Perth: R. A. & J. Hay, 1905), 62.
30. *Edin. Recs*, 1655–1665, 189, 2 March 1660.

31. *Edin. Burgs*, 1406–1760.
32. See the Introduction for an explanation of the two freedoms of burgessship and mastership.
33. Note, this is only of the freemen, and not the larger group of free and unfree craftsmen which made up the wider labour market.
34. Stone, L., *The Family, Sex and Marriage in England, 1500–1800* (London: Penguin, 1990), 37–51; Farr, *Artisans in Europe*, 222–3 and 244–7; and Dolan, C., 'The Artisans of Aix-en-Provence in the Sixteenth-Century: A Micro-Analysis of Social Relationships', in Benedict, P. (ed.), *Cities and Social Change in Early Modern France* (Routledge: London, 1992), 180–4.
35. Farr, J. R., *Hands of Honor: Artisans and Their World in Dijon, 1550–1650* (Ithaca: Cornell University Press, 1988), 134.
36. *Edin. Burgs*, 1406–1700, 189.
37. See Chapter 4.
38. Farr, *Artisans in Europe*, 245. This is supported by Friedrich's study of Nördlingen, though Dolan's study of Aix-en-Provence found examples of endogamous and exogamous patterns for different trades. Friedrichs, C. R., *Urban Society in an Age of War: Nördlingen, 1580–1720* (Princeton: Princeton University Press, 1979), 87, and Dolan, 'Artisans of Aix-en-Provence', 180–4.
39. *Edin. Burgs*, 1406–1700, 126: Patrick Craig, painter, and Marie Tempell, daughter to William Tempell, surgeon.
40. Ibid., 196: Johne Fultoun, mason, and Issobell Sinclair, daughter to Andro Sinclair, stabler.
41. For more on this, as well as some of the problems with seeing craftsmen and merchants as polarised, distinct groups, see Lynch, M., *Edinburgh and the Reformation* (Edinburgh: Edinburgh University Press, 1981), Chapter 4. See also Chapter 4 of this book.
42. In other words, the 50 per cent who married in their own trade, added to the 4 per cent who took a bride from another trade within the Incorporation.
43. *Edin. Burgs*, 1701–1760, 38.
44. NLS, Acc.7056, Box 2, 1733 Petition of Elizabeth Herriot.
45. Lewis, A., *The Builders of Edinburgh New Town, 1767–1795* (Reading: Spire Books Ltd, 2014), 15.
46. NLS, EMS.s.647, James Craig, *To His Sacred Majesty George III . . . this Plan of the new streets and squares, intended for his ancient capital of North-Britain . . .* (Edinburgh, 1768).
47. Nenadic, S., 'Architect Builders in London and Edinburgh, c.1750–1800, and the Market for Expertise', in *Historical Journal*, 55:3 (2012), 600–1, and Stevenson, D., *The Origins of Freemasonry* (Cambridge: Cambridge University Press, 2005), 105 and 108–12.
48. For example: ECA, Mill Recs, B1, f5r: '. . . subscrivit with yer hands on the pen . . .'
49. Numerous examples of Scottish provenance can be found in: Harris, E.,

British Architectural Books and Writers, 1556–1785 (Cambridge: Cambridge University Press, 1990). See also, Lewis, *Builders of Edinburgh New Town*, 26–46; Nenadic, 'Architect Builders', 597–8; and Jackson, S., 'Edinburgh Cabinet Makers' Wage Agreements and Wage Disputes, 1805 to 1826', in *Scottish Archives: The Journal of the Scottish Records Association*, 11 (2005), 79–89.

50. Lewis, *The Builders of Edinburgh New Town*, 27.

51. Anonymous, *A Poem Inscribed to the Members of St. Mary's Chapel. Upon the Most Honourable, Ancient, and Excellent Art of Wright-Craft. By a Brother of the Craft.* (Edinburgh: David Gray, 1757).

52. Houston, R. A., *Scottish Literacy and the Scottish Identity: Illiteracy and Society in Scotland and Northern England, 1600–1800* (Cambridge: Cambridge University Press, 2002), 38, Table 2.3. Of 77 wrights sampled, only 6 per cent were considered illiterate, while the 30 baxters showed 13 per cent illiteracy; the 129 weavers had 26 per cent; the 76 shoemakers had 30 per cent; and the 41 fleshers showed 46 per cent illiteracy. While his sample sizes are not uniform, there is still a clear sense of greater literacy within the wrights than within the other groups of Lowland Scotland.

53. Houston, *Scottish Literacy*, 4–5 and 10–11. Houston quotes Knox from his *Book of Discipline*: '. . . be most careful for the virtuous education and godly upbringing of the youth of this realm.' Lynch has pointed out that provision before the Reformation was not as bleak as is often portrayed. Lynch, *Scotland: A New History*, 259. See also, Thomson, T. (ed.), *Booke of the Universall Kirk: Acts and Proceedings of the General Assembly of the Kirk of Scotland*, vol. 1 (Edinburgh: Bannatyne Club, 1839), 339.

54. Thomson, *Booke of the Universall Kirk*, vol. 1, 17: 'In like manner, to prefer supplication for the poor and their support; for maintainance of schools for instruction of the ȝouth in every parish; and the same to be taken of the twa part of the teinds, and within burrows of the annual rents, and other such things as before served to idolatrie.'

55. Lynch, *Scotland: A New History*, 259.

56. Todd, M., *The Culture of Protestantism in Early Modern Scotland* (New Haven: Yale University Press, 2002), 63, and Lynch, *Scotland: A New History*, 258.

57. Allen, A. and Spence, C. (eds), *Edinburgh Housemails Taxation Book, 1634–1636* (Woodbridge: Scottish History Society, 2014), xxv and 62 (Skinners' mortification 'to serve for a schoole'); Munro, J., Unpublished Transcription, 'Records of the Edinburgh Incorporation of Skinners' (ECA), 1 August 1642, *inter alia,* (Act anent building ane conveining hous and schooll); Munro, J., Unpublished Transcription, 'Records of the Edinburgh Incorporation of Hammermen', vol. 2 (ECA, ED008/1/2), 26 March 1601 (maintaining a beidman 'at the scuill'), and 4 May 1602 ('Quhilk day the deakin and maisteris geiffis libertie and licence to Andro Dalrympill thair clerk to hald ane scuyll within the uttir laich hows of the hospitall and geiffis him libertie be

thir presentis to big ane tofall under the stair of the hous occupeit be him and to repair and bettir the hous in ony sort to his use be thair advyse'); and Durkan, J. and Reid-Baxter, J. (eds), *Scottish Schools and Schoolmasters, 1560–1633* (Woodbridge: Scottish History Society, 2013), 288 ('Edinburgh, Magdalene Chapel').

58. NLS, Acc.7257, Rolled MS Inventory of Writs, Item 12, and Durkan and Reid-Baxter, *Scottish Schools and Schoolmasters*, 288 ('Edinburgh, Niddrie's Wynd, St Mary Chapel').

59. Alexander Cowan's School: '[Margin: 'order to a Committee to visite the Charity schooll belonging to the Incorporatione quarterly'] And Lastly the house appoints the Boxmaster with one quartermaster of the masons & ane other of the wrights To visite the Charity schollars belonging to this Incorporation In Alexander Cowans schooll & in forme themselves, If the number that he be obliged to teach be full and to report to the house And ordaines this visite to be renewed quarterly by their successours in all tyme comeing'. ECA, SL34/1/4, 100, 2 August 1719. See also the 1729 rules for a painting school formed in Edinburgh in 'The Constitution of the Edinburgh School of St Luke' in Appendix VI of Law, A., *Education in Edinburgh in the Eighteenth Century* (London: University of London Press, 1965), 228–9.

60. The sum left was about £11,000 sterling, primarily in jewels. Lockhart, B. R., *Jinglin' Geordie's Legacy: A History of George Heriot's Hospital and School* (Edinburgh: John Donald, 2009), 14–17.

61. Ibid., 60.

62. Ibid., 24.

63. From 1659 to the 1690s, 31 sons of wrights and 11 sons of masons were selected, whilst from the 1700s to the 1740s, 75 sons of wrights and 12 sons of masons were cared for. From the 1750s to the 1790s the figures rose to 85 sons of wrights, with no masons' sons mentioned, and from the first decade of the 1800s to the 1840s, there were 249 sons of wrights; 86 sons of masons; and 63 sons of coopers. The final period, from the 1850s to the 1880s, saw 102 sons of coopers, 94 sons of wrights; and 62 sons of masons. Lockhart, B. R., *Jinglin' Geordie's Legacy*, 316–21, Appendix 2. As the categories used in Lockhart's earlier tables reflect the fourteen incorporations of the town, in addition to merchants and writers, or lawyers, it is safe to assume that the other eight trades were simply grouped with either the wrights or masons, possibly reflecting the later 'denominations' used to organise the ten trades, though the addition of coopers in the 1800s complicates matters. See Chapter 1 and Appendix 8 for details of the 1703 'denominations'. *Edin. Recs*, 1701–1718, 59–60.

64. Colston, *Incorporated Trades of Edinburgh*, 164–5; Towill, E. S., 'The Minutes of the Trades Maiden Hospital', in *The Book of the Old Edinburgh Club*, 28 (1953), 1–43; and Fothringham, H. S., 'The Trades Maiden Hospital of Edinburgh' (Edinburgh: Unpublished Booklet, 2013), 4. I am grateful to the author of the latter for allowing me to see an early draft of his booklet before its publication.

65. Munro and Fothringham, *Act Book of the Convenery*, vol. 2, 216.
66. Colston, *Incorporated Trades of Edinburgh*, 165, and Towill, 'Minutes of the Trades Maiden Hospital', 8–12.
67. Colston, *Incorporated Trades of Edinburgh*, 165–8.
68. Ibid., 169.
69. Ibid., 170.
70. Ibid., 169–70.
71. Ibid., 174.
72. Baptie has shown that in the north-east of Scotland some sons were indentured to their own fathers, so formalised legal agreements did occasionally govern the training of craft sons. How far this applies to Edinburgh or to Mary's Chapel is not clear at present. Baptie, 'Apprentices in the North East of Scotland', 39.
73. Stevenson, D., 'Apprenticeship: Scottish Stonemasons' Indentures, 1573–1740', in *Scottish Archives: The Journal of the Scottish Records Association*, 17 (2011), 63.
74. For details of increasing economic value and apprentice wages, see: Knoop, D. and Jones, G. P., *The Scottish Mason and the Mason Word* (Manchester: Manchester University Press, 1939), 46–7. It might be pointed out that who exactly received these wages – master, for covering his expenses, or the apprentice themselves for their labour – is not wholly clear.
75. Ibid., 37; Stevenson, 'Apprenticeship', 56, especially note 1; and Knoop and Jones, *Scottish Mason*, 43–7.
76. See for one national example from parliamentary legislation regulating manufactories (1661 Act for Erecting of Manufactories), see: *RPS*, 1661/1/344 (last accessed 27 August 2016).
77. '. . . and gif any prentis of quhatsumeuir of the saidis craftismen, or yit his feit man, pasis away or the ische of his termes but leif of his master, and quha that resauis the prentis or feit man thai sall pay to the altar ane pund of walx the first falt, the secund falt twa pundis of walx, the third falt to be pvnist be the provest and ballies of the towne as efferis'. *Edin. Recs*, 1403–1528, 32.
78. Grant, I. F., *The Social and Economic Development of Scotland Before 1603* (Edinburgh: Oliver and Boyd, 1930), 438.
79. ECA, SL34/1/2, 11, 9 January 1687.
80. Stevenson, 'Apprenticeship', 61.
81. 'Item, that na master nor persone of ony of the craftis tak ony prentis for les termis than sevin yeirs, and ilk prentis to pay at his entre to the said altar half a merk'. *Edin. Recs*, 1403–1528, 32.
82. Stevenson, 'Apprenticeship', 61.
83. Ibid., 58–9.
84. ECA, SL34/1/2, 83–4.
85. *Edin. Burgs*, 1701–1760, 63.
86. *Edin. Burgs*, 1701–1760, 72–3.
87. Ibid., 1406–1700, 122.

88. Friedrichs, C. R., *Urban Society in an Age of War: Nördlingen, 1580–1720* (Princeton: Princeton University Press, 1979), 85.

89. Rappaport, S., *Worlds within Worlds: Structures of Life in Sixteenth-Century London* (Cambridge: Cambridge University Press, 2002), 309.

90. Dolan, C., 'The Artisans of Aix-en-Provence in the Sixteenth-Century: A Micro-Analysis of Social Relationships', in Benedict, P. (ed.), *Cities and Social Change in Early Modern France* (London: Routledge, 1992), 181.

91. Farr, J., *Artisans in Europe, 1300–1914* (Cambridge: Cambridge University Press, 2000), 248.

92. Evidence for Edinburgh's burgesses is recognised as being occasionally inaccurate, though it is the best data we have on the freemen of the town. Stevenson, D., 'Apprenticeship: Scottish Stonemasons' Indentures, 1573–1740', in *Scottish Archives: The Journal of the Scottish Records Association*, 17 (2011), 57, and Allen, A., *The Locksmith Craft in Early Modern Edinburgh* (Edinburgh: Society of Antiquaries of Scotland, 2007), 19.

93. Unfortunately, this tells us nothing of the unfreemen, demonstrating a weakness in the historical record.

94. *Edin. Burgs*, 1406–1700 and 1701–1760.

95. Lynch has estimated that only about 30 per cent of householders in 1635 actually held burgesship. Lynch, *Edinburgh and the Reformation*, 10.

96. *Edin. Recs*, 1403–1528, 112–13, and *Edin. Burgs*, 1406–1700, 2. Marwick appears to have mistakenly put down 'lxiii' instead of 'xiii', as the prices note that the cost for daughters followed that of second sons. Prices for guildry are also given and followed suit.

97. See Allen, A., *The Locksmith Craft in Early Modern Edinburgh* (Edinburgh: Society of Antiquaries of Scotland, 2007), 43–4, and *Edin. Recs*, 1528–1557, 148.

98. *Edin. Recs*, 1573–1589, 274.

99. Not all of these 24 sons had fathers who were coopers, though. Mechants, brewers, maltmen and a sievewright were also represented in the burgess fathers of coopers found in the burgess rolls. *Edin. Burgs*, 1406–1760.

100. Coopers' and wrights' figures taken from *Edin. Burgs*, 1406–1760. Equally interesting would be to look at the occupational paths of those who did not follow in their fathers' footsteps, as with son of the wright David Callender, who became a writer, and took burgessip and guildry in 1672 while working as a servitor to Sir William Sharp, his majesty's 'cash keeper'. Ibid., 92. How common was it for children of craft families to enter the professions? Perhaps a full study of the burgess rolls would shed light on this.

101. NLS, Acc.8617, Bundle 1: Legal Papers and Accounts, 1601–80, Item 2: 'Act In favours of David Andersones children 1680'.

102. ECA, SL34/1/2, 11, 29 January 1687.

103. *Edin. Burgs*, 1406–1700, 391.

104. For more on the advantages and prestige of guildry, see Chapter 4.

105. For 'prentice silver', see ECA, Mill Recs, B1–B5. For a limit to the number

of apprentices taken at one time, see Carr, H., *The Mason and the Burgh* (London: Quatuor Coronati Lodge, 1954), 34–7, though admittedly these are specifically from the Lodge rather than the Incorporation. Regardless, they would have impacted upon the working life of at least part of the Incorporation, and are therefore relevant here.

106. *Edin. Burgs*, 1406–1700, 10.
107. *Edin. Recs*, 1655–1665, 9, 1 February 1656.
108. Devine, T. M., 'The Merchant Class of the Larger Scottish Towns in the Later Seventeenth and Early Eighteenth Centuries', in Gordon, G., and Dicks, B. (eds), *Scottish Urban History* (Aberdeen: Aberdeen University Press, 1983), 95, and Carr, *Mason and the Burgh*, 46.
109. ECA, SL34/1/1, 2, Charge to the Compter, 1669–1670, and SL34/2/1, 143, Accompt of Charge and Discharge, 1769–1770.
110. For more on this important topic, see Ben-Amos, I. K., 'Failure to Become Freemen: Urban Apprentices in Early Modern England' in *Social History*, 16:2 (1991). Dr Tawny Paul of the University of Exeter is also working on related issues, in what is provisionally titled, 'Precarious Lives: Economic Culture and the Lower Middling Sort in Eighteenth-Century Britain'.
111. Take, for examples, the 1722 supplication of Patrick Thomson, a seventy-year-old journeyman wright, who was no longer able to work (NLS, Acc.7056, Box 1, Bundle 4, Supplication of Patrick Thomson), or the 1783 petition for relief of Margaret Watson, relict of John Page, who was a journeyman wright for 33 years (NLS, Acc.7260, Petition of Margaret Watson).
112. This is, of course, very different from who *did* work and who did not. Still, status mattered.
113. Fraser, *Conflict and Class*, 3.
114. Farr, *Artisans in Europe*, 29.
115. Farr, *Artisans in Europe*, 29.
116. ECA, Mill Recs, B1, f8v, 18 February 1553–4.
117. How this compares to other journeymen or even to general labourers is difficult to say. Gibson's and Smout's table of building labourers' daily wages shows that Edinburgh council wages for 1553 and 1554 were 1 shilling 6 pence per day. Using the multiplier of 312 *potential* days of work, assuming that of the fifty-two weeks in a year, only six days could be worked in each, this would work out as 468 shillings per year, or £23 8s, though this did not include room and board, and there is little indication that all potential days would have actually brought gainful employment. Gibson and Smout, *Prices, Food and Wages in Scotland*, 316. To compare the council's payment to labourers with that of the wright Patrick Schang, more work would need to be done on the cost of rent and food.
118. *Edin. Burgs*, 1406–1700, 423.
119. ECA, Mill Recs, B3, f2v.
120. Fraser, *Conflict and Class*, 3.
121. Ibid., 23.

122. Ibid., 23.
123. Adam Robertson was certainly supposed to receive meat, drink and bedding in 1553, implying he was in the master's household (ECA, Mill Recs, B1, f8v, 18 February 1553–4), but a 1691 act of the Incorporation against taking in journeymen who left their masters stipulates that as long as the original master was 'alwayes paying his wages [and] dueling', then no other freeman of that art was to 'resett him, upon any termes'. ECA, SL34/1/2, 99, 28 May 1691.
124. ECA, Mill Recs, B4, f4v, 6 August 1568.
125. This minute of 1568 foreshadows the later regulations of the Lodge of Freemasons against 'cowans', who were likewise semi-skilled dykers. See Carr, H. (ed.), *The Minutes of the Lodge of Edinburgh, Mary's Chapel, No. 1, 1598–1738* (London: Quatuor Coronati Lodge, 1962), 36–9 and 42, and Smith, A. M., *The Three United Trades of Dundee: Masons, Wrights & Slaters* (Dundee: Abertay Historical Society, 1987), 49.
126. ECA, Mill Recs, B5, f6r, 1 May 1575: '. . . Johne quhytelaw wrycht band and obleist him self of his awin fre motive will voluntarilie uncompellit or coactit Nocht to wirk ony uyer wark in tyme coming bot . . . Lattrounis (lecterns) cofferis chairis and stules and that in his awin buith and of his awin tymber and sall wark na warkis within this burgh in ony housses yereof except under past maister of the wrycht craft for wages . . .'
127. Farr, *Artisans in Europe*, 70.
128. For example, see the minutes of the convenery of 'Certain wrights having more servants than they should': Munro and Fothringham, *Act Book of the Convenery*, vol. 1, 19, and ECA, SL34/1/1, 14, 30 July 1670, 'Act for booking of Journaymen'.
129. See, for example, the 'Act against Journeymen deserting their masters' service', ECA, SL34/1/2, 99, 28 May 1691, or the 1724 complaint about George Hay, wright, 'deverting and intyceing one Charles Condie journyman wright', ECA, SL34/1/5, f1r-f1v. Carr's transcription of the seventeenth- and eighteenth-century minutes of the Freemason's Lodge of Mary's Chapel includes a 1705 minute about 'masters of this house that tolleratt jurnmen to work up an down this Citie Contrair to yeir oath of admission . . .' Intriguingly, deacon Nisbet is singled out for tolerating Thomas Paterson to work on chimneys. Any further cases were to be 'punished acording to yeir fault or priveledge of this brough', highlighting the Lodge's subservience to burgh law, and therefore to the Incorporation. Carr, *Minutes of the Lodge of Edinburgh*, 226.
130. See, for example, the minutes of the Ayr Wrights and Squaremen, which also imposed fines for masters who, 'shall tak any journeymen without they come and acquent The present deacon for the tyme and the rest off his Brethren'. Ayrshire Archives, B6/24/1, 'Minute Book of the Wrights and Squaremen of the Burgh of Air. 1556, Apr. 7–1724, Oct. 10', 30 April 1655.
131. Fraser, *Conflict and Class*, 3 and Chapter 2.
132. Stevenson, *Origins of Freemasonry*, 192.

133. Ibid., 192 and 210.

134. Ibid., 210–11.

135. Fraser, *Conflict and Class*, 3 and 19.

136. Stevenson, *Origins of Freemasonry*, 192.

137. ECA, SL34/1/4, 95–6, 11 April 1719.

138. Ibid.

139. ECA, Mill Recs, A4, and Mill, 'Inventory', A4, 1508 'alienation by Walter Maiȝone, mason (lathanius), burgess of Edinburgh, of an annual rent of 40 s. in favour of James Scury, mason, John Duncan, wright (carpentario) and Master James Gibson, Chaplain, in name and behalf of all the brethren and sisters of the Craft and their successors . . .'

140. The London Carpenters's charter of 1477 would seem to explicitly refer to craft *families* rather than craftswomen: '. . . and of the brethren and sisters of freemen of the said mystery . . .' Jupp, E. B., *An Historical Account of the Worshipful Company of Carpenters of the City of London Compiled Chiefly from Records in their Possession* (London: William Pickering, 1848), 4, 13 and 161.

141. Munro and Fothringham, *Act Book of the Convenery*, vol. 2, 119.

142. *AMW*, 1529–1615, xlix and 55.

143. Ibid., 1529–1615, 80, 101, and 114.

144. Ibid., 1529–1615, 20.

145. For numerous examples see, Ibid., 1529–1615, 19, 26–7, 57, 59–64, 67, 70, 78–9, and 87.

146. Ibid., 1616–1649, 37.

147. 'Item to Effie McDull for 7 cart draucht hewin wark led be hir cart fra Innerleith craig to the castell at 3[0] s. the draucht x lib. x s.

To hir men to drink vi s.

To the quarriouris of Innerleith craig for winning of the saidis stanes led be our awin cartes being sex scoir futes at xvi d. the fute viii lib.' Ibid., 1616–1649, 68.

148. ECA, SL144/7/1, Dean of Guild Manuscript Tradesmen Accounts, 1735–1781, 477, 18 March 1778.

149. Ibid., Cowan: 479, 28 May 1778.

150. Brodie's son, who was later executed for his crimes, was the Deacon William Brodie who inspired Robert Louis Stevenson to write *The Strange Case of Dr Jekyll and Mr Hyde*. See Allen, A., 'A Pernicious and Wicked Custom: Corporate Responses to Lock Picking in the Scottish Town, 1488–1788', in *Proceedings of the Society of Antiquaries of Scotland*, 137 (2007), 471–86.

151. ECA, SL144/7/1, Dean of Guild Manuscript Tradesmen Accounts, 1735–1781, Cowan: 479, 28 May 1778 and Brodie: 479, 27 May 1778.

152. It is worth noting that Dalrymple was not the first lady to take up japanning, or lacquering, in Edinburgh. Whilst not made a burgess, Jean Montgomery was given a two-year licence by the council in 1692 for japanning work. *Edin. Recs*, 1689–1701, 88.

153. *Edin. Recs*, 1701–1718, 173, 10 August 1709.

154. ECA, SL34/1/4, 15–22, 6 August 1709 to 11 February 1710; SL34/1/4, 67–87, 20 June 1716 to 22 November 1718; and SL34/1/4, 100, 26 March 1720.

155. The admitted assumption that 'Mrs' denoted marital status is based on the fact that the Incorporation used the title 'Mr' only for degree holders, such as 'Mr James Smith'; the only man given the title in the list of 129 freemen for 1727. ECA, SL34/1/6, 11, 1727 'Roll of the Members . . .' A record of her marriage has not yet been found in the published marriage rolls.

156. NLS, Acc.7056, Box 1, Bundle 2, 'Inventory of unfinished work in Mrs Sara Dalrymples shope & workehouse, 1717'. The inside text reads:
'Inventory of the unfinished worke in Mrs Sarahe Dalyrumples shope which her servants are allowed to ffinish betuixt & the fifteen day of May next
Imprimus Tuo litle cabinets for Ladies closet.
Item fyve dressing tables
Item Tuo more dressing tables with drawers
Item one duzon Archt glass frames
Item Three more dressing tables
Item foure more glass frames
Item ane union box
To be finisht betuixt and the fifteen day of May next
The Inventary taken up this 24 January 1717'.

157. The following quotations are all from NLS, Acc.7056, Box 1, Bundle 1, 1720 Contract betwixt Gilbert Couper, wright burgess of Edinburgh and Mrs Sara Dalrymple, merchand. The text of the contract reads: 'Binds & Obliges him To patronise all manner of Finneired & Japanned Work That the sd Mrs Sara Dalrymple shall be imployed in for the space of one year . . . And that by Owning the said Work to be done or Wrought by his men & by defending the same to ye utmost of his power against the Incorporation of the Wrights of Edinr. And ye sd Gilbert Couper Binds & obliges himself to hire what servants the sd Mrs Sara Dalrymple shall want for her working her sd Work & own them as his and go along with any of the forsd Work that she shall be imployed in & see the same Delivered to the Employers . . . Binds & Obliges her To pay the Work men or servants which the said Gilbert Couper shall imploy yr Wages as they used to be formerly And To Refound & Repay to the said Gilbert Couper whatever charges & Expenses he may be put to on account of any suits to be intended against him by the sd Incorporation of Wrights for giving The said Mrs Sara Dalrymple his protection in her said business of Finneiring & Japanning . . .'

158. ECA, SL34/1/4, 106, 26 March 1720.

159. ECA, SL34/1/5, 4, 22 April 1721.

160. Ibid., 4, 22 April 1721.

161. Ibid., 5, 1 June 1721 and 6, 3 June 1721.

162. Pryke, 'Furniture Trade', 18.

163. Fraser, *Conflict and Class*, 23.

Plate 1 'Chimney piece', *The Edinburgh Trades*, 1720 (Chalmers)

Included are the ten Mary's Chapel trades in order of precedence, with what appears to be the most senior trades closest to the middle. The masons and wrights are at the centre, flanked by the coopers and bowers; the glaziers and painters; the slaters and plumbers; and finally at the outside edges, the sievewrights and upholsterers, reflecting the order given in the surviving ECA minute books. Held by the Trades Maiden Hospital. Used with kind permission of the United Incorporation of Mary's Chapel.

Plate 2 'The Four Conditions of Society: The Craftsman or Work' (Bourdichon)
Note that while the craftsman planes a board, the child cleans up shavings in the shop and the woman spins yarn. Technically, only the craftsman is making furniture, though it is clear that all are contributing their labour to the domestic economy. Photo © RMN-Grand Palais, courtesy of the Bibliotheque de l'École des Beaux-Arts, Paris, France.

Plate 3 'Procession for Corpus Christi' (Master of James IV of Scotland)
Note the banners and different-coloured clothing of the separate fraternities processing before
the sacrament in the upper right-hand corner. Flemish, sixteenth century. Original held by John
Paul Getty Museum, Ms. Ludwig IX 18, fol. 48v. By kind permission the J. Paul Getty Museum.

Plate 4 Detail of the building site of the Royal Institution (later the Royal Scottish Academy, Princes Street), 1825 (Nasmyth)
Note the masons at work, their lodge (middle left), the scaffolding and the crane. Alexander Nasmyth (1758–1840), *Princes Street with the Commencement of the Building of the Royal Institution* (1825), NGS, NG 2542. By kind permission of National Galleries of Scotland. Presented by Sir David Baird, 1991.

3

Craft and Kirk: Security, Status and Shelter

It is well known that European society was traditionally divided up into three estates: the church, the nobility and the peasantry, and it is no accident that the church was given first place in this feudal structure. What is also well known, is that throughout Europe groups of craftsmen banded together into craft guilds, often with a specifically-religious focus. The pre-Reformation Incorporation of Masons and Wrights, which by the seventeenth century took on the new title of 'Incorporation of Mary's Chapel', received a grant of an altar in the town's collegiate kirk on the very same day that they were officially given their legal charter, or seal of cause, demonstrating the overlapping role of 'confraternity' alongside their incorporated status. The published council minutes present these two items within contiguous records of a single day's business. Despite the fact that one might read this as being a single charter with two parts, the recent rediscovery of the missing originals shows that they were indeed separate legal documents.[1]

The first was a grant of religious privileges, including an aisle and chapel for the use of the craftsmen. The second was a charter of legal status in regards to their work. Though these two documents were distinct, the connections of the religious and occupational aspects of the group of craftsmen were far more intertwined, which appears to have been a common feature of European confraternities. This raises the question as to just how separate the confraternities were from the incorporated trades within the capital.

The term 'incorporated trade' has already been established in earlier chapters as the proper contemporary term in Scotland for describing what modern historians tend to call 'craft guilds'. When looking at relations between the crafts and the kirk, the situation is further complicated by the parallel descriptor of 'confraternity'. So with the terminology already being quite complicated, what exactly was a confraternity? For reasons explained below, a precise definition is not easily found. To help us unpack this, several useful points can be taken from the work of Christopher Black. In his study of Italian confraternities, Black suggested that a working definition might be '. . . a voluntary association of people who come together under the guidance of certain rules to promote their religious life in common.'[2] This was caveated by an acknowledgment that such bodies were not always voluntary, as, for example, when they overlapped with a trade guild, but the religious aspects would seem to be the crucial element in defining a corporate body as a confraternity.[3] Terpstra agreed that confraternities could be 'more than "purely" devotional groups', pointing to issues of charity, gender and class.[4] Still, both put heavy emphasis on the 'religious culture of confraternities', as have several other historians.[5]

A more precise definition might be found in the ecclesiastical records of the day; in particular, the *legal* definition. Black, in his book *Italian Confraternities in the Sixteenth Century*, explained that the old canon law distinguished between 'pious unions', which were 'associations established for some work of piety and charity'; 'sodalities', which were institutions 'constituted as organic bodies'; and 'confraternities', which were 'established for the increase of public worship'.[6] Using this legal definition, the worship-focussed confraternity was quite different to the other forms of corporate bodies, despite the fact that piety and other Christian virtues could clearly impact upon all forms. In light of this, it is quite plausible that a body of craftsmen and their families could be both a confraternity and an incorporated trade. While legally they may have been distinct institutions, the historical record does not often explicitly delineate their differences.

This leads to problems, as often the religious and the trade-regulatory functions of a corporate group overlapped. Farr, in his study of wider artisan culture, noted that a confraternity and a guild might share officers, with parallel administration and even financial accounts.[7] Legally, they may have been distinct, but socially, politically and economically they could be quite intertwined. Hence both contemporaries and modern historians alike have often used the terms 'confraternity' and 'guild' interchangeably.

In the twentieth century, Black chose to use the terms, 'confraternities, fraternities, sodalities, brotherhoods, and companies interchangeably, without implying categorical differences . . .'[8] Even in Scotland in the seventeenth century such broad usage was justifiable. Fountainhall, in his relation of the legal wrangling of the Incorporation, referred to the ten trades of Mary's Chapel as '*confratri* (for *confratres*)'[9] With both of these two historians, despite their very different contexts, the focus of their use of the term was on the aspects of brotherhood rather than on either religious observance or trade regulation. Despite the fact that the Edinburgh council abolished confraternities in 1561,[10] some element of this institution was still recognisable more than a century later, and this equally translates to more modern historiography. Clearly certain aspects of the confraternity and the trade guild overlap.

Part of the problem behind this overlap is that both religious and trade matters might have been dealt with at meetings of tradesmen in an ecclesiastical property.[11] Perceptions of a difference between such corporate business and spiritual matters would probably have been blurred by the centrality of Christianity across most aspects of life. Many simply would not have recognised a difference between a religious confraternity and a pious incorporation, which has potentially coloured the surviving records.[12]

Several historians have taken note of this problem. Epstein, while commenting on Church protection of secular guilds as well as confraternities, noted the challenge of distinguishing between guild members and a group of individuals gathered to pray for the departed.[13] Black, in explaining his carefully-considered choice of terminology, pointed out that most contemporaries were simply not concerned with 'the niceties of strict categorisation.'[14] Others, such as Meersseman, have seen a clearer division of the interests of the two institutions, with guilds focussing on mutual help for temporal matters, while confraternities looked to spiritual health and eternal salvation.[15] This would certainly fit with the canon law mentioned above. Epstein, however, argued that such judgments about primary concerns remained subjective in light of the problem of sufficient sources, and that a basic rule of thumb should be that 'virtually every guild was also a confraternity but that many of the latter were purely religious associations'.[16] Farr's summation would back this up, based on their common concerns:

> By serving as an association of individuals through which trust, reputation, and salvation could be simultaneously pursued, the confraternity was the conscience of the guild, shoring up the solidarity that countervailing tensions within the guild continually challenged.[17]

Whether overlapping, or distinct legal entities, the problem of the relationship between confraternity and craft guild clearly needs further attention.

Moreover, questions are raised about the relationship between corporate work and corporate religion. Fortunately the Edinburgh Incorporation has much to show us for this last point. In particular, we see in the Masons and Wrights clear evidence of a legal dichotomy between confraternity and incorporated trade due to the fact that their grant of an altar and their seal of cause as an incorporation were separate charters. While canon law may indeed have had a bearing, it was in fact the local municipal laws which defined the privileges of the Masons and Wrights. Firstly, the council granted them an altar, which, it is argued here, equated to confraternal status. Secondly, and on the same day, the council granted them a seal of cause erecting them as an incorporated trade. The fact that this one body received two legal charters demonstrates a clear division between confraternity and incorporation. Still, as the historiography quite rightly suggests, the overlapping functions were not easily separated. Piety and fraternity transcended the legal boundaries between the two. Although the confraternal status was lost with the Reformation, the corporate body continued, and as shall be seen, so too did their relationship with the church. So what was the nature of the relationship between the kirk and Incorporation of Masons and Wrights, and how did this change with the Reformation? Why was this relationship so important to the Incorporation? As we shall see, it was absolutely formative.

CONTRIBUTIONS TO PUBLIC WORSHIP

The Christian church, as the first estate in the feudal system, was absolutely crucial to early modern Scottish society, and the prominence of the kirk in Edinburgh is best exemplified by the central placement of the High Kirk – the collegiate church of St Giles – right at the very centre of the Scottish capital's High Street. Indeed, such a costly and prestigious building speaks to the esteem and importance of Christianity in the history of the Scottish capital, and the building trades were in a rather privileged position in terms of being able to support the church. They not only offered their skills and labour to build and maintain the fabric, but they also gave of their resources to uphold the complex and sophisticated system of public worship within the capital; a unique set of contributions within their parish.

In the earlier periods only important buildings were normally made of costly stone, and most structures were of wooden or earthen construction. While much of Edinburgh was still being built of wood in the seventeenth century, it is likely that the kirk employed masons for more than just the lucrative 'kirk warks' at St Giles. Evidence from ecclesiastical centres, such as Glasgow, with its fifteenth-century stone-built housing for clerics (e.g. the surviving Provand's Lordship, and similar buildings in the area, which are no longer extant) or the small fishing settlement of Cellardyke, in Fife, with its fifteenth-century 'Bishop's House', suggest that the kirk patronised the mason craft for domestic structures as well, greatly multiplying the amount of work given to masons outside the actual buildings related to worship. The kirk was an important employer, and there is little doubt that the building crafts in Edinburgh benefitted greatly from the ecclesiastical contracts, both spiritual and domestic. This, of course, is not to mention the kirk's pastoral role in tending to the crafts as part of the wider flock.

Despite the popular imagination tending to think that the Reformers physically and purposely attacked all church buildings in an iconoclastic rage, the records demonstrate that many of the post-Reformation regimes were every bit as concerned with the upkeep and maintenance of the church fabric as their predecessors, and the Masons and Wrights figure heavily in the 'kirk warks' after 1560. Partition walls were needed to make the space fit for purpose. There was the addition of seating and pulpits for teaching, as well as the renovation of spaces for storage.[18] Windows were repaired, as were the roof and the steeple. After reform, as before, the builders were still very much needed.

Aside from their role in the production of material culture for the church, which both relied upon their skill and allowed them to showcase their abilities in a public forum, the crafts of the Incorporation of Masons and Wrights also acted as consumers of kirk culture through their contributions to public worship. They were in a unique position in burgh society, as they both built the kirk and used it; they sustained the fabric and they worshipped God inside it. Indeed, not all public worship required a church, and the Incorporation, like their neighbours, played a role in religious processions, giving further chances to be seen publicly as an incorporation; an incorporation that was unified, pious and skilful. Some of these aspects survived the Reformation, though the way they were displayed changed slightly.

Upholding of the Altar

The earliest contribution to public worship was the Incorporation's support of the altar of Saints John the Baptist and Evangelist, a dual dedication to two prestigious saints, granted to the Masons and Wrights in October 1475.[19] It would appear that this was not a new foundation, but instead the assignment of an existing altar to the crafts, both from the language of the grant, but also from a late-fourteenth-century charter of Robert III, confirming John Peebles' grant to 'St. Johns chappell in the north side of St. Geyllis kirk Edinburgh.'[20] This appears to have been a fairly common occurrence for craft guilds to inherit existing, or at least defunct, dedications. The Wrights and Coopers of Aberdeen had St John the Evangelist's altar in St Nicholas Church by 1527, though it would appear that there had been an altar dedicated to the apostle by 1277.[21]

Individual craftsmen might have contributed to any altar, but with the assignation of this aisle and chapel to the Masons and Wrights, they were able to participate as a *recognised* corporate body in the worship of their parish, mirroring the continental trends and suggesting a certain level of prestige.[22] St Giles, as the parish kirk of Edinburgh, was dedicated to the town's patron saint. Inside it had an estimated forty altars with numerous dedications.[23] The kirk had received collegiate status in 1466, allowing for an entire college of priests to serve at the numerous altars.[24] This college of priests and altars demonstrates the complexity and crowdedness of the ecclesiastical topography of Edinburgh's primary church; a topography in which both private piety and public prestige were established, and the Masons and Wrights no doubt sought both at their altar to Sts John.

As mentioned, the Masons' and Wrights' altar, which the provost, bailies, dean of guild and craft deacons gave 'consent and assignatioun' to, was already an enfeoffment of Sir John Skaithmuir, who appears to have been a canon of the chapter of St Giles.[25] The details of the canon's enfeoffment are not given, but it is clear that the Masons and Wrights were not the only party with an interest in the altar. As with the phenomenon of inheriting an older, established altar, this aspect of multiple parties having interest in a single altar is also in keeping with what is known of other craft dedications, such as the altar of St Eloi, which came to be under the Incorporation of Hammermen of Edinburgh in 1494.[26] This particular altar in the nave of St Giles, near the pulpit, was founded by John Dalrymple in 1477, and he apparently continued to support it after the Hammermen were incorporated 1483. Their seal of cause stipulated that craft fines were to go to the altar, though it has been argued that they were relieved of the full expense of its upkeep until Dalrymple's death.[27]

With the grant of the aisle and chapel of Sts John to the Incorporation of Masons and Wrights, they obtained considerable liberties to enjoy its freedoms, profits and easements, 'with power to edify big reparell and put it ony pairt thairof to polesy or honour of the saidis sanctis eithir in werk or divine service . . .'[28] In many ways, this was a blank canvas for the Incorporation to publicly display their skills, and piety. The physical space alone would have been most impressive, and it is quite interesting that those who the council relied upon to build and maintain their precious collegiate kirk in a manner befitting their aspirations, would be granted not just any altar, but an entire aisle and chapel in the north transept; a relatively large and impressive space, with not one, but two dedications to elite saints. One was a friend and disciple of Jesus Christ,[29] while the other was actually a family member of the Lord.[30] The grant of the aisle and chapel was no ordinary grant, but a prestigious gift to trusted servants of the town.

Despite the fact that the altars were removed with the Reformation, much can be learned about the physical space and characteristics of the chapel. The grant of 1475 specifies that their aisle and chapel were to be 'fra the ald hers of irne inwarts'. A 'hers' was an iron frame for holding candles which could be placed over coffins during funerals. A 1508 charter states that it was on the north side of St Giles and immediately after the altar of 'St Coberti'.[31] Intriguingly, part of the fabric of St John's aisle survived the renovations of the nineteenth century, including a fifteenth-century window, which must have lit the Masons' and Wrights' aisle.[32]

The accounts of the dean of guild give important details about the fabric of St John's aisle, including several payments for window glass. In February 1554–5, 32 feet of new glass and 21 feet of old glass were used for 'ane greit windo on the north syde of the croce kirk, aboun the heid of Sanct Johnis ile', demonstrating winter hours for both kirk works and glaziers, as well as suggesting substantial windows shedding natural light on Sts Johns' aisle.[33] Further payments were made for glass in St John's aisle sometime between Candlemas (2 February) and Pasche (Easter) of 1555–6, and in January 1560–1, keeping with the winter repairs for glazing.[34]

Clearly window light was very important, though how much natural light actually fell on the St John's chapel, being in the north transept, is somewhat doubtful. More problematic, was the phenomenon of market infill, as the luckenbooths, or the Booth Raw, was erected to the north of the kirk from the 1400s. This created a narrow, dark, and apparently less-than-clean, passage, known as the 'Stinking Style'; a feature of the capital lampooned by the court makar, William Dunbar, in his famous poem to the Edinburgh merchants of c.1500: 'ʒour stinkand Styll that standis dirk, Haldis the lycht fra ʒour parroche kirk . . .'[35] As seen in Figure 3.1, there was very little space between the 'greit windo' on the north gable of St John's Aisle and the south side of the luckenbooths, which were not demolished until 1817.[36]

With the luckenbooths already hemming the kirk in, there was probably little point in objecting to the eastern window of St John's Aisle also being blocked. With the heightening of the revestry over the eastern window, which is thought to have taken place around 1550, there might not have been a serious impact on the level of natural light from the north and east falling on the Masons' and Wrights' altar in St John's chapel and aisle.[37] Indeed, many altars were curtained, so perhaps the crafts lost little here in the way of prestige. The luckenbooths and the revestry were both heightened over time, as public space on the High Street gave way to commercial and demographic pressures. Perhaps this was more problematic for their chaplain, who worked in the chapel daily, though the dean of guild did invest in the windows, which was perhaps some consolation to the Incorporation.[38]

The loss of natural light was far from ideal, but the addition and heightening of the revestry brought several benefits for the Masons and Wrights. It brought contracts; it made for more useful space; and it modernised the medieval fabric surrounding their aisle and chapel. In 1554–5 an unnamed wright was paid to build, 'ane litill hous at the back of Sanct Johnis alter', with a lockable door.[39] Following on from this were three-and-a-half days of work for an unnamed mason, 'to big up Sanct Johnis windois, and the dur cheiks of it,' preparing the way for the upward extension of the revestry.[40] Altars appear to have been 'oriented', so that they faced east,[41] the direction of God's holy city, Jerusalem.[42] As this was the case, we can be fairly certain that the formentioned alterations, along with the various loads of lime, sand, nails, and lath, as well as the work of the slater who 'thacked' the house, pertain to the revestry, directly eastward of the altar of Sts John the Baptist and Evangelist.[43]

The few excerpts recorded by Mill in her 1923 'Inventory' also suggest that the aisle and chapel took up a large space. 'St John's Chapel' was used as a meeting place, so the space must have been considerable.[44] In 1554 a mail, or rent, of 4 merks was paid to the kirkmaster for the rental of 'ye sellar vnder ye chapell'.[45] In 1559 in the midst of the Reformation crisis, only three months after the wright and kirkmaster Robert Fender had made a 'compotum', or account, of all the goods and gear pertaining to St John, the same kirkmaster undertook to 'compleit ye chymnay of ye chapell'; a job large enough that it was estimated to £5.[46] Indeed, in May of 1559 there had been a tenant living above the chapel: 'gilliam ye franche payntir quha duells abone ye chapell'.[47] Although there were other chapels dedicated to one or both Sts John in Edinburgh, it would appear that these references are to the Incorporation's aisle and chapel in St Giles, meaning that the French painter's 'house' was the space above the revestory, as can be seen in the eighteenth-century depiction of St Giles' north façade in Maitland's *History*.[48]

The tower-like revestory structure, as shown by Maitland in 1753 (Figure 3.2), or by nineteenth-century sources, such as Laing's plate 7, or 'St Giles Church Looking West', gives us some very important clues as to the physical space inhabited by the Incorporation, though the records of the now missing fabric are quite puzzling.[49] The square tower of four storeys, with a gable-end chimney appears to the untrained eye to be sixteenth-century in its architectural style and, as MacGibbon discovered in 1899, was built against an apparently fifteenth-century window.[50] At some point this window was blocked up, possibly suggesting that the pointed arch was no longer in fashion, though it might also have been for greater security in the revestory, which was used in the 1550s and 1560s as both jewel-house, clerk's chamber and charterhouse.[51] Hay was of the opinion

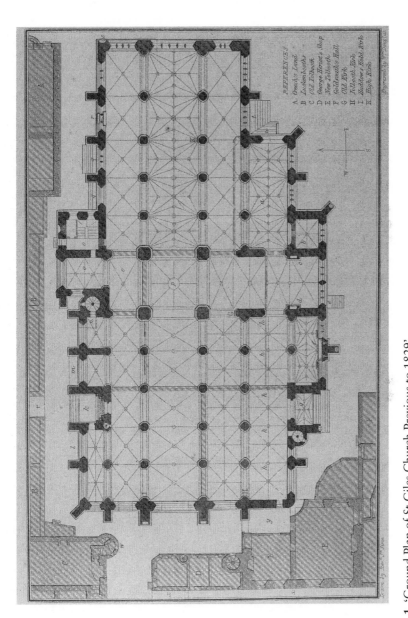

Figure 3.1 'Ground Plan of St Giles Church Previous to 1829'

From the 1891 edition of Wilson's *Memorials of Edinburgh in the Olden Time*, II, 296–7. Note how St John's Aisle in the north transept, flanked by the revestory to the east, juts out into the 'Stinking Styll' passage between the north of the kirk and the luckenbooths at the very top of the illustration. By kind permission of the University of Edinburgh, Special Collections.

The Northern Prospect of St. Giles's Church

P. Fourdrinier sculp.

Figure 3.2 'The Northern Prospect of St Giles Church'

From Maitland's *History*, 184–5. Note the two white-coloured central structures: the revestory, with a doorway, three windows, and a chimney, and the north transept, with a single, north-facing, arched window. The eastern window, which survives, would have looked into the revestory, and was blocked up at some unknown point. By kind permission of City of Edinburgh Council Libraries.

that the blocking of the window dated from the sixteenth century,[52] which might correspond with either the 1554 payment to 'ane masoun thre dayis and ane half to big up Sanct Johnis windois', or the 1561 'beiging upe of the windo in the revestrie with stane and lyme'.[53] While the evidence might not tell us all that one would like, the few surviving clues point to spacious accommodation for the altar and chaplain of the Masons and Wrights; space which was surely most valuable in a collegiate institution with forty altars.

Of the altar of Sts John itself, we have much less to go on, as the 1475 altar grant and seal of cause give very few clues as to its physical appearance. The grant refers simply to the, 'ile and chapell of Sanct Jhone fra the irne hers inwart with the pertinentis to the saidis craftismen'.[54] The seal mentions fines of wax, which fit with our general understanding of how altars were lit, and suggest rich decoration that needed artificial lighting.[55] We know that the Incorporation owned a fine chalice, though in the summer of 1555 this had to be put in 'wed & plege of ten pundis', as there was not enough money in the craft box. All debts to St John were to be 'socht with all regour', due, no doubt, to the Queen Regent's demands for an extent to be raised by the crafts.[56] On 18 February 1553–4, a payment of 2s was recorded for the washing of the altar cloths, while 13s was spent on oil 'brunt yis lest winter in ye lamp'.[57] Were these plain cloths, or richly embellished imported cloths? Was the 'vly' used in the lamp domestically-produced fish oil, or the finer imported olive oil?

Though only a few details survive for the physical traits of the Masons' and Wrights' altar, a great deal survives for other comparable altars, such as that of the Aberdeen Incorporation of Coopers, Wrights and Masons. Their 1527 seal of cause states that every master was to give

> ... every week one penny of offering, which entry silver, apprentice silver, weekly offering, and yearly pound of wax of the servants shall be well, truly, and faithfully gathered by certain masters of the said crafts, and truly spent in the decoring, upholding, and repairing of St. John, Evangelist's Altar within the parish kirk of Aberdeen, their special patron in Imagerie, vestments and towels, chandeliers, desks, lights, and all other ornaments required to the service of God and of their said patron ...[58]

Similarly, at Haddington, a detailed list from 1533 survives of the rates to be paid by the Wrights and Masons to St John the Evangelist's altar, demonstrating the considerable investment by both the craft and individuals. Every first entry, which presumably refers to booking, was to pay 6s 8d, while the freemen were to pay 13s 4d for their first work in the town. Each master was to pay a penny weekly, and every servant a half-penny.

Any person who came to the town to sell wood or to work in the crafts was also to pay one penny weekly, demonstrating the connections between freemen and merchants, as well as the need for outside labour.[59] A further document from 1530 mentions the images, as well as wax to illuminate them, and mass cloths.[60]

Even more is known about the altars of other crafts, such as the rather rich example of St Eloi of the Edinburgh Incorporation of Hammermen.[61] Their altar was wooden, covered with red- and green-coloured Holland cloth and Bruges satin, and decorated with silver armorial bearings. On the altar sat various gilded, silver and earthenware vessels, as well as a tabernacle with carved angels at each corner. Greenery and flowers were used as decoration, as was a statue of St Eloi holding a hammer, firmly connecting saint and craft. Lighting was provided by candles, torches and a lamp. A lectern held St Eloi's mass book, an illuminated vellum manuscript, which the Hammermen replaced at a fair expense of 22d in 1523.[62] A wooden canopy decorated underneath with red and yellow buckram cloth, and taffeta curtains suspended from iron rods encased the altar, making for a sumptuous and intimate space for the celebration of mass. Finally, and crucially, certain insignia of the craft, such as the hammer and crown, were suspended above the altar, making it clear to all and sundry that it was an important incorporation which had bestowed such expense on this altar in the collegiate kirk of Edinburgh.[63] While it was not the altar of Sts John, the Hammermen worked closely with the Masons and Wrights in the Corpus Christi processions, suggesting a parity between the standing of the crafts.

Altars upheld by the crafts required clergymen, and along with the 'chapel and ile' of Sts John came the support of a chaplain. As McKay has pointed out, the term chaplain was a general one for 'priest'. There were parish chaplains, who assisted the rector or vicar at the high altar of the parish church. There were chaplains who served individuals or families, who celebrated mass in a private chapel and possibly undertook secretarial and educational duties. There were chaplains employed by chapels and side altars within collegiate churches and, as with the Incorporation of Masons and Wrights, there were chaplains who served one of the various forms of guilds.[64] Names of each successive chaplain to the Edinburgh Hammermen survive,[65] though we only know the names of three of the chaplains for the crafts incorporated with the Masons and Wrights. In 1508, Master James Gibson was chaplain,[66] and in 1532, Sir James Moffet appears to be the chaplain for the Masons and Wrights.[67] Two entries in the early minute books from 1555 mention the third chaplain for the Incorporation, Sir Robert Ewyn.[68] We may not know the names of all the Incorporation's chaplains, though there is little doubt as to how important they were to the Incorporation's contributions to public worship.

A ratification of their seal of cause by Andro Forman, Archbishop of St Andrews (1514–21), notes that the Incorporation was to pay the chaplain of their altar and his successors 'for his interteinement in meat and drink' alongside the usual fee, and warns that craftsmen who did not contribute to this might be first excommunicated, then aggravated, and finally that they should languish in purgatory: '. . . these quhom the feare of god calles not back from evil, severitie of discipline sould restraine, And that the heavier thair sines be, the langer thair vnhappie saule sould be deteineit wnder bandis . . .'[69] Failure to pay dues and to maintain the Incorporation's chaplain might have much to say about the individual craftsman's experience of the inflationary economy of the early-sixteenth century, but what is crucial here is the corporate nature of maintaining a chaplain. This was not the private chaplain of a single nobleman's family, but instead of the entire incorporation, meaning that the chaplain had sizeable obligations in terms of prayer for souls, all of which fitted into a complex clockwork of public worship across the forty altars and numerous saints' days within the liturgical calendar.[70]

One added benefit of craft support of altars was the increased access to legal provision through publicly-available chaplains. A fine example of this is the chaplain of St John's Aisle in St Giles, Sir James Moffet. As a chaplain, Moffet worked in the collegiate kirk, meaning that he was accessible when an official witness was needed. Hence, many contracts recorded in protocol books tend to have been signed at an altar. In June of 1530, he witnessed an instrument '. . . in the aisle of St John the Evangelist, situated within the collegiate church of Edinburgh . . .'[71] As chaplain of the Masons and Wrights, he was listed along with Sir John Smyth, the chaplain of the Hammermen, in an official testimonial by the deacons of the two incorporations as to the order of the crafts for Corpus Christi and other processions.[72] This testimonial was used by the provost and council of Edinburgh to send an official account of the order to the Sheriff of Haddington and the burgh council.[73] Indeed, the protocol book of the notary who drew up the letter to Haddington records three other occasions between 1529 and 1533 where Moffet witnessed legal proceedings for a range of individuals at various altars within St Giles.[74] Clearly altars and chaplains had their legal uses, and craft support helped provide access for both the Incorporation and for the wider community.

Processions and Feast Days

Aside from altars and chaplains, the incorporated trades also contributed to public worship through participation in processions and feast days. Processions on saints' days and religious feasts were a key part of urban culture in pre-Reformation Europe; an 'urban spectacular', where the upper echelons of burgh society paraded through the town, demonstrating both community and exclusivity at the same time.[75] By the mid-thirteenth century Corpus Christi day festivals were being observed in Scotland, with their focus on the body of Christ, both literally, through the carrying of the eucharist out of the church and into the streets, and metaphorically, suggesting that the single parish community was a united body in Christ. By the fifteenth century we have clear evidence of their celebration in Edinburgh.[76]

Naturally, late-medieval Edinburgh also marked other religious feasts, such as St Eloi's day (1 December) and St Giles' day (1 September), or the celebrations on Candlemas day (2 February), Yule (Christmas) and Pasche (Easter).[77] Many of these festivals appear to have been raucous celebrations, with music and drums, processions through the town with candles, torches, banners and sacred objects, pageants and plays, and the election of festival officials, such as the 'Abbot of Bonaccord' at Aberdeen, or the 'Abbot of Narent' (no rent) at Edinburgh.[78] Some of the festivals were more solemn than others, and it is important to remember that prior to the Reformation, those in authority, both religious and secular, usually approved of the observation of these public festivals, as they afforded further opportunity for communal religious instruction, despite the constant problems of overindulgence.[79] Indeed, when crisis loomed, processions could be used as a way of making corporate petition to God,[80] though previous linkage of Corpus Christi celebrations and the disasters of Flodden and the burning of Edinburgh in 1544 are problematic.[81] Flodden was well after Corpus Christi day in 1513, and Corpus Christi day was nearly two months after Hertford's attack on Edinburgh in 1544. Whether for tradition's sake, for amusement, or for an honest attempt to seek God, processions were an important urban institution, firmly linking burgh community with Christian practice, and the Masons and Wrights made important contributions.

Processions, such as that of Corpus Christi day and its octaves, were more than simple parades of the sacrament. The eucharist was taken out of the kirk and into the community, which, it has been observed, allowed for wider participation amongst the laity.[82] Furthermore, it was escorted by the burgh establishment, allowing guilds and confraternities an opportunity to publicly lead in communal worship. While the guilds went before it, carefully ordered by precedence, the procession of the eucharist became both an elaborate ceremony for the honour of God, and a public spectacle, with minstrels and drummers, food and drink, colourful banners and a welcome distraction from the monotony of work.

Along with the spectacle of communal procession through the town, drama was also included at various points to illustrate both biblical and ecclesiastical stories, reinforcing Christian teaching and traditions. Although the specifics of the dramas are not always clear, this still serves to emphasise the importance of a visual culture for religious education before the Reformation; a visual culture which enabled a largely-illiterate populace to understand the basics of the scriptures. The building trades, through their pre-Reformation activities of adorning church interiors with sculpture, carvings, paintings and stained glass, played a critical role in the religious education of the parishioners. The processions allowed them further opportunities to contribute through the use of scriptural drama in corporate procession.[83] Though we know that the Hammermen were responsible for the provision of 'Herod' for the biblical narrative of the birth of Jesus, records of the Masons' and Wrights' contribution do not survive.[84]

It is known that the Masons and Wrights played an important part in these processions, and as we shall see, they held a particularly good place in one of the most important of such festivals, the Corpus Christi day procession. They also had their own saint's day for public celebration. The 1475 grant of the aisle and chapel included the 'day of Sanct Jhone the Baptist', which presumably referred to the saint's nativity feast on 24 June, giving further opportunities for both public piety and worship.[85]

BENEFITS OF PUBLIC WORSHIP

The Incorporation of Masons and Wrights played several key roles in the religious life of the medieval burgh. Their skills and labour were crucial to the production and maintenance of the devotional spaces, and whether through the upholding of an altar and provision for a chaplain in the parish church, or by processing through the town in times of celebration and concern, they made considerable contributions to public, communal worship. Indeed, it is quite telling that the seal of cause for the Masons and Wrights refers to 'honour and worschipe of the towne'.[86] Clearly they were integral as producers to the *Corpus Christianum* that was the capital, but it is also important to consider their role as consumers.

Public contributions to communal worship and piety were important ways in which to serve, but the relationship between craft and kirk also had several benefits for the Incorporation itself. It allowed them to seek assurance of eternal security, by looking after the souls of the craftsmen and their families. It brought status and standing in the community, and it provided shelter for their meetings. All of these aspects changed markedly with the Reformation, though security, status and shelter continued to be important issues to the Incorporation, and Christianity remained a critical part of corporate life. To better understand these three critical issues, we must now look at each in turn.

Security and Building Assurance

As mentioned, the building crafts which were incorporated in 1475 were also granted an altar, just before their seal of cause, but on the same day.[87] Support of this altar was critical, as altars represented an attempt to corporately obtain salvation in the afterlife. It is telling that the cutlers of Bologna stated that the purpose of their institution was 'for curing our sins'.[88] One aspect of the privileges granted in 1475 was the support of an altar for very similar reasons.

The comfort which came from the medieval church was predicated on the concept of purgatory. The medieval church taught that those destined for Heaven still had to spend time in purgatory, atoning for their earthly sins, before being allowed to pass to the presence of God.[89] As the provision of masses at their craft's particular altar was thought to take time off of the sufferings of purgatory, the chaplains and altars were absolutely crucial. They were thought to be a means of expediting the transition. In the context of a belief in purgatory, it is difficult to overestimate the relief the altar must have engendered for the craftsmen and their families.

This raises an important point about the Incorporation of Masons and Wrights, as it is well known that the medieval church relied on a visual culture for teaching the populace about Christian doctrine. The building trades played an important role in the production of this visual culture, as is still visible in the surviving artefacts from interiors of a number of medieval churches throughout Scotland.[90] The carved timber of rood screens, or the painted images of the last judgement on walls and ceilings pointed the faithful towards salvation, and the careless to damnation. The sculpted stone of vaulting and pillars illustrated parables that the majority of the populace could not read, reinforcing the work of the priests and demonstrating how intimately involved the building trades were in the teachings of the church.[91] As they were the ones who envisaged the images of suffering, did the builders therefore feel that much more anxiety about purgatory? They were certainly invested, and like the rest of burgh society, they too found both comfort and unity of purpose in the support of an altar.

With the Reformation, the anxiety about salvation changed dramatically. Purgatory was exposed as a medieval construct, with no scriptural basis, and the altars to saints were removed. The son of God had been given to redeem all believers, so there was no need to earn salvation through the saying of masses. This meant that the altar was not only redundant, but – even worse – it was idolatrous. The first commandment stated plainly that there should be no other gods before the triune God, so worshipping at the altar of a saint was redundant at best, heretical at worst. The altars simply had to go, and this meant that a central feature of corporate unity – that of the religious confraternity – was removed.

Even those altars dedicated to aspects of Christ, such as the Holy Blood, were removed. Altars were for sacrifice, and Christ had made the ultimate sacrifice on the cross, so altars were simply no longer needed. The death and resurrection of Jesus had paid the full price of sin. Not all of the craftsmen shared the same opinion on which version of Christianity was most appropriate, and many also grieved the loss of what they felt was rightly their property. Hence there was an attempt to retain what had been granted with the altars, even as the pulpit and the sermon replaced the altar and the mass at the central place within the Scottish kirk.[92]

By 1 August 1560, when the Tailors tried arguing that they should be allowed to use the space in St Giles formerly held by their altar to St Ann, the provost, bailies, council – and, interestingly, the deacons – declared that, 'in respect of the godlie ordour now taikin in religioun all title and clame to altaris and sic vther superstitious pretenssis ar and sould be abolischit,' and there was to be, 'na further word nor clame thairof . . . in tymes cuming'.[93] Although questions loomed about who would enjoy the wealth of the old church, whether it be the crown, the landed interests or the new church, movements were made to secure certain sections of the benefices for charitable uses.

In 1561–2 the queen annexed the ecclesiastical property in free burghs for hospitals, schools, 'and utheris godlie usis'.[94] By 1566–7 a gift had been made to Edinburgh of such properties, including chaplainries.[95] The sentiments were repeated in a 1579 act of parliament in favour of an Edinburgh hospital, which cited Mary's gift of,

> . . . all lands, annualrents, obits and alms money, mails, rents, revenues and duties whatsoever pertaining of before to whatsoever benefice, altarage or chaplainry within the said burgh and freedom thereof, or owing out of the said burgh or tenements thereof to whatsoever other benefice or chaplainry, as the said gift in itself at more length bears . . .[96]

It would appear from the rather inclusive language of the gift that every benefice, including the Incorporation's chaplainry of Sts John the Baptist and Evangelist, was included in the property appropriated by the town for the use of the poor. Still, the repetition of the legislation by privy council, queen and parliament over a period of nineteen years following the Reformation suggests a council unable to secure the full benefits of the appropriated benefices. Did the Incorporation of Masons and Wrights loose out? Or did they gain, as they no longer had the burden of providing for the chaplain? Their aisle and chapel had been granted by the provost, bailies and council, so was it therefore included in the benefices taken? It certainly appears to have been. The 1560 wording of the council declaration against claims to altars would indicate that the physical altar and the mass were removed,[97] and the 1561 act of council abolishing 'confraries' removed the more-controversial religious aspects of the groups which had supported them.[98]

The altars themselves were clearly gone, but the lands and chaplainries pertaining to them were not as easily disposed of. It would appear that the council simply appropriated the altarages and chaplainries and redirected their funds towards hospitals, pointing to the new direction of craft charity. Previously they had supported altars to care for the souls of the craftsmen, but after the Reformation souls were entrusted to the death and resurrection of Christ, and corporate funds were instead channelled into the care of the poor.[99] Yet this was not a true secularisation of the Incorporation; prior to 1560, priests were paid for prayers at an altar, but after the craft started saying their own prayers to both open and close meetings of craft business.[100] Prayers remained, and of course God remained, but the way that the incorporated trades interacted with the kirk was changed drastically.

In the reformed Scottish church, the pulpit replaced the altar in primacy of place, and the mass was replaced by the sermon.[101] As the visual culture of the church gave way to one based on the written and spoken word – an intellectual culture which laid the foundations for Scottish education, the enlightenment, and all that came with it – the building trades continued to play a central role through the necessity of their skill for changing the kirk interiors. It was the wright who made the pulpit; the glazier who ensured there was suitable light for study of the scriptures. It was the mason who looked after the kirk fabric, and the slater who kept the building watertight for the congregation to gather to hear God's Word. A new kind of assurance came from the pulpit, but first the pulpit needed to be built, and for this, the town continued to look to the builders.

Status and Standing

As mentioned, the position of the pre-Reformation altar of the Masons and Wrights was most advantageous. They were not sharing the nave with the majority, but instead had a more secluded and private space, suggesting the favour they found themselves in with the council in 1475. As they invested in their own altar, they also invested in the community's kirk, using their skill for the fabric needs of communal worship. Indeed, the placement of the crafts' altar highlights another aspect of what they received for their investment in the medieval kirk, and this is the prestige of their particular dedication. Before the Reformation swept away unbiblical ideas about purgatory and intercessory patron saints, the particular saint to which one had their altar suggested a hierarchy of closeness to God. Having a patron saint who had been canonised and sainted by the church suggested a connection to the miraculous, but having one who was an apostle was that much closer to the Creator himself. How much more prestigious was a dedication to a family member of Christ? Indeed, by the fifteenth century there is evidence in Scotland that proximity mattered.[102] It has been pointed out that fifteenth-century fashions in piety 'saw an increasing preoccupation with the Passion of Christ or with the Virgin and the Holy Family'.[103] While the individual piety of craftsmen is nearly impossible to gauge, the dedication of the Masons and Wrights, who corporately represented the building trades in the Scottish capital, must be viewed in this hierarchical context.

The uniqueness of the Scottish capital in comparison to other Scottish settlements has, understandably, received a degree of attention.[104] How unique – or not – the capital was in relation to its craft altars is a question which has not really been asked, though looking specifically at the dedications of the few known altars of building trades suggests that such research would prove fruitful. While numerous burghs had incorporations pertaining to wood and stone workers, such as the Wrights of Inverness,[105] or the Kirkcudbright Squaremen,[106] very few have surviving evidence of a pre-Reformation foundation charter. It is highly likely that many of these corporate bodies had some form of organisation before 1560, but the records remain silent about their activities, religious or secular. Fortunately, the seven known pre-Reformation building-trade incorporations in Scotland have all left some indication of their particular altar dedication, allowing us to make some tentative observations.

As can be seen in Table 3.1,[107] Edinburgh, Perth, Aberdeen, Haddington, Glasgow and Ayr all had craft altars for their building trades. South Leith also appears to have had an altar, as they were still referred to as the

Table 3.1 Known Saint Dedications for Scottish Incorporations (building trades)

Burgh	Incorporation of	Year	Dedication	Location of Altar
Edinburgh	Masons and Wrights	1475	Sts John the Baptist and Evangelist	North transept, St Giles Collegiate Kirk
Perth	Wrights, Bowers, Coopers & Chirugeons	by 1522–4	Our Lady of Pity	St John's Parish Kirk
Aberdeen	Coopers, Wrights and Masons	1527	St John the Evangelist	St Nicholas Parish Kirk
Haddington	Wrights and Masons	1530	St John the Evangelist	St Mary's Parish Kirk
Glasgow	Masons, Wrights, Coopers, Slaters, Sawars and Quarriers	1551	St Thomas the Martyr	Nave (by Crossing), Glasgow Cathedral
Ayr	Wrights and Squaremen	by 1556	St Ninian	St John's Parish Kirk
South Leith	Coopers ('Brethren of St John')	by 1569	St John	N/A (South Leith Parish Church?)

'brethren of St John' after the Reformation. Six of the seven had dedications in known church buildings, and in at least two, the locations within their kirks are also known. Only the capital had a joint dedication, to Sts John the Baptist and Evangelist, though it is known that the Haddington Wrights and Masons were required to make an image for a separate saint as part of their altar grant to St John the Evangelist.[108] In the seven known dedications for the Scottish building trades, three of the dedications include St John the Evangelist, who was a fisherman before being called to be a 'fisher of men'.[109] South Leith was apparently dedicated to one of the Johns, while Perth had a Marian dedication, to 'Our Lady of Pity', emphasising the later-medieval focus on the mother of Christ. Glasgow and Ayr, on the other hand, had dedications to saints from much closer to home: St Thomas Becket of Canterbury and St Ninian, respectively.

Intriguingly, none of the dedications were to St Joseph, which would seem the obvious choice for any corporate body of carpenters. None were to St Luke, though many included painters. Several northern-European dedications included these rather typical saints, as with St Joseph for the carpenters of Gouda or Bruges.[110] Delft had St Joseph for the carpenters; St John for the coopers; St Luke for the painters; and St Michael for the roofworkers and dyers.[111] In most Scottish burghs, which tended towards conglomerations of crafts within a single corporate body, crafts tended to be under a single saint, possibly to avoid typical dedications which would promote divisions. If the painters could not have St Luke, at least the wrights did not have St Joseph. Perhaps more important are the dedications which *were* given. Of the seven known dedications, the five east-coast

incorporations all had biblical dedications, while the two west-coast incorporations had British saints. Would this division translate to other craft
altars within these burghs as well?

With such a small sample, it is difficult to draw firm conclusions for
these few dedications, though it is noteworthy that within our sample a
hierarchy is visible in terms of the sites of the altars. The majority were
located within their burgh's parish church, though Glasgow and Edinburgh
had more prestigious accommodation. Glasgow had the honoured position
of being within the cathedral, which was used by the parish. Edinburgh,
from 1466, was not in a parish church, but in a collegiate one, with over
forty altars.[112] Data on the precise positions of altars within the parish
kirks do not survive, but the locations of those for the two larger kirks do.
Glasgow's building trades had their altar to St Thomas the Martyr in the
nave, near the crossing.[113] Edinburgh's altar to Sts John the Baptist and
Evangelist was in the north transept, in a separate aisle and chapel, giving
greater privacy from the crowded nave.

Although the sample of pre-Reformation dedications is somewhat
narrow, the data suggests some interesting differences between the building
trades of the capital and those of other burghs. They not only had one, but
two prestigious biblical dedications; one to an apostle and one to a family
member of Christ. Their altar was not simply in the parish kirk, but in a
collegiate foundation, though the Edinburgh altar was given a position of
relative quiet and seclusion from the rest of the forty altars crammed within
the nave, choir and aisles. It would appear that the Edinburgh builders
enjoyed a rather privileged place.

Place was, of course, of the utmost importance in the status-conscious
society of late-medieval and early-modern Scotland. The status and standing of the Masons and Wrights was further projected through their participation in processions, and it is interesting that their seal of cause
explicitly pointed to Bruges as the pattern for their processing; a crucial
link with an important centre of late-medieval religious fashion, such
as the cult of the Holy Blood.[114] While the continental connections are
important, it was their proximity to the eucharist in the Corpus Christi
day and octaves processions which gives the clearest indication of standing. Order mattered, and it was not those who went first in the processions
who had the most honoured position. Rather, it was those toward the
back, as they were closest to the sacrament (see for example Plate 3). The
communion bread was thought to be physically changed into the body
of Christ through the institution of the mass. The feast day dedicated to
the body of Christ – the *Corpus Christi* – was an opportunity to take the
sacrament out of the church and into the community, but it was also an

opportunity for the guilds to receive recognition of their precedence, and the Incorporation of Masons and Wrights held a very privileged position indeed. From 1529 they shared both place and expenses with the Incorporation of Hammermen, putting them at the back, right next to the eucharist.[115] From this it is quite clear how highly the sixteenth-century Masons and Wrights ranked in the hierarchy of Edinburgh's incorporated trades.

The order within the processions was often disputed. For example, in Edinburgh in 1531 there was an argument about whether the producers of cloth or those who finished it should go first, and the council had to step in to arbitrate.[116] Cowan astutely observes that disputes over precedence can be interpreted as 'meaning that such processions were more forces for division than they were forces for unification in Scottish towns'.[117] The dispute over order and precedence between the Edinburgh cloth producers and cloth finishers would certainly seem to back this statement up, but the Edinburgh Hammermen and the Masons and Wrights prove an interesting exception. Instead of bickering, they decided to share both precedence and burdens.[118] This is hardly surprising, considering the close business links through the necessity of architectural hardware and fittings on the building site, as well as the considerable trade done in sharpening of tools.[119] Why one group of crafts chose dispute, while the other chose co-operation is not readily apparent, though this does lend itself to demonstrating that inclusion and exclusion were to be negotiated, and the communal procession gave ample opportunity for assertion of standing.

Although the first generation after the Reformation proved reticent to give up their much beloved festivals, as demonstrated by the Perth observance of Corpus Christi plays in 1577, or the St Andrews Baxters holding a 'sancttobertis play' in 1588, over time the more controversial religious aspects of processions were removed, though the act of processing remained important to corporatism in Scotland.[120] With the Corpus Christi processions, it was the veneration of the sacrament which had proved problematic. Parliament turned its attention to these public religious festivals in 1581 when an act was passed 'Aganis passing in pilgramage to chapellis, wellis and croces, and the superstitious observing of diverse uther papisticall rytes'.[121] This included 'the superstitious observaris of the festvall dayis of the santes, sumtimes namit thair patronis, quhair thair is na publict fayris and mercatis, setteris oute of bainfyris, singeris of caroles within and about kirkis, and of sic utheris superstitious and papisticall rytis'. The religious festival was no longer deemed fit for public consumption.

Other secular events remained, however, such as the wappenshaw, which was a public muster of the town militia, or the royal entry, whereby the town honoured the monarch with secular processions, which included craft banners and public drama.[122] In 1575, when James VI made his entry into Edinburgh, the Masons and Wrights spent 35s on a new banner, made from an ell of blue taffeta and half an ell of white taffeta, 'to mak ane croce to the bennar', suggesting the inclusion of a national symbol rather than iconography related to St John.[123] That said, the following entry notes that certain members had been poinded for not riding on All Hallows' Eve, so some of the pre-Reformation festivals were clearly hard to part with. Over time, those festivals associated with religion were stamped out, though craft processions of a secular nature did indeed remain, offering opportunities for the crafts to reinforce corporate unity and to distinguish themselves from the wider burgh community. Indeed, a published book from 1791 relating to a craft procession in Musselburgh demonstrates that the issue of craft precedence in public procession was still taken very seriously.[124]

But what of religion in its Reformed state? The church was intent on the focus being on Christ, though many of the congregation continued to seek status through the kirk, and the public display of identity was often found in lairds' lofts, or seats located nearest to the seat of repentance, which no doubt frustrated ministers throughout the land.[125] In the same way that craft altars were used to project corporate identity, church seating allowed reformed crafts to publicly display their status.[126] While many incorporated trades in Scotland's smaller burghs were able to retain their public displays of corporate identity through the use of craft lofts, desks or pews, those of the capital seem to have been denied this tradition. In August of 1560, the Edinburgh Tailors argued that they should be allowed to build exclusively corporate seating on the site of their former altar, but the town council unequivocally refused. Craft altars were declared abolished, and it was stated that no one had any claim to them anymore.[127] They did, however, encourage the crafts to sit together, respecting rank of course, though this seems not to have worked in the longer term, partly because of the tremendous growth of the capital in the years after the Reformation.

The traditional Scottish burgh was a single-parish unit, with the whole, or at least the majority, of the community worshipping in one place; a 'single spiritual community' which, it has been observed, was synonymous with the *Corpus Christianum*, or the body of Christ.[128] By the mid-seventeenth century, Edinburgh had tripled in size.[129] From 1592 there were attempts by James VI to reorganise his capital in multiple parishes, responding to the clear growth of Edinburgh. Aside from rationalising the ecclesiastical administration of the burgh, it also led to a departure of the Scottish capital from the usual model of the single-parish town, making it unique in Scotland's urban system.[130] Although it appears that initial efforts were less than successful, further attempts at development of the parish system followed in the 1620s.[131] By 1641 there were six parishes in Edinburgh;[132] by 1698 there were eight.[133] This departure from the single-parish model had significant ramifications for Edinburgh's incorporated trades, as it denied them the standing afforded to their counterparts in smaller towns.[134]

Trades in many smaller burghs enjoyed the ability to display their status publicly through craft lofts in their parish churches, as did those of Selkirk, Perth and Arbroath.[135] Dundee's trades used their seating to make public statements about their importance to the burgh community. The baxters adorned their pews with the biblical words 'Bread is the staff of life', while the fleshers countered with the quote 'Man shall not live by bread alone'.[136] These crafts had a form of advantage over those of the capital, in that they still adhered to the single-parish urban structure, and could therefore be visible to the whole parish as a corporate entity within the congregation. Edinburgh's trades did not have a single-parish church for their members; instead they were distributed across a growing number of parish churches, making it a costly business to display corporate status through corporate seating.

In 1746 we see tradesmen mixed in with the rest of burgh society, men and women; merchants and craftsmen; professionals and labourers, all sitting together. Hence, in the Upper Galleries of the Tolbooth Church in seat 109 was the slater, John Mein, while seat 107 was the tailor, George Spakie, and seat 108 the candlemaker, John Spott. Seats 110 and 111 were John Bell and Helen Lithgow, and 112 was the merchant, Thomas Trotter.[137] Though there was still the potential for conspicuous display through one's position in the church, such as George Riddle, wright, who sat between James Scott of Houden and Bailie George Dunbar in the New North Church,[138] it would appear that there is no evidence of corporate seating; instead the individuals rented their own personal seats, with advocates, cordiners and merchants all together.[139] Occasionally there appear to be pockets of craftsmen together, as with 'John Brounlie mason & others' in the Upper Galleries of the New North Church, but other than the thirteen unlabelled seats after 'others', no concrete indication of a grouping of masons is given.[140] Indeed there are other masons elsewhere, as with John Robertson, mason, who shared seat 50 of Lady Yester's Church with Mrs Reocks, and sat between two brewers.[141]

Shelter and a New Identity

Church buildings were often used for secular meetings,[142] and one of the benefits of the 1475 grant of aisle and chapel was the space this gave for meetings of the craft, though with the complex arrangement of masses and feast days, it is doubtful that this would always have been an option for the Incorporation. Indeed, Mill noted from her perusal of the early minutes that the crafts occasionally met elsewhere, such as the meeting 'on St Leonard Hill' in June of 1554, which was to the south-east of the burgh, near Holyrood Park.[143] This particular summer meeting appears to have been outdoors, as were various meetings of Dundee craftsmen at the Howff,[144] those of Perth at the South Inch,[145] or of Arbroath craftsmen on Boulzie Hill,[146] but the majority of the surviving references to the meetings of the Edinburgh Masons and Wrights were indoors, 'in St. John's Chapel', in winter, spring and summer months.[147] Indeed, the rather privileged possession of both 'aisle and chapel', being in a quiet transept rather than in the crowded nave, must have been greatly appreciated for privacy and space.

With the loss of their chapel and aisle in the collegiate kirk after 1560, and the practical problems of meeting in remote sites, such as St Leonards, it makes sense that the Incorporation would seek to obtain their own property where they could meet. By 1601 they seem to have achieved this, through the purchase of a former private chapel in Niddry's Wynd, but the process of how they came to control this building – leaving aside the complexities of the adoption of its rather Catholic-sounding name into the official title of their Incorporation – is all rather complicated. The chapel was originally a private chapel of Elizabeth Livingston, countess of Ross, who founded the '*Nova Capella B.V.M. De Nativitate, per se construeta in le Nudryis Vynd infra burgum de Edinburgh*', in 1505.[148] This chapel of the blessed virgin went through a series of private hands, predominantly crown officials and lawyers, before finally being sold to the Masons and Wrights in 1601.[149]

As their Incorporation was increasingly complex, with new trades being brought in over the sixteenth and seventeenth centuries, the issue of precedence in the name of the Incorporation was no doubt a sore point. Why should a slater or an upholsterer settle for being part of the Incorporation of Masons and Wrights? Why shouldn't it be the Incorporation of Wrights and Masons? Order mattered, and increasingly there were more crafts who desired recognition.[150] When the chapel was purchased, it offered the ideal resolution. At some point after 1601, the Incorporation began using the moniker, 'The Incorporation of Mary's Chapel'. While the loss of their pre-Reformation aisle and chapel created problems in terms of shelter for corporate meetings, it ended up being formative for the establishment of a corporate identity; an identity which was inclusive for an incorporation which was exclusive.

CONCLUSION

For the Incorporation of Masons and Wrights there was both continuity and change with the Reformation. Whilst the altar and the confraternity were lost, the legal rights of the Incorporation itself remained intact. This was because only the grant of the altar was revoked; the seal of cause, on the other hand, was retained and later confirmed. Though the Masons and Wrights received both charters on the same day in 1475, some incorporated trades did not receive their seals of cause until years after they had been granted corporate rights to support an altar, suggesting an existing division between the overlapping religious confraternities and trade-regulating incorporations.[151] After the Reformation chaplainries and lands associated with the abolished altars remained valuable property, but in a burgh context the crown annexed and redirected them to charitable uses.[152] While the precise details of when the Incorporation's physical altar was removed, or what happened to the fabric remain hazy, the loss of the craft altars with the Reformation is clear, pointing towards the wider changes in the aspects of security, status and shelter which the kirk had traditionally provided for the trades.

As producers of kirk fabric, there was again much change, but at the core there was also continuity, as it was the builders who executed the new reformed styles in the building projects that continued, unabated. Perhaps stained glass fell out of favour until the ecclesiological movement of the later 1800s, but domestic stained glass remained in fashion for some time.[153] Churches continued to be stone-built, keeping masons employed. Roofs still required wooden trusses and slate roofs. If anything, the 'kirk work' became more important, as the establishment was determined to provide a spiritual basis for a reformed society. This meant building the kirk, both metaphorically and literally. The realisation of their vision, however, proved challenging.

NOTES

1. The text in the first volume of Marwick's *Extracts of the Records of the Burgh of Edinburgh* presents these together, as they were, no doubt, recorded on the day, but the original charters were indeed written on separate sheets,

each with their own signatures and wax seals, demonstrating that the grant of an altar and the seal of cause were separate and distinguishable groups of privileges. ECA, Mill Recs, A1 and A2, and *Edin. Recs*, 1403–1528, 30–1.

2. Black, C. F., *Italian Confraternities in the Sixteenth Century* (Cambridge: Cambridge University Press, 1989), 1.

3. Black, *Italian Confraternities*, 1 and 23–4.

4. Terpstra, N., *The Politics of Ritual Kinship: Confraternities and Social Order in Early Modern Italy* (Cambridge: Cambridge University Press, 2000), 4.

5. Terpstra, *Politics of Ritual Kinship*, 4; Black, *Italian Confraternities*, 1 and 23–4; Farr, J. R., *Artisans in Europe, 1300–1914* (Cambridge: Cambridge University Press, 2000), 228–9; Epstein, S. A., *Wage Labor and Guilds in Medieval Europe* (Chapel Hill: University of North Carolina Press, 1991), 156.

6. These quotations are from Black, *Italian Confraternities*, 24, footnote 2.

7. Farr, *Artisans*, 229–30.

8. Black chose to 'use the words confraternities, fraternities, sodalities, brother-hoods, and companies interchangeably, without implying categorical differences . . .' Black, *Italian Confraternities*, 23.

9. Lauder of Fountainhall, Sir John, *Historical Notices of Scottish Affairs*, vol. 1, 1661–1683 (Edinburgh: T. Constable, 1848), 97.

10. *Edin. Recs*, 1557–1571, 111.

11. Epstein, *Wage Labor and Guilds*, 163–4.

12. Ibid., 52, and Black, *Italian Confraternities*, 24.

13. Epstein, *Wage Labor and Guilds*, 164.

14. Black, *Italian Confraternities*, 24.

15. This assessment of Gilles Meersseman's views is from Epstein, *Wage Labor and Guilds*, 157.

16. Ibid.

17. Farr, *Artisans*, 229.

18. For examples, see the 1607–8 treasurer's accounts in *Edin. Recs*, 1604–1626, Appendix xi, page 333–4.

19. *Edin. Recs*, 1403–1528, 30–1. See Appendix 1 for text of the grant of the altar, which was given on the same day as their seal of cause.

20. The University of Edinburgh's 'Database of Dedications to Saints in Medieval Scotland' [http://www.shca.ed.ac.uk/Research/saints/] records no less than nineteen entries for dedications to 'St John' in Edinburgh, though some of these refer to the same altar. Entry EN/JD/166 refers to the 1396 charter of Robert III, and is also noted in *RMS*, vol. 1, App. 2, 632, no. 1739. Hay has shown that there were other dedications to St John the Baptist and St John the Evangelist in St Giles. Hay, G., 'The Late Medieval Development of the High Kirk of St Giles, Edinburgh', in *PSAS*, 107 (1975–6), 255.

21. Bain, E., *Merchant and Craft Guilds A History of the Aberdeen Incorporated Trades* (Aberdeen: J. & J. P. Edmond & Spark, 1887), 238–9; Lynch, M., DesBrisay, G., and Pittock, M. G. H., 'The Faith of the People', in Dennison,

E. P., Ditchburn, D., and Lynch, M., (eds), *Aberdeen Before 1800: A New History* (East Linton: Tuckwell Press, 2002), 292; and Cooper, J. (ed.), *Cartularium Ecclesiae Sancti Nicholai Aberdonensis*, vol. 2 (Aberdeen: New Spalding Club, 1892), lv.

22. See, for example, Brown, A., *Civic Ceremony and Religion in Medieval Bruges, c.1300–1520* (Cambridge: Cambridge University Press, 2013).

23. Durkan, J. (ed.), *The Protocol Book of John Foular, 1528–1534* (Edinburgh: SRS, 1985), xi–xii, and Hay, 'High Kirk of St Giles, Edinburgh', 254.

24. Lamond, 'Scottish Craft Gild as a Religious Fraternity', 204. Hay gives the example of the altar of the Incorporation of Goldsmiths having had five separate dedications. Hay, 'High Kirk of St Giles, Edinburgh', 254.

25. *Edin. Recs*, 1403–1528, 30–1 and Marwick, J. D. (ed.), *Charters and Other Documents Relating to the City of Edinburgh*, A.D. *1143–1540* (Edinburgh: SBRS, 1871), 142–5.

26. For details of John Dalrymple's 1477 foundation of St Eloi's altar, and the council's 1483 seal of cause to the Incorporation of Hammermen, see Smith, J., *The Hammermen of Edinburgh and Their Altar in St Giles Church* (Edinburgh: William J. Hay, 1906), xvi. Smith argues that after Dalrymple's death, the Hammermen obtained control of the altar and chaplaincy, though he was unable to explain what happened to the altar after 1558. Perhaps control of the altar was not the same as ownership.

27. Smith, *Hammermen of Edinburgh*, xvi.

28. *Edin. Recs*, 1403–1528, 30–1.

29. Habakkuk Bisset's *Rolment of Courtis* noted the 'ordoure of the Evangelistis', with John coming in fourth, behind Peter, Andrew and James in the book of Matthew, or third in the book of Mark. Bisset started a biography of John with: 'Sanct Johnne the brother of James quha wes also ane Evangilist quhome oure lord loved . . .' Hamilton-Grierson, P. J. (ed.), *Habakkuk Bisset's Rolment of Courtis*, vol. 2 (Edinburgh: Scottish Text Society, 1922), 281 and 286.

30. John the Baptist's mother, Elizabeth, was Mary's cousin. Luke 1:36.

31. Mill, on page 1 of her 'Inventory', quotes a Latin phrase from the charter: 'ex parte boreali et immediate post altare sancti coberti versus boream eiusdem ecclesie.' I'm grateful to Dr Aaron Pelttari for his assistance with the Latin, which is paraphrased above. 'St Coberti' would appear to refer to St Hubert, whose altar was just south of that of Saints John the Baptist and Evangelist. See the map of the altars in St Giles in Hay, 'High Kirk of St Giles, Edinburgh', 255.

32. This east-facing window, which was blocked up with the building of the revestry, is still visible today. It was also depicted in MacGibbon, D. and Ross, T., *The Ecclesiastical Architecture of Scotland*, vol. 2 (Edinburgh: David Douglas, 1896), 438–9, which can be accessed via the Internet Archive (https://archive.org/). See also Hay, 'High Kirk of St Giles, Edinburgh', 246 and 249.

33. 'Dean of Guild's Accounts, 1552–1567', in Adam, R. (ed.), *Edinburgh Records: The Burgh Accounts*, vol. 2 (Edinburgh, 1899), 39.

34. Ibid., 56 and 131.

35. William Dunbar, 'Satire on Edinburgh (Quhy will ʒe, merchantis of renoun)', in Small, J. (ed.), *The Poems of William Dunbar*, Vol 2 (Edinburgh: Scottish Text Society, 1893), 261, lines 15 and 16.

36. Hay, 'High Kirk of St Giles, Edinburgh', 244.

37. Ibid., 251.

38. There are numerous other examples of the dean of guild investing in the fabric of St John's Aisle, such as work on the roof. 'Dean of Guild's Accounts, 1552–1567', in Adam, R. (ed.), *Edinburgh Records: The Burgh Accounts*, vol. 2 (Edinburgh, 1899), 43 and 161.

39. 'Dean of Guild's Accounts, 1552–1567', in Adam, R. (ed.), *Edinburgh Records: The Burgh Accounts*, vol. 2 (Edinburgh, 1899), 43 and 219–20.

40. 'Dean of Guild's Accounts', 43.

41. Durkan, J. (ed.), *The Protocol Book of John Foular, 1528–1534* (Edinburgh: SRS, 1985), xi–xii.

42. Psalms 48:1 & 8 and Matthew 5:35.

43. 'Dean of Guild's Accounts', 43:
   'Item, to ane wrycht to big ane litill hous at the back of Stanct Johnis alter, iiij dayis ½, ilk day iijs; summa . . . xiijs vjd
   Item, cost vj laids lyme, cost, . . . vijs
   Item, for vj laids sand, . . . xxxd
   Item, cost ijc½ dur naillis, cost the jc, xvjd; summa, . . . iiijs
   Item, cost j dosone garroun nallis, cost, . . . xijd
   Item, ½c planscheor nallis, . . . xvd
   Item, cost ij dallis to be ane dur and ane gutter to it, cost the pece iijs; summa, . . . vjs
   Item, for ane loke and ane pair of bands to it, . . . xjs
   Item, for bussumis to deycht the kirk with, the hail yeir, . . . vjs viijd
   Item, to ane masoun thre dayis and ane half to big up Sanct Johnis windois, and the dur cheiks of it, ilk day iijs; summa, . . . xs vjd
   Item, cost laith to theik it with, cost, . . . viijs vjd
   Item, to ane sklater to theik it, . . . xiiijs'

44. Mill, 'Inventory', 14–16, e.g. 'Meeting in St. John's Chapel'. See also the 1475 grant in Appendix 1.

45. Ibid., 15. It is worth noting that a cellar survives under the north transept of St Giles today, though it appears to have been altered in the nineteenth century. The dean of guild's accounts for 1553–4 also list a payment for a lock to the vault door of St Thomas's aisle, suggesting that cellar space beneath the kirk was a common feature of aisles and chapels. 'Dean of Guild's Accounts, 1552–1567', in Adam, R. (ed.), *Edinburgh Records: The Burgh Accounts*, vol. 2 (Edinburgh, 1899), 23.

46. Mill, 'Inventory', 17.

47. She goes on to refer to it as a 'house', for which rent was paid each term. Ibid., 17.

48. Ibid., 17, and Maitland, W., *The History of Edinburgh From its Foundation to the Present Time* (Edinburgh: Hamilton, Balfour and Neill, 1753), 184–5, figure 10. For more on the alterations to St Giles, including the removal of most of St John's aisle in the north transept, see Hay, 'High Kirk of St Giles, Edinburgh', 249, 254–5, and Laing, D. (ed.), *Registrum Cartarum Ecclesie Sancti Egidiide Edinburgh* (Edinburgh: T. Constable, 1859), 32 and plate 7. For details on the revestry, see Hay, 'High Kirk of St Giles, Edinburgh', 251.

49. Laing, D., *Registrum Cartarum Ecclesie Sancti Egidiide Edinburgh* (Edinburgh, 1859), plate 7, and Britton, J., *Modern Athens! Displayed in a Series of Views: Or Edinburgh in the Nineteenth Century* (London, 1829), 'St. Giles' Church, looking West, Edinburgh', between pages 32–3. See also M'Culloch, W. T., 'Note Relating to "Haddo's Hole," in St Giles's Church, Edinburgh', in *Proceedings of the Society of Antiquaries of Scotland*, 4 (1860–2), 289–90.

50. Hay, G., 'The Late Medieval Development of the High Kirk of St Giles, Edinburgh', in *Proceedings of the Society of Antiquaries of Scotland*, 107 (1975–6), 251–2, and MacGibbon, D., and Ross, T., *The Ecclesiastical Architecture of Scotland: From the Earliest Christian Times to the Seventeenth Century*, Vol. II (Edinburgh, 1896), 436–9.

51. *Edin. Recs.* 1557–1571, 30; 'Dean of Guild's Accounts, 1552–1567', in Adam, R. (ed.), *Edinburgh Records: The Burgh Accounts*, vol. 2 (Edinburgh, 1899), 157 and 176; and Hay, 'Late Medieval Development of St Giles', 251.

52. Hay, 'Late Medieval Development of St Giles', 251–2.

53. Adam, 'Dean of Guild's Accounts, 1552–1567', 43 and 157.

54. *Edin. Recs*, 1403–1528, 31–2.

55. Ibid., 32. For more on wax and the lighting of altars, see Allen, A., 'Production and the Missing Artefacts: Candles, Oil and the Material Culture of Urban Lighting in Early Modern Scotland', in *Review of Scottish Culture*, 23 (2011), 23, 29–30, 36 and 45.

56. Mill, 'Inventory', 16. For more on the extent, or tax, see Ritchie, P. E., *Mary of Guise in Scotland, 1548–1560* (East Linton: Tuckwell Press, 2002), 131–2.

57. Mill, 'Inventory', 14.

58. Bain, E., *Merchant and Craft Guilds A History of the Aberdeen Incorporated Trades* (Aberdeen: J. & J. P. Edmond & Spark, 1887), 239.

59. NRS, GD98/11/7, Translation of 16 July 1533 notarial instrument in favour of the masons and wrights of Haddington, as to the support of the altar of St. John in the parish church.

60. NRS, GD98/11/8, Extract from the Burgh Court Books of Haddington of decreet arbitral finding that the masons and wrights shall have the image and offering of St. John, the Evangelist, to be their patron, under condition of upkeep etc., 1 April 1530.

61. The description of the Hammermen's altar which follows relies heavily on Mairi Cowan's excellent study, *Death, Life and Religious Change in Scottish Towns, c.1350–1560* (Manchester: Manchester University Press, 2012), 71–2, citing John Smith's *The Hammermen of Edinburgh and Their Altar in St Giles Church* (Edinburgh: William J. Hay, 1906), Chapter 4, and J. Cameron Lees' *St Giles', Edinburgh* (Edinburgh: W. & R. Chambers, 1889), 313–33.

62. Smith, *Hammermen of Edinburgh*, xlviii.

63. Cowan, *Death, Life and Religious Change in Scottish Towns*, 72.

64. McKay, D., 'Parish Life in Scotland, 1500–1560', in McRoberts, D. (ed.), *Essays on the Scottish Reformation, 1513–1625* (Glasgow: Burns, 1962), 88.

65. Smith, *Hammermen of Edinburgh*, xxxix.

66. Mill, 'Inventory', 1.

67. See *Edin. Recs*, 1528–1557, 35, where in June of 1530 Sir James Moffet witnessed an instrument '. . . in the aisle of St John the Evangelist, situated within the collegiate church of Edinburgh . . .' He was listed as one of two chaplains 'for the crafts', alongside Sir John Smyth, who we know was chaplain of the Incorporation of Hammermen. This was in a testimonial for the Edinburgh council regarding the Hammermen, Wrights and Masons, meaning that Moffet must have been chaplain to the Masons and Wrights. NRS, GD98/11/10/1, Testimonial by the deacons of the Hammermen, Masons, and Wrights of Edinburgh, as to the procession of the crafts, 26 May 1532. Mill's Inventory mentions a fee of 2 merks being paid to him in 1554. Mill, 'Inventory', 14. A further chaplain is noted for 'Sanct Johnis alter, scituat within thair College Kirk of Sanct Geyll', though it is impossible to say which St John's altar this meant. Was it that of the Baptist and Evangelist, or one of the individual dedications in the choir? *Edin. Recs*, 1528–1557, 60 and Hay, 'High Kirk of St Giles, Edinburgh', 255.

68. Mill, 'Inventory', 16, and ECA, Mill Recs, B2, f5v and f8v.

69. Mill, 'Inventory', 3.

70. Brown, *Civic Ceremony*, 165.

71. *Edin. Recs*, 1528–1557, 35.

72. NRS, GD98/11/10/1, Testimonial by the deacons of the Hammermen, Masons, and Wrights of Edinburgh, as to the procession of the crafts, 26 May 1532.

73. NRS, GD98/11/9, Letters from the provost, etc., of Edinburgh, to the sheriff of Haddington, bailies and council thereof, anent precedence in processions of the Crafts, 27 May 1532.

74. Durkan, J. (ed.), *Protocol Book of John Foular, 1528–1534* (Edinburgh: Scottish Record Society, 1985), 69, 157 and 164.

75. Dennison, E. P., 'The Myth of the Medieval Burgh Community', in Harris, B. and MacDonald, A. (eds), *Scotland: The Making and Unmaking of the Nation, c.1100–1707*, Vol. 3 (Dundee: Dundee University Press, 2006), 137.

76. Dennison, 'Myth of the Medieval Burgh Community', 137. Dennison takes

a more sceptical view of how united the communities were in the Corpus Christi processions, focussing more on the hierarchical nature of participation, with the elite processing and the rest merely observing. Cowan differs here, acknowledging the hierarchy, but focussing more on the 'beneficial effects of processions', which, she argues, reached beyond the processors themselves. Cowan, *Death, Life and Religious Change*, 113.

77. Cowan, *Death, Life and Religious Change*, 110, and Mill, A. J., *Mediaeval Plays in Scotland* (Edinburgh: William Blackwood & Sons Ltd, 1927), 61–4.
78. Mill, *Mediaeval Plays*, 61, and Smith, *Hammermen of Edinburgh*, lxix.
79. Smith, *Hammermen of Edinburgh*, lxv.
80. Cowan, *Death, Life and Religious Change*, 113, citing a 1456 act of parliament requiring processions in a time of plague.
81. Smith, *Hammermen of Edinburgh*, lxix.
82. Cowan, *Death, Life and Religious Change*, 113.
83. Smith, *Hammermen of Edinburgh*, lxv.
84. For more on the various characters of these plays, see Smith, *Hammermen of Edinburgh*, chapter IX; Mill, *Mediaeval Plays*; and Mill, A. J., 'The Perth Hammermen's Play: A Scottish Garden of Eden', in *The Scottish Historical Review*, 49:148:2 (1970), 146–53. It is worth noting that in 1531 in Aberdeen, the Wrights, Masons, Slaters and Coopers were responsible for provision of 'the Ressurection'. Chambers, E. K., *The Medieval Stage*, Vol. 2 (Oxford: Oxford University Press, 1903), 332.
85. *Edin. Recs*, 1403–1528, 30–1.
86. *Edin. Recs*, 1403–1528, 31. See Appendix 1 for text of seal of cause.
87. *Edin. Recs*, 1403–1528, 31–2.
88. Text and translation quoted in Epstein, S. A., *Wage Labor and Guilds in Medieval Europe* (Chapel Hill: University of North Carolina Press, 1991), 164.
89. Purgatory was thought to be a 'place of purging in wise fire'. MacCulloch, D., *Reformation: Europe's House Divided, 1490–1700* (London: Penguin, 2004), 11–16.
90. See, for example, the fifteenth-century painted ceiling-boards in the National Museum of Scotland from Guthrie Church, Angus: NMS, H.KL 221.
91. See, for example, the interior of Rosslyn Chapel.
92. Jackson, S., 'Kirk Furnishings: The Liturgical Material Culture of the Scottish Reformation', in *Regional Furniture: The Journal of the Regional Furniture Society*, 21 (2007), 1.
93. *Edin. Recs*, 1558–1571, 71.
94. *RPC*, vol. 1, 202 (1561–2). See also: Donaldson, G., 'The Parish Clergy and the Reformation', in McRoberts, D. (ed.) *Essays on the Scottish Reformation, 1513–1625* (Glasgow: Burns, 1962), 131.
95. *RSS*, vol. 5, xiv and 313, no. 3334 (1566–7).
96. *RPS*, 1579/10/68 (last accessed 18 August 2015).
97. *Edin. Recs*, 1557–1571, 71.

98. '. . . thairfor ordanis proclamatioun to be maid at all pairttis of this burgh neidfull, dischargeing the confrarie of Sanct Anthonis, the Hally Blude, and all vther confrareis quhatsumeuir quhilk hes bene heirtofore in tyme of ignorance, and all sic dewiteis as wes gevin thairto according to the statutis maid heiranent, to be vptaikin and applyit to the pure . . .' *Edin. Recs*, 1557–1571, 111.

99. Lamond, R., 'The Scottish Craft Gild as a Religious Fraternity', in *The Scottish Historical Review*, 16:63 (1919), 211.

100. ECA, SL34/1/1, Minute Books 1669–1686, f1v; SL34/1/2, Minute Books 1686–1696, 1 and 2; etc.

101. Jackson, 'Kirk Furnishings', 1.

102. See for example, Hall, M. A., 'Wo/men Only? Marian Devotion in Medieval Perth', in Boardman, S. and Williamson, E. (eds), *The Cult of Saints and the Virgin Mary in Medieval Scotland* (Woodbridge: The Boydell Press, 2010), 111.

103. Lynch, DesBrisay and Pittock, 'The Faith of the People', 292.

104. For details of further readings on this topic, see Allen, A., 'Conquering the Suburbs: Politics and Work in Early Modern Edinburgh', in *Journal of Urban History*, 37:3 (2011), 424 and 436, footnote 9.

105. Perry, D., 'Inverness: An Historical and Archaeological Review', in *The Proceedings of the Society of Antiquaries of Scotland*, 128 (1998), 840.

106. Dickie, W., 'Scottish Burghal Life in the 16th and 17th Centuries, Illustrated by Extracts from Kirkcudbright Records', in *The Transactions and Journal of Proceedings of the Dumfriesshire and Galloway Natural History and Antiquarian Society*, 17 (1906), 91.

107. The sources for Table 3.1 are: Edinburgh: *Edin. Recs*, 1403–1528, 30–2; Perth: NLS, Ms.19288, 'Perth Wrights' Minutes', f.7r, f.9r, f.12v, f.18r, f.19v, f.22r, f.24v; Aberdeen (New): Bain, E., *Merchant and Craft Guilds A History of the Aberdeen Incorporated Trades* (Aberdeen: J. & J. P. Edmond & Spark, 1887), 239; Haddington: NRS, Douglas Collection, GD98/11/8, 1 April 1530; Glasgow: Cruikshank, J., *Sketch of the Incorporation of Masons; and the Lodge of Glasgow St John* (Glasgow: W. M. Ferguson, 1879), 3–6; Durkan, J., 'Notes on Glasgow Cathedral', in *The Innes Review*, 21:1 (1970), 48 and 60; Marwick, J. D. (ed.), *Charters and Other Documents Relating to the City of Glasgow. A.D. 1175–1649*, Vol. 1, Pt. 1 (Glasgow: Scottish Burgh Records Society, 1897), lxxiii and 17; Original 1551 seal of cause held by Glasgow City Archives, GB243/T-TH12; Ayr: Ayrshire Archives, B6/24/1, 'Minute Book of the Wrights and Squaremen of the Burgh of Air. 1556, Apr. 7–1724, Oct. 10', f3r, f4v and f5r; and ECA, SL220/2/2/1, 17 April 1569, Charter in Favour of the Brethren of St John with Precept of Sasine for Infeftment of the said Cowpar Craft.

108. This image was to be of 'St Doicho'. NRS, GD98/11/8, Extract from the Burgh Court Books of Haddington of decreet arbitral finding that the masons and wrights shall have the image and offering of St. John, the Evangelist, to be

their patron, under condition of upkeep etc., 1 April 1530. See also, Marshall, R., *Ruin and Restoration: St Mary's Church, Haddington* (Haddington: East Lothian Council Library Service, 2001), 11–12.

109. Matthew 4:21 'And going on from thence, he saw other two brethren, James the son of Zebedee, and John his brother, in a ship with Zebedee their father, mending their nets; and he called them.'

110. Van der Sterre, G., *Four Centuries of Dutch Planes and Planemakers* (Leiden: Primavera Press, 2001), Fig. 80, and Brown, *Civic Ceremony*, Appendix 5, 325.

111. Montias, J. M., *Artists and Artisans in Delft: A Socio-Economic Study of the Seventeenth Century* (Princeton: Princeton University Press, 1982), 13–14.

112. Hay, 'High Kirk of St Giles, Edinburgh', 243 and 254.

113. Durkan, 'Notes on Glasgow Cathedral', 48 and 60.

114. They were to 'haue thair placis and rowmes in all generale processiouns lyk as thai haf in the towne of Bruges or siclyk gud townes'. *Edin. Recs*, 1403–1528, 31–2. For more on Bruges, see Brown, A., *Civic Ceremony and Religion in Medieval Bruges, c.1300–1520* (Cambridge: Cambridge University Press, 2013).

115. Smith, *Hammermen of Edinburgh*, lxx and 161 and GD98/11/9, Letters from the provost, etc., of Edinburgh, to the sheriff of Haddington, bailies and council thereof, anent precedence in processions of the Crafts, 27 May 1532. See Appendix 4 for text.

116. This was between the websters on one part, and and the walkers, shearers and bonnetmakers on the other, '. . . anent all and syndry debaitis contrauer-siis actionis causis and querellis that athir of the saidis partiis has to say . . . anent the ordering of thame to pas in the processioun on Corpus Christi day and the octauis tharof, and all vthir generall processionis and gatheringis in all tymes tocum . . .' *Edin. Recs*, 1528–1557, 48–50.

117. Cowan, *Death, Life and Religious Change in Scottish Towns*, 112.

118. Mill gives several examples of these shared costs, including two new banners in 1552, and the following excerpt: 'Item on corpus Christi day and ye octaue of ye samyn betuix ws ye masonis & wrychtis to menstralis waigis novn-schankis [4:00 pm repast] disiouns [breakfast] and for breyd and wyne bayth ye dayis In ye processiouns and to childer yat bur ye samyn and to ye men yat bure ye baunaris bayth ye dayis & all vyer necessaries ye sovme of all Is xj lbis viij s iiij d our part yairof v lbis xiiij s ij d'. Mill, *Mediaeval Plays*, 234.

119. As Chapter 1 has demonstrated through the dispute over plumbers and pew-terers, they did not always work so well together.

120. Mill, *Mediaeval Plays*, 92.

121. Ibid., 91 and *RPS*, 1581/10/25 (last accessed 11 August 2015).

122. For more on royal entries, see Guidicini, G., 'Municipal Perspective, Royal Expectations, and the Use of Public Space: The Case of the West Port, Edinburgh, 1503–1633', in *Architectural Heritage*, 22 (2011).

123. Mill, 'Inventory', 20. While it is not clear that St John ever figured on the Incorporation's pre-Reformation banner, it is known that the Edinburgh council replaced the image of St Giles with the thistle on the town banner. See *Edin. Recs*, 1557–1571, 137. The key point here is that national symbols were approved of by the post-Reformation regimes.

124. Crawford, J., *To the Praise of the Honourable Society of Magistrates, Treasurers, Counsellors, and Incorporate Members* (Edinburgh: A. Robertson, 1791). Accessible through SCRAN or Midlothian Council, Local Studies Library.

125. Todd, M., *The Culture of Protestantism in Early Modern Scotland* (New Haven: Yale University Press, 2002), 319.

126. Ibid., 318–27.

127. *Edin. Recs*, 1558–1571, 71.

128. Dennison, E. P., 'The Myth of the Medieval Burgh Community', in Harris, B. and MacDonald, A. (eds), *Scotland: The Making and Unmaking of the Nation, c.1100–1707*, Vol. 3 (Dundee: Dundee University Press, 2006), 137.

129. Lynch, M., *Scotland: A New History* (London: Pimlico, 2000), 171, and Lynch, M., *Edinburgh and the Reformation* (Edinburgh: Edinburgh University Press, 1981), 3 and 9–14.

130. Lynch, M., 'Burghs: Development of Edinburgh 1550 to 1650', in McNeill, P. G. B. & MacQueen, H. L. (eds.), *Atlas of Scottish History to 1707* (Edinburgh: The Scottish Medievalists, 1996), 456 and *Edin. Recs*, 1589–1603, xiv and 75.

131. *Edin. Recs*, 1604–1626, xi–xii and 277–9, 289–90, 292–4.

132. *Edin. Recs*, 1626–1641, 253–4; *Edin. Recs*, 1655–1665, 40–1, 43–4, and 310–11.

133. *Edin. Recs*, 1689–1701, 78, 119, 124, 227 and 257. See also Dingwall, H., *Late Seventeenth-century Edinburgh: A Demographic Study* (Aldershot: Scolar Press, 1994), 12–14.

134. Lynch, M., 'Continuity and Change in Urban Society, 1500–1700', in Houston, R. A., and Whyte, I. D. (eds), *Scottish Society 1500–1800* (Cambridge: Cambridge University Press, 1989), 89–90.

135. Todd, *Culture of Protestantism*, 318–27, and Hay, *History of Arbroath*, 302.

136. I'm grateful to Dr Pat Dennison for sharing this with me. See Dennison, E. P., 'The Myth of the Medieval Burgh Community', in Harris, B. and MacDonald, A. (eds), *Scotland: The Making and Unmaking of the Nation, c.1100–1707*, Vol. 3 (Dundee: Dundee University Press, 2006), 138.

137. ECA, SL154/5/1, 1746–1747 Ledger of Seat Rentals, Tolbooth Church, Seats No. 107–112.

138. Ibid., New North Church, Seats No. 27–29.

139. Ibid., New North Church, Seats No. 90–92. Perhaps further work in the Dean of Guild's various records might reveal a group of corporate seats in one of the sundry churches within the town in an earlier period, but at

present there is no such indication of status and standing being pursued by craft seating.

140. ECA, SL154/5/1, 1746–1747 Ledger of Seat Rentals, New North Church, Seats No. 116–129.

141. Ibid., Lady Yester's Church, Seat No. 50.

142. See Cowan, *Death, Life and Religious Change in Scottish Towns*, 99–100, and Allen, A., *The Locksmith Craft in Early Modern Edinburgh* (Edinburgh: Society of Antiquaries of Scotland, 2007), 6.

143. Mill, 'Inventory', 15.

144. Smith, A. M., *The Nine Trades of Dundee* (Dundee: Abertay Historical Society, 1995), 63–4.

145. NLS, Ms.19288, Perth Wrights' Minutes, f9r, f28r and f37r. I am grateful to Dr Michael Pearce for kindly sharing his notes on this manuscript source with me.

146. This was apparently *after* their Michaelmas elections, for the distribution of apples to the local children. Still, the corporate connection between assembly and the outdoors is clear. Hay, G., *History of Arbroath to the Present Time, With Notices of the Civil and Ecclesiastical Affairs* (Arbroath: Thomas Buncle, 1876), 288.

147. There are seven notes of meeting in St John's Chapel in the months of February, May, June, and July, for the years 1554, 1555 and 1559. Mill, 'Inventory', 14–16.

148. *RMS*, vol. 2, 617, no. 2905 and Oram, R. (ed.), *The Lordship of the Isles* (Leiden: Brill, 2014), 33 and 167. For examples of her support of the king financially, see *TA*, vol. 1, clv, 313–14, 317, 359, and vol. 3, 30.

149. NLS, Acc.7257, Rolled MS Inventory of Writs, numbers 14–17. The process by which the chapel came to the Incorporation of Masons and Wrights is a complex one, with an apparent division of the chapel from its associated tenement of land and patronage of the chaplainry. The 1601 sale of the chapel was ratified in 1618, while in 1631 the associated tenement and patronage went to Mr William Chalmer, Treasury Clerk, who five years later alienated the same to the Incorporation of Masons and Wrights of Edinburgh, giving them full ownership of the chapel, its grounds, the patronage of the chaplainry and the tenement lands which funded it. Mill, 'Inventory', 10; and NLS, Acc.7257, Rolled MS Inventory of Writs, numbers 7 (crossed out '25') and 19. See also NLS, Acc.8617, Bundle 1, Legal Papers and Accounts, 1601–80 for the 1601 contract from James Chalmers.

150. See Chapter 1 for examples.

151. For example, see Lamond, 'Scottish Craft Gild as a Religious Fraternity', 206.

152. *RPC*, vol. 1, 202 (1561–2) and *RSS*, vol. 5, xiv and 313, no. 3334 (1566–7).

153. This is emphasised by the unspecified 1568 essay of a 'painter and glaisinwricht': 'The quhilk day andro jhonesoun hes produceit his assay of payntrie and glasynwrychts befoir ye brodir & maisters of payntours and glasyn-

wrichtis and yai have tane inspectioun of ye saids assayis and think it qual-
ifeit and yerfor yai have admittit him fre man & maister to work of bayth
ye said occupatiouns . . .' ECA, Mill Recs, B4, 6 August, 1568, f4v. The fact
that such a craftsman was still being set an essay demonstrates the surviving
market for their work.

4

Craft and Burgh: Conflict or Partnership?

On 13 September 1753 the foundation stone for the new Exchange and Town Hall[1] was laid on the north side of the High Street. The pomp and ceremony included a 'grand Masonic procession, with the usual honours'; an address by Provost Drummond as 'Grand Master'; the striking of commemorative medals; an historical account recorded in W. A. Laurie's *History of Free Masonry*; and circulation of printed copies of the 'Contract of Agreement for building an Exchange in the City of Edinburgh, between the Magistrates and Town-Council and the Tradesmen', which carried an engraving of the forthcoming south elevation.[2] The contractors for this important symbol of the capital's affluence and commercial ambitions included a mason, four wrights, and an architect, who – crucially – were 'all Burgesses, Freemen Members of Mary's Chapel of Edinburgh'.[3]

As the last exchange had burned down half a century before,[4] this new phoenix-like structure not only beautified the aging High Street, but also promised a reinvigorated commercial and municipal heart for an expanding capital of 'North Britain'; a heart not removed to the fashionable New Town, but one adjacent to the traditional marker of burgh privileges, the Market Cross. While reaffirming the commercial importance of the Old Town, this ceremony also demonstrated the traditional structures of the town council, with tradesmen firmly ensconced in the magistracy.

Although it offers a slightly 'rose-coloured' perspective on the relations between the council and the Incorporation of Mary's Chapel, Laing's account of the foundation stone ceremony contrasts wonderfully with the much less collegial atmosphere in the first century of corporatism within the capital. From the fifteenth century to 1583, when royal arbitration provided a new 'sett', or constitution, for Edinburgh, relations between the trades and the council were more often characterised as a 'struggle', as the crafts sought political representation.[5] Indeed, it was, and is, often explained as a struggle between the merchants and the trades.

The second quarter of the sixteenth century clearly saw merchant-craft conflict, culminating in the notorious 1543 incident where several craft deacons took the very symbol of craft privileges, the 'Blue Blanket', and drew their swords in front of the merchant-dominated town council in the burgh's tolbooth. In resolving this crisis Governor Arran had to get involved, demonstrating the seriousness of the affair.[6] While the deacons were protected, the tensions continued, with various spikes, such as the 1555 abolition of craft deacons, followed by their return the next year for a money payment.[7]

By the 1560s a form of collective action can be seen amongst the crafts, in the formation of the Edinburgh 'convenery' of trades. Apparently active from 1562, by 1577 regular records were kept of meetings of the fourteen deacons of the incorporated trades, under the leadership of the deacon convener.[8] Though at first the council did not recognise the authority of the convener of trades, by the eighteenth century it was a firmly established part of the council.[9] Whether formally accepted or not, the convenery gave the crafts a form of political voice through lobbying and hiring suitable legal protection, all of which no doubt helped bring about the eventual compromise with the town council in 1583 over council seats for some of the crafts.[10]

Parliamentary legislation from 1469 had theoretically given the crafts a voice in the election of town officers, though the crafts were still denied council seats until the 1530s.[11] The 1583 arbitration did not give equal representation with the merchants on the council, but it did give greater access, with six 'ordinary' council deacons and two craft councillors.[12] The offices of the provost, the four bailies, the dean of guild and the treasurer were all denied to craftsmen, as they were to be 'of the estaitt and calling of merchants'.[13] With the additional ten merchant councillors, the merchants had a total of seventeen seats to the crafts' eight.[14] Still, from 1583 the crafts were very much invested in the government of the capital.

But how are we to read these events? Is it as straightforward as conflict resolution and gradual integration; a transition from conflict to partner-ship between crafts and merchants? Was it a case of political mobility for the crafts and, if so, did all crafts experience this? There were certainly plenty of instances of disagreement with the council, and these were – and are – often framed as merchants oppressing the craftsmen.

Though not all historians agree on the extent of the burgh tensions, it is clear that there were problems in burgh society. Smith argued that from a craft perspective, the lack of political representation and the economic restrictions of burgh councils were central to these tensions, and were caused by 'the weakness of the policy of the highest courts of the land', and 'the important place held by the merchants in municipal affairs'.[15] Lamond, giving a thorough account of the relevant fifteenth- and sixteenth-century parliamentary legislation, pointed to the various issues the authorities took exception to. These issues included sufficiency of craft work; craftsmen trading in raw materials, which were technically 'merchandise'; independent pricing; and the danger of 'leagues and bands' amongst groups of craftsmen.[16]

These tensions created strife between craftsmen and the council in Edinburgh, in a time of dramatic demographic and economic change.[17] Traditionally such tensions have been viewed as 'a struggle between merchants and craftsmen, which came to dominate all towns.'[18] Some historians, such as Grant and Lynch, have argued against the universality of such merchant-craft conflict, but it is not disputed that tension was seen along merchant-craft lines at various times in certain burghs.[19] Although tensions were often labelled by contemporaries as being between these two groups, the reality was more complex.[20]

The revised view of the merchant-craft conflict has emphasised several problems. First of all, the terms 'merchant' and 'craftsman' are too vague to hold absolute meaning across Scotland's burghs. A merchant could be an itinerant peddler, a petty retailer, or an affluent importer and exporter. Such shipping magnates were the 'merchant princes' of the Scottish burghs. Some merchants only became burgesses, as with the father and son, John and Archibald Ferguson.[21] Others had the resources to join the more prestigious Guild,[22] as with William Dick of Braid.[23] Not all of these 'merchants' had access to the council, and not all of them would have been opposed to craftsmen, who were, of course, customers.

Alternatively, the 'craftsman' was not a homogenous type either. A humble candlemaker was not likely to accrue the wealth of a goldsmith; nor were all goldsmiths likely to have the same level of wealth. Indeed it has already been shown in a previous chapter that there was a clear aristocracy within the Incorporation of Mary's Chapel, with too much division to simply lump them all together as 'craftsmen' in common opposition to the 'merchants'.[24]

While contemporary commentators found it expedient to use the two labels to describe a tangible tension within burgh society, it was also pointed out that such vague lines were often crossed. Fountainhall was justified in his phrasing when in 1677 he wrote about the 'old controversy . . . betuixt the Merchands and Trades of Edinburgh', as this was certainly the way the tensions were understood.[25] He was also quite correct when the year before he caustically remarked in regards to '. . . the present agreement betuen the merchands, and wrights, and masissons, against thir other trades . . .', that it was a case of the 'old politique maxime *Divide et impera*.[26] Such social labels were only meant to be a shorthand; an expedient which was just as easily disregarded by contemporaries. This was especially true after 1583, when it became easier for craftsmen to attain guildry and act as merchants.[27]

Aside from problems with the terminology, there also was too much diversity in terms of the burghs themselves to speak about a universal merchant-craft conflict. Few burghs had as wide of a range of crafts as Edinburgh, and some did not have a merchant guild.[28] The larger settlements, such as Aberdeen, did have more in common with Edinburgh, and there is some indication of the crafts from such burghs working together in defence of their 'liberties' against the merchants, though the occasional reference is far from indicative of a universal conflict.[29]

It is more accurate to say that there were examples of merchant-craft conflict amongst some sections of burgh society. Grant argued that

> The quarrels between the craftsmen and the burghal authorities were often not class conflicts between craftsmen and merchants, but struggles against the small clique of the most influential merchants who monopolized the burghal offices.[30]

Lynch, in his study of the capital after the Reformation, came to a similar conclusion, pointing to the political and economic power held by, 'a relatively small section of the merchants', and a similarly influential craft aristocracy.[31]

Although there was a merchant-craft conflict in Edinburgh society, this was not part of a wider urban culture, but dependent on its own isolated circumstances. There were plenty of examples of interaction between the merchants and the crafts. The wright, William Bailie, married the daughter of a merchant brother of the Guild, and in doing so, secured access to the Guild for himself in 1692.[32] In 1733 the son of a Lord Provost became a mason burgess and guild brother.[33] Even in the sixteenth century there was social interaction across merchant-craft lines. When Mause Udwart passed away in 1587, her testament described her husband as 'glassinwright and merchant'.[34] The burgess entry for one of his apprentices listed him solely as a 'glassinwricht', but his apprentice as a 'merchant'.[35] Considering the need to import glass prior to the beginning of domestic production, such arrangements made sense. Other instances are more general, as when the former boxmaster of the Incorporation, Gilbert Clewcht, was mentioned in a deposition as having entertained at his house in the Canongate the baxters, Alexander Bartilmo and Herculis Methven, the mason, Johnne Inglis, and the merchant Henry Kynloch.[36] Tensions there were, but they were often overcome.

So, in terms of the Incorporation of Mary's Chapel, how were relations with the council? Were they oppressed by merchants, or were they fully integrated into the burgh establishment? To explore these questions further, it is helpful to use Grant's assessment of the tensions between the crafts and the burgh authorities. In her book, *Social and Economic Development of Scotland Before 1603*, Grant pointed to three causes of tension between the crafts and the councils of Scotland's burghs. These were participation in government; participation in foreign trade; and the setting of prices.[37] These make a helpful yardstick with which to consider just how integrated the Mary's Chapel crafts were with the merchant-controlled town council. Before these will be looked at in turn, it will be useful to consider several crucial external influences which impacted upon relations between the crafts and the council. These issues relate to questions of authority, in that the capital had not only the crown and the court interfering in burgh politics, but also a growing array of 'suburbs', all of which complicated craft participation in burgh affairs.

BLURRED LINES: CONSUMERS, PRODUCERS AND THE QUESTION OF PLACE

Residency and Status: The Problem of the Suburbs

Whether merchants and craftsmen were in conflict or not, freemen by the nature of their corporate privileges usually sought to exclude unfreemen. Rising population levels within the town created problems in keeping track of who was free and who was not, but there was an additional complication in the various non-royal burghs immediately adjacent to the town's walls.[38] While the town sought to impose suburban status on these settlements, they were legally burghs in their own right, though their legal status was not that of a *royal* burgh. Instead they were 'inferior' burghs of barony or regality, depending on their charters and landlords. While a royal burgh was held by the crown in feudal infeftment, a baronial or reglity burgh was granted by a subject of the crown, and usually held more limited trading rights.[39]

In the 1980s an important study of Edinburgh's social and economic structures used tax records to show that as the population of the capital grew, and inflationary pressures and increased taxation put pressure on individual incomes, many craftsmen left the capital for the suburbs.[40] Some crafts, such as weavers and walkers (fullers of cloth), appeared to have had many of their members leave the capital to take up residence and work in the suburbs. The building trades, however, seem to have had a slightly different experience. The data presented in the aforementioned study only gives figures for coopers, masons and wrights, which interestingly mirrors the hierarchy of the Incorporation through its three most senior trades. While the coopers were shown to drop from nine taxable members in 1583 to none in 1634, the wrights went from nineteen to twenty-nine and the masons from thirteen to twelve, suggesting that the builders were drawn to the town while the makers of casks were not.[41] It would appear that many of the builders were not fleeing to the suburbs, though as we shall see, they too faced a rather complex problem in trying to enforce their control over their suburban rivals.

As the freemen were not all leaving, though the suburbs were attracting unfreemen within Edinburgh's 'liberties', or area of jurisdiction, clearly the flight to the suburbs was not wholly from *within* the capital. Some Edinburgh crafts fled to the suburbs; others stayed in the town while unfreemen from their trades came into the suburbs from outside. The growing population was clearly increasing demand for housing, both within and immediately without the town walls, which no doubt encouraged the incomers. Crucially, this gave a degree of common cause with the merchants, as both groups sought to control suburban competition. It was therefore in the Incorporation's interests to work with the council, though as shall be seen, the council and the Incorporation did not always see eye-to-eye on how best to deal with the problem.

For the Incorporation, part of the problem with unfreemen was the very nature of their work. While some of their trades were more static and shop-based, such as the coopers or sievewrights, the majority were quasi-peripatetic, often taking work outside of the town as available.[42] This itinerancy caused problems both for the Incorporation and the town council.

The requisite freedoms of the town and incorporations both had stipulations about residency.[43] While burgesship was no longer predicated on ownership of land within the town, one still had to live within the town walls. Though more common in seventeenth-century burgess entries, from the later-sixteenth century conditions were often stipulated that the incoming burgess or guild brother had to move 'within this burgh' by a set quarter day, such as Martinmas or Witsunday.[44] To ensure compliance, a complicated system of fines and surety was instituted. In 1669, Francis Aird, merchant in Leith, was told to 'come to Edinburgh and reseed with his familly at Whitsonday nixt under the paine of ane hundreth punds Scots money', suggesting a level of trust in that he was deemed trustworthy enough not to need surety.[45] Nearly a century earlier a slater, Matthew Duncan, had to have Francis Kynet act as surety for his ability to pay extents, participate in the town watch with his own armour, and reside within the town.[46] Intriguingly, the person who gave these assurances, under pain of fines himself should the slater fail, was in fact not a craftsman, but a merchant. Such arrangements between the supposedly conflict-ridden groups were in fact quite common.

Residency within the town walls was important for several reasons. It gave access to markets, as suggested by the eighteenth-century name for the last street before the town walls – the 'World's End Close'. To be outside the walls was like being beyond the ends of the Earth, which was not wholly inaccurate.[47] While access was important, perhaps the most important aspect was administrative necessity. As the population of the capital grew, it became too difficult to even keep track of the freemen, let alone the unfreemen. In January of 1689, shortly after the 'Glorious Revolution', the council minutes recorded a discussion regarding a convention of estates to greet the new king. It was suggested that there be an election of commissioners by popular vote of the burgesses of the royal burghs, though Edinburgh's lawyers pointed out that for the capital:

> If the election were by the whole burgesses the meetting would be so numerous that it would be impossible to avoid confusion and as it cannot be expected but all popular elections must be tumultuous much more in such a popular Cittie as Edinburgh . . .[48]

By the seventeenth century, if not earlier, the burgess community had grown considerably. It was simply too large to keep track of individuals within it. Although rules about residency were difficult to enforce, they were also absolutely necessary for the administration of burghal privileges.

While administrative need made residency worth pursuing, increased specialisation often worked against it. Edinburgh was not near the sea, though its suburb of Leith was one of Scotland's busiest and most important ports. Shipping containers and naval goods were in constant demand, so it made sense for coopers and blockmakers to work near the docks.[49] Although the 1633 ratification of the Incorporation's seals of cause stipulated a three-mile exclusion zone for the work of the ten arts,[50] stopping all work in the suburbs was simply not possible.

Indeed, not all freemen saw the suburbs as a threat. Several officers of the Edinburgh Incorporation had connections with the neighbouring Canongate. Mason Gilbert Clewcht, a former boxmaster to the incorporation, was still living in the Canongate in 1562, despite a stipulation in his 1561 entry as brother of the Guild that he must take up residency within the town.[51] Deacon Joshua Mansion's widow also lived in the regality burgh, though where her late husband had resided is less clear.[52] Deacon Miller was deposed by the council in 1764 because he lived on the north side of the Head of the Canongate, and therefore outside the town.[53]

Despite the council rules about residency, the reality for the building trades was far more complicated, as financial interests were simply not limited by burgh jurisdictions. Some craftsmen had interests in property outwith the town, as with the Edinburgh mason who owned land in Glasgow.[54] Another Edinburgh mason was involved in quarrying operations just north of the Canongate, which again transcended burgh boundaries.[55] At times, the council themselves were happy to bend the rules, as when there was a dearth of skilled slaters available in the capital. As the Incorporation could not find enough slaters to meet demand, the council made a Glaswegian slater a burgess of Edinburgh.[56] Burgh boundaries were rigid when it suited the interests of those in power, though economic pressures often betrayed a more permeable jurisdiction.

Legal Battles

As the capital grew in both size and prominence, so too the 'inferior' settlements on its doorstep also grew, bringing both challenges and opportunities for the craftsmen. The municipal response was initially focussed on completely denying the suburban settlements the rights to work or trade, though over time a more flexible system of controlled toleration came into being through the purchase of feudal 'superiority' over the neighbouring burghs of barony or regality.[57] In the century from 1565 to the 1660s, Edinburgh became landlord over South Leith, West Port and Potterrow, which were joined into 'Portsburgh', and Canongate, which had its own suburbs.[58] This gave the incorporated trades of Edinburgh leverage over their suburban counterparts, though their position and rights were not always clear.

Details of this process are often difficult to ascertain, but the net effects are more apparent. The problem of outland men[59] seeking to use Edinburgh's markets had long been a thorn in the capital's side. Occasionally, this was dealt with through violence.[60] More often, the courts were seen as the avenue for protecting corporate privileges. From at least the 1400s it was understood that a firm legal basis was the best way to protect against unfreemen. Hence the coopers' 1489 seal of cause complained about 'outlandisfolkis ... passand fra hous to hous mendand and spoilland nychtbouris wirk and stuf, hafand nother stob nor stake within this towne'.[61] These outsiders did not contribute to the town watch, nor did they pay taxes, and according to the incorporated coopers, their work, which they took away from freemen, was substandard in execution. Hence the seal of cause specified that officers were to go with the free coopers to forbid the outland men from working within the town – unless they took

up residence and joined the Incorporation.[62] Granting legal status therefore was intended to stop 'outlandismen' from usurping burgh privileges,
though it is telling that the charter did not allow them to stop unfreemen
from joining.

It was not just the craftsmen of the capital who had troubles with the
suburbs, as the merchants also resented suburban competition. A 1570 act
of the Edinburgh town council claimed that, 'the chief liberty and freedom
of a free burgh of royalty consists in two things, the one in using of merchandise, the other in using of crafts.'[63] The reality was more complex, as
the privileges of foreign trade and incorporated crafts were also granted to
certain lesser burghs, but from this 1570 act we see an important element
of common cause. Whether merchant or craftsman, it was in the interest of
all of Edinburgh's burgesses and guild brethren to work together in defending their privileges against the 'outlandisfolk'. Therefore, one would expect
the crafts of the Incorporation of Mary's Chapel to have worked with the
council, and at times they did so.

After the initial purchase of superiority over the port of South Leith, a
legal complication known as 'reversion' threatened to undo the gains of
the capital over its new suburb. In 1581 the fourteen incorporated trades
were given a writ for an unspecified amount of silver loaned to the council
in order to buy the superiority over the port.[64] Nearly forty years later,
when troubles over Leith's crafts surfaced again, several craftsmen were
sent by the convenery to 'travail' with the council, demonstrating their
understanding of the need to work with the merchants on this common
problem.[65]

Though some aspects of this legal battle with the suburbs were pursued
corporately, either through the convenery or with the council, other aspects
were advanced by the individual incorporations, which set a dangerous
precedent against working together. Even within a composite incorporation such as that of Mary's Chapel, there was not always consensus as to
how to proceed. In 1610, when relations between the masons and wrights
and the coopers were breaking down over the exclusion of the coopers from
holding office, the convenery had to step in and decree that any 'lauchfull
appointment' with the suburban coopers in Leith was to be undertaken only
with 'universall consent' within the whole Incorporation.[66] Interestingly, in
1608 an 'agreement' had been made between the masons and wrights of
Edinburgh with the masons, wrights and slaters of Leith, though the suburban coopers were not actually included.[67] Clearly this early contract was
not in everyone's best interests, though in 1619 the council stepped in to
declare that they would admit new coopers in Leith, which would be tested
for sufficiency by the Incorporation.[68]

While there were apparently problems with this 1608 attempt to finalise arrangements with suburban workers in Leith, it was an example of the final solution to the problem of suburban work for the building trades. By obtaining legal contracts with the suburban crafts, the Incorporation was finally able to wield influence in the burghs they insisted were suburban. Often these contracts needed to be refined and ratified, but they gave a firmer foundation for the protection of the Incorporation's privileges.

Not all contracts with suburban crafts survive, though several important examples do. Often they refer to other contracts, which are now missing. In 1608, 1638 and 1658, contracts were made with various building trades in South Leith, and the 1658 document refers to earlier contracts with the coopers of Leith from 1607 and 1628.[69] In 1649 a contract was made with the relevant trades of Portsburgh, though the situation with the Canongate proved more complicated.[70] These contracts were not uniform; nor is it likely that they were given without some degree of dissent, though for most of the suburban crafts the Incorporation was successful in establishing contractual superiority. In part, this was by not *stopping* suburban work, but instead seeking to tax and control it.

Although the Portsburgh contracts are now missing, the surviving Leith contracts are informative as to the Incorporation's attitudes and concerns. These documents dealt with access, by ensuring that no suburban apprentices were taken without the Incorporation's consent, and by setting essays to be tried and examined before admission of new freemen.[71] As with access to work within the capital, sufficiency was key, and was used to exclude those who were not approved of by the Incorporation.

Issues of control were enshrined in the contracts. These included the right of Edinburgh's deacons and masters to punish the suburban craftsmen who disobeyed the ordinances of the contracts, as well as the right of the Edinburgh Incorporation to elect the 'deacons in Leyth at Michelmas ȝeirlie as ane oversman To gyde thair brethren In keiping of gude ordour'.[72] While the 1619 act of council had decreed that they would manage access for suburban workers, with the Incorporation only testing sufficiency, by 1658 Edinburgh had enhanced and affirmed their control by claiming in the new contract, 'To be yeir superiors In all tyme coming', though they did acknowledge that this was under the Provost.[73]

Aside from ensuring oversight of their suburban counterparts, the Incorporation also managed to obtain a degree of financial control over them. Booking fees and upset silver were to be 'equally dividit', with half of the income going to the Edinburgh Incorporation.[74] This would appear to have been a particularly beneficial aspect of allowing suburban work. In 1678, according to a scrap of paper apparently used for rough working by the boxmaster or clerk, the upsets in Portsburgh brought in £40, while those of Leith brought in £33 6s 8d. The upsets of Edinburgh were greater, at £208 for the same year, though the suburban upsets together were more than a third of the value of the usual upset payments for Edinburgh masters, making, no doubt, for a welcome addition to the Incorporation's coffers.[75]

Contracts made strategic sense to the Edinburgh Incorporation, but they were not without benefits to the suburban crafts which signed them. Many included clauses obliging the Edinburgh Incorporation to 'menteane and defend' the suburban workers,[76] and several stipulated that if the Edinburgh craftsmen had too much work, Leith craftsmen were to be engaged 'befor any uther outlandis craftismen of the saidis craftis for the waiges as they can aggrie upoun'. In giving up control, they did receive a degree of access.[77]

Problems of Control

Whereas the Incorporation was able to exert influence over the smaller suburban burghs of barony, they appear to have had less success with the larger burgh of regality, the Canongate.[78] As Canongate began at the very edge of Edinburgh, the two burghs had long been rivals. In part this stemmed from David I's c.1143 charter, which gave Canongate both burghal privileges and access to Edinburgh's markets.[79] Edinburgh managed to purchase the right of superiority over the Canongate in 1636, though being the landlord over the settlement apparently did not give it the legal right to remove their established craft privileges.[80] In part this was due to a series of ratifications which entrenched the rights of the Canongate crafts, despite protests and counter-protests to the parliament.[81]

Prior to the purchase of superiority over Canongate, a policy of exclusion was pursued by the Edinburgh building trades against their 'suburban' counterparts in the Canongate. According to the minutes of the convenery, on 8 September 1631 an act was made by the Incorporation of Mary's Chapel that none of their freemen should fee or give work to any master or servant in either the Canongate or its suburbs.[82] This did not stop members, such as Johne Hay, slater, from taking work in the burgh of regality, which was perceived as both a breach of oath and an acknowledgement of Canongate's legitimacy.[83]

After the acquisition of superiority, it was recognised that such policies of exclusion were not always tenable. The Edinburgh magistrates, apparently taking their legal position as superior quite seriously, set up a committee in 1650 to 'consider quhat is fitting to the counsell to graunt to and to requyre fra the Cannogait in the presente differences and to report their opiniouns . . .'[84] Apparently their opinions were not welcomed by all, as a rift opened up between the crafts and the rest of the council when without the 'consent of the ordinar deakynes and craft counsellouris', the Canongate crafts' seals of cause were apparently ratified.[85] Through the Edinburgh convenery of trades it was decided that all craft deacons were to refuse to attend council meetings until their unilateral decision was reversed.[86] Importantly, the convenery's discourse explicitly referred to the controversy in terms of merchants versus craftsmen. The town council that took the decision was declared to be, 'consisting onlie of merchantis without the consent of the deakynes ordinar and craftis counsellouiris who is the uther pairt'.[87]

The council responded a few days later by setting up another committee, which was to include the provost, 'to resave any prejudices' the crafts could show against the ratification of Canongate's seals of cause. One of the bailies was appointed to collect all the charters from the Canongate crafts so that they could be compared with those of Edinburgh, though what came of the committee's findings is not recorded. Within a few months the capital was to be occupied by a Cromellian army, though the 'bussines of the craftis of the Canogait' was taken up again a few years later.[88] Perhaps the earlier ratifications by crown and parliament simply made it too difficult for the new feudal superior to remove the established privileges, though they certainly didn't stop the council from putting a blanket ban on the exercise of the skinner craft in any suburb in 1659.[89]

A generation later, in 1677, the Edinburgh lawyer, Sir John Lauder of Fountainhall, noted down rather mischievously in his *Historical Notices* that the failure to control the Canongate crafts was down to merchant spite:

> ane old controversy betuixt the Merchands and Trades of Edinburgh . . . and what bursts furth with much bitternesse upon all occasions, they being jealous one of another; and it's for this cause why the Merchands, ever since the Toune acquired the Cannogate . . . have ever refused to annex it to the royalty of Edinburgh, leist, by that accession it would too much increase and strenthen the Trades, the Cannogate being most inhabited by such, and oft tymes better craftsmen than the tounsmen . . .[90]

A compromise seems to have been reached by 1674 for a payment of 100 rex dollars by the Canongate trades 'for the use and mantinance of the privilidges of the haill trads of the kingdome'.[91] A degree of the Incorporation's honour was restored, while Canongate was apparently allowed to carry on in its privileges.

Being a burgh of regality, Canongate was able to fend off some of the attempts of the Edinburgh crafts to exclude them from craft production, though merchant spite might indeed have influenced the council's decision, as suggested by Fountainhall. Not all crafts had equal success in this, but it would appear that the legal position of the Canongate building trades was fairly solid, and the Incorporation of Mary's Chapel therefore had to cope with their competitors being next door. Tellingly, although they managed to establish the right to choose an oversman for the Leith and Portsburgh crafts, they were not able to impose such an office in Canongate.[92]

Even with an oversman elected annually for Leith and Portsburgh, the level of control enjoyed by the Incorporation was not absolute, in part because it was the council which held the actual superiority, and therefore the suburban crafts had recourse to legal institutions just as the Incorporation did. In 1676 several Edinburgh craftsmen were not only working in Leith, but had also taken up residence there, so the masons and wrights of Leith complained not only to the Incorporation, but also to the provost, bailies and council.[93] The Edinburgh Incorporation was forced to admit that some of their craftsmen were indeed living in the suburbs, though the convenery decided to back Mary's Chapel against the upstart suburb, as it had 'no priviledge bot be the tolerance of the trades'.[94]

The convenery did not always side with the town's incorporations though, as in the 1682 case when the Portsburgh masons, wrights and coopers put in a petition citing the text of a contract from 7 February 1650.[95] It appears that the masons were refusing to honour the contract, so the convenery told them to comply. While contracts did give certain advantages to the Incorporation over the suburbs in terms of legal standing, these same legal institutions could also be used against them.

As demonstrated by the masons, there was not always unity in the corporate approach to suburban work, which no doubt discouraged any unity with the town council. Despite the convenery's 1682 ruling that the masons must comply with the terms of the contract, two years later the same infraction was again noted, with the masons still delaying in the setting of an essay for the 'outlandish craftsman', John Moutray.[96] Throughout these years no mention is made of infringements from the other arts, but only by the masons. Similar disunity was shown elsewhere, as with the separate Leith contracts for the coopers.[97]

Even the convenery itself occasionally lacked unity in its approach to the suburbs, as with the 1649 negotiations with the Portsburgh trades, which were to be pursued by the fourteen individual deacons rather than by the deacon convener and his court.[98] Though it was stipulated that none were to take any action without first acquainting the deacon convener and the other deacons, this was still far from a united front. When the system began to break down in the eighteenth century, with Leith refusing to let Edinburgh choose their oversmen,[99] this lack of unity proved problematic, as defence of the capital's privileges in the suburbs was to be paid for by only those trades with suburban oversmen.[100] While the 1676 defence against Leith was paid for by the common purse of the convenery, the 1728 'Leith affair' was to be paid for by the individual trades. Perhaps it was obvious to all that the control of Leith's craftwork was simply untenable, as the Leith crafts soon won rulings in the court of session which declared them independent of the Edinburgh trades.[101] On the other hand, it is worth noting that unlike Canongate or Leith, Portsburgh seemed to become more firmly linked to Edinburgh at this period, as in 1726 they petitioned the Incorporation for help in fending off their own unfreemen problems.[102]

Edinburgh was not wholly successful in controlling suburban work, though for a time contractual toleration seemed to work better than outright banning of all economic activity. As there was not a united front between the craftsmen, it is perhaps not surprising that control was not sustainable. Despite the common threat of the suburbs to both merchants' and craftsmen's privileges, it would appear that the lack of unity affected not only the incorporations and the convenery, but the council as well. Discussions in 1649 in regards to the subjugation of the Portsburgh crafts also turned to 'the toune counsel off this burghe (viz the merchandis) intending to wrong the saidis trades of this burghe in the matter concerneing the trademen of Portsburghe'.[103] Similar distrust is visible in the handling of the Canongate seals of cause three years later,[104] so perhaps it should not be surprising that the convenery in 1728 used the inflammatory language of 'arbitrary procedure'; 'incroachments'; and 'the arbitrary will and management of the Merchants or Town Council of Edinburgh'.[105] Incorporation and council did indeed have common cause in fighting the suburban outlandsmen, though clearly there were limits to how unified any of the groups involved actually were.

Issues of burgh jurisdiction could be quite problematic, and occasionally divisive, though they were further complicated by the role of the customer; especially when the customer was the monarch. As the Incorporation sought to control free and unfree labour, the upper echelons of Scottish society sought quality and expediency, and their consumption patterns did not always hinge on legal jurisdictions. Having affluent customers was a necessity for those who made expensive buildings, though having powerful and influential customers could also lead to complications when trying to defend corporate privilege.

Interference: Crown, Court and the Burgh's Crafts

As a royal burgh, Edinburgh held its privileges from the crown, and in turn the Incorporation held its privileges from the town. This feudal hierarchy was predicated on an increasingly complex legal system, but in effect, all privileges of the town and the crafts were derived either directly or indirectly from the crown. This meant that the burgh boundaries and liberties, which roughly corresponded to the jurisdiction of the Incorporation, could be interfered with by the monarch.[106] As the kings and queens made Edinburgh their capital from the later fifteenth century, the court was also usually present, providing a wealthy and influential customer base, though they might just as easily employ craftsmen who were not freemen of the Incorporation. While these unfreemen might be challenged, as with the case previously discussed of the unfree painter being employed through licence of the Abbot of Dunfermline,[107] still it was not easy to go against the crown or the aristocracy.

Although the crown and court wielded a fair degree of power, it was still limited by law, and was not absolute. On the other hand, their power as influential consumers was particularly important to the development of the capital's architectural and material cultures. Foreign masons were not only brought into the town, but also into the Incorporation, bringing new practices and broadening traditions. Over time this had a deep impact on the built environment, as courtly expectations and gentility trickled down through the societal pyramid. By the eighteenth century, even the Incorporation's medieval meeting hall, Mary's Chapel, was remade in the latest Palladian style, firmly linking them into the trends enjoyed by the upper classes and making a very public statement about their skill and taste.[108]

Whether as leaders of architectural and consumer fashions, or as privileged upper-class meddlers, who disregarded the municipal rules for their own selfish ends, the crown and the court were important parts of the Incorporation's customer base. They could enforce the status quo, as when Charles I and the Parliament followed the town council in ratifying the Incorporation's seals of cause in 1635 and 1641.[109] They could also challenge municipal authority, as when James V issued an edict under the Great Seal in favour of Edinburgh's craftsmen.[110] Occasionally, this challenge to municipal authority also went against the privileges of the Incorporation, as with Charles I's ratification of the seals of cause for the Canongate's craftsmen,[111] or with the later institution of the 'King's Freemen', former soldiers who were given gratis burgesship.[112]

The forcing of soldiers on the incorporations would no doubt have annoyed those who sought some degree of control over the labour market, but for certain individuals such royal interference could be a tremendous blessing. Some master craftsmen from the Incorporation were elevated to the status of 'his Majesty's master', which brought access to lucrative royal contracts.[113] Alexander Hay became 'His Majestie's bower', while John Kerr became 'His Majesty's cooper' at Leith.[114] Other examples include 'maister carvour to the king', or 'his majesty's master mason'.[115] Such offices were no doubt welcomed by the holders, but they could also cause problems by crossing traditional lines. One master mason to the crown was not a mason at all, but in fact a slater by training.[116]

Usually such positions brought a degree of authority; occasionally they brought a governmental role, as with the 'herald painters' under the Lord Lyon, King of Arms. Herald painters specialised in coats of arms, which should only have been granted by the crown's official, the Lord Lyon.[117] Hence we see parallels with the English system under their College of Arms, where potential conflict over jurisdiction might arise between the royal institution and the Painters-Stainers' Company.[118] This would have been particularly problematic where a painter could undertake both heraldic devices and other forms of painting, such as landscapes, histories or portraiture. While there was potential for conflict, though, there was also an opportunity for more work. As with the English herald painters, several Edinburgh herald painters, such as George Porteous, were able to 'enjoy parallel careers', with the freedom to work under both institutions.[119] As a freeman of the Incorporation, Porteous was indirectly under the town's authority, though as a herald painter, he also fell under that of the Lord Lyon.

Having such rich and powerful customers as the crown and nobility within the town boundaries created challenges, but it also offered opportunities, and many craftsmen were able to exploit these. Jurisdictional questions might have complicated the labour market, but there were those within the Incorporation who sought to use this to their advantage, as with the painters' parallel organisation under the Lord Lyon, or the masons' parallel organisation of freemasonry. Both were attempts to control specific aspects of labour at a national level, and both came from those within court circles.[120]

Though corporate privileges were granted fairly early in the early modern period, they remained contested throughout, and it was not only council authority which threatened craft agency. The presence of the crown and court within the capital's boundaries was therefore a mixed blessing, especially in terms of the dynamics of jurisdiction, privilege and custom. This certainly complicated relations between the crafts and the council, and hopefully highlights the pressures on both the Incorporation and the magistracy.

As mentioned above, Grant pointed to three aspects of municipal government which had potential to cause divisions between the merchant-dominated council and the craftsmen of the incorporated trades. It has been argued above that the upper echelons of the crafts were increasingly involved in municipal government, but this is not to say that the divisions disappeared; especially with other interested parties so near. It is therefore expedient to turn our focus back to Grant's three points of conflict: a share in government; a share in foreign trade; and the council regulation of prices.

CRAFT AND COUNCIL: INTEGRATION OR INTERFERENCE?

A Share in Government

Aside from the communal burgess duties of scot, lot, watch and ward, the post-1583 incorporated trades also had more of a political role in the capital through increased access to council seats, giving greater influence in town affairs.[121] In 1508 the Edinburgh crafts were firmly rebuffed in their request for six to eight seats on the council, though by 1538 it would appear that they held two seats between all the crafts.[122] While arbitration in 1583 saw this number augmented significantly, it was still only eight seats for fourteen incorporated trades.[123] Before the decreet arbitral, some years saw more access for the crafts than others, as various deacons and 'visitors' were occasionally brought in alongside the two craft councillors, but for some, at least, 1583 was a tremendous victory.[124] The 'craft aristocracy' did very well out of the new municipal sett, though the other trades did not necessarily see as much benefit.[125]

The Incorporation of Masons and Wrights, well before they purchased St Mary's Chapel, had a small degree of success in securing council seats, but it would appear that at least politically, they were not on equal footing with the more successful trades, such as the hammermen or skinners. According to Lynch's lists of councillors from 1551 to 1583,[126] the Incorporation of Masons and Wrights had one of two seats in 1559–60 (a wright); one of two in 1573–4 (a bowmaker); and one of two in 1582–3 (a bowmaker).[127] Even though this was not complete political exclusion, the period from 1551 to 1583 still only saw councillors from the Incorporation of Masons and Wrights for three of thirty-three years.[128]

In the first election after the decreet arbitral, the six new seats for craft deacons went not to the masons and wrights, but to the surgeons, hammermen, tailors, goldsmiths, skinners, and furriers.[129] The two craft councillors from the previous year, however, had included the tailor, Jhonn Bairnisfather, and the bower, James Fergussoun, so the Incorporation appears to have had some influence over the choice of the new council deacons on the eve of the new burgh constitution.[130]

Although complete lists of the craft councillors are not always given in the published council records, a petition to the town council in 1648 demonstrates how the council seats in the next generations were monopolised by a small oligarchy of the more influential incorporated trades. In that year, the deacons of the furriers, wrights, masons, baxters, fleshers, websters, walkers, and bonnetmakers presented a bill to the council complaining that for the past twenty years the craft council seats had been monopolised by the remaining six incorporated trades.[131] The council found the supplication 'reasonable', and declared that the future elections of the 'most qualified' deacons would conform to the sett rather than perpetuating the aristocracy.[132]

Clearly this suggests that the building trades continued to be passed over even after the decreet arbitral, but one should not read into this equal access from 1648 onward. The phrase 'most qualified' gave much latitude for the council, and certain trades, such as the baxters and fleshers, were prohibited from public office due to the fact they produced necessary food stuffs for the burgh community:

> And, it is a very just ordinance of the Toune of Edinburgh, among it's other statutes, that nather the deacon of the Flechers nor of the Baxters be upon the ordinar Councell of the burgh, consisting of 25 persones, because they selling things absolatly necessar for the life of man, if they were sitting their, might obstruct usefull and expedient regulations and checks to be made against them.[133]

Intriguingly, there does not seem to have been a similar proscription against the building trades, despite the potential problems of combining the housing interest with local politics.

While proscription of the building trades was not overtly legislated, there were other ways in which the council wielded influence over those in charge of the building trades, such as the use of leets for selecting the deacons of masons and wrights. The 1583 decreet arbitral declared that the council would use a system of lists, or 'leets', to include the worthiest candidates for the office of deacon of the fourteen incorporations.[134] The decision of who would be deacon from the leet of names was up to the particular trade, but it was the council which chose the names to go on the leet in the first place. By the seventeenth century, the system involved a 'long leet', which was given to the council by the deacons, from which they chose a 'short leet' to be sent back to be voted on, but even this system was open to abuse, as complained about by the goldsmiths in 1686. The fourteen deacons met that year to discuss a controversy, where some crafts' deacons made the lists to be handed in to council, whereas others were made by vote of the whole incorporation.[135]

A case involving Mary's Chapel, in 1764, shows the potential for abuse from above. In that year, there was a political divide over the re-election of the deacon convener of trades. The deacon of the masons, who was the glazier, Alexander Miller, had been elected from a short leet approved by the council, but when he was subsequently encouraged to support the re-election of the council's choice for deacon convener, he made it clear that he would not vote for him. A complaint was made against Miller, on the grounds that he lived in the Canongate rather than Edinburgh, and the council proceeded to remove him from office. A 'memorial' was published of the ensuing legal battle, explaining that although the council's choice for convener was 'grazed', or retired, the Incorporation's choice of deacon was still removed.[136] How divided the Incorporation was on the matter is not clear, though what the *Memorial* records about the partisan politics of the leet, is particularly revealing.[137]

While there was clearly some political participation for the Incorporation of Mary's Chapel, it does not appear that they were hugely successful in wielding influence through council seats. Other crafts clearly had less of a voice in municipal government, though several had much greater access. Though it cannot be said that politically there was only conflict with the council, neither can it be said that the Incorporation was fully integrated with the magistracy. Perhaps the potential conflicts over raw materials and finished products will help to explain this.

A Share in Foreign Trade

Participation in municipal government, though important, was not the only issue which promoted division between the council and the crafts, as the merchant-dominated council also held sway over trade. The Incorporation relied on raw materials for their businesses, and though some were sourced domestically, such as stone from Abbeyhill or the Burghmure,[138] or lime from Cousland,[139] others, such as the larger pieces of timber, had to be imported from Scandinavia or the Baltic.[140] Even after Scotland started producing its own glass in 1610, glaziers still relied on imports, bringing them closer to the merchants.[141] Of course, such proximity to the privilege of the merchants – the 'use of merchandise' – was not always perceived as a blessing. The craftsman as customer was most welcome, but the craftsman as importer was a clear threat.

With the 1583 decreet arbitral, though, it would appear that craftsmen gained greater access to the merchant body that controlled foreign trade, or 'the Guild'. The Guild was a body of merchants of some antiquity. Legislation on the merchant guilds can be found in a codified set of laws, known as *Leges Burgorum*, which apparently date to the reign of David I (1124–53), and in the laws of William I (1165–1214), demonstrating the early origins of this exclusive 'friendly society' of merchants.[142] Although the exact origins are unclear, some historians, such as James Colston, have argued that the early guilds were the very basis of burgh government; the 'first inception of proper civic administration'.[143] Others, such as Pat Dennison, have questioned the validity of such claims, offering alternative readings of the sparse early evidence, such as the *Statuta Gilde*.[144] Although the *Statutes* deal in part with municipal organisation, Dennison took the view that this implied an attempt by the municipal authorities to control the Guild rather than acceptance of control by the Guild. Though the early structures might be somewhat confusing, it is without doubt that throughout the early modern period, the merchants of the Guild were firmly intertwined with the town council.[145]

By the early modern period, most of the larger royal burghs had a merchant guild, which helped differentiate the upper echelons of the burgess community. Guildry was a step above mere burgess ship. To be a member of the Guild implied wealth and influence.[146] A 1467 act of parliament stated that brethren of the Guild were to be 'famous and worshipful', implying a level of honour and piety befitting the leaders of burgh society and the public face of Scotland's international trade.[147]

A statute from the *Leges Burgorum*, entitled 'Of thaim that may nocht be in the gylde', declares that fleshers, litsters (dyers), or soutars (shoemakers) were not allowed in the Guild unless they forswore to not practise their trade with their own hands, but instead 'wyth servandis under hym'.[148] Though only certain trades were mentioned, legislation against working with one's hands was often repeated in relation to the Guild. To join was therefore to become a merchant, who could employ others to make things, but was to disdain the dirtying of their own hands.

In theory only guild brethren had the right to trade abroad, or 'use merchandise', but in reality this was very difficult to enforce. Several inland burghs like Edinburgh relied on port facilities at some distance from their actual towns. What the port of Leith was to Edinburgh, so Aberlady was to Haddington, which no doubt made it more challenging to keep track of just who was using merchandise. It seems that many craftsmen, who either sought raw materials direct from the source, or wished to export their goods, were attempting to bypass the merchant middlemen. In response to this, parliament passed legislation in 1467, '. . . that na man of craft use merchandise be himself, his factouris or servandis, bot gif he lefe and renunce his craft . . .'[149] If the craftsman were to join the Guild and renounce his craft, then all would be well with his mercantile activities, but to do this one needed the resources and connections to join the exclusive merchant body. Apparently, many craftsmen simply ignored the act of parliament, as by 1500 the council books recorded both a judgment of the Court of the Four Burghs and a further affirmation from the king regarding the same issue. The former bemoaned 'craftismen vsand merchandice within the borrowis', and reaffirmed the 1467 parliamentary legislation, while the latter gave the king's affirmation.[150] Hence we see that craftsmen were not to act as merchants, though some clearly continued to do so.

This difference between the accepted activities of merchants and craftsmen must have done much to inflame the rivalries. Merchant honour was partly predicated on clean hands, which appears to have been in emulation of the nobility who did not labour. Just as merchants were seeking landed estates, they too sought gentility through carefully defined commercial activities. In such a context, it was important for the merchant elite to exclude those who did not reinforce such ideals about merchant standing. Before the decreet arbitral it was much less common for craftsmen to meet this stringent code, though some craftsmen did manage to make the transition to 'brother of the Guild'. Even after 1583 there were still careful rules about acceptable activities for not only the guildry, but for their families and households as well. On 1 March 1587–8, the skinner Robert Vernour was made guild brother providing that he bound and obliged himself:

> to obserue and keip the lawes and consuetudes of burgh concerning the gild brether thairof, and to desist and ceis fra all tred and occupatioun in his awin persoun that is nocht comely and decent for the rank and honesty of ane gild brother, and that his wyfe and seruands sall vse and exerce na poynt of commoun cwikry[151] outwith his awin hous, and namely that thai sall nocht sell nor cary any meitt dishes or courses throw the toun to priuat chalmers, hostillare howssis, or ony vther pairt owtwith his awin howse, vnder quhatsumeiur cullour or pretense, nor pas to brydellis or bankets within or without this burgh to vse the occupatioun of commoun cuikry, or yitt be sene in the streits with thair aiprunes and seruiets as commoun cuikis and thair seruands vses to do; and that vnder the payne of tynsall of his liberty and fredome of ane gild brother without all favour for evir.[152]

As a brother of the Guild, Vernour and his entire household were expected to conform to guild expectations, and this touched on all aspects of their household economy.

As the 1583 decreet arbitral made it clear that craftsmen were to have access to the Guild, it became more difficult to enforce the class aspirations of the merchant elite, especially as corporate privileges were challenged in the seventeenth century. After the Restoration, the council noted bitterly the much more liberal granting of freedom which they had been forced to undertake during the Cromwellian protectorate:

> Seeing, praised be God, we ar delyvered from the yok of bondage wnder the late tyranous vsurpatioun, which laid a kynd of necessitie upon the magistratts and counsell to be somewhat profuselie prodigall in creatting burgesses and conferring gild tickets, some expedient would be thoght wpon be the magistrats and counsell for hedging wp of that priviledge of gildrie, that the vulgar throng may not find so easie accesse, and even these who have right be birth or service according to the true meaning of the sett, efter exact tryell, be not found a persone of competent estate and sufficientlie qualified with congruous endowmentis, that they be not capable of admissioun, for even efter passing all these previous tryells they of old tymes wer admitted, so highlie did they pryse and of such golden worth did they esteem that soveraigne cittie priviledge the gildship . . .[153]

This 'vulgar throng' challenged not only their control of trade, but their sense of honour and rank as well.

Despite the 1583 sett giving greater access for craftsmen to both burgh government and to the merchant guild, there were still attempts to retain clear definitions between merchants and craftsmen. In 1634 the council used a letter from the king to insist that all men on the leets for deacons had to be practising craftsmen, which had implications for their council roles, as they would not be merchants.[154] On the other hand, they might still pursue merchant-type activities by joining the Guild, as council legislation from 1585 made it clear that both practising and non-practising craftsmen could attain guildry. The distinction between them was about wealth. Merchants were only to join the Guild if they had at least 1,000 merks in moveable goods. Craftsmen who continued to pursue their craft had to be worth 500 merks, but those not using their craft were to be worth 1,000 merks, just like the merchants.[155]

The Incorporation of Mary's Chapel certainly had reason to join the Guild, as the profit of the middlemen on timber, glass and other necessary raw materials could be quite considerable when it came to a product as large as a building, but building solid relations with the body which controlled importation was only one facet. Indeed, there were other aspects of the Guild which had an impact on the craftsmen of Mary's Chapel. Possibly the most important was the institution of the 'dean of guild court', which was presided over by the dean of guild.

The office of dean of guild was a very old part of the municipal government. The title, 'dean', was borrowed from the hierarchy of the church, where the dean was over the chapter, demonstrating the pre-Reformation religious functions of the Guild.[156] Long before the merchants were given a seal of cause and their own altar in St Giles kirk, the deans of guild had wielded influence in the burgh.[157] As the head of the merchant guild, the oversight over merchandise was naturally part of their remit, but over time several other functions came under the jurisdiction of the dean of guild court.[158]

The dean of guild's court, or occasionally 'council', was to consist of an equal number of merchants and craftsmen to the number of six persons.[159] As the 1583 decreet arbitral brought more craftsmen into the Guild, it also allowed craft representation on this influential municipal body. The remit of this group was indeed far reaching. In 1593 the by-laws of the Guild court were ratified by parliament, as based on fifteen 'articles', which had been drawn up nearly a decade before, in the year following the decreet arbitral.[160] By these articles, the dean of guild and his court were recognised as having jurisdiction over various issues affecting the burgh community.

First to be listed were 'questions of neighbourhood', referring to the dean of guild's right to stop building works. The court was to hear and adjudicate on the complaints given in between neighbours about their built environment.[161] Wood's discussion of the earliest volume of the dean of guild court's 'Nichborheid buik' reveals the business related to this aspect of their jurisdiction, as the court arbitrated over issues of encroachment on public space; failure to maintain properties; building works which restricted access to backlands; drainage; middens; blocked sunlight; and many other such potential conflicts in an increasingly congested urban environment.[162] While the court was really concerned with the customers, rather than those undertaking the building work, it is still apparent how this particular remit might have affected the work of the building tradesmen. Indeed, after corporate privileges were abolished in the mid-nineteenth century, the building regulation and town planning aspects of the dean of guild court were retained.[163]

Other aspects of the dean of guild court's remit had a potential impact on the Incorporation. As ratified in 1593, the court was also tasked with pursuing unfreemen, which might have been a source of common cause with the tradesmen.[164] As they also were responsible for all apprenticeship bookings and the granting of burgesship and guildry, there was no guarantee that the dean of guild would necessarily be an ally in matters of freedom.[165]

The dean of guild court was also to 'oversee and reform the mets and measures, great and small, of pint and quart, peck and firlot, of all sorts'.[166] This would have covered the gallon and chopin measures so crucial to the work of the coopers.[167] Though commonly thought to be a shape of vessel, the 'barrel' was actually a specific capacity, as with 'tun' or 'hogshead'.[168] As these were the usual method of packing and transporting goods, the coopers were obliged to make accurate casks to ensure that both seller and purchaser received a fair deal.

The dean of guild's remit gave authority over 'all questions of compt and reckoning anent merchandise', that might happen to arise between guild brothers.[169] An extension of this was their authority to freight all outgoing and incoming ships, giving direct control over all aspects of foreign trade.[170] The remaining articles and by-laws deal with enforcement of parliamentary statutes, taxation, and administration.

While previously the dean of guild court would have effectively excluded most craft involvement, after the decreet arbital more craftsmen could join the Guild and therefore participate in foreign trade.[171] With half of the court expected to be craftsmen, the building trades might have had more input into the decisions of the dean of guild, though clearly there was also potential for conflict when a decision of the court was contrary to the wishes of the building trades. It is known from nineteenth-century lists of the dean of guild court that in the 1830s it was quite common for 'builders' or 'masons' to make up the craft half of the dean's court, though how common this was in the early modern period is not clear.[172] There were certainly protests in the seventeenth century against certain arts of Mary's Chapel being allowed to sit on the dean of guild's council. In 1673, when relations between the ten arts were less than amicable, several deacons of the wrights and of the masons protested against the slater, Andrew Cassie, being on the council.[173]

Clearly the remit of the dean of guild could be somewhat controversial, as it could interfere with the agendas of the Incorporation's members. Though the Incorporation would have liked to have had the final say as to who could work in their arts and who could not, it was actually the dean of guild and his court who controlled legal access to the labour market.[174] Although the craftsmen relied on imports for much of its raw materials, foreign trade was the prerogative of the Guild; not the Incorporation. As imported timber was 'merchandise', the council was responsible for pricing this commodity,[175] and therefore it was the council which controlled the timber market, or 'timber bourse', down at Leith.[176]

When relations between the Incorporation and the municipal authorities were good, there could be favourable legislation ensuring access to timber, as with the 1554 ordinance that when timber was landed at Leith, a part of it was to be delivered, 'of the tounis pryce to the brether of the wrichtis and cowperis be yair maister of wark for the tyme that thay may wyrk the samine The biggaris within the burgh for the tyme beand served with yaim of the said pryce'.[177] Did this extend to all of the Incorporation? Or was it only to those working on municipal contracts? The 'biggars', or builders, certainly seems to be general rather than specific. Either way, there are examples of the Incorporation securing bargains of timber for its own members, which suggests that corporate action was one strategy for negotiating a volatile market for necessary materials.[178] As will be seen, others simply took on the role of merchant.

Still, such control over imports affected not only the raw materials, but also the products which were produced. The council intervened in 1618 to forbid the use of oak for 'deid kists', or coffins.[179] Little is said about why this was enacted, but perhaps, as most oak was imported, it was deemed an immodest use of the precious material. Occasionally the use of such imports was regulated, though how long such a statute was observed is difficult to know.

The subsequent impact on products highlights an important point about Grant's three aspects of municipal government which caused conflict, in that it was not just foreign trade that proved controversial. The council also interfered with domestic trade. In part, this was due to the fact that urban markets were taxed to provide revenue for the crown, and therefore the physical market place needed to be regulated. The Incorporation had an important role in this, as they were to act as searchers in the markets to ensure sufficiency of products for the crown's lieges. While the crafts looked to quality, the other aspects of the markets were regulated by the council, such as ensuring equal access to commodities, or that the laws about when and where goods were to be sold were obeyed.

Despite the richness of the records for Edinburgh, surprisingly little is known about the mechanics of the markets for the trades of Mary's Chapel. More is known about the *general* regulation of open-air markets in the capital. From a very early period we can see evidence of formally-regulated and taxed markets firmly centred within the jurisdiction of Edinburgh. When David I (1124–53) granted the Abbey of Holyrood the right to have a burgh, which became the 'Canongate', it was stipulated that they were to use Edinburgh's markets. The charter therefore mentioned the 'common right of selling their wares, and of buying, in my market', as well as the canons being 'quit of claim and custom in like manner as my own burgesses' in Edinburgh.[180] Markets and market tolls were clearly established well before William the Lion (1165–1214) decreed that all merchandise had to be presented 'at the mercat and mercat croce of burghis', demonstrating a fair degree of inherited regulation from the medieval period.[181]

The 1633 ratification of the seals of cause mentions a Monday market for unfreemen to sell their wares, as well as sworn visitors to ensure quality:

> And that also to inhibit all persounes duelling within thrie mylles of this burgh frome bringing in anye of thair said worke . . . bot upone the Mononday allanerlie which they salbe haldin to present first to the commoun mercatt in mercatt tyme to the effect the samin may be visited be the suorne visitouris to be apointed to that effect whither the same be sufficient or nott that his Ma. liedges be nott thairby dissavit and prejudged under payne of conficatioun of all such worke as they salbe fund working or setting up or fund bringing in af the said mercatt day the one halff thairof to the use of the guid toun and the uther to be applyed for the sustentatioun of the poore of the craft . . .[182]

While the 1475 seal of cause stipulated that the Incorporation was to 'serche and se all wirkis',[183] by 1633 the punishment of offenders was explicitly 'at the discretioun of the Magistrattis', though fines were to be split between the crafts and the council.[184]

Later in the seventeenth century Edinburgh appears to have had several market places, all on a Wednesday, for all wright and mason work, including that of the other ten crafts, such as sievewrights and coopers.[185] Just how specialised these markets were is difficult to surmise. Were finished products sold alongside raw timber? Other burghs could have very specific markets, such as the 'cart market' and 'cooper market' at Elgin.[186] Though the mechanics of the markets pertaining to Mary's Chapel are not as clear as one would like, the role of the council in regulation is much more apparent.

Occasionally municipal legislation tackled perceived problems of quality, as with the 1658 demand by the council that the wrights stop using 'vycenaillis' in coffins, as they were damaging the mortcloths.[187] While the fifteenth-century charters had implied a degree of self-regulation through the institution of the essay as a test of the sufficiency of the incoming craftsmen's skills, the increased roll of craftsmen on the council made it much more difficult to argue with council interference in product regulation. Though portable goods such as casks, sieves or ploughs might have been brought to the Wednesday market, where visitors could easily assess their quality, larger-scale buildings were not quite as easy to regulate.

For some aspects of domestic trade, such as the lucrative public contracts, the council simply ignored the Incorporation and took their own craft specialists for municipal works. These craftsmen were known as the 'town's masters'. By 1646, Edinburgh had a town glazier, a town mason, a town wright and a town plumber.[188] Some of these public contracts went to freemen of the Incorporation, as in 1554 when Andro Mansion was pensioned and obliged to serve the town in its works.[189] Others were given out to men who were not even burgesses. Alexander Miller and his son Andrew, who were calsaylayers, or paviours (someone who lays paving stones or cobbles), were given a lifetime tack of the duties on shod carts and coaches payable to the town in return for maintaining the capital's streets.[190] Within a fortnight of the act of council setting them in the town's employment, both were given burgesship, though neither appears to have joined the Incorporation.[191]

A similar situation was seen with the town's wells, as Thomas Dods, plumber, was engaged in 1631 to maintain the well pumps, though it was found in 1670 by the Court of Session that plumbers were not one of the trades of the Incorporation until after 1646.[192] When the town needed a millwright in 1595, it was not to a master of the Incorporation they turned, but instead to William Lyntoun in Dalkeith.[193] These last two are important examples, as sometimes there were technological considerations which had to outweigh existing corporate privileges. This was perhaps less of an issue in the later eighteenth century, when the Incorporation issued a remonstrance to the provost, magistrates and town council over the employment of unfree masons on the pier at Leith.[194]

While the council or the dean of guild court might have prioritised the common well over corporate privileges in public contracts, such considerations could also be extended to the private contracts of the Incorporation as well. The dean of guild's oversight of issues relating to 'neighbourhood' gave a form of veto to the continuation of building works when they proved controversial in any way. By the later seventeenth century, the danger of fire meant that demands were being made by the burgh authorities about what materials were being used in building projects, which helped bring about a shift from timber to stone and from thatch to slate.[195] By prioritising certain building materials, the dean of guild was effectively influencing the work of the building site, and it is therefore quite interesting that relations between the ten arts of the Incorporation saw such strain in the last three decades of the seventeenth century.[196]

Hence the influence of the council over trade was not only relevant to importation and exportation. These aspects were crucially important for the supply of certain building materials, but they also had an impact on more localised trade. In part this was due to the influence of municipal bodies, such as the dean of guild court, which touched not only on trade, but also on issues of labour, building regulations, and the choice of materials. Though the Incorporation was more involved after 1583, this is not to say that they as a corporate entity had any more autonomy. Using Grant's third point of conflict – price setting – this will hopefully become clearer.

Regulation of Prices

As well as political control, town councils were also supposedly responsible for overseeing the economic regulation of the burgh's inhabitants. From at least the 1100s these economic activities were both protected and constrained by the *Leges Burgorum*.[197] This legal basis for economic activity was usually predicated on the concept of the 'commonweal', though corporate privileges and outside influences often complicated matters. The provost, bailies and town council sought to oversee municipal affairs, but as Edinburgh rose to prominence in the medieval period with the loss of Berwick, and became the capital by the reign of James III, parliament, court and crown were often in residence, making for a rather influential customer base. This further complicated municipal regulation, as the special interests of council, crafts, court and crown were not always in alignment.

The differing interests added complexity to the economic relationship between regulator, producer and customer. By 1426 parliament made an act which gave oversight of pricing to town councils, who were expected to bring into consideration all relevant factors.[198] The price of materials as well as the cost of labour, or 'travale', were to be taken into account, and the final cost was to be publicised, whether for bread or for building.

Being that the council already regulated their own markets, while the bailies ensured taxation was collected, it made sense for the council to also oversee prices. Still, it was a complex business, often requiring the specialist knowledge of producers, and often leaving either customer or producer short-changed.[199] As with many aspects of the commonweal, trying to set accurate prices which allowed an acceptable profit to the producer above the ever-fluctuating costs of materials and labour, was a difficult balance to achieve. Indeed, the right balance was often not achieved, which brought the dangers of either one group or another being unhappy with the municipal leadership.

Baxters and fleshers are known to have protested what they perceived as unfair prices set at the annual assizes, which occasionally bordered on riots.[200] Such tensions no doubt ebbed and flowed, though it is worth remembering that the first century and a half of corporatism in Edinburgh coincided with what some historians refer to as the 'Price Revolution', when the debasement of the nation's coinage, amongst other factors, such

as population increase, pestilence and famine, contributed to severe inflation across a range of daily necessities.[201] Though prices of foodstuffs in
the capital were indeed rising,[202] Lythe has suggested that the 'top-grade'
craftsmen also saw a three-fold increase in their wages, suggesting that the
craft aristocracy was better placed for weathering the economic storm.[203]
What percentage of the craftsmen of Mary's Chapel enjoyed such a rise in
wages is difficult to say with any authority, but the fact that they held a
stake in prices through the period is clear.

The 1426 parliamentary grant of the right and obligation to set prices
of materials and labour for craftsmen was reaffirmed in 1551, which highlights the fact that the council's prerogative was occasionally usurped,
either by the Incorporation or by individuals.[204] In fact, throughout the
early modern period the council had to reassert its role in setting prices at
several points. Complaints were made to the parliament about craftsmen
charging exorbitant prices for their work in 1540.[205] Similar complaints
were made by the baxters to the council in 1577, over the high price of
building an oven,[206] and in 1610, which led to weekly rates for masters
and servants being specifically laid out.[207] Despite this reassertion of prerogative over prices, acts were made by the Incorporation in 1671 about
wages for journeymen[208] and prices to be given to turners and sawers for
their work.[209] Similar examples can be found in the eighteenth century as
well, suggesting rather patchy observance of the 1426 act across the early
modern period.[210]

Whilst there was no annual assize on building materials, as there was for
bread, ale or tallow, it is doubtful that the headship of the Incorporation
would have welcomed such continuous interference. It is clear that the
deacons of the Incorporation often chose to disregard the council's prerogative over pricing, but just how the craftsmen of the building trades felt about
a merchant-dominated council imposing prices and setting wages is not fully
known. In the 1690s, when corporate unity appears to have been at a low
point, one disgruntled master wright was less than enamoured with the two
recently-elected deacons. John Hislop therefore used the 1426 legislation on
prices as leverage. A complaint was made about the election leets in 1691,
citing an act of the Incorporation made by the two deacons in question
setting out their own prices for the Incorporation's work. As this was contrary to the 1426 act of parliament, the council responded by ordering the
act to be struck from the Incorporation's books.[211] How relations between
Hislop and the two deacons fared is not clear, though the incident does
betray a lack of unity in pricing strategy even within the Incorporation itself.

There is evidence that the council sought expert advice on prices in
certain situations. When James Smith, slater, was made burgess by act of

council in 1652, 'for old dews', it was stated that they would 'agree with him for a settled price of the rood of his worke'.[212] Such negotiation was not common, though, and perhaps has more to do with council contracts than with the autonomy of the crafts themselves.

Although parliament decreed and later affirmed the right of the council to set prices, the records would seem to indicate that they failed to keep up-to-date prices. Indeed, few councillors would have had the expertise on building operations to keep up an effective pricing strategy, so throughout the early modern period examples of disregard for the parliamentary legislation are clearly visible. By the nineteenth century it was recognised that these laws were ineffective. In 1813 an act of parliament repealed the previous legislation and removed the right of 'magistrates of cities and burghs to rate wages or fix prices for work of artificers, labourers, and craftsmen'.[213] Perhaps this was not truly a free market, but there was at least a recognition of market forces in the equations dealt with on a daily basis by the building trades.

FROM CONFLICT TO PARTNERSHIP? THE INCORPORATION'S GUILDRY

Masters, Burgesses and Brethren of the Guild

From 1406, when the first recorded burgess was listed in the official rolls, to 1583, when the decreet arbitral revised the rules about access, very few craftsmen were accepted into the elite body of merchants known as the Guild. In terms of the building trades, only nine burgesses of the relevant trades were able to become brethren of the Guild (see Table 4.1).[214] Of these, four were masons, three were wrights, and two were glaziers. From 1583 to the arbitrarily-picked date of 1650,[215] forty-four such tradesmen took up guildry. Of these, the wrights had the most, at seventeen, and the bowers second most, at eight, suggesting the importance of the timber trade in terms of the building trades entering the Guild.

Some of the Incorporation's trades appear to have benefitted fairly dramatically from the 1583 decreet arbitral; others saw little change. As seen in Table 4.1, the painters and plumbers saw only a single member each joining the Guild before 1650, while the sievewrights and uphoslsterers had none. The slaters and coopers saw only two members each, while the masons and glaziers were not far behind the bowers.

Guildry attainment for the trades represented by the Incorporation of Masons and Wrights clearly grew in the short term, at least for most of the ten arts, though the longer term trends are perhaps even more telling. As

Table 4.1 Entrants as Guild Brethren

	Before 1583 Decreet Arbitral	After, to 1650
Masons	4	6
Wrights	3	17
Coopers	0	2
Bowers	0	8
Glaziers	2	7
Painters	0	1
Slaters	0	2
Plumbers	0	1
Sievewrights	0	0
Upholsterers	0	0
Total	9	44

Numbers are by trade for the period before the 1583 decreet arbitral, and for the period after, up to 1650. Data taken from *Edin. Burgs*, 1406–1760.

with other data taken from the burgess and guildry rolls for earlier chapters, the data is based on Watson's first two published volumes of the rolls, and therefore only covers the period from 1406 to 1760.[216] Table 4.2 looks at all burgess and guildry entrants for the ten trades of the Incorporation. Though being a burgess and guild brother was separate from being a master of the Incorporation, these numbers should be fairly close, and therefore they give a rough estimate of how many masters were accepted into the Guild. Imprecise as this may be, the broad trends are apparent.

In terms of the longer trends, there are some substantial problems with the very-early numbers and the eighteenth-century numbers. The fifteenth- and sixteenth-century rolls do not appear to be complete, as explained in the earlier chapters, while the eighteenth-century data ends forty years before the end of the century. Still, the trend of growth is apparent, even with a few potentially missing names, so as a very rough index the data still has much to tell us.

As seen in Table 4.2, out of 1,295 burgess entrants from the trades represented by the Incorporation of Mary's Chapel from 1406 to 1760, 273 also attained membership of the Guild, or 21 per cent. As demonstrated above, most of these guild entrants were after the 1583 decreet arbitral. No entrants to the guildry were listed for the fifteenth century, while only 13 per cent of burgesses from the building trades took guildry in the sixteenth century. By the seventeenth century, 22 per cent joined the Guild, whilst the first sixty years of the eighteenth century showed a similar percentage. These figures are nearly double that of the preceding sixteenth century. At no time in the available records were guild brethren in the majority, speaking to the exclusiveness of the affluent merchant body.

Table 4.2 Burgesship and Guildry Entrants for the Crafts of Mary's Chapel

	1400s	1500s	1600s	1700s (to 1760)	Totals
Masons	1 / 0 (0% G)	55 / 5 (9% G)	131 / 26 (20% G)	64 / 14 (22% G)	251 / 45 (18% G)
Wrights	3 / 0 (0% G)	44 / 5 (11% G)	313 / 89 (28% G)	225 / 54 (24% G)	585 / 148 (25% G)
Coopers	0 / 0 (0% G)	20 / 2 (10% G)	55 / 7 (13% G)	42 / 11 (26% G)	117 / 20 (17% G)
Bowers	0 / 0 (0% G)	12 / 3 (15% G)	24 / 5 (21% G)	3 / 0 (0% G)	39 / 8 (21% G)
Glaziers	1 / 0 (0% G)	14 / 6 (43% G)	45 / 4 (9% G)	41 / 6 (15% G)	101 / 16 (16% G)
Painters	0 / 0 (0% G)	4 / 0 (0% G)	39 / 9 (23% G)	46 / 12 (26% G)	89 / 21 (24% G)
Slaters	0 / 0 (0% G)	13 / 0 (0% G)	36 / 8 (22% G)	19 / 3 (16% G)	68 / 11 (16% G)
Plumbers	0 / 0 (0% G)	0 / 0 (0% G)	11 / 1 (9% G)	9 / 1 (11% G)	20 / 2 (10% G)
Sievewrights	0 / 0 (0% G)	0 / 0 (0% G)	11 / 0 (0% G)	2 / 0 (0% G)	13 / 0 (0% G)
Upholsterers	0 / 0 (0% G)	0 / 0 (0% G)	5 / 0 (0% G)	7 / 2 (29% G)	12 / 2 (17% G)
Totals	5 / 0 (0% G)	162 / 21 (13% G)	670 / 149 (22% G)	458 / 103 (22% G)	1,295 / 273 (21% G)

The data for each century is presented in the following format: *Number of Burgesses / Number of Guildry (percentage of Burgesses to attain Guildry)*. Note: The data for this table comes from the *Edinburgh Burgess Rolls*, and therefore is independent of the Incorporation. It represents the numbers of craftsmen who attained freedom of the town (burgesship) and freedom of the town's Guild, which allowed one to trade abroad. *Edin. Burgs*, 1406–1760.

The two senior arts of the masons and wrights show fairly substantial growth in guild-brethrenship. From none in the fifteenth century, the masons rose to 9 per cent in the sixteenth century, and 20 per cent in the seventeenth century. The wrights were even more dramatic, going from none to 11 per cent, and then to 28 per cent in the same time frame. This contrasts markedly with the more humble arts, such as the sieve-wrights, which saw not a single guild entrant over the period. Intriguingly, the upholsterers, which had need of expensive cloth, saw only two guild entrants over the period.

Here we see another form of hierarchy, which no doubt reflected on the Incorporation as well as the burgess and guildry communities. In terms of percentages of guild entrants across the 1406–1760 period, the wrights saw the highest figure of 25 per cent of its burgesses, whilst the painters were second, with 24 per cent. Third, were the bowers, at 21 per cent, followed by the masons at 18 per cent of its members. The coopers and upholsterers, were next at about 17 per cent each, followed by the glaziers and slaters at 16 per cent. Finally, the plumbers trailed at 10 per cent of their members.

Looking at change, perhaps the glaziers are most striking. In the sixteenth century, more glaziers took guildry than any other art represented by Mary's Chapel. While only 11 per cent of wrights joined the Guild in that century, 43 per cent of the glaziers joined. In the seventeenth century, however, the percentage for the glaziers dropped to 9 per cent, reflecting the changes in the market for glass. Previously, glass had been an import, but by 1610 glass was being made in Scotland.[217] Just over a decade later in 1621, the Privy Council legislated against all imports of glass in an attempt to become self-sufficient for glass production.[218] How successful the ban was is difficult to say, though it would appear to have had a drastic impact on glaziers entering the merchant guild.[219]

Although there are problems with the figures in Tables 4.1 and 4.2, as the burgess entrants were not necessarily identical to the freemen of the Incorporation, the data still works as a rough guide, due to sufficient overlap. Hence we can find meaning in the figures in several important areas. First of all, in terms of the craft aristocracy, guildry was clearly a crucial aspect. The masons and wrights saw the most benefit in terms of shear numbers of craftsmen becoming guild brethren with forty-five and 148 respectively. This reflects the wider trend of political and administrative access described in the first chapter. It also shows differentiation within a particular art, no matter how senior. Only 25 per cent of wrights and only 18 per cent of masons were in the Guild, so even within these privileged senior trades there was a clear hierarchy.

In terms of economy and trade, it would appear that certain arts had greater reliance on foreign materials. The top five arts in terms of actual numbers of guild brethren were the wrights, at 148; the masons, at forty-five; the painters, at twenty-one; the coopers, at twenty; and the glaziers, at sixteen guild entrants. Here we see a potential reflection of the importance of the timber trade, as well as the components for paints and the (declining) appetite for imported glass.[220] While importation of such merchandise had once been the prerogative of merchants, after 1583 we see craftsmen joining them through the Guild. Indeed, we even have evidence of the Incorporation taking an interest in ship-ownership through a 1616 legal battle over the equal half of a bark or crayer called the 'Robert'.[221]

By the eighteenth century, we also have evidence of the importation of ready-made parts. Arnot, in his history of Edinburgh, included a list of imports around the year 1778. From Norway came a range of woods and wooden wares, including oak spokes for cartwheels, wooden hoops for coopers, and sieve rims for sievemakers.[222] Intriguingly, the coopers decreased in number of burgesses from the seventeenth century into the first part of the eighteenth, but they increased in the number of guild brethren, making for a higher percentage of coopers with access to foreign trade. Were they becoming more reliant on imported components? Perhaps they were involved in export, and not just as the trade that made the containers? According to Arnot, various other types of timber and wooden parts were available from around the globe, demonstrating that both the raw materials and some component parts were available for the woodworkers of Edinburgh.

For some, guildry meant more than just political representation or access to the importation of raw materials; for some it meant diversification. Donald Baine, bower burgess and guild brother from 1632,[223] was listed in 1636 as owning property in the affluent north-east quarter worth £317 6s 8d. He also paid a further £100 in rent for additional property, making for a long list of chambers and houses which he apparently occupied himself. As owner-occupier, he had a high fore chamber; a turnpike house; three additional fore chambers; a cellar; a low house; and a yard with archery butts. Further to these he apparently occupied, but did not own, a high house; a high fore booth; and a low fore tavern.[224] Guildry would have given him access to the importation of wine for his tavern, which also might have facilitated the rental of the various chambers as an innkeeper.[225] Guildry clearly went with wealth, as his 'mails' or rental-levels were well above the £41 average for the town,[226] but perhaps it also facilitated a more diversified occupational portfolio. The archery butts suggest the testing of the products made either by him or his employees, while the tavern suggests a secondary occupation, quite possibly reliant on imported wine.

By comparing entrants to the Guild with entrants to mere burgesship, a range of aspects are illuminated. Hierarchy, whether political or social, is clear, giving us further insight into the craft aristocracy within the building trades. The proclivity of certain materials is suggested, reinforcing previous work on imported raw materials, and highlighting what cannot be seen in terms of an export market for those craftsmen who focussed on the built environment. Wealth and occupational diversity, especially in terms of secondary occupations, are also visible, though any conclusions must be approached carefully. The data represents not the Incorporation itself, but the overlapping institutions of burgesship and guildry. However, in light of the heavy involvement of the council in Incorporation affairs, which this chapter has sought to explore, this overlap between municipal and corporate membership proves to be particularly significant.

CONCLUSION

This brings us back to our introductory questions and the test of Grant's three points of conflict between craftsmen and the town council. Throughout the broad period covered by this study, there are many examples of conflict between what was perceived as the merchants on one side and the crafts on the other. While it has been demonstrated that such simplistic terms as 'merchant' and 'craftsman' do not accurately represent the diverse and hierarchical groups involved, there can be little doubt that such broad brushstrokes were useful to contemporaries. Whilst the convenery was happy to label the town council as 'the merchanddis' when they were not supporting their claim against suburban competition,[227] there were also craftsmen who embraced the label 'merchant' and joined the merchant guild, though perhaps more so after the burgh's constitution, or 'sett', was revised in 1583. But should this be seen as a transition from conflict to partnership? Broadly speaking, yes – but only when it suited the parties involved.

Using Grant's three causes of tension between crafts and councils in Scotland's burghs, which were: participation in government; participation in foreign trade; and the setting of prices,[228] we can see that the relations between the Incorporation of Mary's Chapel and the town council of Scotland's capital were highly characterised by self-interest. When it suited them to work together, as in the defence of commonly-held corporate privileges, there was a great deal of partnership. Other times saw clear divisions, but at all times there was an increasing importance put on the legal framework of the carefully defined, and often refined, burgh laws. But how long could this last?

NOTES

1. This quadrangular structure is the present-day Edinburgh City Chambers, home to the Edinburgh City Archives.
2. Laing, D., 'Note respecting the Royal Exchange, Edinburgh, and the Original List of Subscribers in 1752', in *Proceedings of the Society of Antiquaries of Scotland*, 4 (1860–2), 597.
3. Ibid., 597.
4. Ibid., 593.
5. Fraser, W. H., *Conflict and Class: Scottish Workers, 1700–1838* (Edinburgh: John Donald, 1988), 17.
6. For an account of the affair, see Smith, J., *The Hammermen of Edinburgh and Their Altar in St Giles Church* (Edinburgh: William J. Hay, 1906), lxxxii–lxxxiv.
7. Smith, and Ritchie, P. E., *Mary of Guise in Scotland, 1548–1560* (East Linton: Tuckwell Press, 2002), 131–2. The Incorporation had to pay £50 as their part of the apparent total of £1,000 promised to the queen. ECA, Mill Recs, B2, f3r: '. . . ye extent of L lib ptenand to y pt of ye sowme of jm lib . . .' Note that this differs with other accounts of the total equalling 4,000 merks, as in Lynch, *Edinburgh and the Reformation*, 71, and Ritchie, *Mary of Guise in Scotland*, 132, or of the total equalling £168 13s 4d, as given by Smith in reference to the Hammermen's payment of £38 6s. Smith, *Hammermen of Edinburgh*, xc. Perhaps the £1,000 was Edinburgh's contribution? More work is needed on the background and meaning of this notorious episode, though it is clear that as Lynch has argued, the queen was exploiting burgh tensions. Lynch, *Edinburgh and the Reformation*, 71–2.
8. Munro, J. and Fothringham, H. S. (eds), *Act Book of the Convenery of Deacons of the Trades of Edinburgh 1577–1755*, vol. 1 (Edinburgh: Scottish Record Society, 2011), ix–xi.
9. Colston, J., *The Incorporated Trades of Edinburgh* (Edinburgh: Colston & Co., 1891), xliv–xlvi. The 1583 decreet arbitral contains a clause against conventions of either merchants or craft deacons. *Edin. Recs*, 1573–1589, 270. A cursory survey of the indices from the published *Extracts* suggests that after this 1583 clause, the deacon convener was not even mentioned in the council records until the later seventeenth century. *Edin. Recs*, 1681–1689, 120. See also Lynch, *Edinburgh and the Reformation*, 61.
10. For more on the 1583 decreet arbitral, or the burgh 'sett', see Lynch, *Edinburgh and the Reformation*, 14–17 and 60–2, and Calderwood, D., *The History of the Kirk of Scotland* (Edinburgh: Wodrow Society, 1843), 635–6 and 698–9.
11. Lamond, R., 'The Scottish Craft Gild as a Religious Fraternity', in *The*

Scottish Historical Review, 16:63 (1919), 202 and Lynch, M., 'Social and Economic Structure of the Larger Towns, 1450–1600', in Lynch, M., Spearman, M. and Stell, G. (eds), *The Scottish Medieval Town* (Edinburgh: John Donald, 1988), 264–5.

12. *Edin. Recs, 1573–1589*, 275: election of 14 May 1583. The remaining 'extraordinary' deacons from the fourteen trades, who were not formally part of the council, did occasionally figure in later council minutes. For an explanation of the 'ordinary' and 'extraordinary' deacons, and the two 'trades councillors', see ECA, Acc.622/8, 142, 11 July 1834.

13. *Edin. Recs, 1573–1589*, 266–7.

14. Ibid., 266–7 and 275.

15. Smith, *Hammermen of Edinburgh*, lxxix–lxxx.

16. Lamond, 'Scottish Craft Gild as a Religious Fraternity', 200–4. See also, Smith, *Hammermen of Edinburgh*, lxxx, and Grant, I. F., *The Social and Economic Development of Scotland Before 1603* (Edinburgh: Oliver and Boyd, 1930), 425–35.

17. Lynch, M., *Edinburgh and the Reformation* (Edinburgh: Edinburgh University Press, 1981), 5 and 9.

18. Lynch, M., 'Towns and Townspeople in Fifteenth-Century Scotland', in Thomson, A. F. (ed.), *Towns and Townspeople in the Fifteenth Century* (Gloucester: Alan Sutton, 1988), 174. For examples of proponents of the traditional stance which Lynch argued against, see Colston, *Incorporated Trades of Edinburgh*, xxxii–xxxiii; Mackenzie, W. M., *The Scottish Burghs* (Edinburgh: Oliver and Boyd, 1949), 114; and Johnston, T., *The History of the Working Classes in Scotland* (East Ardsley: EP Publishing Ltd, 1974), 133–9.

19. Grant, *Social and Economic Development of Scotland*, 382; Lynch, *Edinburgh and the Reformation*, Chapter 4; Lynch, 'Towns and Townspeople', 174–5; Lynch, M., 'Social and Economic Structure of the Larger Towns, 1450–1600', in Lynch, M., Spearman, M. and Stell, G. (eds), *The Scottish Medieval Town* (Edinburgh: John Donald, 1988), 264–5; and Lynch, M., 'Whatever Happened to the Medieval Burgh? Some Guidelines for Sixteenth and Seventeenth Century Historians', in *Scottish Economic & Social History*, 4:1 (1978), 12–13.

20. For contemporary examples see: Anonymous, *A Diurnal of Remarkable Occurents That Have Passed Within the Country of Scotland Since the Death of King James the Fourth Till the Year M.D.LXXV. From a Manuscript of the Sixteenth Century in the Possession of Sir John Maxwell of Pollock, Baronet.* (Edinburgh: Bannatyne Club, 1833), 347–8; James VI, *Basilikon Doron. Devided Into Three Bookes.* (Edinburgh: Robert Walde-graue, 1599), 59–62; and Calderwood, *History of the Kirk of Scotland*, 635–6 and 698–9.

21. *Edin. Burgs, 1406–1700*, 179.

22. The 'Guild', or the 'guildry', was the corporate body of merchants in a

Scottish burgh, as opposed to the 'incorporated trades', which are often called 'craft guilds' in modern usage. Throughout this chapter, 'guild' refers to the exclusive merchant body, while 'trade' refers to the crafts.

23. *Edin. Burgs*, 1406–1700, 148.
24. See Chapter 1.
25. Lauder of Fountainhall, Sir John, *Historical Notices of Scottish Affairs*, vol. 1, 1661–1683 (Edinburgh: T. Constable, 1848), 160.
26. Ibid., 96.
27. The 'merchanting' of the crafts is an aspect which needs further work, as there were certain caveats. For example, a 1661 act of parliament forbade tradesmen from importing and vending made work pertaining to their trade. *RPS*, 1661/1/388. Date accessed: 14 May 2015.
28. Lynch points out that Brechin had no organised crafts prior to the seventeenth century, while Dumfries had no guild. Lynch, *Edinburgh and the Reformation*, 51.
29. Munro and Fothringham, *Act Book of the Convenery*, vol. 1, 29.
30. Grant, *Social and Economic Development of Scotland*, 383.
31. Lynch, *Edinburgh and the Reformation*, 52–3.
32. *Edin. Burgs*, 1406–1700, 43.
33. *Edin. Burgs*, 1701–1760, 152.
34. NRS, CC8/8/16, Udwart, Mause, 1587, and *Edin. Burgs*, 1406–1700, 263.
35. NRS, CC8/8/16, Udwart, Mause, 1587, and *Edin. Burgs*, 1406–1700, 263.
36. Angus, W. (ed.), *Protocol Book of Mr. Gilbert Grote, 1552–1573* (Edinburgh: Scottish Record Society, 1914), 48.
37. Grant, I. F., *The Social and Economic Development of Scotland Before 1603* (Edinburgh: Oliver and Boyd, 1930), 424–5.
38. For a contemporary illustration, see the 1647 view of the capital by Gordon of Rothiemay, *Edinodunensis Tabulam*. This is available online through the National Library of Scotland's digital map collection at http://maps.nls.uk/towns/rec/211.
39. For more on suburbs and the distinctions between royal and non-royal burghs, see Allen, A., 'Conquering the Suburbs: Politics and Work in Early Modern Edinburgh', in *Journal of Urban History*, 37:3 (2011), 429–30.
40. For more on this sixteenth-century 'flight to the suburbs', see Lynch, M., 'Social and Economic Structure of the Larger Towns, 1450–1600', in Lynch, M., Spearman, M. and Stell, G. (eds), *The Scottish Medieval Town* (Edinburgh: John Donald, 1988), 276.
41. Ibid., Table 2, 274, and footnote 59, 284.
42. Knoop, D. and Jones, G. P., *The Scottish Mason and the Mason Word* (Manchester: Manchester University Press, 1939), 47–8. See also the details from the contract for Edinburgh mason, Alexander Nisbet, to build 'the Place', which was the 1663 manor house of Anstruther Easter. Included are prices and notes of comparative structures on which details of the house were to be modelled. While Anstruther Easter was a royal burgh, Nisbet still

took work within the town – and therefore outside of the capital. Gourlay, G., *Anstruther: Or Illustrations of Scottish Burgh Life* (Anstruther: George Gourlay, 1888), 16.

43. Lord Dreghorn, in a 1764 memorial relating to a court case about a deposed deacon of the masons who lived in the Canongate, argued that 'Non-residence is a Term of Ecclesiastical Extraction, being introduced by the Canon Law, to prevent Pluralitites, and oblige Clergymen to perform their Pastoral Duties.' The parallel was meant to show that the concept was irrelevant, as the deacon could separate the domestic chores from his work, just as he could separate home from work. Dreghorn, John Maclaurin, Lord, *Memorial for the United Incorporations of Mary's Chapel, and for Alexander Miller Glazier, deacon, duly elected by them, of the Incorporation of Masons, pursuers, against Alexander Nicolson, the pretended deacon of the said incorporation, and the magistrates and town-council of Edinburgh, and others, defenders*, (Edinburgh: s.n., 1764), 12–13.

44. *Edin. Burgs*, 1406–1700, 9, 12 and 16.

45. Ibid., 9.

46. Ibid., 164.

47. It is worth noting that part of the 'Head of the Canongate', which was the south side of the Canongate High Street to St John's Cross, was technically part of Edinburgh's liberties. Allen, A., and Spence, C., *Edinburgh Housemails Taxation Book, 1634–1636* (Woodbridge: Scottish History Society, 2014), xxii, and Dreghorn, *Memorial for the United Incorporations of Mary's Chapel . . .*, 1

48. *Edin. Recs*, 1681–1689, 261.

49. A blockmaker made wooden blocks for ships' rigging, or 'block and tackle'. ECA, SL34/1/2, 35, Charge: 27 October 1688 to 26 October 1689, and SL34/1/4, Charge: 20 September 1707 to 15 September 1709.

50. *Edin. Recs*, 1626–1641, 125. This was reiterated in 1677 regarding 'all sort of work in use to be wrought be the friemen members of the said Incorporatione within this Citie and priviledges thereof . . . viz. masson work, wright work, couper work, upholsterer work and other work that is propper to be wrought be the friemen of that Incorporatione of Mary Chapell . . .', unless it was sold only in the Wednesday market, and was subject to the Incorporation's quality controls. *Edin. Recs*, 1665–1680, 301–2. Perhaps the market stipulation was the loophole which perpetuated suburban work, though the legal complications of baronial- and regality-burgh status certainly made exclusion policies difficult to enforce.

51. Angus, W. (ed.), *Protocol Book of Mr. Gilbert Grote, 1552–1573* (Edinburgh: Scottish Record Society, 1914), 48.

52. In a 1630 stent roll (tax) for the burgh of Canongate is an entry for the 'Widow of Joshua Mansion'. She was listed at 200 merks, and apparently paid a tax of £7 10s. Wood, M. (ed.), *Book of Records of the Ancient Privileges of the Canongate* (Edinburgh: Scottish Record Society, 1956), 32.

Joshua Mansion was listed as deceased in 1623 in the burgess entry of his son-in-law, Thomas Hendrie. *Edin. Burgs*, 1406–1700, 247.

53. Dreghorn, *Memorial for the United Incorporations of Mary's Chapel . . .*, 1.

54. 17 November 1558: 'Memorandum narrating that Johnne Bargillo, son and heir of umquhile Thomas Bargillo, burgess of Glasgw, granted that he had received payment from Alane Roger, mason and burgess of Edinburgh, of all sums of money, goods, and gear, which he could claim from him before the date hereof, and specially for the tenement of land lying in the Briggait, on the north side of the city of Glasgw, which he sold to the said Alane; and discharged him thereof.' Angus, W. (ed.), *Protocol Book of Mr. Gilbert Grote, 1552–1573* (Edinburgh: Scottish Record Society, 1914), 37.

55. 16 March 1692: 'The Councill Recommends to Baillie Halyburtoune to call for Robert Milne Master Mason and presently to order him or any concerned in the Quarry at the Abbayhill to fence the highway adjoyning to the said Quarrie with ane dyke of stone and lyme of ane elne and ane half high upon his owne expences . . .' *Edin. Recs*, 1689–1701, 88. John Adair's c.1682 manuscript 'Map of Midlothian' shows two quarry sites between Abbeyhill and Leith. NLS, Adv.MS.70.2.11 (Adair 9), available online at http://maps.nls.uk/joins/adair09.html.

56. 'Gray, (blank), B., sklaitter, ordinarily residing in Glasgow, gratis, by act of C, finding great necessity of more able sklaitters 18 Aug. 1648' *Edin. Burgs*, 1406–1700, 220.

57. Allen, 'Conquering the Suburbs', 431–6.

58. Ibid., 430–1.

59. The term 'outland' is meant to imply someone from the landward, or countryside, rather than from the town. The act books of the convenery used the variant 'outlandish craftsmen', suggesting that they were both in the wrong place, and that they were an anathema to the established, legal order. Munro and Fothringham, *Act Book of the Convenery*, vol. 2, 36 and 35.

60. For example, Canongate made several complaints to the privy council about violent attacks on its wrights in the 1620s and early 1630s. Stewart, L. A. M., *Urban Politics and the British Civil Wars: Edinburgh, 1617–53* (Leiden: Brill, 2006), 140–1. Even with superiority violence continued to be resorted to by a few individuals. In 1732 George Lamb, a wright in the Potterrow, was attacked in Niddry's Wynd by John Yetts, an Edinburgh wright, while taking a chest of drawers to an inhabitant of Edinburgh. NLS Acc.7056, Box 1, Bundle 1, 1732 Statement of George Lamb. Of course, the Canongate wrights and masons were not above using violence themselves, as in 1683 against 'country masons, unfree-men' who were working on Lord Hatton's lodging in the burgh. Lauder of Fountainhall, *Historical Notices*, 293.

61. *Edin. Recs*, 1403–1528, 57–8.

62. Ibid., 1403–1528, 57–8.

63. Ibid., 1557–1571, 273.

64. Munro and Fothringham, *Act Book of the Convenery*, vol. 1, 77.

65. Ibid., 99.

66. Ibid., 81.

67. ECA, Mill Recs, A24. Being on a series of hills, with its port a mile distant, the physical topography of the capital surely complicated the relationship between the Incorporation's coopers and their suburban counterparts, who quite naturally set up near the port. Shipping required packaging, of which the coopers were essential providers. It would appear that the threat posed by these suburban coopers was less concerning to the masons and wrights.

68. *Edin. Recs*, 1604–1626, 195.

69. ECA, Mill Recs, A24, A38 and A42. See also Mill, 'Inventory', 9, 12 and 13.

70. Mill 'Inventory', 22, B6 (Portsburgh records, currently missing), and Mill Recs, A40 (Canongate).

71. ECA, Mill Recs, A24 and A38. See also Mill, 'Inventory', 9 and 12.

72. ECA, Mill Recs, A24. See also A38 and Mill, 'Inventory', 9 and 12.

73. ECA, Mill Recs, A42 and Mill, 'Inventory', 13.

74. ECA, Mill Recs, A24 and A38. See also Mill, 'Inventory', 9 and 12.

75. The Edinburgh figure does not include the £100 for 'upsets of stallangers' for the same year. ECA, Mill Recs, A47f. See also Mill, 'Inventory', 13B.

76. For examples from 1607, 1628 and 1658, see ECA, Mill Recs, A42.

77. ECA, Mill Recs, A24 and A38. See also Mill, 'Inventory', 9 and 12.

78. For parallels with the metalworkers, see Allen, 'Conquering the Suburbs', 432–5.

79. Marwick, J. D. (ed.), *Charters and Other Documents Relating to the City of Edinburgh*, A.D. *1143–1540* (Edinburgh: Scottish Burgh Records Society, 1871), 7.

80. Allen, 'Conquering the Suburbs', 430–1.

81. *RPS*, 1641/8/467 and 1641/8/484 (last accessed 3 December 2016).

82. They were also barred from packing and peeling, or importing and exporting, with them. Munro and Fothringham, *Act Book of the Convenery*, vol. 1, 185.

83. Ibid., 184–6.

84. *Edin. Recs*, 1642–1655, 231.

85. Munro and Fothringham, *Act Book of the Convenery*, vol. 1, 221–2. Interestingly, this does not appear in the printed version of the council records. *Edin. Recs*, 1642–1655, 231–4.

86. Munro and Fothringham, *Act Book of the Convenery*, vol. 1, 221–3.

87. Ibid., 223.

88. *Edin. Recs*, 1642–1655, 226, 234 and 305.

89. For the ban on skinner work in Canongate, Leith and Portsburgh, see *Edin. Recs*, 1655–1665, 175. For the 1626 and 1627 ratifications of Canongate's seals of cause, see Wood, *Book of Records of the Ancient Privileges of the Canongate*, 25, and for the 1641 ratification, see *RPS*, 1641/8/447 (last accessed 3 December 2016).

90. This followed shortly after an account of the 'Murder Acre' riot, where

he'd given a less-than-objective account of the craft youth. It is difficult to determine how accurate his assessment was, though similar arguments about picking and choosing when it suited them to hold sway over the Canongate were also levelled against the Edinburgh council in a court case in 1764. Lauder of Fountainhall, *Historical Notices*, 160, and Dreghorn, *Memorial for the United Incorporations of Mary's Chapel . . .*, 16–17 and 45.

91. Munro and Fothringham, *Act Book of the Convenery*, vol. 1, 303.
92. This is shown by the lack of an election of a Canongate oversman along with those for Leith and Portsburgh oversmen in the minute books. ECA, SL34/1/1–14 and Acc.622/1–8 & 73. See also the example of a similar situation for the Hammermen: Allen, 'Conquering the Suburbs', 432 and 435.
93. Munro and Fothringham, *Act Book of the Convenery*, vol. 1, 317–20.
94. Ibid., 318.
95. Ibid., vol. 2, 34–6.
96. Ibid., vol. 2, 64–6.
97. Ibid., vol. 1, 80–1.
98. Ibid., vol. 1, 217.
99. Ibid., vol. 2, 356–7.
100. Ibid., vol. 2, 358–9.
101. Marshall, J. S., *Old Leith at Work* (Edinburgh: Edina Press, 1977), 16.
102. The Incorporation gave them £28 Scots towards their legal fees. NLS, Acc.7332 Box 2, Group 9, Petitions, 1725–7, Item 6: 1726 Petition of Masons, Wrights and Coopers of Portsburgh.
103. Munro and Fothringham, *Act Book of the Convenery*, vol. 1, 218.
104. Ibid., 221–3.
105. Ibid., vol. 2, 357.
106. The 1633 ratification, for example, simply stipulates a three-mile exclusion zone for the work of unfreemen, demonstrating how jurisdiction did not precisely equate to within the burgh boundaries. *Edin. Recs*, 1626–1641, 125. See Appendix 7 for text.
107. See the Introduction of this book for discussion of the incident. *Edin. Recs*, 1528–1557, 194–5.
108. See Figure 1.1 in Chapter 1, 'A View of St Mary's Chapel'. Maitland, W. *The History of Edinburgh From its Foundation to the Present Time* (Edinburgh: Hamilton, Balfour and Neill, 1753), 167.
109. Mill, 'Inventory', 11–12, nos A34, A35, A36 and A39. See also Appendix 7.
110. This was in response to 'vexious, sinister and wrangus information . . . be merchands of our realm'. Smith, *Hammermen of Edinburgh*, lxxxi–lxxxiv.
111. Wood, M., *Book of Records of the Ancient Privileges of the Canongate* (Edinburgh: Scottish Record Society, 1956), 25, and *RPS*, 1641/8/447 (last accessed 3 December 2016).
112. Fraser, W. H., *Conflict and Class: Scottish Workers, 1700–1838* (Edinburgh: John Donald, 1988), 21, and *Edin. Burgs*, 1406–1700, 8, 9 and 11.
113. There are clear parallels here between the phenomenon of the 'estate'

craftsmen. Certain landed gentry kept skilled craftsmen in their employment rather than seeking workmen from the towns. See Pryke, S., 'The Eighteenth Century Furniture Trade in Edinburgh: A Study Based on Documentary Sources' (University of St Andrews PhD thesis, 1995), 121–6, and Pryke, S., 'Pattern Furniture and Estate Wrights in Eighteenth-Century Scotland', in *Furniture History*, 30 (1994), 101.

114. *Edin. Burgs*, 1701–1760, 104 and *Edin. Burgs*, 1406–1700, 289, respectively.

115. *RSS*, vol. 1, 494/2 and *Edin. Burgs*, 1406–1700, 375, respectively.

116. The second burgess entry for John Mein reads: 'Mein, John, B., sclaiter, as p. to Andrew Cassie, his majesty's mason, B. (17 Feb. 1658) 22 Feb 1689'. *Edin. Burgs*, 1406–1700, 346. Cassie was a freeman slater in the Incorporation, but a master mason to the crown.

117. In George Seton's nineteenth-century study of Scottish heraldry is an excerpt from Scott's *Marmion*, which attempts to distil the roll of the herald to attending the Lord Lyon and helping to quell 'feudal strife'. Seton, G., *The Law and Practice of Heraldry in Scotland* (Edinburgh: Edmonston and Douglas, 1863), 38.

118. Tittler, R., *Portraits, Painters, and Publics in Provincial England, 1540–1640* (Oxford: Oxford University Press, 2012), 108–10.

119. *Edin. Burgs*, 1406–1700, 347, and Tittler, *Portraits, Painters, and Publics in Provincial England*, 109. For more on George Porteous, see Burnett, C. J., *Officers of Arms in Scotland, 1290–2016* (Edinburgh: Scottish Record Society, 2016), 111, and Apted, M. R. and Hannabuss, S. (eds), *Painters in Scotland 1301–1700: A Biographical Dictionary* (Edinburgh: Edina Press Ltd, 1978), 72–5.

120. For herald painters, the first is thought to have been George Workman, who was granted a monopoly by James VI in 1592. This same year the jurisdiction of the Lyon Court was clarified by an act of parliament, showing the increased concern over issues of heraldry in tandem with the first specialist painter of coats of arms. From this point to 1800, eleven other herald painters are known to have worked for the Lyon Court. Apted and Hannabuss, *Painters in Scotland*, 9–10; Seton, *Heraldry in Scotland*, 42–4; Grant, F. J., *Court of the Lord Lyon: List of His Majesty's Officers of Arms and Other Officials With Genealogical Notes, 1318–1945* (Edinburgh: Scottish Record Society, 1945), 9; and Burnett, *Officers of Arms in Scotland, 1290–2016*, 58–9. For masons with the complicated nature of jurisdictions in and outside of towns, there were attempts in the later 1500s to create wardens over masons within the shires. By 1598 William Schaw was attempting to organise the mason trade throughout the whole realm; a movement towards national regulation of labour. Issues of jurisdiction overlapping with burgh privileges complicated the matter, though attempts continued into the seventeenth century at least. The best account of the evidence for all this can be found in David Stevenson's *The Origins of Freemasonry* (Cambridge: Cambridge University Press, 2005), 32–76, but especially 68–71.

121. For more on the burgess duties, see the Glossary and Allen, *Conquering the Suburbs*, 430.
122. Lynch, 'Social and Economic Structure of the Larger Towns', 264–5, and *Edin. Recs*, 1403–1528, 118–19.
123. For the 1508 request for six to eight seats, see Lynch, 'Social and Economic Structure of the Larger Towns', 264–5, and *Edin. Recs*, 1403–1528, 118–19.
124. Lynch, *Edinburgh and the Reformation*, 226–58: Appendix I, 'Lists of Edinburgh town councils and deacons of crafts, 1551–1584, with index to members of council'. Various deacons were also listed in addition to the councils prior to the revised sett.
125. Ibid., 64.
126. The list technically goes to 1584, with the end of the 1583 council's tenure, though the election for 1584 is not actually included.
127. Ibid., Appendix I, 233, 247 and 256.
128. Ibid., 226–58: Appendix I.
129. *Edin. Recs*, 1573–1589, 275.
130. Ibid., 265 and 275.
131. Ibid., 1642–1655, 169.
132. Ibid., 1642–1655, 169.
133. This 1677 commentary comes from Lauder of Fountainhall, *Historical Notices*, 159.
134. *Edin. Recs*, 1573–1589, 267–8.
135. Munro, J. and Fothringham, H. S. (eds) *Edinburgh Goldsmiths' Minutes, 1525–1700* (Edinburgh: Scottish Record Society, 2006), 278–9.
136. The perspectives of the Incorporation, which appear to show division, can be found in the minute books in the Edinburgh City Archives. See for example the opposing views and the grudging acceptance of the council's choice of deacon from 12 September 1763 to 22 September 1764: ECA, Acc.622/1, 279–85, 298–304. Note also how Alexander Nicholson's name was deleted from the list of deacons in 1764: ECA, Acc.622/1, 22 September 1764, 303.
137. Dreghorn, *Memorial for the United Incorporations of Mary's Chapel . . .*, 1–5.
138. *Edin. Recs*, 1689–1701, 88, and Ibid., 1528–1557, 193. In later centuries a particularly good source of free stone was the quarry at Craigleith. McMillan, A. A., Gillanders, R. J., and Fairhurst, J. A., *Building Stones of Edinburgh* (Edinburgh: Edinburgh Geological Society, 1999), 3–4, 54–5, and 118–24. I'm grateful to Dr Angus Miller for our discussions of Edinburgh's geology and the role of the materials in the history of the Incorporation of Mary's Chapel.
139. For example: 'Dean of Guild's Accounts, 1552–1567', in R. Adam (ed.), *Edinburgh Records: The Burgh Accounts*, vol. 2 (Edinburgh, 1899), 27–8.
140. See for examples: Lillehammer, A., 'The Scottish-Norwegian Timber Trade in the Stavanger Area in the Sixteenth and Seventeenth Centuries', in Smout, T. C. (ed.), *Scotland and Europe, 1200–1850* (Edinburgh: John Donald,

1986); Lorvik, M., 'Mutual Intelligibility of Timber Trade Terminology in the North Sea Countries During the Time of the "Scottish Trade"', in *Nordic Journal of English Studies* 2:2 (2003); Newland, K., 'The Acquisition and Use of Norwegian Timber in Seventeenth-Century Scotland', in *Vernacular Architecture*, 42 (2011); and Smout, T. C., MacDonald, A. R., and Watson, F., *A History of the Native Woodlands of Scotland, 1500–1920* (Edinburgh: Edinburgh University Press, 2005).

141. Turnbull, J., *The Scottish Glass Industry, 1610–1750: 'To Serve the Whole Nation with Glass'* (Edinburgh: Society of Antiquaries of Scotland, 2001), 82.

142. Innes, C. and Renwick, R. (eds), *Ancient Laws and Customs of the Burghs of Scotland*, vol. 1, A.D. 1124–1424 (Edinburgh: SBRS, 1868), 46 and 81–2, no. xxxix. For a good introduction to the medieval guilds, see (Dennison) Torrie, E. P., *The Gild Court Book of Dunfermline, 1433–1597* (Edinburgh: Scottish Record Society, 1986), xiv–xviii.

143. Colston, J., *The Guildry of Edinburgh: Is it an Incorporation?* (Edinburgh: Colston and Company, 1887), x.

144. (Dennison) Torrie, *Gild Court Book*, xvi.

145. Grant, *Social and Economic Development of Scotland*, 385 and 389.

146. Allen, A., *The Locksmith Craft in Early Modern Edinburgh* (Edinburgh: Society of Antiquaries of Scotland, 2007), 38–49.

147. Lynch, 'Towns and Townspeople', 183, quoting from: *RPS*, 1467/1/3 (last accessed 16 December 2016).

148. Innes, C. and Renwick, R. (eds), *Ancient Laws and Customs of the Burghs of Scotland*, vol. 1, A.D. 1124–1424 (Edinburgh: SBRS, 1868), 46.

149. *RPS*, 1467/1/2 (last accessed 17 December 2016).

150. *Edin. Recs*, 1403–1528, 86–7 and 88–9.

151. 'Cwikry' should be translated as 'cookery'.

152. *Edin. Recs*, 1573–1589, 514–15.

153. Marwick, J. D., *Edinburgh Guilds and Crafts* (Edinburgh: Scottish Burgh Record Society, 1909), 179–80, quoting the manuscript minutes of the Edinburgh council for 4 October 1661.

154. *Edin. Recs*, 1626–1641, 153.

155. Ibid., 1573–1589, 383.

156. This was also the case with 'deacons'. See Lamond, R., 'The Scottish Craft Gild as a Religious Fraternity', in *The Scottish Historical Review*, 16:63 (1919), 197.

157. The 'haill merchandis and gild brether' were granted their seal of cause on 10 December 1518. This charter included the power to 'hald courtis quhilkis sall be callit courtis of Gildry'. See *Edin. Recs*, 1403–1528, 181–6.

158. This court has been described as a 'sub-committee of the General Court of the Guild', which 'performed the function of municipal arbitration . . .', amongst other things. For more on this important institution and its impact on Scotland's urban environments, see Rodger, R., 'The Evolution of Scottish

Town Planning', in Gordon, G. and Dicks, B., *Scottish Urban History* (Aberdeen: Aberdeen University Press, 1983), 71–91.

159. As per the decreet arbitral: *Edin. Recs*, 1573–1589, 274.

160. For the ratified 1593 by-laws, see Colston, *Guildry of Edinburgh*, Appendix II, 115–18. For the original 1584 articles, see *Edin. Recs*, 1573–1589, 395–8.

161. Colston, *Guildry of Edinburgh*, Appendix II, 116, and Wood, M., 'The Neighbourhood Book', in *The Book of the Old Edinburgh Club*, 23 (1940), 83.

162. Wood, 'The Neighbourhood Book', 88–98.

163. Rodger, 'The Evolution of Scottish Town Planning', 79–80. Ian Gray argues that the scope of their jurisdiction over 'nuisances' was reduced by an 1834 Court of Session ruling to those disputes dealing with the structure of buildings. Gray, I., *A Guide to Dean of Guild Court Records* (Glasgow: University of Glasgow, 1994), 4.

164. Colston, *Guildry of Edinburgh*, Appendix II, 116.

165. Ibid., 117.

166. Ibid., 116.

167. See, for example, the 1641 'Act anente loyall packing of sallmond', where the whole coopers of the kingdom were ordered to use sufficient wood, 'without worme bolles', and to ensure that their barrels contained no less than ten gallons according to the Stirling pint. *RPS*, 1641/8/210 (last accessed 12 November 2016). A 1615 example shows coopers being consulted in a question over the volume of foreign barrels of fish, showing how important such gallon and chopin measures could be to municipal regulation. *Edin. Recs*, 1604–1626, 129. For more on Scottish weights and measures, see Connor, R. D., Simpson, A. D. C. and Morrison-Low, A. D. (eds), *Weights and Measures in Scotland: A European Perspective* (Edinburgh: NMS Enterprises Ltd & Tuckwell Press, 2004).

168. While the volume was occasionally adjusted by the Scottish government, in 1487 the salmon barrel equalled 14 gallons, but was later reduced to 10. Connor, Simpson and Morrison-Low, *Weights and Measures*, 242–4.

169. Colston, *Guildry of Edinburgh*, Appendix II, 116.

170. Ibid., 117.

171. Some crafts were involved in export and had guildry representation before 1583, though numbers were small. See, for example, the leather and textile crafts discussed in Lynch, 'Towns and Townspeople', 184–5.

172. Ibid., Appendix VIII, 204–8.

173. *Edin. Burgs*, 1406–1700, 9–10.

174. As with the 1648 dearth of slaters and the subsequent admission of a Glasgow slater to the freedom of Edinburgh: *Edin. Burgs*, 1406–1700, 220.

175. Grant, *Social and Economic Development of Scotland*, 356 and 398.

176. The 'Timber Bush', as it came to be called, appears to have been started in 1582 for 'the hail Norway tymmer quhilk is to come in at Leyth'. *Edin. Recs*, 1573–1589, 235: 4 May 1582. For the best discussion of the Timber

Bush at Leith, see Mowat, S., *The Port of Leith: Its History and its People* (Edinburgh: John Donald, 1994), 268–79.

177. Mill, 'Inventory', 5, A10, 20 September 1554. See also *Edin. Recs*, 1528–1557, 198 and 310.

178. ECA, SL34/1/1, 13, 22 July 1670, about 'bargains' being offered to fellow freemen before sale to the public, and 22, 16 December 1671: 'The same day the deacons masters & brethren of the wrights amongst themselves ordered that the most able men amongst them should (with advice of the deacons & masters of wrights) joyn in each of them the soume of ane hundred pounds scotts for keeping of ane Common stock of timber for service of the wholl brethren of wrights when occation offers that timber is scarce to be hade'.

179. 30 September 1618: 'Dischargis any aickyn kistis to be maid for burial of the deceist persones within this burgh in the burial place thairof and the belmen to mak intimatioun to the parties as occasioun offerris.' *Edin. Recs*, 1604–1626, 182.

180. Marwick, J. D. (ed.), *Charters and Other Documents Relating to the City of Edinburgh*, A.D. 1143–1540 (Edinburgh: Scottish Burgh Records Society, 1871), 7.

181. Innes and Renwick, *Ancient Laws and Customs of the Burghs*, vol. 1, 61. See also the undated fragment 'Anent the mercat and wares' on page 188.

182. *Edin. Recs*, 1626–1641, 125. See Appendix 7 for full text.

183. Ibid., 1403–1528, 30–1. See Appendix 1 for full text.

184. Ibid., 1626–1641, 125. See Appendix 7 for full text.

185. See for example the 1677 reference to the Wednesday market for the work of the ten trades of Mary's Chapel: '. . . upon the mercat day being Weddinsday and that to the mercat places which is to remain therein from nyne of the cloak in the foir noon to two of the cloak in the efter noone . . .' *Edin. Recs*, 1665–1680, 301–2.

186. For examples from 1765 and 1784, see: Watson, W. E., *The Convenery of the Six Incorporated Trades of Elgin* (Elgin: Privately published; copy held at Moray Local Heritage Centre, 1960), 2 and 5.

187. 23 April 1658: 'Complaint being made that of lait the wrights of this brugh in making of the dead kists doe make the samen with yroun vycenaillis quhich sticke so farr out that the mortcloths ar torne and riven theirby drawing them aff at the graves Theirfoir the Counsell ordaines the deaken Alexander Cleghorne to make intimatioun to the craft that none of them preysume in tyme comeing to make use of any vycenaillis to dead kists under the paine of Twentie punds scotts . . .' *Edin. Recs*, 1655–1665, 92.

188. Ibid., 1642–1655, 105.

189. Ibid., 1528–1557, 196–7.

190. Ibid., 1665–1680, 107.

191. *Edin. Burgs*, 1406–1700, 349. The Millers are not listed in the Incorporation's minutes. ECA, SL34/1/1. Another Andrew Miller, mason, later took burgesship in 1689, and even became deacon by 1693, though it would appear that

this was a different Andrew Miller to the calsaymaker. If they were the same man, then he was entered as a burgess twice. *Edin. Burgs*, 1406–1700, 349.

192. *Edin. Recs*, 1626–1641, 87, and Dalrymple of Stair, Sir James, *The Decisions of the Lords of Council & Session, In the Most Important Cases Debate Before Them; From July 1671 to July 1681 . . . Part Second* (Edinburgh: Heir of Andrew Anderson, Printer to His most Sacred Majesty, 1687), 405. Dods was not a burgess until 1644. *Edin. Burgs*, 1406–1700, 152.

193. 23 May 1595: 'Comperit William Lyntoun, mylne wricht in Dalkeyth and wes content . . . to serve the guid toun as their mylne wricht at thair common mylnis in maner . . . contenit in the acts of counsall maid of before betuix the guid toun and William Stenhope, last mylne wricht . . . and band himselff to observe . . . the samyn for his part and that he sall enter the townes service at Witsounday nixtt.' (*Edin. Recs* 1589–1603, 133).

194. ECA, Acc.622/2, 109–15.

195. For more on the dean of guild and this important transition, see Campbell, I., and Stewart, M., 'The Evolution of the Medieval and Renaissance City', in Edwards, B. and Jenkins, P. (eds), *Edinburgh: The Making of a Capital City* (Edinburgh: Edinburgh University Press, 2005), 32–4, and Rodger, 'The Evolution of Scottish Town Planning', 76–9.

196. For more on the internal relations between the ten arts of Mary's Chapel, see Chapter 1.

197. Innes and Renwick, *Ancient Laws and Customs of the Burghs*, iii and 8–58.

198. 'Item it is ordanit that the alderman and the consel of ilk toune sworn sal se and priss the mater of ilk craft and consider the price of the mater and the cost and the travale of the werkman ande thare eftir priss the maid werk how it sal be sauld and that price mak knawin to the kingis commonis and be opyn cryit.' *RPS*, 1426/36 (last accessed 7 December 2016).

199. For more on this complex process of setting prices, see the following: Gibson, A. J. S. and Smout, T. C., *Prices, Food and Wages in Scotland, 1550–1780* (Cambridge: Cambridge University Press, 1995), and Gemmill, E. and Mayhew, N., *Changing Values in Medieval Scotland: A Study of Prices, Money, and Weights and Measures* (Cambridge: Cambridge University Press, 2006).

200. Lynch, M., *Edinburgh and the Reformation* (Edinburgh: Edinburgh University Press, 1981), 19 and 70, and Grant, *Social and Economic Development*, 421.

201. For more on general trends, see Fischer, D. H., *The Great Wave: Price Revolutions and the Rhythm of History* (Oxford: Oxford University Press, 1996). For specific discussion of inflation in Edinburgh, see Lynch, *Edinburgh and the Reformation*, 5, 19–20, 140–1, 147–8 and 151; Lythe, S. G. E., *The Economy of Scotland in its European Setting, 1550–1625* (Edinburgh: Oliver and Boyd, 1960), 28 and 30; Knoop, D. and Jones, G. P., *The Scottish Mason and the Mason Word* (Manchester: Manchester University Press, 1939), 34–40; Gibson and Smout, *Prices, Food and Wages in Scotland,*

5–14; and Gemmill and Mayhew, *Changing Values in Medieval Scotland*, 361–81.

202. Gibson and Smout, *Prices, Food and Wages in Scotland*, 162–3.

203. Lythe, *Economy of Scotland*, 30. Compare with Gibson and Smout, *Prices, Food and Wages*, Figure 9.3, 361.

204. *RPS*, 1426/36 and A1552/2/18 (last accessed 7 December 2016). See also: Smith, T. B., 'Master and Servant', in Lord Normand, et al., *An Introduction to Scottish Legal History* (Edinburgh: The Stair Society, 1958), 139–40.

205. Anentis conductioune of craftismen: *RPS*, 1540/12/84 (last accessed 12 February 2016).

206. 16 April 1577: 'The provest, baillies, and counsall vnderstanding that the wrychtis and masonis of thair pretendit maner had stoppit certan masonis, vnfremen, to big ane cone in Grayes clois becaus the baxteris wald nocht geve thame sic exhorbitant prices as thay desyrit, for remeid quhairof the provest, baillies, and counsall foirsaidis hes statute and ordanit that the saidis vnfre masones, conforme to the act of parliament, sall compleit and end the said wark and nane vtheris, and commandis this ordour to be kepit in all tymes cuming quhen wrychtis or masonis becomis vnresonabill on thair prices.' (*Edin. Recs*, 1573–1589, 58).

207. 27 April 1610: 'In respect of the acts of parliament geving power to the magestrats of ilk burgh to sett pryces upoun the wedges of craftismen and in considderatioun of the exorbitant pryces raysit . . . be the deykin and brether of the wrichts and masouns crafts within this burgh, Thairfor settis the pryces and owlklie wedges following . . . To witt the maister to haif owlklie foure li. and the servands sufficient men ilk persoun foure merk and sex schillings aucht penneis for drynk and drynk sylver and the lads and boyes as thai ar worth.' *Edin. Recs*, 1604–1626, 61.

208. 16 December 1671: 'The same day the deacons and brethren aforsaid takin to ther Consideration the skaith & damnage that they have be the Exorbitant pryces given to ther Journaymen for remeid wherof they have all at one Consent agreed that a peremptor price be putt upon the days wadg of the best Journayman and ane peremptor pryce alsoe upon the worst Journayman and the price of ilk mane betuixt them to be as it shall occur and therto the brethren of the house to stand to thes settled pryces . . .' ECA, SL34/1/1, 22, 16 December 1671.

209. 16 December 1671: '. . . the prices of the turners and sawers be Rectified with advice of the deacon & masters of wrights and that the same shall stand in force in tyme Coming as alsoe that the turners & sawers shall be Inacted and bound to serve the brethren of wrights befor any other within burgh in all tyme Coming' ECA, SL34/1/1, 22, 16 December 1671.

210. See for example the 3 June 1721 'Act & Resolutione anent the pryces to be given to sawers of timber':
'The same day The brethren of the wrights takeing to their seriouse consideration That the people commonly Imployed for sawing of timber, are in use

very often to impose upon the members of this house, In exacting exorbitant pryces for yeir worke, and much more from one master then from another, and thereby introduces ane unequalitie in that sort of business, and considering that it would tend very much to the advantage of the members of this house To have that matter sett on ane equall footting Have unanimously resolved, statut and ordained That only the following pryces be payed to sawers for the severall demensions of timber underwritten

Viz ffor each sueds dale of Holland plank Tuo shilling & six pennies scots –

ffor each dale below Tuelve and above ten foot one shilling eight pennies scots

ffor each dale above nyne & below Ten foot one shilling ffoure pennies scots

ffor each daill above Eight & below nyne foot one shilling Tuo pennies scots –

ffor each double tree Tuo shilling six pennies scots

ffor each single tree one shilling six pennies scots &

ffor each ffyve foot knappell Ten pennies pr draught and the –

Incorporation seriousely recomends to the members yereof this house to observe the above rules in tyme coming' ECA, SL34/1/5, 3 June 1721.

211. *Edin. Recs*, 1689–1701, 75–6.
212. *Edin. Burgs*, 1406–1700, 456.
213. 53 Geo. III, c. 40, as quoted in Smith, 'Master and Servant', 139–40.
214. *Edin. Burgs*, 1406–1700.
215. This date was chosen simply for convenience.
216. *Edin. Burgs*, 1406–1700 and 1701–1760. There is a third volume which takes the rolls up to the nineteenth century, but I did not have access to this when undertaking the research.
217. Turnbull, J., *The Scottish Glass Industry, 1610–1750: 'To Serve the Whole Nation with Glass'* (Edinburgh: Society of Antiquaries of Scotland, 2001), 63.
218. Ibid., 82–4.
219. Dr Turnbull has argued that the prohibition appears to have worked, which would seem to be backed up by the guildry figures above. Ibid., 84.
220. For timbers, see Lillehammer, A., 'The Scottish-Norwegian Timber Trade in the Stavanger Area in the Sixteenth and Seventeenth Centuries', in Smout, T. C. (ed.), *Scotland and Europe, 1200–1850* (Edinburgh: John Donald, 1986), 97–111. For paint, I'm grateful to Dr Michael Pearce for sharing an unpublished paper on the paintwork at Gladstone's Land, Edinburgh, which shows the prevalence of both domestic and imported pigments in paint, as well as the connections with apothecaries and merchants in their supply. See for example, the 'Certane painteris cullors' worth over £284 in the 1645 testament of the apothecary John Livingston: NRS CC8/8/64, 572–3, John Livingstone, apothecary. For glass, Turnbull, *Scottish Glass Industry*, 82–4.
221. 'That forsamekle as Johnne Andersoun messinger haveing laitlie providit & apprysit fra ye said George Cranstoun the equall halff of ane bark or crear

callit ye Robert with ye halff of hir ornamentis perteneing to him ffor ye sowme of thrie hundreth and fyftie markis money at ye Instance to ye behaiff of ye saids maissonis and wrichtis & thair brethering . . .' NLS, Acc.7056, Box 1, Bundle 1, 1616 at the instance of George Gibson, bower burgess of Edinburgh and boxmaster of Mary's Chapel, against George Cranston, indweller.

222. Arnot, H., *The History of Edinburgh, from the Earliest Accounts to the Year 1780* (Edinburgh: Thomas Turnbull, 1816), 448.
223. *Edin. Burgs*, 1406–1700, 42.
224. Allen, A. and Spence, C. (eds), *Edinburgh Housemails Taxation Book, 1634–1636* (Woodbridge: Scottish History Society, 2014), 245–6.
225. This can only be a guess, though other taverns in 1630s Edinburgh both sold wine and provided lodgings. See for example, James Howell's 1639 letter to Lord Clifford from Edinburgh: '. . . my lodging, which is a tavern . . . and my landlord, who is a pert smart man, brought up a chopin of white wine; and for this particular, there are better French wines here than in England and cheaper, for they are but a groat a quart, and it is a crime of a high nature to mingle or sophisticate any wine here.' Reprinted in Brown, P. H. (ed.) *Early Travellers in Scotland* (Edinburgh: D. Douglas, 1891), 160. Marwick gives two references to wine being reserved for guild brethren alone to sell. Marwick, *Edinburgh Guilds and Crafts*, 76 and 142.
226. As based on the work of Walter Makey and Michael Lynch – see Allen and Spence, *Edinburgh Housemails Taxation Book*, xvii, and Allen, A., 'Occupational Mapping of 1635 Edinburgh: An Introduction', in *Proceedings of the Society of Antiquaries of Scotland*, 136 (2006), 260.
227. For examples, see Munro and Fothringham, *Act Book of the Convenery*, vol. 1, 218 and 221–3, and vol. 2, 357.
228. Grant, I. F., *The Social and Economic Development of Scotland Before 1603* (Edinburgh: Oliver and Boyd, 1930), 424–5.

Conclusion
The Decline of Corporatism and the Rise of the Unfree

The context for work in nineteenth-century Edinburgh was very different from that in the fifteenth century. Though many institutions had proven remarkably resilient, still it is change rather than continuity which stands out as most apparent when comparing the two periods. A poignant symbol of these changes can be found today in the rather empty space at the intersection of the High Street and St Mary's Street. This space once held the Netherbow Port, but now is a mere outline of brass bricks in amongst the cobbles. At one point this was the most significant gateway in the town walls of the Scottish capital, where imported wine was taxed, where invasions were resisted, and where kings and queens were honoured with civic processions.[1] Possibly more important was its symbolic message to those entering the town. To stand before the early-seventeenth-century structure left one in no doubt that they were entering a town of some importance.

The imposing fabric, shown in Figure 5.1, implied the strength and authority of a town which would resist enemies, whether political, in the form of a foreign army, or economic, as with the lesser burgh of Canongate over which it looked. The cockerel weather vane spoke to the town's Christian virtue; this was a town which remembered the example of Peter, and would not deny Christ. The clock suggested modernity; the crenellation made it clear that this was a *royal* burgh, pointing to the institution from which the town's authority derived. In short, the Netherbow Port was an overt statement of power and privilege. It was a symbol of the socio-economic and political advantages held by those freemen within, and it was intended for those unfreemen without.

Blunt as this architectural statement might have been, the reality was naturally far more complex. Simply being inside the town walls was no guarantee of access to freedom, nor was being outside an indication of access having been lost. But as a metaphor for the early-modern system of privilege, the Netherbow Port works remarkably well. This is particularly true when we consider its removal in 1764. Long before the eighteenth

Figure 5.1 'A View of the Netherbow Port', c.1753

The Netherbow Port as seen from outside the town in the neighbouring burgh of Canongate. From Maitland's *History*, 140. By kind permission of City of Edinburgh Council Libraries (http://www.capitalcollections.org.uk).

century, the defensive capabilities of the port were obsolete, as were its regulatory functions. By 1693 the gate was being left open all night,[2] meaning that this once-powerful icon of protectionist privilege was becoming a nuisance; a hindrance to trade rather than a guardian of the town's privileged place in Scotland's economy. Hence, in 1764 it was simply swept away (Figure 5.2).[3]

The removal of the port opened up the way between the two High Streets which form the main part of the Royal Mile of today's Edinburgh. While market infill had removed public space over the centuries, the new focus was on freeing up space; space for transport and trade which reflected the wider changes in Scotland's economy. Indeed, one might argue that this was merely a speeding up of processes already underway. Restrictions on non-royal burghs participating in foreign trade had been removed in 1672, and only three years prior to this there had been an unsuccessful attempt to remove restrictions on unfree craft work in royal burghs.[4] More to the point, for the building trades the privileges of exclusive right to work had always been disputed, as demonstrated by the phrasing of the seals of cause, or the 1518 confirmation from the Archbishop of St Andrews. Even James VI wrote in his 1599 *Basilicon Doron* that foreign craftsmen should be encouraged to settle in Scotland for the 'wealth and policie' it would promote.[5] Perhaps this was not exactly free-market thought, though it certainly expressed doubts about the benefits of traditional corporate privileges.

The Incorporation had never had the level of control that its upper echelons would have liked, but the context of corporatism ensured that the freemen usually had the upper hand, as they were the judges of 'sufficiency'. Even after their altar grant had been taken away by the religious reforms of the 1560s, the trade privileges of the seal of cause remained intact, though defence of these privileges remained a fairly constant struggle. By the later eighteenth century, however, the context had changed markedly. Certain societal changes were clearly visible by this period, all of which help to illuminate the erosion of the Incorporation's control over building works. Importantly, these were not unique to Edinburgh, but instead they had parallels with wider trends across Europe.[6]

While the corporatism of the early modern was focussed on protecting the interests of those within a particular group, such as the Incorporation of Mary's Chapel, the eighteenth century was increasingly influenced by liberal free-market thought, and the individual, whether free or not, was taking on greater importance in this increasingly laissez-faire system.[7] Although protectionist policies and corporate privileges remained well into the nineteenth century, public opinion was beginning to turn against them

Figure 5.2 The removal of the Netherbow Port, as seen from inside the town

Note the caption at the top relating to the port's removal in 1764, which reads 'Nether Bow, Port, bought & taken down, by Wil^m. Mylne.' John Runciman (1744–68), 'The Netherbow Port', NGS, P 6709, Etching on Paper. By kind permission of National Galleries of Scotland.

by at least the century before.[8] Trade and trades were becoming more free as both physical and societal restrictions were removed. One cannot help but wonder if the men who took down the Netherbow Port appreciated the parallel deconstruction of corporate privileges, no matter how slow the work.

THE CAPITAL REFORMED

Growth of Edinburgh

Through the eighteenth and nineteenth centuries the political and economic systems which governed Scotland went through a series of reforms. Similarly, the physical fabric of Edinburgh underwent drastic growth, and as such, it too was re-formed. In 1707 the parliament left for London, expanding the physical distance between municipal and national governments. Suburban expansion with the New Town and George Square took the town elite beyond the traditional municipal boundaries, making it harder to enforce exclusive privileges of work through the former mechanism of enforcing residency.

As political boundaries took on greater importance with the electoral reforms of the nineteenth century, worries over the relationship between municipal expansion and jurisdiction over work and workers played out in the meetings of the Incorporation.[9] With the careful redefining of the political boundaries as part of the national reforms of 1832, Edinburgh's boundary was set well north of the Water of Leith, which had loosely been the traditional north-west extent of the capital's 'royalty', or jurisdiction.[10] Voting boundaries went further north, but it would appear that the Incorporation's authority remained within the traditional boundaries of the burgh.[11] Perhaps this is why they argued for the Water of Leith being the northernmost boundary in regards to the Police Act which followed the 'Representation of the People (Scotland) Act 1832'.[12] The town was getting bigger, but the influence of the Incorporation did not necessarily expand in proportion.

As the physical space of the town was changing, the number of inhabitants was also growing, creating further need for housing and public buildings. One recent study has suggested that from 1790 to 1827 the population doubled to 120,000.[13] Although increased demand for the products of the Incorporation's crafts was an encouragement, the growth of the town was in fact a mixed blessing. Urbanisation was increasing in many cities across Britain, as people flocked to the cities in search of work. Many of these were Irish migrants, which prompted concerns about Irish labour.[14]

Others were from closer to Edinburgh, but still beyond the traditional burgh boundaries. From the conservative perspective of the Incorporation, urbanisation both created jobs and threatened to take them away.

With the expanding boundaries and growing population, it became much more difficult and much more expensive to fight off the encroachments of the unfreeman, though these rituals of exclusion continued. Some cases proved more tractable than others, but many ended up in court, incurring legal expenses for all involved. By the eighteenth century there were enough such cases to justify the printing of a legal document, or 'summons of declarator', for use by the Incorporation in pursuing those who encroached upon the privileges of Mary's Chapel. On the form, blank spaces were left for the name of the encroaching unfreeman to be inserted, demanding their attendance before the court of session.[15]

Occasionally it was a single unfree craftsman, though at other times it was the town council employing unfree masons. When in the late-eighteenth century the council decided to employ unfree masons to work on the pier at Leith, the Incorporation could do little other than to send a harsh letter of remonstrance. The clerk noted that they were 'justly alarmed at this conduct', and therefore authorised the Incorporation's representatives on the council to enquire into the cause of the infringement of their privileges.[16] Furthermore, the Incorporation sought the moral high ground by appealing to the council's sense of history and of embattled privilege. To such ends, they asked for:

> every aid and Assistance in a design so laudable and praise worthy in handing doun to posterity uncorrupted those privileges they now plead for and as a proof of their concurrence hope they will immedieately dismiss from Work the Unfreemene Masons now employed at the Pier of Leith and for the future employ in the necesary Execution of the Publick Works None but thos who are Freemen Burgesses of this City.[17]

What seemed a corruption of ancient privileges to the men of Mary's Chapel no doubt seemed common sense to the council which had apparently never intended for the Incorporation to hold complete autonomy over who worked and who did not.

Though some incorporated trades were granted the right to stop unfreemen from working, the 1475 seal of cause for the masons and wrights had no such clause. It did not exclude others from building, so long as they were found sufficient in their work by the searchers of the Incorporation.[18] From the fifteenth century, the sufficiency of one's work was to be the deciding factor in the admission or exclusion of unfreemen, though subsequent legislation complicated this issue.[19] Still, sufficiency of work was a valuable tool for the Incorporation, and therefore the traditional institutions of controlling sufficiency, such as apprenticeships and essays for mastership, remained intact all the way through to 1846.

Despite such conservatism, the increasing size of the capital brought home the realities of defending corporate privileges. One practical response to this was to simply tax the unfreemen, though this had drawbacks. As with the stallanger payments of the early modern period, the unfree craftsman of the nineteenth-century could pay an 'encroachment' fine and apparently continue to work.[20] Eventually, the discussions over how much to charge gave way to discussions over whether to charge such fines, betraying a loss of confidence in the battle against the unfreemen.[21]

Through the declining determination to exclude the unfreemen, there was not necessarily a disregard for the labour force which worked for the masters. Three guineas were given in 1844 to the 'Association in Edinburgh for providing Baths for the Working Classes', showing concern for free and unfree alike.[22] The minutes of the Incorporation also recorded a response to a bill proposed in parliament for abolishing imprisonment for small debts.[23] Although the petitioners 'warmly' approved of the bill, they took exception to the first section, which declared that it would be illegal for any creditor to imprison someone for debts of less than £8 6s 8d Sterling. The grounds on which they opposed this section were in regards to their stated sympathy for the 'labouring class of the community', who they argued would no longer be able to obtain the necessary credit to makes ends meet.[24] Of course, it also would have left them powerless for chasing debtors, and they admitted that many of the accounts incurred to themselves did not exceed the specified sum.[25] Despite the obvious self interest, it is clear that some sense of obligation to the labour force remained in the Incorporation of the nineteenth century. However, while paternalism remained, control was ebbing. Indeed, not all members of the Incorporation agreed on the propriety of attempting to wield such control.

By the 1830s some members were beginning to question the former policy of pursuing unfree workers in the ten arts of the Incorporation. In 1834 the mason Robert Patterson declared his intention to make a motion at the next quarterly meeting that from Lammas quarter day, 'no proceedings should be instituted against any individual practising any of the arts'.[26] When it was proposed, the motion was tabled until the next meeting, though by November Patterson had withdrawn his motion.[27] In 1840 the issue was again raised by Patterson, this time as a deacon of the Incorporation.[28] Apparently it was two years before this motion to allow unfreemen to work without being fined was actually discussed. Deacon Dodds moved that the motion be adopted, which was seconded by Mr

John Cousine, though others moved against it. Upon putting the motion to a vote, it was defeated by twenty-one votes to three, demonstrating continued conservatism despite society's increasing liberalism.[29] Whilst the clear majority were keen to maintain the Incorporation's exclusive privileges over unfreemen, there were still voices of dissent; voices that used a dialectic focussed not on the privileged corporate body, but on the merit of the unprivileged individual.

Political and Municipal Reforms, 1832–1846

The well-known reforms of the nineteenth century had a profound impact on corporatism, both in Edinburgh and across the United Kingdom, though the process of reform was relatively slow. Liberal ideas from the American and French revolutions made a deep impression, and by the early 1830s the need for some form of electoral reform was widely recognised. Though 1832 did much to address the need for wider political representation, it was a far cry from universal suffrage. In terms of municipal reforms, dissatisfaction with the narrow representation in local government, such as on town councils, led to the petitioning of parliament in the late eighteenth century. Aside from various committees of enquiry and reports, little impact was made until after the 'Great Reform Act' of 1832.[30] The Scottish version, or the 'Representation of the People (Scotland) Act, was passed on 17 July of that year, though debate over the extent of the reforms had been a feature in many of Scotland's burghs for some time.[31]

Support for the 1832 act appears to have been quite popular in Edinburgh, though not everyone was in favour of changes to the old system. Before they were passed, the Incorporation of Mary's Chapel debated the detail of the proposed acts in their meetings, and sent various petitions explaining their support for reform and their anxiety about the bill's progress.[32] Clearly they were interested in parliamentary reform, but they also wanted stability and reassurance of their position in society. Ironically, 1832 opened the door for the complete removal of any exclusive privileges.

Shortly after the parliamentary reform bill passed into law in July of 1832, there were celebratory parades organised by the Edinburgh Trades Union, including sixty-three different trades. The purpose of this body was fairly diverse:

For co-operating with others in the obtainment of Union, Burgh Reform Repeal of the Corn Laws, Free Circulation of Knowledge, Revisal of the Militia Laws, Separation of Church and State, Extinction of all unmeritted Pensions, Free Representation in Parliament, Equitable Settlement of the National debt,

Sobriety, Industry, Economy, Improvement of the Working Classes, Employer and Employed United, Abolition of Slavery, Free Trade.[33]

Parliamentary reform had a broad base of popular support, but with it came a multitude of other agendas which did not necessarily correspond with the wishes of the Incorporation. The minutes of the Incorporation show that they supported electoral reform, so long as they retained a degree of control over the process. As it turned out, their anxieties were well founded, as municipal reforms followed fairly soon after the parliamentary reforms of 1832.

The attention shifted from questions of parliamentary representation to concerns over corruption in municipal taxation and administration.[34] Mismanagement had long been a problem, as municipal governments struggled to pay their debts.[35] In 1819 a parliamentary commission had investigated Aberdeen, Dundee, Dunfermline and Edinburgh, only to discover that all four burghs were bankrupt.[36] Unfortunately, reform was slow, as the legislation meant to correct the problems was ineffective, creating the context in which the limited parliamentary reforms of 1832 inspired further-reaching reforms of the burghs.[37]

Hence, on 15 July 1833, shortly after the municipal reform acts of the same year altered the election process for town councils, a royal commission was established to investigate the current state of municipal institutions in Scotland.[38] In order to make their recommendations as to the extent and nature of the reforms needed, questions were sent out to the burgh councils regarding their exclusive privileges and practices. Nine such questions in regards to the exclusive privileges of work were recorded in the minutes of the Incorporation of Mary's Chapel, along with their answers. Recorded in intimate detail were their responses as to their laws, privileges, membership, funds and property.[39]

Though reform often prompted strong reactions, the language of the questions was quite conciliatory, asking, for example, how far their privileges were still enforced, and how far they could 'be safely abolished, always reserving funds and other advantages to the Incorporations'.[40] The clerk responded that they continued to enforce their privileges as formerly, and that as to abolition, it was

for the Legislature to determine this matter, but in so far as the Incorporation of Marys Chapel are concerned, they by a late vote declared that it would be exceedingly injurious to their pecuniary interest the abolition of these privileges.[41]

Although exclusive privileges were increasingly untenable in a climate where the public will was for reform, the issues of corporate funds and property made the process much more complex.

Within two years the royal commission had finished its report, which recommended the abolition of exclusive burgh privileges.[42] Tellingly, it took a further eleven years before the exclusive privileges were actually abolished with the 1846 'Act for the Abolition of the exclusive Privilege of trading in Burghs in Scotland'.[43] Over that decade, there was much lobbying by some of the more influential incorporated trades in Scottish burghs, as with the efforts of Glasgow's Trades House to secure the retention of not only the office of deacon, but also of deacon conveners on the town councils, ensuring a degree of continued influence in municipal matters for the incorporated trades.[44]

For the Edinburgh Incorporation of Mary's Chapel, the period between 1833 and 1846 saw further attempts to petition the government over new legislation, as with the police acts or the water company bill.[45] At first they continued to pursue unfreemen, but their resolve began to fade as it became clear that this aspect of the Incorporation belonged to a different era.[46] While masters continued to be admitted, and widows and orphans continued to be provided for, the focus seems to have shifted towards consolidation, with, for example, the revision of their laws and the seeking of legal advice over their corporate property and funds.[47] Just as with the loss of the Netherbow Port nearly seventy years earlier, the final barriers to working in the burgh were coming down.

CONTINUITY AND CHANGE IN THE BUILDING TRADES

For the work of the building trades, there was both continuity and change through the eighteenth and nineteenth centuries. Some of these changes affected only a few of the ten arts of Mary's Chapel; others impacted across the whole of burgh society. Certain aspects affected not the masters of the Incorporation, but instead the labourers that had once been under their roofs and under their authority. Yet others aspects of their work changed very little, right up to the twentieth century.

For example, building technology proved remarkably conservative. Despite the culture of improvement and modernisation that came with industrialisation, most of the Incorporation's tools and techniques went largely unchallenged.[48] Though certain aspects of building materials saw innovation and change, such as factory brick production, or the application of steam power to the dimensioning of timber, for the most part the hand tools of the sixteenth century were basically the same as those of the nineteenth century.[49] As late as the 1950s, apprentices in the Glasgow shipyards were still trained on hand tools rather than power tools, though one early-twentieth-century treatise on employments argued for much greater use of machinery.[50] Likewise, the impact of new technologies on the Incorporation would appear to have had little impact while they still held any sway over the labour market.

Training saw much more change, though some trades experienced greater changes than others. Some changes affected only those trades which involved the design of structures. One such change was the increased separation of the roles of the architect and the builder. By the 1830s the design of buildings was becoming increasingly professionalised, and therefore less often undertaken by masons.[51] Though aspects of this can be observed at a much earlier period, by 1835 there was a national, external body offering accreditation and training in the Institute of British Architects.[52] Eventually one would go to a university to learn architecture rather than doing an apprenticeship with a mason.

Other aspects of the changes in training were more universal, such as the effective deregulation of apprenticeships. Essays and apprenticeships had continued up to the 1840s, but as the trades were no longer allowed to test the sufficiency of entrants after 1846, such formal training was no longer regulated by the Incorporation.[53] Apprenticeships continued for the training of builders, but the traditional statutes governing the process no longer applied. Tellingly, arguments involving British trade unions in the later nineteenth century often mentioned the lack of regulation of apprenticeships.[54]

Deregulation was becoming an important economic force, largely due to the rise of liberalism and free-market thought.[55] Traditional corporate structures were increasingly seen as outdated, ineffective, and as a hindrance. Such ideas had particular sway in relation to the labour market, as relations changed between masters and servants. In Edinburgh such relations had once been largely governed by 'the House' and within the household, but these institutions were increasingly embattled in the fight for control over labour. For the first half of the nineteenth century, it has been argued that:

> the central characteristic of industrial relations – and not in building alone – was the absence of any formal, institutional structures to systematise worker-employer relations, to provide rule-making procedures and to mediate issues of contention.[56]

With liberal thought having eroded traditional economic structures for some time, systems of authority in much of the nineteenth century have been described as 'informal and voluntary'.[57] The focus had shifted to a large degree from corporatism to liberalism; from the privileges of the group towards the rights of the individual.[58] In Edinburgh, we see clear

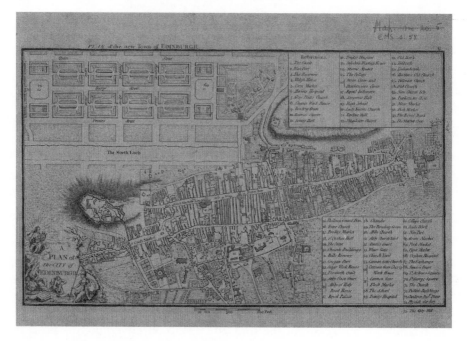

Figure 5.3 'Plan of the New Town of Edinburgh'
NLS, EMS.s.58: *Plan of the City of Edinburgh* (London: s.n., 1771). Courtesy of the National Library of Scotland.

signs of this process at work well before the nineteenth century, particularly through the rise of the unfreemen.

As mentioned in earlier chapters, the corporate framework gave advantage to the free, legitimate masters within the Incorporation. From the very beginning there had been challenges from unfree workers in an increasingly-crowded labour market, which was often complicated by the more powerful consumers from the upper tiers of society. The Incorporation had largely managed to sustain their privileges, forcing unfreemen into the accepted and controlled roles of stallangers, journeymen, or servants. When this battle over the privileges of work had moved beyond the town walls to the suburbs, in part due to inflationary and demographic pressures, the discourse had focussed on the *legal* position of the freemen of the town.

By the eighteenth century this discourse was changing, as emphasised by the changing context. A new, more modern form of suburb, populated by the elite and projecting classically-influenced gentility, gave very similar opportunities to the unfree builders, only this time the council did not have common cause with the crafts in stemming the tide. One such modern suburb was the expansion of the city with the building of the New Town (Plate 4).[59] As the New Town nearly doubled the footprint of the capital (Figure 5.3), one would think that such guaranteed building work would be a blessing to the Incorporation. In reality it created such demand for labour that keeping the unfreemen out was simply impractical. Ideologically, those behind the New Town plan, such as the lord provost, George Drummond, or the chief designer, James Craig, held more free-market principles.[60]

Hence, the discourse over work showed the ascendancy of liberal principles over the increasingly outdated corporate rational. It was not the privileges of the establishment, but the practical demands of the market which governed the building site. Certain sections of society, such as the crown and the court, had always had a large degree of liberty to override corporate privileges even within burgh boundaries, but such practices were becoming more common across the rest of society. Suburbs had been a challenge to the standing of the Incorporation in the labour market since at least the sixteenth century, but by the eighteenth century they were much more difficult to oppose effectively.[61] Society's outlook was fundamentally changing.

Journeymen, in particular, were moving away from their traditional role as 'semi-skilled' labour towards a more levelled role as 'builders' in their own right.[62] Despite opposition from the Incorporation, the New Town development went ahead, and the labour market was ready to respond with little regard to customary privileges.[63] Even before the New Town was begun, Edinburgh's journeymen had already started to organise into their own societies, which increasingly became independent from the masters of the incorporated trades.[64]

The organisation of these journeymen societies centred on a box in which a communal fund for the charitable support of journeymen and their families was held.[65] Such journeymen's boxes mimicked the charitable functions of their masters' incorporations, as did the 'stock or box' of the Edinburgh Society of Journeymen Wrights.[66] In the early eighteenth century, the funds of this box society were managed by an 'overseer' who was a freeman of the Incorporation, such as the master wright Thomas Herron. Just as the funds of the Incorporation were used for the relief of the masters and their families, the stock of the journeymen was also for the relief of their 'poor distresst bretheren relicts & Orphants', though not all journeymen joined the box society. Indeed, the Incorporation had to pass an act in 1719 requiring journeymen to join, though it is difficult to tell how effective this legislation was. What is more important, is that the Incorporation not only gave their blessing to the journeymen's box society, but sought to impose control over it.

Such control would appear to have been limited, as by mid-century there is clear evidence of independent organisation within the journeymen in the Edinburgh building trades. In the summer of 1764 the journeymen masons went on strike for higher wages, followed shortly by the journeymen wrights.[67] Though the official records of the Incorporation remain silent about the walkout, the local newspapers were used by the journeymen to inform the public as to their intentions.[68] Tapping into the liberal sentiment of the readership, their unnamed author asserted that, 'the Journeymen are resolved, one and all, to show the world that they are free men and not bond slaves, as the Masters would insinuate'.[69] Apparently the council decreed against them, demanding that they take their traditional place working under the masters.[70] Whether successful or not, the 1764 strike demonstrates a very different labour market from that of the early modern period.

The journeymen were no longer under their master's roofs, and were beginning to show signs of effective organisation, heralding the rise of trade unionism.[71] By the 1820s, there were committees of Edinburgh journeymen meeting to decide policy and prices for cabinetmaking.[72] Laws were made against such 'combinations' of craftsmen, but their long-term effect was fairly limited.[73] Society was moving away from corporate privileges to liberal, free-market thought, making the Incorporation's privileges harder to defend.

In part, this was driven by economics, as laissez-faire capitalism became more influential across Scottish society.[74] For the Incorporation and the wider building trades it was struggling to influence, this emphasis on capital impacted upon two areas in particular. The first was the rise of general contracting within the labour market, and the second was the funding of building projects within Edinburgh. Both demonstrate considerable continuity of practice.

The traditional unit of craft production was thought to be the single master, working with a few journeymen and apprentices, in a single art such as masonry, painting or plumbing. By the nineteenth century general contracting was an important alternative to such small firms, where many different arts were under a single enterprise, meaning that the one large firm could cover all parts of the building process.[75] With general contracting came greater emphasis on sub-contracting and specialisation, and a blurring of traditional distinctions, such as the labels 'master' and 'servant'.[76] Hence an element of proletarianisation might be suggested by the general contract system, especially where craftworkers took work for such firms in response to the volatilities of the labour market.[77]

The Incorporation had traditionally contained numbers of privileged small firms, with a single master and a handful of servants. Occasionally the papers of the Incorporation betray an acceptance of the larger firm, as with the accounts which note payments not to an upholsterer, but to 'the Upholstery Company'.[78] This is most likely the 'Edinburgh Upholstery Joiner and Mirror Glass Company', which was located at Carrubber's Close off the High Street, and consisted of the upholsterer, James Cullen, and a group of wrights and cabinet makers.[79] The periodic lists of freemen within the Incorporation's records had always been names of single masters, disregarding their journeymen and apprentices who were usually only mentioned when booking money was paid. With the Upholstery Company we see the Incorporation not only acknowledging a larger unit of production, but hiring them for work on an Incorporation property.

While large firms do appear in nineteenth-century Edinburgh, it has been demonstrated that they were far from the normal mode of craft production.[80] Richard Rodger has shown that in 1851 just over half (52.2 per cent) of the building firms in Scotland's principal burghs employed less than five workers, and 69.6 per cent employed fewer than ten, which highlights both the prevalence of the small firm, but also the disproportionate importance of the large firm.[81] For example, Rodger found that 13.2 per cent of the masonry firms accounted for half of the employment.[82] Though the larger, general-contracting firms made a significant contribution to the wider industry, the traditional model of the small firm remained the usual mode of production. This may have been much more compatible with the conservative attitudes of the Incorporation, which continued to seek control up until the 1840s, but it did not promote stability in the wider industry, as most of the small firms were unable to compete in terms of influencing the labour market, or raising the substantial capital for larger-scale projects.[83]

Evidence of building finance in early modern Scotland is difficult to find, though even the smallest of buildings naturally called upon considerable capital.[84] Some customers would have had access to resources sufficient to pay for an entire building, either upfront, or as needed, but larger-scale speculative building of multiple structures required capital often beyond the means of the average builder.[85] This was due, in part, to the prevalence of the small firms mentioned above.

Aside from personal wealth and credit, finance could be obtained from the land itself. One traditional form of such finance involved the 'sub-infeudation' of land. Feuing was a process of permanently alienating a piece of land for a fixed perpetual payment, or 'feu duty'.[86] Along with such annual payments were other occasional payments or 'casualties', as when a property passed to a holder's heir.[87] Such feuing was permanent, and offered security of tenure, though this encouraged higher feu prices to compensate the landowner for longer-term depreciation of the feu duty.[88] The feuar would in turn feu parts of the land out to sub-feuars, whose combined feu duties would both cover the original costs and generate a continuous profit.[89] Hence, feus could be used as collateral for securing further funding. Aside from feuing, developers could also create certain annuities on the land known as 'ground annuals'. As soon as they were created they could be sold to generate further capital.[90] As this process has been explained more eloquently and in better detail elsewhere, there is no need to elaborate on this system.[91] Suffice it to say that the holding of land was a crucial component of raising capital for the wider building industry.

Information on building finance in the early modern period is difficult to find, though it would appear that certain features of nineteenth-century finance have their roots well-established in the past.[92] It has been suggested that certain legal changes in the nineteenth century made this system easier to exploit, encouraging absenteeism and the commodification of property values.[93] Feu duties were often exported out of the town, highlighting complex networks of finance which connected Edinburgh properties with landlords in distant locations such as London or Dublin.[94] To what extent the 1603 Union of Crowns helped to open up such financial opportunities is not clear, though connections between and beyond the capitals were clearly significant.[95] Indeed, to fully understand this process, one would need to look at ecclesiastical investment, which might shed further light on the process of financing through feuing. Although the sources available for this study have not disclosed building finance, those which are available have suggested continuity rather than change in several areas.

Clearly technology, professionalisation, liberalism and capitalism had significant effects on both the wider building industry and the Incorporation in particular, though whether these should be deemed continuity or change is not always clear. Some crafts were more susceptible to changes in technology or professionalisation than others, whilst liberalism had a strong impact across the ten arts, as attitudes toward exclusive privileges changed in the wider society. Capital had always been necessary for commencement of building operations, and remained so for both the small firm and the general contractor. Though their abilities to martial resources were markedly different, the small firm remained the numerically-dominant unit of production, despite the importance of the fewer, but larger, firms. Land and sub-infeudation remained important components of building finance, though some aspects of the legal standing were altered. Capitalism might have been increasingly important to both the Incorporation and the wider building industry, but it is not clear that this wholly represents change.

UNITY IN DECLINE?

Regardless of changes to the wider building industry, the Incorporation itself underwent a massive change in 1846 through the loss of its privileged status. Clearly these privileges had always been contested, but the context in the early modern period was predicated on corporatism and the rights of the group. With the rise of liberalism and free-market thought, the Incorporation found itself unable to defend such exclusive privileges, so as Colston quite rightly observed, they continued, 'only as a benefit society'.[96] Gone was any influence over the labour market, though charitable functions, such as the distribution of pensions, still remain today.

Also surviving was a continued role in burgh affairs, politically in the short-term, and culturally up to the present day. Thanks to the efforts of Glasgow's Trades House, a political role on the town council remained, through the continuation of deacon conveners as municipal officials.[97] Although this role was later abolished, the Edinburgh incorporated trades have recently been involved in the revival of civic ceremonies, such as the 'riding of the marches'. Culturally, the Incorporation has much to offer to a capital city which consciously seeks to foster its heritage sector. This survival of the Incorporation is what makes this study so very important, as it is strikingly counterintuitive that such a disparate collection of individual arts managed to maintain unity through the vicissitudes of the last 543 years.

This returns us to the central question of this study. As a composite group of trades, how did the Incorporation build unity? Because of their composite nature, the Incorporation of Mary's Chapel had greater need for unity. A divided house was less able to protect its members' privileged position in the complex society of a European capital. To achieve this, they modelled themselves on two other composite institutions: the family and the wider household. These were the very building blocks of a stable, godly society, yet they too faced similar challenges of bringing together different individuals with potentially conflicting agendas into one corporate unit. By looking to the household, they found a model which included both the privileged kinship group, along with outsiders allowed to be co-resident. To the master, mistress and children were added the servants, while to the masons and wrights were added not only the other eight trades, but also the journeymen, apprentices and tolerated stallangers. Of course, there were also many who remained outside the House, as with the many unfree challengers who sought a place in the growing labour market. The very idea that the Incorporation was a household implied legitimacy for the few within, and illegitimacy for those without, but as any observer would surely have noticed, the family unit rarely survived intact. Death, remarriage, growth to adulthood and the leaving of the parental household all pointed to the complicated nature of the household, raising questions about just how stable it really was as an institution.[98] Likewise, the Incorporation was also complicated, and building unity as 'the House' was therefore a central strategy for its survival.

As elaborated on in earlier chapters, the phenomenon of corporatism is an important aspect of Europe's urban social structure, from the largest capital city, to many of the smaller aspiring towns. Paradoxically, to maintain the 'common well' for all, privileges were maintained for the few. For example, the seal of cause for the Masons and Wrights claimed that it was for the good of the whole town, as incorporating the privileged few was 'proffitable baith for the wirkaris and to all biggaris'.[99] Regardless of these privileges, many unfreemen were employed by the same council which granted the seal of cause, not to mention the court and crown. Still, the idea of corporate privilege was maintained.

Internally, the two senior trades enjoyed a large degree of control for the first two centuries of the Incorporation's history. Afterwards they had serious challenges to their authority from several of the other arts, especially from the later seventeenth century. As external pressure removed the monopoly of the masons and wrights on the headship of the House, they needed to be more flexible and to adapt to their changing circumstances, or the whole institution of their corporate privilege would have ceased. Even after 1846 the masons and wrights remained the nominal senior trades within the surviving Incorporation, but they were forced to compromise on certain issues in order to secure their often-tenuous hold on these corporate privileges. Through numerous threats, such as an expanding population of unfreemen, price uncertainties in wages and costs, suburban competition, and shifting markets with new types of wood and stone products, success in securing their position had to be carefully negotiated with both internal and external forces. Such pressures were not dissimilar to the challenges faced by the head of any Edinburgh household. The very fact that they began in 1475 as the 'Masons and Wrights', but ended after 1846 as the 'United Incorporations of Mary's Chapel', highlights the need they faced to rebuild their corporate identity. Rigidity, whether in policies or identity, had to go hand-in-hand with well-judged flexibility in order to maintain unity. As a composite craft, this is perhaps even more true than for single-craft incorporations, though further comparative work would be needed to test this.

Naturally, not every individual involved in craftwork features as prominently in the historical records as the privileged masters. Beyond the craftsmen of the 'House' were the wider households, including both craft families and their lodgers. As the household was the basic unit of society, the clear modelling of the Incorporation on the familial ideal reinforced the legitimacy of the privileged masters. Just as they used the symbols of their trades to imply authority and skill, so too they used the language of the family to project brotherhood within 'the House'. Of course the brethren of the ten arts did not always get along, which was often detrimental to the standing of the Incorporation. A divided house implied social breakdown, and this raised questions about legitimacy.

There were strategies for reinforcing the household model, as with marriages between craft households, though how effective this was corporately is questionable. Half of the known craft marriages were endogamous, suggesting a strengthening of corporate ties through the marriage bond, but of these endogamous marriages within the wider Incorporation, only 4 per cent crossed the dividing lines between the ten arts.[100] A mason's daughter was far less likely to marry a slater than to marry a mason. Not only was the Incorporation separated from the unfree labour force of the wider industry, but they were also quite compartmentalised within the corporate framework. Composite corporatism therefore shows a strong sense of the individual, despite the attempts to build unity as 'the House'.

This aspect of individuality is not necessarily out of keeping with the purposes of corporatism, as care for the individual members was an integral feature of the incorporation. This took many forms at different times. Occasionally it was through charitable giving, but at other times provision was in the form of work, education, or prayers for the eternal souls of members and their families.

The Reformation did much to alter some of the forms of charity and care provided by the Incorporation, though relations with the church continued to be important. Indeed, they proved formative, as the loss of the Incorporation's chapel at the Reformation led to the purchase of the disused medieval St Mary's Chapel, which gave a new name and a more-inclusive corporate identity for the ten trades of the former 'Incorporation of Masons and Wrights'. Modelling the Incorporation on the household helped build unity, and changing their name helped avoid the uncomfortable questions of who exactly got to be the head of that House. External arbitration was still needed to resolve this issue, but having a less-divisive name certainly contributed in the struggle for unity.

Whether through modelling corporate relations on the family and household, or through the formation of a new corporate identity that avoided the problems of headship, the building of unity was not wholly an internal process, as external relationships complicated matters. The legal

status of incorporation came from a municipal council which was domi-
nated by merchants with their own agendas. Occasionally the agendas
of the council and the Incorporation coincided, as with the problem of
the suburbs, but this could be undermined by differing opinions between
the ten trades, or interference from crown or court. The decreet arbitral
of 1583 helped to redefine corporate relations with wider burgh society.
This brought the Incorporation more into the municipal fold, though not
always into positions of power. One still might interpret this as a form of
solidification of the standing of the trades, though the rise of liberalism
and demographic pressures did much to erode their position over the next
two centuries. Still, they remained, despite an apparently severe crisis of
internal relations through the economically challenging later seventeenth
century.

Indeed, despite numerous challenges over the centuries, from the unfree
who sought access to their privileges, or the less-than-brotherly relations
within the Incorporation, the corporate body of the building trades did
not simply fade away into obscurity, as happened to so many other similar
incorporations in Scotland's burghs. Through occasionally troubled relations with municipal authorities, demographic pressures on the labour
market, and inflationary strains, the diverse trades of Mary's Chapel
managed to survive as a composite Incorporation by modelling themselves
on the family and the household. So, despite the loss of privileges in 1846,
the House still stands.

NOTES

1. *Edin. Recs*, 1642–1655, 181; Smith, J., *The Hammermen of Edinburgh and
   Their Altar in St Giles Church* (Edinburgh: William J. Hay, 1906), lxxxv and
   116; and Guidicini, G., 'Municipal Perspective, Royal Expectations, and the
   Use of Public Space: The Case of the West Port, Edinburgh, 1503–1633', in
   Architectural Heritage, 22 (2011), 40–3.
2. Prior to this, the ports had been closed at night to control access to the town
   and its markets. Allen, A., 'Production and the Missing Artefacts: Candles,
   Oil and the Material Culture of Urban Lighting in Early Modern Scotland',
   in *Review of Scottish Culture*, 23 (2011), 21.
3. The minutes of the town council showed little nostalgia or sympathy: 'Did
   Reccomend to Baillie Hamilton to dispose of the materials of the nether Bow:
   port in Such manner as he shall think best for the advantage of the City and
   that without loss of time and Resolve that the Bell there, be put up in the
   College Kirk.' ECA, SL1/1/80, 154–5, 29 August 1764. Other entries related
   to its removal appear in the same volume.
4. For details of the failed 1669 attempt to declare all tradesmen in royal burghs

free, see *General Report*, 1835, 83, quoting from Sir George Mackenzie's *History of Scotland*, 176.

5. James VI, 'Basilicon Doron', as reprinted in James, Bishop of Winton, *The Workes of the Most High and Mightie Prince, James* (London: Robert Barker and John Bill, 1616), 164: 'But for their part, take example by ENGLAND, how it hath flourished both in wealth and policie, since the strangers Craftesmen came in among them: Therefore not onely permit, but allure strangers to come heere also; taking as strait order for repressing the mutining of ours at them, as was done in ENGLAND, at their first in-bringing there.'

6. Farr, J. R., *Artisans in Europe, 1300–1914* (Cambridge: Cambridge University Press, 2000), 24 and 282.

7. Ibid., 276–82, and Fraser, W. H., *A History of British Trade Unionism 1700–1998* (Basingstoke: Macmillan, 1999), 2–3 and 12.

8. See for examples, the 1736 essay suggesting that Scotland's incorporated trades should be more open, like those of London: Lindsay, P., *The Interest of Scotland Considered, with Regard to its Police in Employing of the Poor, its Agriculture, its Trade, its Manufactures, and Fisheries* (London: T. Woodward and J. Peele, 1736), 53–6; or the 1790 notice of a court of session ruling that the Incorporation of Mary's Chapel was obliged to admit unfreemen for a reduced price: Anonymous, *The Scots Magazine*, 52: May (Edinburgh: Murray and Cochrane, 1790), 255. See also Appendix 10 for text of 1790 notice.

9. For examples of the use of maps to rationalise political boundaries in the process of reform, see Fleet, C., Wilkes, M. & Withers, C., *Scotland: Mapping the Nation* (Edinburgh: Birlinn, 2013), 113–15, and Fleet, C. and MacCannell, D., *Edinburgh: Mapping the City* (Edinburgh: Birlinn, 2014), 140–3. For an example of the Incorporation showing a rather conservative interest in the municipal boundaries, see ECA, Acc.622/8, 28, 9 March 1832.

10. While not a perfect line, the north-west boundary appears to have followed the water fairly closely in 1701, from Newhaven through Bonnington, Powderhall, Canonmills, Stockbridge, the Dean, and the 'Water of Leith Village', or Dean Village. The 1832 political boundaries, however, extended to Golden Acre and Comely Bank. See Maitland, W., *The History of Edinburgh From its Foundation to the Present Time* (Edinburgh: Hamilton, Balfour and Neill, 1753), 178, citing the 1701 'council register', and Fleet and MacCannell, *Edinburgh: Mapping the City*, 140.

11. See, for example, the response to the enquiries of the Burgh Commissioners whose report preceded the 1846 abolition of exclusive privileges: ECA, Acc.622/8, 109, 2 October 1833. See Appendix 11 for text.

12. ECA, Acc.622/8, 28, 9 March 1832.

13. Rodger, R., *The Transformation of Edinburgh: Land, Property and Trust in the Nineteenth Century* (Cambridge: Cambridge University Press, 2004), 96. While this was a dramatic change, it also shows a certain level

of continuity for the capital. The estimated population of Edinburgh is thought to have tripled between 1550 and 1650. Lynch, M., *Scotland: A New History* (London: Pimlico, 2000), 171. Clearly there was not a constant level of expansion from the sixteenth to the nineteenth centuries, but it is important to remember that such expansion was not a wholly new phenomenon.

14. Rodger, *Transformation of Edinburgh*, 95.

15. 'I _____ messenger, by virtue of a summons of declarator, whereof this and the seven preceding pages are full double to the will, raised at the instance of the Conveener William Jamieson, present Deacon of the Masons ... as representing the whole members of the said Incorporation, in his Majesty's name and authority, summon, warn, and charge you _____ to compear before the Lords of Council and Session, at Edinburgh, or where it shall happen them to be for the time ...' NLS, Acc.7056, Boxes 1 & 2 (copies in both), 1787 Summons of Declarator.

16. ECA, Acc.622/2, 109–15.

17. Ibid.

18. *Edin. Recs*, 1403–1528, 30–1. See Appendix 1 for text.

19. See, for example, the 1540 act of parliament discussed in the Introduction: Anentis conductioune of craftismen: *RPS*, 1540/12/84. Naturally, cost was also a potential barrier.

20. See for examples, ECA, Acc.622/8, 10, 14 October 1831, or ECA, SL34/2/4, 323, Lammas 1835. See also *General Report*, 1835, 84, which discusses this system as an attempt by the incorporated trades to make exclusive privileges 'less obnoxious'.

21. Compare the 1831 debate about how much the fines should be with the 1845 decision to compromise with the firm of Smith and Son who were encroaching on the Parliament House site. ECA, Acc.622/8, 10, 14 October 1831 and ECA, SL34/1/12, 92–3, 4 August 1845.

22. ECA, SL34/1/12, 55, 12 March 1844.

23. ECA, Acc.622/8, 191–4, 29 May 1835.

24. According to the petition, 'it would expose the labouring class of the community, to great and serious hardship, inasmuch as it would completely deprive them of the means of procuring the common necessaries of life, when owing to the inevitable fluctuations of trade, they happen to be temporarily out of employment, as no Tradesman or shopkeeper would be disposed to deal with them, without ready money, whereas under the present system, they obtain credit to a reasonable extent, till they have the means of extinguishing the debt, while the dread of imprisonment exites every exertion on their part, to redeem the sum due.' Ibid., 192.

25. See full text for further details of the relations between masters, men and 'dealers' of materials. Ibid., 191–4.

26. ECA, Acc.622/8, 139, 19 May 1834.

27. Ibid., 167–8, 4 August 1834 and 173, 17 November 1834.

28. Ibid., unpaginated section, 1 August 1842, citing a minute of 3 February 1840.

29. Ibid., unpaginated section, 1 August 1842.

30. Marwick, J. D., 'The Municipal Institutions of Scotland: A Historical Survey (Concluded)', in *Scottish Historical Review*, 1:3 (1904), 282–3.

31. Ibid., 282.

32. For two examples, see ECA, Acc.622/8, 1–5, 23 September 1831 and 10, 14 October 1831.

33. Fraser, W. H., *Conflict and Class: Scottish Workers, 1700–1838* (Edinburgh: John Donald, 1988), 139, quoting from W. M. Millar (ed.), *An Account of the Edinburgh Reform Jubilee, celebrated 10 August 1832* (Edinburgh, 1832).

34. Mackenzie, W. M., *The Scottish Burghs* (Edinburgh: Oliver and Boyd, 1949), 160–4 and 180–5.

35. Ibid., 180–2.

36. Ibid., 181.

37. Ibid., 182; *General Report*, 1835, 30; and Marwick, 'Municipal Institutions', 282–3.

38. Mackenzie, *Scottish Burghs*, 185, and Marwick, 'Municipal Institutions', 283.

39. ECA, Acc.622/8, 109–14, 2 October 1833. See Appendix 11 for the text of those queries and answers recorded in the minutes.

40. Ibid., 112–13, 2 October 1833: Enquiries 6 and 7.

41. Ibid., 113, 2 October 1833: Answer to enquiry 7.

42. *General Report*, 1835, 88–9.

43. 9 Victoria c.17 (1846). See Appendix 12 for text.

44. Bain, E., *Merchant and Craft Guilds A History of the Aberdeen Incorporated Trades* (Aberdeen: J. & J. P. Edmond & Spark, 1887), 320.

45. For example: ECA, Acc.622/8, 131–4, 17 February 1834 (Police Acts); 180–90, 18 March 1835 to 27 May 1835 (Water Company Bill).

46. Compare ECA, Acc.622/8, 176–9, 9 February 1835 and ECA, SL34/1/12, 79, 3 February 1845.

47. ECA, Acc.622/8, unpaginated section, 6 March 1838 and 1 August 1842.

48. Contrast Rodger, R., *Housing in Urban Britain, 1780–1914* (London: Macmillan, 1989), 19–20, with Price, R., *Masters, Unions and Men: Work Control in Building and the Rise of Labour, 1830–1914* (Cambridge: Cambridge University Press, 1980), 34 and 290, note 56, which suggests more upheaval from machinery for joiners.

49. Ibid., 19, and Sturt, G. *The Wheelwright's Shop* (Cambridge: Cambridge University Press, 1958), 56–61.

50. I'm grateful to Mr Peter Forret, retired joiner in Edinburgh, for sharing this detail of his Glasgow apprenticeship with me. Mr Forret's experiences can be contrasted with Ogilvie-Gordon, M. M., *A Handbook of Employments Specially Prepared for the Use of Boys and Girls on Entering the Trades,*

Industries and Professions (Aberdeen: The Rosemount Press, 1908), 166, which argues for a 'rapid increase' in the use of machinery in the building trades. It is further argued that this cheapened production.

51. For more on the professions and the phenomenon of 'professionalisation', see Dingwall, H. M., *Late Seventeenth-Century Edinburgh: A Demographic Study* (Aldershot: Scolar Press, 1994), 215–44; O'Day, R., *The Professions in Early Modern England, 1450–1800* (Harlow: Longman, 2000), 4, 7–9 and 255–7; and Nenadic, S., 'Architect-Builders in London and Edinburgh, c.1750–1800, and the Market for Expertise', in *Historical Journal*, 55:3 (2012), 597–616.

52. Nenadic, 'Architect-Builders in London and Edinburgh', 601.

53. For essays, see the 1845 admissions of a mason and a wright: ECA, SL34/1/12, 83–4, 18 April 1845, and 85–7, 19 May 1845. For apprentices, compare Chapter 4 of the 1842 laws: ECA, SL34/1/12, 9, 28 November 1842: 'Laws . . . Chapter IV: Of Apprentices', with the discussion of how best to amend the laws in the 'altered circumstances': ECA, SL34/1/12, 121–2, 3 August 1846, and 131 and 133, 8 October 1846.

54. Fraser, *History of British Trade Unionism*, 11–12, and Price, *Masters, Unions and Men*, 42, 61, 90, 92, 170 and 242.

55. Farr, *Artisans in Europe*, 277–82, and Lewis, A., *The Builders of Edinburgh New Town, 1767–1795* (Reading: Spire Books Ltd, 2014), 46.

56. Price, *Masters, Unions and Men*, 55–6.

57. Ibid., 56, citing W. L. Burn.

58. Farr, *Artisans in Europe*, 280–2.

59. Allen, A., 'Conquering the Suburbs: Politics and Work in Early Modern Edinburgh', in *Journal of Urban History*, 37:3 (2011), 426.

60. Lewis, *Builders of Edinburgh New Town*, 15, 23, 33 and 46.

61. The Incorporation certainly tried. Ibid., 33.

62. Ibid., 23.

63. Rodger, *Transformation of Edinburgh*, 55.

64. Fraser, *Conflict and Class*, 39–41.

65. Ibid., 41; ECA, SL34/1/4, 95–6, 11 April 1719; and Jackson, S., 'Edinburgh Cabinet Makers' Wage Agreements and Wage Disputes, 1805 to 1826', in *Scottish Archives: The Journal of the Scottish Records Association*, 11 (2005), 83.

66. The following account of the 1719 box society is from ECA, SL34/1/4, 95–6, 11 April 1719: 'Act of the Incorporation In favours of such of the journeymen wrights as have joyned in the society'.

67. Fraser, *Conflict and Class*, 50.

68. ECA, Acc.622/1 and NLS, *Edinburgh Evening Courant*, 14 July, 23 July, and 1 September 1764.

69. NLS, *Edinburgh Evening Courant*, 1 September 1764.

70. London School of Economics and Political Science Library, Webb Trade Union Collection, A/XIII/441, 'Masons' Strike in 1764', in *Forfar Review*

(Summer, 1892). I am grateful to Dr David Motadel and Dr Paul Horsler for their help in accessing this source.

71. Fraser, *Conflict and Class*, Chapter 3; Fraser, *History of British Trade Unionism*, 1–8; Jackson, 'Edinburgh Cabinet Makers', 79; and Lewis, *Builders of Edinburgh New Town*, 29 and 120–2.

72. Jackson, 'Edinburgh Cabinet Makers', 81–2.

73. For more on the 'Combination Acts' in Scotland, see Jackson, 'Edinburgh Cabinet Makers', 82, footnote 9; Fraser, *History of British Trade Unionism*, 8–13; and 'Section 2: Combination Laws', in Haythornthwaite, J. A., Wilson, N. C., and Batho, V. A., *Scotland in the Nineteenth Century: An Analytical Bibliography of Material Relating to Scotland in Parliamentary Papers, 1800–1900* (Aldershot: Scolar Press, 1993), 209–11.

74. Rodger, *Transformation of Edinburgh*, 3 and Fraser, *History of British Trade Unionism*, 12.

75. Price, *Masters, Unions and Men*, 22–34. Contracting had long been a feature of building in Scotland, though not necessarily with such emphasis on the single firm. Knoop, D. and Jones, G. P., *The Scottish Mason and the Mason Word* (Manchester: Manchester University Press, 1939), 9–15.

76. Price, *Masters, Unions and Men*, 25 and 30. Not all of the building trades experienced this to the same extent, of course. See Fraser, *Conflict and Class*, 28, for variable levels of sub-contracting between masons and wrights, and 34, for marked specialisation from the eighteenth century.

77. Rodger, *Transformation of Edinburgh*, 182.

78. ECA, Acc.622/1, 318, 24 August 1765, and 395, 27 August 1768.

79. Habib, V., 'Eighteenth-Century Upholsterers in the Edinburgh Old Town', in *Scottish Archives: The Journal of the Scottish Records Association*, 11 (2005), 71–2.

80. Price, *Masters, Unions and Men*, 19, and Rodger, R., 'Structural Instability in the Scottish Building Industry 1820–80', in *Construction History*, 2 (1986), 49–51.

81. Rodger, 'Structural Instability', 49–51.

82. Ibid., 51.

83. Ibid., 55, and Price, *Masters, Unions and Men*, 24 and 26–7.

84. This is focussed on new buildings, which were probably not the usual work of the building trades. Indeed, the minutes of the Incorporation note that one reason why they opposed the 1835 bill for abolishing imprisonment for debts below £8 6s 8s, was that most of the accounts incurred to them were below this threshold. Clearly their usual work involved small jobs such as repairs and renovations. ECA, Acc.622/8, 191–4, 29 May 1835.

85. Rodger, 'Structural Instability', 55–6.

86. Rodger, *Transformation of Edinburgh*, 70. It has been described by Rodger as 'the peculiarly Scottish combination of freehold and leasehold tenure systems'. Rodger, *Housing in Urban Britain*, 15.

87. Rodger, *Transformation of Edinburgh*, 70–1.

88. Ibid., 70.

89. Rodger, *Housing in Urban Britain*, 25–6.

90. Rodger, *Transformation of Edinburgh*, 72–3.

91. Ibid., 70–6.

92. Ground annuals were certainly well established by 1641 when a definition of the term was included in the reprinting of John Skene's 1597 book of Scottish legal terms, *De Verborum Significatione*: 'Alwayes, ground annuel is esteemed to be quhen the ground and property of ony land bigged or unbigged, is disponed and annalied for ane annuel to be payed to the annalier thereof, or to ane vther person, sik as ony Chaiplaine or Priest.' Skene, J., *De Verborum Significatione: The Exposition of the Termes and Difficill Wordes* ... (London: E.G., 1641), 8.

93. Rodger, *Transformation of Edinburgh*, 65–8, 70 and 116.

94. Ibid., 116.

95. Finance aside, the aspects of training demonstrate clear links. See Nenadic, 'Architect-Builders in London and Edinburgh', 597–616.

96. Colston, J., *The Incorporated Trades of Edinburgh* (Edinburgh: Colston & Co., 1891), 73.

97. Bain, *Merchant and Craft Guilds*, 320.

98. Flandrin, J., *Families in Former Times: Kinship, Household and Sexuality* (Cambridge: Cambridge University Press, 1979), 50.

99. *Edin. Recs*, 1403–1528, 31. See Appendix 1 for text of seal of cause.

100. See Chapter 2, Tables 2.1 and 2.2.

Appendix 1: Seals of Cause

The following texts are taken from the first volume of the printed extracts of the Edinburgh council records, published by the Scottish Burgh Records Society in 1869. The original 1475 documents were still extant in 1923 when Anna Jean Mill listed them in her 'Rough Inventory of Records Belonging to the Wrights and Masons of Edinburgh', but were then lost until found in the Edinburgh City Archives in early 2016.[1] The 1489 seal of cause that incorporated the coopers with the masons and wrights was not mentioned by Mill, but was again available in the published council records. The text from the council copies are given here.

15 October 1475.

[Grant of the Isle and Chapel of St John in St Giles to the Wrights and Masons.][2]

Till all and syndry quhom it efferis quhais knawlege thir present lettres sall cum. – The prouest ballies counsall dene of gild and dekynnis of the hale craftismen within the burgh of Edinburgh greting in the Sone of the glorious Virgine. Wit ye ws in the honour worschipe and glore of Almychte God and of the glorious virgin Sanct Mary, and of our patrone Sanct Gele, and for the furthering helping eiking and suppleing of diuine seruice daily to be done at the altar of Sanct Jhone the Ewangelist, foundit in the College Kirk of Sanct Geile of Edinburgh, and for reparatioun beilding and polecy to be maid in honour of the said sanct of Sanct Jhone, and of the glorius sanct Sanct Jhone the Baptist, to have consentit and assignit, and be thir our present lettres consentis and assignis, to our lovit nychtbouris the hale craftismen of the Masonis and of the Wrichtis within the said burgh, the ile and chapell of Sanct Jhone fra the ald hers of irne inwarts als frely as it is ouris, with all the fredomis proffittis and esementis thairto pertenand at we haf or may haf richt to, nocht doand nor committand ony preiudice or skaith to Sir Jhone Scaithmure[3] or his successouris in his first feftment or priuilegis that he has broukit or joisit of befor. To be haldin and to be had the said ile and chapell of Sanct Jhone fra the irne hers inwart with the pertinentis to the saidis craftismen the Masonis and Wrichtis of the said burgh and to thair successouris for euir, with power to edify big reparell and put it ony pairt thairof to polesy or honour of the saidis sanctis outhir in werk or diuine seruice quhatsumeuir at the altar or vther wayes, nocht hurtand the auld feftment. And the saidis craftismen to vse occupy and aduoruy the said ile as thair awin proper ile, siclyk as vtheris craftismen occupies within the said College Kirk, nocht doand ony preiudice to our patronage or to the auld feftment or to the auld laus in the said Ile. And at the said craftismen sall adoury and haf the day of Sanct Jhone the Baptist and to thig to the licht of the said altar as vtheris dois in the kirk yerlie. And this till all thame quhom it efferis we mak it knawin be thir our present lettres. And in witnessing hereof our commoun sele of caus of the said burgh, togidder with the selis of Alexander Turing, David Quhytehed, Bartillmo Carnis, balyeis for the tyme, and Alexander Richerdsons sele dene of the gild, in token of gevin consent and assignatioun to the saidis craftismen of the said ile, be the handis of the dekin for them all, ar to hungin at Edinburgh the xv day of the moneth of October the yeir of God j^m four hundreth sevinty and five yeris.[4]

[Seal of Cause to Wrights and Masons][5]

Till all and syndry quhom it efferis quhais knawlege thir present lettres sall cum;– The prowest ballies counsall and the dekynnis of the hale craftismen of the burgh of Edinburgh greting in God euirlestand, Wit your vniuersiteis that our comburgessis and nychtbouris all the craftsmen of the Masonis and the Wrichtis within the said burgh quhilkis presentit to ws in jugement thair bill of supplicatioun desyring of ws our licence consent and assent of certane statutis and reullis maid amangis tham self for the honour and worschip of Sanct Jhone in augmentatioun of devyne seruice, and richt sa for reuling governyng of the saidis twa craftis, and honour and worschipe of the towne, and for treuth and lawte of the saidis craftis proffitable baith for the wirkaris and to all biggaris, the quhilk bill togidder with thair statutis and reullis befor ws red, and thairwith we beand wele awysit, considerit and fand that thai war gud and loveable baith to God and man, and consonand to ressoun, and thairto we assentit and grantit tham thair desyris, togidder with the Ile of Sanct Jhone in the college kirk of Sanct Gele to beild and put to polesy in honour of the said Sanct, and for the sufferage of devyne seruice, and thir ar the artikallis and statutis at we haf approvit and for ws in sa fer as we haf power; In the first it is thocht expedient that thair be chosin four personis of the best and worthiest of the twa craftis, that is to say twa masonis and twa wrychtis, that sall be sworne, quhilkis sall serche and se all wirkis at the craftismen wirkis, and that it be lelely and treulie done to all biggaris; Item, gif ony man beis plentuous of ony wirk or of ony wirkman of the saidis craftis thai to complenye to the dekin and the four men or to ony twa of tham, and thai persons sall caus the scaith and wrang to be amendit, and gif thai can nocht the prowest and baillies to gar it be amendit as efferis. Item, gif ony persoun or persouns of the saidis craftis cummis of newe after this act to the guid towne and schapis to wirk, or to tak wirk apoun hand, he sall first cum to the said four men and thai sall examyn him gif he be sufficient or nocht and gif he beis admittit he sall lay downe to the reparatioun of the altar a merk. Item, that na master nor persone of ony of the craftis tak ony prentis for les termis than sevin yeirs, and ilk prentis to pay at his entre to the said altar half a merk, and gif any prentis of quhatsumeuir of the saidis craftismen, or yit his feit man, pasis away or the ische of his termes but leif of his master, and quha that resauis the prentis or feit man thai sall pay to the altar ane pund of walx the first falt, the secund falt twa pundis of walx, the third falt to be pvnist be the provest and ballies of the towne as efferis; and allswa quhen ony prentisses has completit his termis and is worne out, he sall be examinit be the four men gif he be sufficient or nocht to be a fallow of the craft, and gif he be worthy to be a fallow he sall pay half a merk to the alter and brouke the priuilege of the craft, and gif he be nocht sufficient he sall serf a master quhill he haf lirit to be worthy to be a master, and than to be maid freman and fallow. Item, gif thar be ony of the craft that disobeyis or makis discord amangis the craftismen of ony of the craftis, or that ony of them plenyeis apoun them sall be brocht befor the dekynnis and ouermen of the craftis, and thai to gar amend it be trety amangis thamself, and gif thai can nocht be faltouris to be brocht and pvnist be the prowest and ballies of the towne for thair trespas as efferis. Alswa the saidis twa craftismen sall caus and haue thair placis and rowmes in all generale processiouns lyk as thai haf in the towne of Bruges or siclyk gud townes, and gif ony of the craftismen of outher of the craftis decesis and has na guds sufficient to bring him furth honestly, the saidis craftis sall vpoun thair costes and expensis bring him furth and gar bery him honestlie as thai aucht to do of det to thair brother of the craft; and allswa it sall be lefull to the saidis twa craftis and craftismen of Wrichtis and Masounis to haue power quhatsumeuir vtheris actis statutis or ordinancis that thai think mast convenient for the vtilite and proffet of the gud towne and for tham to statut and ordane with awys of the hale craftis and of our succes-souris, thai to be ratifiit and apprufit siclik as thir actis, and to be actit and transsumpt in the commoun buke of Edinburgh hafand the samyn forme force and effect as this present writ has. The quhilkis actis ordinance and devys shewin to ws and considerate we appruf ratifyes and for ws and our successouris confirmis and admittis in so far as we haf power. In witnes of the quhilk thing to thir present lettres we haf to affixt our commoun sele of caus, togidder with the seles of the ballies of the said burgh for the tyme, in takynyng of appreving of all the thingis aboue writtin, the xv day of October the yeir of God j^m iiij^c seventy and five yeirs.[6]

6 August 1489

[Seal of Cause to the Cooper Craft][7]

Till all and syndry quhais knawledge thir present lettres sall cum, the provest, ballies, and counsall of the burgh of Edinburgh greting in God euirlesting, wit ye that the day of the making of thir present lettres comperit befor ws sittand counsaly gadderit and for jugement within the Tolbuith of the said burgh, in the inner chalmer of the samyn, thir persouns vnder written, Alexander Browne cowpar, Jhone Richartsoun, William Coupar, Jhone Jhonsoun, and Gilbert Turnour, masteris of the Cowpar craft within the said burgh, and thar presentit till ws thair supplication and bill of complant makand mentioun that diverssis personis of the said craft quhilkis ar and has bene of lang tyme obstinat and inobedient in obseruying and keping of gud reull ordinance and statutis maid and ordaint of befor and confirmit be our predecessorires to the maisteris of the wrichtcraft for the uphald of diuine seruice and augmentatioun thairof at Sanct Jhonis altar situat in our College Kirk of Sanct Gele within the said burgh, and speciale in the withhalding and disobeying in the deliuering and paying of the oulkly penny to God and to Sanct Jhone and to the reparatioun of the said altar, and als in the disobeysance in the payment making of thar prentis siluer at thair entre, quhilk is five shilling, to the reparatioun and polesy of the said alter, nor yit will nocht pay thair dewteis at the wpsetting of thar buthis siclyke as the masters of the wrychtis ar ordaint and statut to pay, considering the said Couper craft is conformit to tharis and bundin with tham to fulfill the reulis and pay siclyke dewteis to the Sanct and altar as thai and thai lymmit togidder, and [adionit] to gadder and inbring the samyn dewteis and mak compt and rekynnyng thairof to thair dekyin and kirk maisters of the Wrichtis as efferis, and siclyke as is vsit amangis vther craftis of the said burgh, and as anentis the outlandisfolkis that the said masteris of the Cowpar craft complanit vpoun lauborand and vsand thair craft and practik thairof in this tovne, passand fra hous to hous mendand and spilland nychtbouris wirk and stuf, hafand nother stob nor stake within this towne, nor yit walkis nor wardis nor yit beris sic portable chargis with tham as extentis and vtheris quhen thai occur, nor yit beand sufficient in thair labour and werkmenschip, and thairthrow neuertheles hurtis and scaithis the saidis masteris in thair fredomes and priuilegis contrar to all gud reull ordour and polecy within burgh, Quharupon the saidis masteris of the Cowpar craft besocht ws of remeid for the honour and loving of God and Sanct Jhone, and the sustentatioun and wphalding of divine seruice at his altar forsaid, patrone to the saidis craftis, The quhilk bill and supplicatioun beand red herd and vnderstandyn and diligentle considerit be ws that thair petitioun was consonant to ressoun and to the lovage of God and thair patrone forsaid, and als consonand to the commoun proffet of the said burgh, we decret ordanis and deliueris concordand to thair resonable desyris and petitioun that all the poyntis and articlis contenit in the statutis of the Wrichtis confermit be the tovne be obseruit and kepit to the masteris of the Cowpar craft, and be tham in all thingis accordand to thair craft, and quha that disobeyis tham that ane officer pas with tham and tak a poynd of the disobeyar, and mak penny [payment] thairof to the awale and quantite of the dewteis awand to Sanct Jhone the altar and chaplane thairof for the tyme, siclyk as vse and wont has bene, and at the said officeris sall caus the masteris and ingadderaris of the said dewteis to be answerit and obeyit thairvntill, and thai to mak compt rekynning and payment to the dekin and kirkmaster of the said altar, and at all the laif of the wrichtis statutis forsaid be obseruit and kepit with tham and be tham according to thair faculte; and anentis the outlandismen quhilkis prevenis tham in thair laubouris and proffetis, that officeris pas with tham and forbid and put tham fra the occupatioun thairof in this towne, bot gif thai mak residence thairvntill, and pay thair dewteis to Sanct Jhone and the craft, and be resauit thairvntill be the masteris thairof, and to fulfill the statutis aboue expremit as efferis, sa that the disobeyaris be pvnist be the officeris of the towne efter the tenour of the saidis wrichtis statutis maid of befor and confermit be our predecessouris. In witnes of the quhilk thing we haue gart append our commoun sele of caus to thir present lettres at Edinburgh the xxvj day of August the yeir of God j^m four hundreth auchty and nyne yeiris.[8]

NOTES

1. ECA, Mill Recs, A1 and A2, and Mill, 'Inventory', 1.
2. Bracketed text is from the margins of the printed council records.
3. Sir John Skathmur was a canon of Chapter of St Giles, as indicated by the inclusion of his name in the 'signatures manual of the Canons'. See Marwick, J. D. (ed.), *Charters and Other Documents Relating to the City of Edinburgh, A.D. 1143–1540* (Edinburgh: SBRS, 1871), 142–5: 'Johannes Skathmur manu propia'.
4. *Edin. Recs*, 1403–1528, 30–1.

5. Bracketed text is from the margins of the printed council records.
6. *Edin. Recs*, 1403–1528, 31–2.
7. Bracketed text is from the margins of the printed council records.
8. *Edin. Recs*, 1403–1528, 57–8.

Appendix 2: Mill's Partial Transcription of the 1517 Letter from the Archbishop of St Andrews

The following partial transcription is from Anna Jean Mill's 1923 'Rough Inventory of Records Belonging to the Wrights and Masons of Edinburgh', held by the Edinburgh City Archives.[1] The original has since been found and is also in the Edinburgh City Archives, but is not yet fully transcribed.[2] The letter corresponds to the 20 June 1517 confirmation of the Incorporation's seals of cause by Andrew Forman, Archbishop of St Andrews (1514–1521), which is also amongst the Mill Records in the Edinburgh City Archives.[3] Forman, as Archbishop of St Andrews, had authority over the diocese that included St Giles in Edinburgh.

Andro be the mercy of God archebißope of Saintandro primat of the realme of Scotland, Borne legat of the apostolicke sea, And sic a legate of the said sea, through the hoill realmefoir said, quha hes pouer and authorite of a legate (send) from the papas syde; As lykvyes perpetual commendatar of the abbacie of dumfermeling; Vnto the curatis of the colegiat kirk of Saint Egide of edinburghe, And the pariche kirkis of halyrudhouse, Santcudbertis vnder the castell wall, And of Restalrig, or vnto ony vther chapelane, curate, or nocht curat, celebrating divine ßervice within our diocie Being duelie requyreit vpoun the executioune of thir presents Salvatioune and health with divine benedictioune. (Lately he had a <u>petition from the Wrights and Masons of Edinburgh</u> and their adherents as also of the masters of the fabric of the altar of St John the Baptist in the Church of St Giles, which petition said that some statutes of the Craft had been approved and ratified by the Town Council of Edinburgh under the seal of common causes and asks for ratification of the charter. He commands the curates to warn all the masons, carpentars, coopers, glassinwrights, bowers, slaters, "dykars", to obey the statutes and within nine days thereafter to pay to the masters of the fabric of the altar (?MS. torn here prentiships and entries of masters to the freedom of the craft and to pay and satisfy the present chaplain of the altar and his successors "for his interteinment in meat and drink" and usual fee under pain of (1) excommunication, & (2) "aggravatioune",) "Thridlie gif they sall ʒit abyde with indured hairtis, as befoir is said, sic excommunicatioune and aggravatioune for vther nyne dayes immediatilie following the said aggravatioune, we then taking heade that as wickednes increassis punishment sould lykwayes incresß, That these quhom the feare of God calles not back from evil, severitie of discipline sould restraine, And that the heavier thair sines be, the langer thair vnhappie saule sould be deteineit wnder bandis; And least, the easines of punißment sould gif peartnes to sine We hawe thocht gude to Reaggrawat our foirsaid sentencesß of excommunicatioune and aggravatioune and be the tenor of this presentis we reaggravat the same wpoun them and everie ane of them, chairging ȝow thairfoir, as befoire, that ȝe and evrie ane of ȝow publicklie and solemnlie denunce sic wicked men, not obeying our admonitiounes, bot lying damnablie and filthilie involved in the said sentences of excommunicatioune, aggravatioune and reaggravatioune, In the foirisaid kirkes and all vther places competent for sic purpose, on all and everie festuall and ferial dayes quhen greater multitude conveines to heare divine ßrvice, efter the solemnities or the mesß, and vther divine houres, The bellis being rung, candillis being lichtit and put out, and as custome is, throwen to the ground, going forvard be way of processioune withe the crosß borne vp, and religious habite put on; And singing the psalme, deus laudem to chase away the dewles quha haldis them so captive and bund, And praying that our lord Jesus crist wald degnie him self to reduce them ~~then~~ to the bosome of there holie mother the kirk, And that he suffer them not to end thair dayes in sic wickednes, casting thre stones toward thair duelling housß In signe of eternall maledictioune quhilk the lord gave to core dathan and abiron, quhom the earth for thair wickednes did swallow quick; Not cessing to do sua, quhill that they returne to the bosome of thair holy mother the kirk, humblie to crawe and obteine the benefite of absolutioune And quhill ȝe resave wther command from vs. And ȝe sall rander thir presentes duelie execute to the bearer, given vnder our round seale At Edinburgh the viij day of Julij the ȝeir of God 1517 And the thrid ȝeir of our translatioune

    Be the said moist reverend airchbißope
        And legit
        Johne lauderis

NOTES

1. Mill, 'Inventory', A8, 3–4.
2. ECA, Mill Recs, A8.
3. Ibid., A6, A7 and A8, and Mill, 'Inventory', A6–A8, 2–4.

Appendix 3: 1527–8 Ratification of Seal of Cause by James V

The following text is from the Register of the Great Seal of Scotland, *and details in Latin and Scots the confirmation by James V of the acts and statutes of the 'wrights and masons' of Edinburgh.*

'536. Apud Edinburgh, 12 Jan. [1527–8]
REX confirmavit acta et statuta confecta seu conficienda per ecclesie magistros, decanos et artificiorum magistros CARPENTARIORUM ET LATHAMORUM et alios assistentes et sustentatores divini servitii apud altare SS. Johannis Baptiste et Evangeliste infra ECCLESIAM COLLEGIATAM BURGIDE EDINBURGH, eorumque predecessores seu successores; et specialiter (1) cartam sub hac forma; – [Till all and syndry ... the provost, ballies, counsall, dene of gild and dekynnis of the hale craftismen within the burgh of Edinburgh greting; – wit ye ws ... to have consentit and assignit to our lovit nychtbouris the hale craftismen of the masonis and of the wrichtis within the said burgh, – the ile and chapel of Sanct Johne (in the college kirk of Sanct Gele) fra the ald herse of irne inwort, als frely &c. ...; – not committand ony prejudice to Schir Jhonne Scaithmure or his successouris in his first feftment: — cum communi sigillo dicti burgi, et sigillis Alexandri Turing, David Quhythed, Bart. Carnis, ballivorum, et Alex. Richerdsone decani gilde:— Apud Edinburgh, 15 Oct. 1475]:— (2) cartam sub hac forma;— [Till all &c. the prowest, baillies, counsall and the dekynnis &c. (*ut supra*);— we beand wele awysit &c. grantit our licence, consent and assent of certane statutis and reullis maid be all the craftismen of the masonis and the wrichtis amangis thaim self for the honour and worschip of Sanct Jhonne in augmentatioun of devyne service, and richtsa for reuling governyng of the saidis twa craftis:— (*sequuntur statuta in vulgari*):— cum communi sigillo dicti burgi, et sigillis ballivorum;— 15 Oct. 1475]:— (3) cartam sub hac forma;— [Till all &c., the provest, ballies and counsall of the burgh of Edinburgh greting;— comperit befor ws thir personis under writtin, Alex. Browne cowpar, Joh. Richertsoun, Wil. Coupar, Johnne Jhonsone and Gilbert Turnour, masteris of the cowpar craft within the said burgh, and presentit till ws ther supplicatioun and bill of complant, makand mentioun that diversse personis of

the said craft quhilkis are and has bene of lang tyme obstinat and inobedient in observyng and keping of gude reull, and specialie in the withholding
and disobeyng in the delivering of thir oulkly penny to God and to Sanct
Jhonne &c.; and as anentis the outlandis folkis that the said masteris
complenit apon, lauborand and usand ther craft in this toune, passand fra
house to house mendand and spilland nychbouris werk and stuf, hafand
nether stob nor stake within this towne, nor yet walkis nor wardis, &c.:—
quharupon we decret concordand to ther resonable desyris, that all the
poyntis and articlis contenit in the statutis of the wrichtis confermit be the
towne, be observit and kepit to the masteris of the cowparcraft; and anentis
the outlandis men quhilkis prevenis thaim in ther laubouris and proffettis,
that officeris pas with thaim and forbid and put thaim fra the occupatioun
therof in this towne bot gif thai mak residence therintill and pay ther
dewteis to S. Johnne and the craft, and be resavit therintill be the maisteris therof, &c.:— cum communi sigillo dicti burgi:— Apud Edinburgh,
26 Aug. 1489]:— INSUPER dedit licentiam dictis ecclesie magistris ad
percipiend. ab unoquoque emptitio, viz. *le prentice*, cui intrare conting-
eret ad discend. dicta artificia, 20 sol., et cum forent admisei magistri 30
sol.,— applicand. sustentationi divini servitii dicti altaris, et reparationi
ejusdem:— TEST. *ut in aliis cartis &c.*   xxii. 62.'[1]

NOTE

1. *RMS*, vol. 3, 119–20, no. 536 (12 Jan. 1527–8).

Appendix 4: 1532 Order of Crafts in Processions

The following text is transcribed from a letter from the provost, bailies, and council of Edinburgh, to the sheriff and council of Haddington. In it, the council reiterates to their counterparts in Haddington the order of precedence in processions for the various incorporated trades.

'Till all and syndry quhais knawlege thir p[rese]nt l[ett]ers sall to cum And in speciall to ye ry^t honoraibill sh^{r}ef off haidinton bail3es counsel & communite of ye samin The p[ro]vest bail3es counsel of ye brouch of Edinburgh greeting Sene meid and meritabill thing is to bere lele and suchfast witnessing to ye vate and specialie in caus or causis q^{r}throw ye conceling of the vate preiudice or schaith may be ingenerit to ye innocent theirfor it is to 3^r universate we maik it knawn that it is ye lovaible use and ordour observit and keipit wy^{t}in yis towne amangs the craftsmen in ye passing in p[ro]cession on corps cristi day the octavis^1 y^{r}eftir And all uthir generall processionis and gathererings y^t is to say that hail brethers of hamyrmen of all kynd off sorts to gidd^r wy^t ye masons wrychts glasinvrychts and paynt^{rs} passis all to gidd^r wy^t y^r baneris nixt the sacrame[n]t And nixt yair befor passis the baxstars The thred craft befor yai is the wobstars & waikars to gide[r] The ferd is ye tail3^{rs} The fift place befor ye sacrame[n]t is ye cordanars The sixt place is ye skynars and furrours The vij place befor ye sacrame[n]t passis ye barbour The viij place q^{lk} is ye formest place passand befor ye p[ro]cession is ye fleshars & candillmaikars And this is ye ordour keipit wichtin yis toun amang ye craftsmen in all p[ro]cessions and gatherings The q^{lk} to yow we maik it manifestly knawn be thir pnts subscrivit wy^t our common scrives hand At Edinburgh ye xxvij day of maij ye 3eir of god ane thousand five hundreth thretty twa 3eirs

Ita est Johannes foular notarius publicis communus scriva burgi de Edinburgh de mandate subscription manualibus'^{2}

NOTES

1. Octave refers to the eighth day of the Corpus Christi cycle, when the festival finished.

2. NRS, GD98/11/9, Letters from the provost, etc., of Edinburgh, to the sheriff of Haddington, bailies and council thereof, anent precedence in processions of the Crafts, 27 May 1532.

Appendix 5: Documents Relating to Foundation of Mary's Chapel, 1505–6

The following text is taken from The Register of the Great Seal of Scotland, *vol. 2:* A.D. *1424–1513, and records the foundation of St Mary's Chapel in Niddry's Wynd, Edinburgh, by Elizabeth Livingston, Countess of Ross, at the end of 1505.*

'**2905.** Apud Edinburgh, 1 Jan.
REX ad manum mortuam confirmavit cartam Elizabethe comitisse Rossie, – [qua in puram elemosinam consessit, ad sustentationem unius capellani perpetui, viz. D. Wil. Broun junioris et ejus successorum, in NOVA CAPELLA B.V.M. DE NATIVITATE, per se construeta in *le Nudryis Vynd* infra burgum de EDINBURGH, – terram per se noviter edificatam in dicto burgo ex parte australi ejusdem in dicta venella de *le Nudryis Vynd*, ex parte orientali transitus ejusdem, inter dict. capellam. ex boreali, (tenementum) M. David Vocat ex australi, terram vastam Pat. Forehouse infra tenementum quondam Geo. Grenelaw ex orientali partibus:– Test. Fratre David Andersoun provinciali totius ordinis Fratrum Predicatorum regni Scotie, Alex. Lawder preposito, et Joh. Levingtoun uno ballivorum, dicti burgi, D. Joh. Quhite rectore de Petcokkis, Phil. Colvile, Hen. Strathauchin notario publico, et Alex. Clerk:– Apud Edinburgh, 31 Dec. 1505]:– TEST. *ut in carta* 2734.

xiv. 175.'[1]

Mill included in her 1923 'Rough Inventory of Records Belonging to the Wrights and Masons of Edinburgh' a set of notes and quotations from a 1505–6 confirmation of the Countess of Ross's 'charter of donation and concession', which gives further detail of the foundation of St Mary's Chapel in Niddry's Wynd.[2] The original was recently found and is in the care of the Edinburgh City Archives.[3]

'3. <u>1505/6</u>. Copy (in Scots) of Confirmation by King James under the Great Seal of the "Chartour of donation and concession" by our beloved kinswoman, Elizabeth, Countess of Ross, of all and hail her tenement of land in Niddries Wynd toward the sustentation of a perpetual chaplain, Sir

William Brown and his successors, in the new chapel of the Nativity of the Blessed Virgin Mary built by the said Elizabeth and lying in Niddries Wynd for perpetual divine service to be celebrated for the souls of our umquhile dearest father and mother and of our dearest consort, Margaret, Queen of Scots, and of the said Elizabeth, and others. (The Charter specifies the new Chapel of St Mary "edified and build by us" with the land "foir and bak" and the "pertinents by us newlie builded". Bounds.) The Donation of the Chaplain is to pertain to Elizabeth for lifetime, then to Robert Colville of Hiltonn and his heirs. Conditions to which Chaplain must conform – must be "of sufficient literatour and good and honest conversation" – and his duties. The Chaplain and his successors are to uplift yearly from the lands 20 marks towards their sustentation. Rest of the rents to go to repairing of the Chapel, furnishing of bread, wine and ornaments. If the profit is not more than 20 marks, then the Chaplain is to repair the Chapel and furnish the bread, etc. All of which is to be done with the advice of the patron. <u>Date of Charter – 31st Dec. 1505. Date of confirmation – 1st Jan. 1505/6.</u>

(And see Register of Great Seal, Vol. II, p. 617. No. 2905.).'[4]

NOTES

1. *RMS*, vol. 2, 617, no. 2905.
2. Mill, 'Inventory', 1. For further commentary on Mill's 'Inventory', see Allen, A., 'Finding the Builders: Sources Lost and Extant for Edinburgh's Incorporation of Mary's Chapel', in *Scottish Archives: The Journal of the Scottish Records Association*, 20 (2014), 103–6, and Allen, A., 'The Missing Records of the Edinburgh Building Trades: Mill's 'Rough Inventory' and the Incorporation of Mary's Chapel', in *Architectural Heritage* (Forthcoming: 2018). The charter was found in the Edinburgh City Archives in January 2016, along with most of the items noted in Mill's 'Inventory'. See 'Mill Records' in the bibliography for accession information.
3. ECA, Mill Recs, A3.
4. Mill, 'Inventory', 1.

Appendix 6: Excerpts from Inventory of Writs Relating to 1601 Purchase of St Mary's Chapel, Niddry's Wynd

The undated, itemised 'Inventory of Writs' held by the National Library of Scotland (NLS)[1] includes the following excerpts that relate to the 1601 purchase of the medieval chapel and corresponding lands and entitlements which would give the name 'Mary's Chapel' to the Incorporation. Whilst it is not clear what has happened to all of the documents listed, one 1601 document mentioning James Chalmer and the Incorporation can be found in the NLS.[2] Whilst previously it was thought that the Incorporation purchased Mary's Chapel in Niddry's Wynd in 1618, these excerpts suggest that the process had begun by 1601, and continued into the 1630s with the purchase of rights and properties associated with the chapel.

Followis ane particular inventar of the writtis of and contenyng These tenimentis of land baick and for in front and in taill with housses biggingis close and utheris pertinents thereof . . .

14   Item ane contract maid betwix the said James Chalmer on the ane pairt and the deacones of masones and wrightis of the said burgh of Edinburghe for thame selffis and in name of the remanent masters and bretherin of thair saids craftis and of thair haill societie & yr successors on the uther pairt of the date at Edinburghe the fourtein day of februar ane thowsand sex hundreth ane yeiris quhairby the said James Sellis to the saids craftis & thair successors the said chapel callit saint marie chapel place & ground yrof and trans upon the eist & south syids thairof[3]

15   Item ane charter following thairupon datit the aught day of maij Jaj vjcs and ane yeirs forsd

16   Item the saising following upoun the samen charter datit the threttein day of maij Jajvjcs ane yeiris forsd under the subscriptioun of Alexander dick noter publict

~~16~~ 17   Item ane contract maid betwix the said James Chalmer umqll Bessie rynd his spous and the said umqll Robert chalmer thair sone on the ane pairt and the deacons of the forsaids craftis for thame selffis & in name behalff forsd on the uther pairt datit at edinburghe the sexten day of aprill Jaj vjc & aughten years quhairby the said James with consent of his sd spous, and sone sauld To the saids craftis & yr successers the said chapell ground & place yrof & transs aboue written, with the back land then waist, ratiefeis the auld rightis & writtis abouewrittn, grantit to the saids craftis of the samen chapel. Sua that then the vestit[4] onelie undisponeit[5] to the saids craftis the for tenement of land and patronage of the sd chapell

~~17~~ 18   Item ane charter conforme thairto following thairupoun datit the sextein day of apryill ano Jaj vjcs aughten yeirs forsaid

18   Item the saising following upoun the same charter datit the said sextein day of apryill ano 1618 yers frd under the signe subscriptioun of Johne Stewart noter registrat in the register of saisingis hr at Edinburghe the Threttie day of maij Jaj vjcs aughten yers forsd subscrivit be mr francis hay clerk deput to the clerk of register . . .[6]

NOTES

1. NLS, Acc.7257, Rolled MS Inventory or Writs
2. NLS, Acc.8617, Bundle 1: Legal Papers and Accounts, 1601–80, Item 7: 1601 Writ.
3. This probably refers to the 1601 writ in the NLS mentioned above.
4. Vest: 'To place (property) in someone's possession.' M. G. Dareau, L. Pike, and H. D. Watson (eds), *Dictionary of the Older Scottish Tongue*, Vol. XI: Tra–Waquant (Oxford: 2002), 511.
5. Dispone: 1. 'To set in order, arrange, regulate, dispose (in some way).' W. A. Craigie (ed.), *Dictionary of the Older Scottish Tongue*, Vol. II: D–G (London: 1951), 156–7.
6. NRS, Particular Register of Sasines Etc. for Edinburgh: First Series, RS25/1/170–1.

Appendix 7: 1633 Ratification of Seal of Cause

The following excerpt from 18 April 1633 is taken from the seventh volume of the printed extracts of the Edinburgh council records, published by the Scottish Burgh Records Society in 1936. After a brief paragraph regarding preparations for the royal entry of Charles I, the text of a ratification of the Incorporation's seal of cause by the town council is given. Charles I and parliament followed suit in 1635 and 1641.[1] The original copy given to the Incorporation is included in the recently re-discovered 'Mill Records' in the Edinburgh City Archives, though this version comes from the printed council records.[2]

18th *April* 1633.

[Omitted: text about preparations for royal entry of Charles I]

Being convenit anent the supplicatioun givin in be Thomas Patersoun deykin of the maissouns and Alexander Cleghorne deykin of the wrichtes for them selffes and in name and behalff of thair saids craftis and brethrein thairof and also in name and behalff of the whole coupars glaissinwrichtis bowars sclaitteris paynteris and uthers thair adherents That quhair they have in longe tyme past memorie bein erected in frie craftis and in ane bodye; and for the commoun benefeit of all his Ma. liedges and making of expert and skilfull men in thair saids craftis: thair hes not onlie lawis bein sett doun be oure predicessoures for governing of the saids craftis sic as anent the tyme of prenteisis ressaiving of servands and oversieing of workemens worke; bot also for the floorisching and inritching of the saids craftis that they micht not onlie be the more inhabled to doe thair service and worke the more skilfullie and sufficientlie to all such as should imploy theme bot to the end they micht be the more inhabled to beir all commoun burdeins in watching wairding and in all taxatiounes and impositiounes lyand upone this burgh as ane profitabill member thairof thair hes also bein particular lawis and statuttis sett doun that when anye of the saids craftis sould cum of new to this burgh and schaipe theme to worke or tak worke in hand they sould first cume to the visitoris yeirlie appointed be us

to be tryet if they wer sufficientlie expert in the craft or nott and being fund
sufficient to pay thair dewes and to be admittit be theme to the fellowschip
of the saids craftis and warrand hes being givin be oure predicessoures that
the same statuttis to the maissouns and wrichtes sould be keiped to the
coupers and officers ordaynit to pas with theme and forbid outland folkes
that preveins theme in thair worke and to putt theme frome the occupatioun of thair saids craftis within this toun except they mak thair residence
within the samyn pay thair dewes to the saids craftis and be ressavit to the
fellowschip thairof As at mair lenth is contenit in thair seilles of causes
giftes and donatiounes grauntit be oure saids predecessoures to the saids
craftis and brethrein thairof of the daittes of the yeires respective 1475–
1489 confermit be the Archiebischope of Sanctandroes for the tyme and
be umquhill King James the fyft in anno 1527 Nothwithstanding quherof
they finding thair saids liberties daylie violate thair brethrein daylie decay,
for laick of exerceis of thair craft, and that through the unjust intrusioun
and usurpatioun of sundrie unfrie persounes duelling within and without
this burgh who being les skilfull and subject to fewar burdeins then they
daylie and at all tymes importis all maner of work within this burgh settis
up the samen and takkis frome theme that whairupone they sould intertyne
theme selffes, servandis and families to beir commoun burdein with the rest
of the bodye of this burgh, quhairby they ar redacted to extreame neces-
sitie And if the farther grouth thairof be not tymouslie previned they sall
not onlie ceis to be ane member bot with thair wyffes and childreyne they
salbe castin to be ane commoun burdein upone us Beseikand us thairfore
to tak the causes of thair ruine and decay to our serious consideratioun
and to ratifie and approve unto theme thair former liberties grauntit unto
theme be oure predicessoures in all the heads, clauses and articles thairof
and possessed hithertillis be theme and to renew the same to theme in such
cleir termes as all mater of questioun and debaitt amongst theme selffes
or with utheris craftismen duelling[3] outwith this burgh may be absolutlie
taiken away and they the more not onlie inhabled to serve his Ma. liedges
bot also inhabled to beir thair pairt of all commoun chairges pertening to
this burgh in all commoun effaires [the council ratify the foresaid gifts and
privileges]. And farder considering that the craftismen duelling neir to this
toun without the jurisdictioun of the samin does at all tymes be day and be
nicht bring in thair work wrocht be theme selffes settis up the samen within
this burgh to all persounes quhairby not onlie his Ma. liedges ar prejudgit
in the insufficiencie thairof they not being skilfull nor expert in thair craft
and sumtymes being such who throw thair ignorance and unskilfulnes hes
bein refuised to be ressavit unto anye of the saids craftis and quha without
any ordour or governament amongst theme selffes ar tollerat promiscuou-

slie to worke As lyikwayes consideering that the saids deykins and thair
brethrein and adherents ar subject to all commoun burdeins both of his
Ma. taxatiounes as also of uther burdeins of the toun and ar licklie now
to decay throw laik of exerceis of thair craft being previned therof be the
saids uther persounes duelling neir this burgh and outwith the liberties
thairof Thairfore to inhibite all persounes from working within this burgh
in anye of the saids craftis . . . bot such as salbe fund sufficientlie qualifiet
and admittit to the libertie of sum of the saids craftis except in the cump-
anie and under the commandement of sum of the friemen thairof And that
also to inhibite all persounes duelling within thrie mylles of this burgh
frome bringing in anye of thair said worke . . . bot upone the Mononday
allanerlie which they salbe haldin to present first to the commoun mercatt
in mercatt tyme to the effect the samin may be visited be the suorne visi-
touris to be apointed to that effect whither the same be sufficient or nott
that his Ma. liedges be nott thairby dissavit and prejudged under payne of
conficatioun of all such worke as they salbe fund working or setting up or
fund bringing in af the said mercatt day the one halff thairof to the use of
the guid toun and the uther to be applyed for the sustentatioun of the poore
of the craft and furder punischement of thair persounes at the discretioun
of the Magistrattis and the samin being presentit it salbe lawfull to the said
worker to sett up the worke provyding they sett up na uther worke under
cullour And ordanis officeris to pas with the saids deykins for executioun
heirof at command and discretioun of the Magistrattis so oft as occasioun
requyres in whose handis not onlie the executioun of thir presentis does
and sall consist Bot also to sett doun such uther lawis and statuttes be
advyse of the counsall for governing of the saids craftis and apointing of
thair tymes of working as they sall think guid for the better services of all
his Ma. liedges and ordanis thair clerk to subscryve thir presentis and to
append the seill of caus thairto . . . [4]

NOTES

1. Mill, 'Inventory', 11–12, A34, A35, A36 and A39.
2. ECA, Mill Recs, A34, and Mill, 'Inventory', 11.
3. dwelling
4. *Edin. Recs*, 1626–1641, 123–5.

Appendix 8: Record of the 1703 Court of Session Decreet Arbitral from the Edinburgh Council Records

Following a lengthy dispute over the rights of the ten trades within Mary's Chapel to be elected as one of the two deacons, several senators of the College of Justice acted as arbitrators, establishing two 'denominations' of masons and wrights, with the other eight arts grouped under these two trades within the 'United Incorporation'. The 5 March 1703 decreet was officially recorded in the town council's minutes later in the year:

8th September 1703

Anent the petition given in be the deacons and ten Crafts of the airts of Maries Chapell shewing that wherby ane decreit Arbitrall pronounced be John Earle of Lauderdaill and Sir James Stewart of Goodtrees, her Majesties Advocat, Sir Colline Campbell of Aberuchell, Sir John Lauder of Fountainhall, and Sir Archibald Hope of Rankeillor Senatores of the Colledge of Justice judges arbitrators and amicable compositors mutually chosen be the petitioners *hinc inde* severall matters debaitable among the petitioners are composed and determined And the Decreit is Recommended to the Counsell to be recorded in ther books ther Authoritie to be interponed therto as the said Decreit dated the fyfth of March 1703 . . . more fully bears . . . The tennor wherof followes: They decerne and ordeane the bowers, glasiers plummers and upholsterers to be joyned with the measones under the denominatione of the deaconrie of the measones . . . the coupers painters sclaitters and sevewrights to be joyned with the wrights under the denominatione of the deaconrie of the wrights . . . decernes and ordeans the electione of the long leitts as lykewayes the electione of the deacones out of the short leitts in all tyme comeing to be by the poll votts of the haill united Incorporatione consisting of all the ten trades above mentioned or so mony therof as shall hapen to be existing and in being for the tyme And declairs that as all the members are capable to vote in the electiones so all of them are capable of being elected in all tyme comeing . . . they decerne and ordeane that ther shall be two quarter masters of the wrights out of the number of the wrights and other two quarter masters out of the number of the Coupers painters sclaitters and seivewrights . . . as also there shall be two quartermasters of the measones out of the number of the measones and other two quartermasters out of the number of the bowers Glassiers plummers upholsterers . . . And that the way and maner of electing the said eight quartermasters shall be by the pole vott of *the haill United Incorporation consisting of the haill ten trades* . . .[1]

NOTE

1. *Edin. Recs*, 1701–1718, 59–60.

Appendix 9: 1718–21 Chimney Piece Debate

The following excerpts are taken from the minute books of the Incorporation of Mary's Chapel, and relate to an apparently missing 'chimney piece' painted by James Norrie, which was later replaced by the more famous Roderick Chalmers painting in 1720 (see Plate 1).

[Margin: 'Complaint Deacon Smyth of Deacon Brownhill & oy[rs] for removeing the chimney peece in the Conveening hall']

Lykeas Deacon Smyth Complained to the house Mentioning That whereas James Norie painter haveing very Lately handsomely painted a Representation of the severall arts of this Incorporat[io]ne upon the Chimney peece of the Conveening hall & Complemented the Incorporat[io]ne therewith Which peece of painting haveing by their order been brought to this house & afterwards affixed in the ordinary place Nevertheless James Brownhill Late Deacon of the wrights with Thomas Herron Robert Denholm William M[c]lean John Yeats & Laurence Andrew wrights & John Jack Sclater had in a clandestine manner came to the Chappell & without any warrand from the house had at their oun hand taken doun the said Chimney peece & quite altered the same from the manner it was formerly in And therefor craveing they might not only be censured for so doeing But also ordained to put the same in the condition it was formerly in Which being Considered by the said Incorporation And they haveing called the persons above named and Complained upon befor them who acknowledged themselfs to b the persons who had altered the said Chimney peece They therefor ordained them betwixt & the next sederunt to put the samen in the condition it was at first put up in at he sight of the boxm[r] which was done accordingly

R[o] Alison Clerk[1]

[Margin: 'Gilb: Smiths protestatione anent the precedencie of the masons.']

Att Maries Chaeppell the twenty nynth day of November Jaj vij[c&]
& Eighteen years Deacon Antoniouse preses

The which Day William M^clean wright being one of these concerned in the Late unwarrantable alteration of the Chimney peece of the Conveening house Being absent Last sederunt & now present He publickly acknowledged the offence befor the Incorpora[tio]ne Begged the houses pardon & was thereupon excused And the said Chimney being in obedience to the last sederunt reformed & put in the condition It was formerly in when painted by James Norie There arose a Debate in the house annent precedencie Gilbert Smyth present Deacon of the masons & severall others of his bretheren affirmeing that in the old painteing of the said Chimney peece befor the same was Last renewed The measons were placed on the right hand of the wrights And the same remained in that condition for a Long tyme And James Norie haveing now Complemented the house with the se[ver]al arts thereof painted on the old chimney peece in the same manner though on different figures. And the same haveing not only been by order of the house brought thereto & put up therein, and the said James Norie getting the publick thanks of this Incorpora[tio]ne for his Complement But also after the same had been unwarrantably altered haveing been againe by order of this house put in the Condition It was formerly in, He contended that the same could not now be altered without the plaine violat[io]ne of the rights & privilidges of the Incorporation of the measons, whose right of being first called in the rolls of this house is expressly reserved to them By the Decreet arbitral following upon the submission betwixt the masons & wrights & eight airts And therefor he protested against any new alterat[io]ne of the painteing on the said Chimney peece otherwayes there as it is at present, and that no superiority of voyces of the Incorporat[io]ne (where the wrights & airts joined with them by reason of their superiority of number are sure to carrie) Could deprive them of their undoubted right of precedencie in the Chappell which they had enjoyed past memory of man To which protestation se[ver]al of the measons & members of the four arts joined with them adhered To which It was agred by the bretheren of the wrights first That they did not conceive that the painting of figures on a Chimney peece could give either partie any right of precedencie secondly that the new painteing thereon neither is nor could beafter the forme of the old where the airts had been painted promiscuously[2] and not conform to the order They are now classed in by the said Decreet arbitral Nixt that the said Decreet Did no wayes Concern the precedencie betwixt wrights & masons But only regulates & accommodates the pleas & differences That had formerly been betwixt them & the eight arts And altho any right or privilidge that the masons had of being first called in the rolls of this In Corporat[io]ne be thereby reserved to them The wrights privilidge of being first mentioned in the Sett of the good toun of Ed^r & called in the Councill rolls thereof Is by that Decreet arbitral also reserved to them But the question not being here annent precedencie in being in the rolls But annent the painteing of a Chimney peece as a decorement to the Hall The forsaid Decreet arbitral hath no manner of concern therein And albeit it had, Yet they oppone the same Whereby it is expressly provided That all differences ariseing anent the implement of any part of that Decreet shall be determined by a pole voice of the whole united Incorporat[io]ne, But however the bretheren of the wrights humbly Conceived that the painteing of the said Chimney peece either with them or the masons on the right hand ought not to be made a handle off to make arent or breed divisions or animosities in this Incorporat[io]ne And it being therefore proposed that the same should be taken doun and divided into two halfs and each half put within a handsome black frame And that which concerned each trade & arts joyned with them hang up in their oun side of the hall and a plaine chimney peece with Landskip painted thereon put on the Chimney in place thereof which proposall being put to a vote of the house Was by the plurality of voices thereof approven of, But the said Gilbert Smyth & severall of his bretheren masons & some of the four arts joyned with them Refused to vote therein But adhered to his former protestat[io]ne

R° Alison Clerk[3]

[Margin: 'The Chimney peece ordered to be rectified as to the Coupars & Bowers']

And in lyke manner the house haveing reconsidered the grivances represented to them at the Last meeting by the bretheren of the Coupers of their airt being wrong placed in the painteing of the Chimney peece Lateli done by James Norie painter They ordained the same to be rectified And the Coupars and bowars to be placed thereon in the same manner as it was befor it was renued

R° Alison Clerk[4]

[Margin: 'The house appoynts a new chimney peece to be put up & the se[ver]al airts painted yron']

The same Day The house appoynted a chimney peece to be made to the Conveening house and the se[ver]al airts of this house to be painted thereon In the same order & figures they were formerly painted on the old Chimney peece befor it was taken doun Conform to a sedurunt signed by the Deacons in presence of the house And appoynted the same to be done upon the Incorporat[io]ns expences

R° Alison Clerk[5]

... It: To Roderick Chalmers painter & present boxmaster for painting the Chimney peice of the Chappell With a Representation of the Whole trades and arts yron per Discharged acco^td_____£100 0s 0d ...[6]

[Margin: 'Act approving the painting of the chimney peice']

The Chimney peice of the conveening house being now putt up in its place with the severall airts or trades of this incorporation handsomly painted yron conforme to the skeme and Act of this house of the Twenty Thrid of ffebry last The house unanimously approved thereof

R° Alison Clerk[7]

NOTES

1. ECA, SL34/1/4, 87–8, 22 November 1718.
2. DSL/DOST: Promiscuously – 'a. Without distinction, discrimination or order; indiscriminately; at random; in confusion. b. Of dancing etc.: Mixed, between the sexes.'
3. ECA, SL34/1/4, 88–9, 29 November 1718.
4. Ibid., 100, 2 August 1719.
5. Ibid., 106, 23 February 1720.
6. Ibid., Accompt of Charge and Discharge Betwixt the Incorporation of Marys Chapell And Roderick Chalmers painter burges of Edinburgh Boxmaster thereto from the 12th of September 1719 to the 16th of September 1721, Discharge by tradesmens accounts (unpaginated, towards back of volume).
7. ECA, SL34/1/5, f3v, 18 March 1721.

Appendix 10: Unfreemen Declared Able to Join the Incorporation in 1790

The following extract is from the 'Historical Affairs in Scotland' section of The Scots Magazine, May 1790 edition. It notes the ruling by the Court of Session in regards to a court case against several unfree masons who were employed on the building of the new South Bridge, over the Cowgate.[1] Importantly, the Court of Session ruled that the Incorporation was obliged to accept unfreemen for half of the exorbitant price they had apparently been charging, though no mention is made of the traditional factor of sufficiency of work in regards to entry.

'Friday, May 28. the court determined a cause of importance to incorporations. Two masons, not belonging to the incorporations of Mary's Chapel, Edinburgh, had proceeded to build on some areas on the south bridge. The incorporations insisted, that non-freemen had no right to build within the ancient royalty of the city, and demanded a fine from the masons; but they afterwards came to a resolution of admitting persons not freemen to the privileges of the incorporations, on paying 100 l. The court of session found the incorporations obliged to admit non-freemen, and reduced the sum they were to pay for the privileges they were to enjoy from 100 l. to 50 l. It was formerly a received, but an erroneous opinion, that the different incorporations had a right to reject all persons but those who served apprenticeships to members for their freedom, or married a member's daughter.'[2]

NOTES

1. For more on this case, see also: Morison, W. M., *The Decisions of the Court of Session, From its Institution until the Separation of the Court into Two Divisions in the Year 1808, Digested Under Proper Heads in the Form of a Dictionary* (Edinburgh: Archibald Constable and Compay, 1811), 229.
2. Anonymous, *The Scots Magazine*, 52: May (Edinburgh: Murray and Cochrane, 1790), 255.

Appendix 11: Responses to the Questions from the Royal Commission on Municipal Corporations

The following excerpt is from the minutes of the Incorporation of Mary's Chapel,[1] and record a series of questions and responses from the Royal Commission which was set up to enquire into the state and condition of the cities, burghs and towns of Scotland. This Commission collected this information from across Scotland and used it to produce their 1835 General Report.[2]

Mary's Chapel the second day of October, Eighteen hundred and thirty three.

Committee Meeting – on Burgh Reform

Deacon Henderson. Preses.

There was read to the Meeting the following answers to the Enquiries of the Burgh Commissioners:

"Answers for the Incorporations of Marys Chapel of the City of Edinburgh. To the Note of Enquiries issued by the Commissioners "appointed under a Royal Commission to enquire into the <u>State</u> . . .

Wm Gardner Clerk

[p.] 109

" . . . State and Condition of the Cities, Burghs and Towns of Scotland.

"Enquiry 1st. Brief statement of the Constitution and history of the Corporations, with reference to, and production of any Charters or Documents printed or otherwise connecte with these points.-

"Answer. Reference is made for an account of the origin of the United Incorporations, to the printed Laws herewith sent – They have hitherto enjoyed the exclusive right of working, and debaring others from working within the ancient Royalty of Edinburgh.

"Enquiry 2nd.- Boundaries within which, the exclusive privilege is, or may be exercised.

"Answer. The limits of the ancient Royalty of the City.

"Enquiry 3^d. Fund of the Incorporations, either Heritable or Moveable, how raised, how invested, and how applied for Corporation and other purposes.

"Answer. The fund was raised from the entry money of Members, and the transference of the Capital belonging to the Widows fund as aftermentioned – In answer to Enquiry fourth, it is chiefly Heritable – the sum lent out on Bonds amounts to £32 11/0, whereof £2600 is heritably secured on Land – In 1820 the Incorporations purchased a shop on North Bridge Street for £1950, which was let on a Lease which expired at Whitsunday 1833 for £135. 15/, but it is since let for only £65 on a Lease for five years. In 1822 from the general reduction of the rate of interest, it was resolved to rest the funds in the purchase of Heritable subjects: accordingly property in Saint Andrews Square called the Union . . .

Wm Gardner Clerk

[p.] 110

. . . Union Hotel was purchased for £6,200, on which very material alterations were made by adding an additional flat, and converting the two under flats into shops. In 1825 the first and second flats above the shops in the south corner Tenement in London Street were purchased for £2700. The Rental of the House property for the year ending at Whitsunday 1833 amounts to £593. 17/- The Corporations draw an annual Dividend of £77.4.5 from their interest in the Friendly Insurance Company - £21 from the joint stock Water Company – besides ten shares of the Union Canal stock which cost £939 and yields at present little more than one per cent.- The Fund is applied toward the support of decayed Members, Widows and children – The Members at present receive an annuity of £10, Widows £9. Sons o Daughters of deceased Members £4. 10/. The Charity thus paid for the year ending at Lammas 1833 amounted to £761.15.6., there being nine Members, Sixty Widows, and thirty two Sons or Daughters, the fund is no otherwise applied, except in the repair of property and expense of management.

"Enquiry 4. Any Widows Scheme or other charitable Institutions of Corporation, wither with, or without Parliamentary authority.

"Answer.- None under Parliamintary authority – there was a Widows Scheme belonging to the Incorporations instituted in 1768 for providing annuities for the Widows of such Members as acceded to it – the fund of this Scheme amounting to £4180.14*l*. was . . .

Wm Gardner Clerk

[p.] 111

. . . was transferred to the Incorporations, with this declaration, that those who were then, or should thereafter become entitled to the benefit of the Scheme, should receive an annuity from the funds of the Incorporations of £15., the Members having gradually decreased to three in number. In 1820 a Widows Scheme was established, by which each subscriber contributes ten shillings per annum, and his Widow derives an annuity of two pounds as a matter of right. The fund of this Scheme at Martinmas 1832 amounted to £982.1.9.- £800 of which are vested on Heritable security, and £100 are lent to the City of Edinburgh. There were at Martinmas last twenty seven Widows on the Roll, and the sum paid for annuities for the year preceding that term amounted to £53. vide Chap. 14th, page 25. of the printed Laws.

"Enquiry 5th. The Clerk might give a comparative List of prosecutions for last 30 years – of Intrant Members, Apprentices, for same period distinguishing the number each year.

"Answer:[3] Year	Number of Entrants	Number of Apprentices	No of Prosecutions
1803	9	12	
1804	5	17	
1805	6	8	
1806	4	13	
1807	6	14	
1808	6	12	
1809	23	7	
1810	85	19	
1811	5	12	

Wm Gardner Clerk

[p.] 112

"Year	Number of Entrants	Number of Apprentices	No of Prosecutions
1812	4	24	
1813	5	17	
1814	3	11	
1815	11	22	
1816	5	23	
1817	9	12	
1818	6	20	
1819	3	14	
1820	3	13	
1821	12	15	
1822	10	18	
1823	5	14	
1824	7	19	2
1825	10	20	1
1826	5	7	1
1827	9	10	3
1828	5	11	4
1829	4	9	
1830	7	6	2
1831	7	4	3
1832	10	6	2
1833	None	None	None

"Enquiry 6. How far the Exclusive privileges now inforced compared with what they were formerly – are those privileges any considerable inducement to enter.

"Answer: The privileges continue to be enforced as formerly they were at one time, but are now supposed to afford little inducement to enter.-

"Enquiry 7. How far they could be safely abolished, always reserving funds and other advantages to the Incorporations . . .

Wm Gardner Clerk

[p.] 113

. . . Incorporations, what these other advantages are.

"Answer. It is for the Legislature to determine this matter, but in so far as the Incorporation of Marys Chapel are concerned, they by a late vote declared that it would be exceedingly injurious to their pecuniary interest the abolition of these privileges.-

"Enquiry 8. Right of presentation to Hospitals.

"Answer:- Reference is here made on this very important subject to the interests of the Incorporations of Marys Chapel, to the Memorial presented to the Lord Advocate, and Petition to the House of Lords, copies of which are subjoined hereto.-

"Enquiry 9. Present state of the Incorporation generally, if not prosperous, state causes, and suggest improvements.

"Answer. The Funds of the Incorporations are greatly diminished, since the introduction and passing of the Burgh Reform Bill, and will continue to decrease, principally from their Deacons being excluded from the Town Council,[4] and perhaps eventually from a share of the Government of George Heriot's Hospital, and the probable abolition of the exclusive privileges.- The Sum paid for Charity at Lammas 1827 was £1011 9 6

Ditto 1828	£1022	4	6
Ditto 1829	£899	4	0
Ditto 1830	£884	0	6
Ditto 1831	£719	7	6
Ditto 1832	£751	2	0
Ditto 1833	£761	15	6

And a considerable additional reduction must of necessity immediately take place, from the reasons . . .

Wm Gardner Clerk

[p.] 114
. . . reasons before mentioned, and the very great depression in the value of House property, and the low rate of Interest.- Edinburgh 8 October 1833"

The above Answers were approved of by the Meeting and ordered to be forthwith transmitted to the Burgh Commissioners.-

Wm Gardner Clerk

258		BUILDING EARLY MODERN EDINBURGH

NOTES

1. ECA, Acc.622/8, 109–14, 2 October 1833.
2. Greenshields, J. B., *General Report of the Commissioners Appointed to Inquire into the State of Municipal Incorporations in Scotland* (London: His Majesty' Stationery Office, 1835).
3. Note that the format of the table needed to be changed slightly so that it would fit.
4. See Bain, E., *Merchant and Craft Guilds: A History of the Aberdeen Incorporated Trades* (Aberdeen: J. & J. P. Edmond & Spark, 1887), 320, where it is argued that 'through the efforts of the Glasgow Trades House, the bill was amended in the House of Lords, and the deacons and conveners were allowed to remain constituent members of the Town Councils.' Colston suggests that it was only the Dean of Guild and Convener of Trades which retained council seats along with the elected council. Colston, J., *The Incorporated Trades of Edinburgh* (Edinburgh: Colston & Company, 1891), xlix–l.

Appendix 12: Burgh Trading Act 1846

Below is the text from the 1846 Act of Parliament which formally abolished exclusive privileges of trade within Scotland's Burghs.

ANNO NONO
VICTORIAE REGINAE

CAP. XVII

An Act for the Abolition of the exclusive Privilege of trading in Burghs in *Scotland*.

[14th *May* 1846.]

Whereas in certain Royal and other Burghs in *Scotland*, the Members of certain Guilds, Crafts, or Incorporations possess exclusive Privileges of carrying on or dealing in Merchandize, and of carrying on or exercising certain Trades or Handicrafts, within their respective Burghs; and such Guilds, Crafts, or Incorporations have corresponding Rights, entitling them to prevent Persons not being Members thereof from carrying on or dealing in Merchandize, or from carrying on or exercising such Trades or Handicrafts, within such Burghs: And whereas it has become expedient that such exclusive Privileges and Rights should be abolished: Be it therefore enacted by the Queen's most Excellent Majesty, by and with the Advice and Consent of the Lords Spiritual and Temporal, and Commons, in this present Parliament assembled, and by the Authority of the same, That from and after the passing of this Act all such exclusive Privileges and Rights shall cease, and it shall be lawful for any Person to carry on or deal in Merchandize, and to carry on or exercise any Trade or Handicraft, in any Burgh and elsewhere in *Scotland*, without being a Burgess of such Burgh, or a Guild Brother, or a Member of any Guild, Craft, or Incorporation: Provided always, that in lieu of the Stamp Duties of One Pound and Three Pounds now payable on the Admission of any Person as a Burgess or into any Corporation or Company in any Burgh in *Scotland*, for the Enrolment, Entry, or Memorandum thereof in the Court

Books, Roll, or Record of such Corporation or Company, there shall from and after the passing of this Act be paid on every such Admission a Stamp Duty of Five Shillings.

II. And be it enacted, That notwithstanding the Abolition of the said exclusive Privileges and Rights all such Incorporations as aforesaid shall retain their Corporate Character, and shall continue to be Incorporations, with the same Names and Titles as heretofore; and nothing herein contained shall anywise affect the Rights and Privileges of such Incorporations, or of the Office Bearers or Members thereof, except as herein-before enacted.

III. And whereas the Revenues of such Incorporations as aforesaid may in some Instances be affected, and the Number of the Members of such Incorporations may in some Instances diminish, by reason of the Abolition of the said exclusive Privileges and Rights, and it is expedient that Provision should be made for facilitating Arrangements suitable to such Occurrences; be it therefore enacted, That it shall be lawful for every such Incorporation from Time to Time to make all Bye Laws, Regulations, and Resolutions relative to the Management and Application of its Funds and Property, and relative to the Qualification and Admission of Members, in reference to its altered Circumstances under this Act, as may be considered expedient, and to apply to the Court of Session, by summary Petition, for the Sanction of the said Court to such Bye Laws, Regulations or Resolutions; and the said Court, after due Intimation of such Application, shall determine upon the same, and upon any Objections that may be made, thereto By Parties having Interest, and shall interpone the Sanction of the said Court to such Bye Laws, Regulations, or Resolutions, or disallow the same in whole or in part, or make thereon such Alterations, or adject thereto such Conditions of Qualifications, as the said Court may think fit, and generally shall pronounce such Order in the whole Matter as may to the said Court seem just and expedient; and such Bye Laws, Regulations, or Resolutions, subject to such Alterations and Conditions as aforesaid, shall be, when the Sanction of the said Court shall have been interponed thereto, valid and effectual and binding on such Incorporations: Provided always, that nothing therein contained shall affect the Validity of any Bye Laws, Regulations, or Resolutions that may be made by any such Incorporation without the Sanction of the said Court, which it would have been heretofore competent for such Incorporation to have made of its own Authority or without such Sanction.

IV. And be it enacted, That this Act may be amended or repealed by any Act to be passed in the present Session of Parliament.[1]

NOTE

1. 9 Victoria Cap. XVII, 241–2.

Glossary[1]

Accompts – accounts.

Aggravation – an ecclesiastical censure for those who disregard a reprimand.

Annualrent – an interest payment.

Calsay – paving stone.

Chirugeon – surgeon.

Biggers – builders, or those who 'big' something up.

Boxmaster – treasurer, or keeper of the boxes.

Deacon – head or chairman of an incorporated trade.

Decreet arbitral – a decree of arbitration, such as the famous 1583 decreet arbitral between the merchants and craftsmen of Edinburgh, which formed a new burgh 'sett', or constitution.

Disjones – breakfast.

Drink-silver – customary payment for drink paid to workers.

Enfeoffment – act of 'infefting', or investing a person with some heritable property.

Essay – a test of skill for becoming a master of an incorporated trade.

Essay masters – those who judge the sufficiency of an essay for entry into an incorporated trade.

Extent – a tax.

Leet – list.

Mell – mason's mallet.

Noneschankis – light repast at 4:00 pm; a workman's break.

Oversman – one who is put over others, as with the Incorporation's officials in the suburban crafts.

Pattens – overshoes with a wooden sole, intended to keep the owner's shoes out of the muck.

Poinding – impounding of.

Prentice – apprentice.

Qu – w, as in 'quhat' (what) or 'qhua' (who).

Quheels – wheels.

Relict – 'relic', or widow.

Rex dollar – a large silver coin from one of a number of European countries, often used for international trade; also called *inter alia* a rix dollar, a reichsthaler, or a rijksdaalder.

Rood – cross.

Rood screen – partition between nave and chancel (with the choir and high altar), which held a cross.

Scot and lot – burgess duties of taxation and financial burdens. To avoid them was to get off 'scot free'.

Seal of Cause – a charter of incorporation giving official, legal status; so called due to the use of wax seals to verify the charter.

Sett – a form of municipal constitution brought about by the 1583 decreet arbitral.

Square – right-angle gauge of precisely 90 degrees, intended to check that joints or sides were truly square.

Stallanger – one who pays fees for the right to trade or hold a stall in the market.

Umquhile – late / deceased.

Warding – guarding or imprisoning.

Watch and ward – burgess duties of watching and guarding, or town watch and militia responsibilities. These were expensive duties due to sacrificed time and the provision of arms and armour.

NOTE

1. See also the *Dictionary of the Scots Language/Dictionary of the Older Scottish Tongue* (DSL/DOST) for further explanation of the terms (www.dsl.ac.uk).

Bibliography

MANUSCRIPT AND TYPESCRIPT PRIMARY SOURCES

Ayrshire Archives

B6/24/1, 'Minute Book of the Wrights and Squaremen of the Burgh of Air. 1556, Apr. 7–1724, Oct. 10'.

Edinburgh City Archives (ECA)

Acc.622/1–8 & 73, Minute Books 1755–1842 and 1910–1947 (entitled in catalogue: 'Minutes of Record').

Acc.622/33, Widows' Scheme Annual Rates Book, 1768–98.

Acc.622/35–42: Annuitants' Roll Books, 1838–1890.

Howie Prints.

Mill Records, A1–A46 and B1–B6 (Mary's Chapel Papers, 1475–1678), including charters and minute books. (Recently discovered, on 27 of January 2016, and yet to be given an accession number, but fully inventoried by A. J. Mill in her 1923 'Rough Inventory'. See ECA, SL12/236.)

Munro, J., Unpublished Transcription, 'Records of the Edinburgh Incorporation of Hammermen', vols 2 and 3.

Munro, J., Unpublished Transcription, 'Records of the Edinburgh Incorporation of Skinners'.

SL1/1/80, Town Council Minutes.

SL12/236, A. J. Mill, 'Rough Inventory of Records Belonging to the Wrights and Masons of Edinburgh' (Unpublished typescript, 1923).

SL34/1/1–14, Minute Books 1669–1755 and 1842–1910 (entitled in catalogue: 'Record of the Acts and Statutes of St Mary's Chapel').

SL34/2/1–4, Account Books, 1749–1842.

SL34/3/1-5, Widows' Fund Scheme, 1768–1897.

SL34/5/1-4, Books of Absent Diets, 1743–1835.

SL220/2/2/1, 17 April 1569, Charter in Favour of the Brethren of St John with Precept of Sasine for Infeftment of the said Cowpar Craft.

East Lothian Council Archive and Local History Service (ELCALHS), John Gray Centre

HAD/13/2/4, Minute Book of the Wrights and Masons 1616–1751 (Haddington).

London School of Economics and Political Science Library, Webb Trade Union Collection

A/XIII/441, 'Masons' Strike in 1764', in *Forfar Review* (Summer, 1892).

National Library of Scotland (NLS)

Acc.7056, Box 1
Bundle 1:
1720 Contract betwixt Gilbert Couper, wright burgess of Edinburgh and Mrs Sara Dalrymple, merchand.
1732 Statement of George Lamb.
Bundle 2:
'Inventory of unfinished work in Mrs Sara Dalrymples shope & workehouse, 1717'.
Acc.7056, Box 2
1733 Petition of Elizabeth Herriot.
1795–6 Bill of Jo Ritchie, Slater.
1787 Summons of Declarator.
Acc.7056, Box 4
1722 Supplication of Patrick Thomson.
Acc.7257
Petition from Collectors for the Episcopal Ministers 1735.
Rolled MS Inventory of Writs.
Acc.7260
Petition collections for the Episcopal ministers & their widows to the Incorporation of Masons & Wrights in Edinburgh 1732.
Petition of Margaret Watson.
Acc.7332, Box 2: Accounts and papers of the Deacons and Boxmaster [Treasurer] of the Incorporation 1676–1793
Group 2: 'Complaints' of members and related memoranda 1666–7.
Group 9: Petitions to Deacons and Treasurer, 1725–7.
Group 12: Petitions, 1757–8.
Acc.8617, Bundle 1, Legal Papers and Accounts, 1601–80
Item 7: 1601 Writ.
Craig, J., *To His Sacred Majesty George III . . . this Plan of the new streets and squares, intended for his ancient capital of North-Britain . . .* (Edinburgh, 1768), EMS.s.647.
Edinburgh Evening Courant (1764).
Ms.19288, 'Perth Wrights' Minutes'.

National Records of Scotland (NRS)

GD98/11/7, Notarial instrument in favour of the masons and wrights of Haddington, as to the support of the altar of St. John in the parish church, 16 July 1533, and modern translation.

GD98/11/8, Extract from the Burgh Court Books of Haddington of decreet arbitral finding that the masons and wrights shall have the image and offering of St. John, the Evangelist, to be their patron, under condition of upkeep etc., 1 April 1530.

GD98/11/9, Letters from the provost, etc., of Edinburgh, to the sheriff of Haddington, bailies and council thereof, anent precedence in processions of the Crafts, 27 May 1532.

GD98/11/10/1, Testimonial by the deacons of the Hammermen, Masons, and Wrights of Edinburgh, as to the procession of the crafts, 26 May 1532.

GD98/11/10/2, Extract act of the Burgh Court of Haddington as to payment by the craftsmen of their weekly penny for augmentation of God's service at St. John's altar in the parish kirk of Haddington, 30 June 1530.

Testaments:

CC8/8/61, George Smyth, Heilmaker, 30/3/1646.

CC8/8/63, James Stevinson, 9/6/1647.

Stirling Council Archives Services

GB224/CH2/723, Presbytery of Dunblane, 'Ministers' Widows Fund, 1759'.

University of Edinburgh Special Collections

Papers of David Laing (1793–1878), La.IV.20, Notes, drafts, etc. on subjects: artists, architects and engravers: La.IV.20.J2, George Jamieson, and La.IV.20. W4, Johnne Warkman.

PRINTED PRIMARY SOURCES

Adam, R. (ed.), *Edinburgh Records: The Burgh Accounts*, vol. 2 (Edinburgh, 1899).

Allen, A. and Spence, C. (eds), *Edinburgh Housemails Taxation Book, 1634–1636* (Woodbridge: Scottish History Society, 2014).

Angus, W. (ed.), *Protocol Book of Mr. Gilbert Grote, 1552–1573* (Edinburgh: Scottish Record Society, 1914).

Anonymous, *A Poem Inscribed to the Members of St. Mary's Chapel. Upon the Most Honourable, Ancient, and Excellent Art of Wright-Craft. By a Brother of the Craft* (Edinburgh: David Gray, 1757).

Anonymous, *A Diurnal of Remarkable Occurents That Have Passed Within the Country of Scotland Since the Death of King James the Fourth Till the Year*

M.D.LXXV. From a Manuscript of the Sixteenth Century in the Possession of Sir John Maxwell of Pollock, Baronet (Edinburgh: Bannatyne Club, 1833).

Arnot, H., *The History of Edinburgh, from the Earliest Accounts to the Year 1780* (Edinburgh: Thomas Turnbull, 1816).

Brown, K. M., et al. (eds), *The Records of the Parliaments of Scotland to 1707* (St Andrews, 2007–15), http://www.rps.ac.uk (last accessed 17 December 2016).

Brown, P. H. (ed.) *Early Travellers in Scotland* (Edinburgh: D. Douglas, 1891).

Burton, J. H., et al. (eds), *The Register of the Privy Council of Scotland*, vol. 1, A.D. 1545–1569 (Edinburgh: H. M. General Register House, 1877–2009).

Calderwood, D., *The History of the Kirk of Scotland* (Edinburgh: Wodrow Society, 1843).

Carr, H. (ed.), *The Minutes of the Lodge of Edinburgh, Mary's Chapel, No. 1, 1598–1738* (London: Quatuor Coronati Lodge, 1962).

Chambers, E. K, *The Mediaeval Stage*, vol. 2 (Oxford: Oxford University Press, 1903).

Cooper, J. (ed.), *Cartularium Ecclesiae Sancti Nicholai Aberdonensis*, 2 vols (Aberdeen: New Spalding Club, 1888–92).

Crawford, J., *To the Praise of the Honourable Society of Magistrates, Treasurers, Counsellors, and Incorporate Members* (Edinburgh: A. Robertson, 1791).

Dalrymple of Stair, Sir James, *The Decisions of the Lords of Council & Session, In the Most Important Cases Debate Before Them; From July 1671 to July 1681 . . . Part Second* (Edinburgh: Heir of Andrew Anderson, Printer to His most Sacred Majesty, 1687).

Donaldson, G. (ed.), *Accounts of the Collectors of Thirds of Benefices, 1561–1572* (Edinburgh: Scottish History Society, 1949).

Dreghorn, John Maclaurin, Lord, *Memorial for the United Incorporations of Mary's Chapel, and for Alexander Miller Glazier, deacon, duly elected by them, of the Incorporation of Masons, pursuers, against Alexander Nicolson, the pretended deacon of the said incorporation, and the magistrates and town-council of Edinburgh, and others, defenders* (Edinburgh: s.n., 1764).

Dunbar, W. H., Fordyce, G. D., and De Maria, J., *Reports of Cases Decided in the Supreme Courts of Scotland, and in the House of Lords on Appeal from Scotland, &c. &c.: House of Lords Cases from 16th March 1837, to 2d February 1838 . . .*, vol. 10 (Edinburgh: M. Anderson, 1838).

Durkan, J. (ed.), *The Protocol Book of John Foular, 1528–1534* (Edinburgh: Scottish Record Society, 1985).

Gray, A., *The Plough-Wright's Assistant; or, A Practical Treatise on Various Implements Employed in Agriculture* (Edinburgh: Archibald Constable & Co., 1808).

Greenshields, J. B., *General Report of the Commissioners Appointed to Inquire into the State of Municipal Incorporations in Scotland* (London: His Majesty' Stationery Office, 1835).

Hamilton-Grierson, P. J. (ed.), *Habakkuk Bisset's Rolment of Courtis*, vol. 2 (Edinburgh: Scottish Text Society, 1922).

Hannay, R. K. (ed.), *Rentale Sancti Adnree: Being the Chamberlain and Granitar Accounts of the Archbishopric in the Time of Cardinal Betoun, 1538–1546* (Edinburgh: Scottish History Society, 1913).

Health and Safety Executive, 'Falls and Trips in Construction', available at: www.hse.gov.uk/Construction/campaigns/fallstrips/index.htm (last accessed 7 September 2016).

Incorporation of Mary's Chapel, *Act of the Incorporations of Mary's Chapel. Instituting a Scheme for Providing Annuities to Widows of the Members. Passed 8th March 1768. With Obligations by the Contributors Subjoined* (Edinburgh: Balfour & Smellie, 1776).

Innes, C. and Renwick, R. (eds), *Ancient Laws and Customs of the Burghs of Scotland*, vol. 1, A.D. 1124–1424 (Edinburgh: Scottish Burgh Record Society, 1868).

James VI, *Basilikon Doron. Devided Into Three Bookes* (Edinburgh: Robert Walde-graue, 1599).

Kirk, J. (ed.) *The Books of Assumption of the Thirds of Benefices: Scottish Ecclesiastical Rentals at the Reformation* (Oxford: The British Academy, 1995).

Laing, D. (ed.), *Registrum Cartarum Ecclesie Sancti Egidiide Edinburgh* (Edinburgh: T. Constable, 1859).

Lauder of Fountainhall, Sir John, *Historical Notices of Scottish Affairs*, vol. 1, 1661–1683 (Edinburgh: T. Constable, 1848).

Lindsay, P., *The Interest of Scotland Considered, with Regard to its Police in Employing of the Poor, its Agriculture, its Trade, its Manufactures, and Fisheries* (London: T. Woodward and J. Peele, 1736).

Livingstone, M., et al. (eds), *Registrum Secreti Sigilli Regum Scotorum (Register of the Privy Seal of Scotland)*, 8 vols (Edinburgh: H. M. General Register House, 1908–82).

Lumsden, H., *The Records of the Trades House of Glasgow*, A.D. *1605–1678* (Glasgow: Trades House of Glasgow, 1910).

Maitland, W., *The History of Edinburgh From its Foundation to the Present Time* (Edinburgh: Hamilton, Balfour and Neill, 1753).

Marwick, J. D., et al. (eds), *Extracts From the Records of the Burgh of Edinburgh*, 13 vols and Index (Edinburgh: SBRS, 1869–1967).

Marwick, J. D. (ed.), *Charters and Other Documents Relating to the City of Edinburgh*, A.D. *1143–1540* (Edinburgh: Scottish Burgh Records Society, 1871).

Marwick, J. D. (ed.), *Charters and Other Documents Relating to the City of Glasgow*. A.D. *1175–1649*, vol. 1, Pt 1 (Glasgow: Scottish Burgh Records Society, 1897).

Morison, W. M., *The Decisions of the Court of Session, From its Institution until the Separation of the Court into Two Divisions in the Year 1808, Digested Under Proper Heads in the Form of a Dictionary* (Edinburgh: Archibald Constable and Company, 1811).

Munro, J. and Fothringham, H. S. (eds) *Edinburgh Goldsmiths' Minutes, 1525–1700* (Edinburgh: Scottish Record Society, 2006).

Munro, J. and Fothringham, H. S. (eds), *Act Book of the Convenery of Deacons of the Trades of Edinburgh 1577–1755*, 2 vols (Edinburgh: Scottish Record Society, 2011).

Ogilvie-Gordon, M. M., *A Handbook of Employments Specially Prepared for the Use of Boys and Girls on Entering the Trades, Industries and Professions* (Aberdeen: The Rosemount Press, 1908).

Paton, H., and Grant, F. J. (eds), *Register of Marriages for the Parish of Edinburgh*, 3 vols: 1595–1800 (Edinburgh: Scottish Record Society, 1906–1922).

Paton, H. M., Imrie, J., and Dunbar, J. G. (eds), *Accounts of the Masters of Works*, 2 vols (Edinburgh: Her Majesty's Stationery Office, 1957 and 1982).

Pennecuik, A., *An Historical Account of the Blue Blanket: or Crafts-Men's Banner* (Edinburgh: David Bower, 1722).

Registrum Magni Sigilli Regum Scotorum (Register of the Great Seal of Scotland), 11 vols, eds J. M. Thomson et al. (Edinburgh, 1882–1984).

Renwick, R., *Extracts from the Records of the Burgh of Peebles, 1652–1714* (Glasgo: Scottish Burgh Record Society, 1910).

Skene, J., *De Verborum Significatione: The Exposition of the Termes and Difficill Wordes . . .* (London: E. G., 1641).

Small, J. (ed.), *The Poems of William Dunbar*, Vol. 2 (Edinburgh: Scottish Text Society, 1893).

Smith, J., *The Hammermen of Edinburgh and Their Altar in St Giles Church* (Edinburgh: William J. Hay, 1906).

Stark, J., *Picture of Edinburgh: Containing a Description of the City and its Environs* (Edinburgh: John Fairbairn, Manners and Miller Etc., 1825).

Stow, J., *A Survey of London Written in the Year 1598* (Stroud: The History Press, 2005).

Thomson, T. (ed.), *Booke of the Universall Kirk: Acts and Proceedings of the General Assembly of the Kirk of Scotland*, Vol. 1 (Edinburgh: Bannatyne Club, 1839).

Thomson, J. M., et al. (eds), *Registrum Magni Sigilli Regum Scotorum* (Register of the Great Seal of Scotland), 11 vols, (Edinburgh, 1882–4).

United Incorporations of St Mary's Chapel, *Laws of the United Incorporations of St Mary's Chapel* (Dingwall: U.I.S.M.C., 2001) [Copy held by the Incorporation].

Vitruvius and Morgan, M. H. (translator), *The Ten Books on Architecture* (New York: Dover, 1960).

Watson, C. B. B. (ed.), *Roll of Edinburgh Burgesses and Guild-Brethren*, 2 vols: 1406–1700 and 1701–1760, (Edinburgh: Scottish Record Society, 1929 and 1930).

Watson, W. E., *The Convenery of the Six Incorporated Trades of Elgin* (Elgin: Privately published; copy held at Moray Local Heritage Centre, 1960).

PUBLISHED SECONDARY SOURCES

Ackerman, J. S., *Palladio* (London: Penguin, 1991).

Allen, A., 'Occupational Mapping of 1635 Edinburgh: An Introduction', in *Proceedings of the Society of Antiquaries of Scotland*, 136 (2006).

Allen, A., *The Locksmith Craft in Early Modern Edinburgh* (Edinburgh: Society of Antiquaries of Scotland, 2007).

Allen, A., 'A Pernicious and Wicked Custom: Corporate Responses to Lock Picking in the Scottish Town, 1488–1788', in *Proceedings of the Society of Antiquaries of Scotland*, 137 (2007).

Allen, A., 'Conquering the Suburbs: Politics and Work in Early Modern Edinburgh', in *Journal of Urban History*, 37:3 (2011).

Allen, A., 'Production and the Missing Artefacts: Candles, Oil and the Material Culture of Urban Lighting in Early Modern Scotland', in *Review of Scottish Culture*, 23 (2011).

Allen, A., 'Finding the Builders: Sources Lost and Extant for Edinburgh's Incorporation of Mary's Chapel', in *Scottish Archives: The Journal of the Scottish Records Association*, 20 (2014).

Allen, A., 'The Missing Records of the Edinburgh Building Trades: Mill's 'Rough Inventory' and the Incorporation of Mary's Chapel', in *Architectural Heritage* (Forthcoming: 2018).

Anonymous, 'Hammermen Trade of Old Aberdeen: Extracts From the Minutes', in *Aberdeen Journal Notes and Queries*, Vol. 2, No. 73 (1909).

Apted, M. R. and Hannabuss, S. (eds), *Painters in Scotland 1301–1700: A Biographical Dictionary* (Edinburgh: Edina Press Ltd, 1978).

Baptie, D., 'Apprentices in the North East of Scotland', in *Scottish Archives: The Journal of the Scottish Records Association*, 9 (2003).

Bain, E., *Merchant and Craft Guilds A History of the Aberdeen Incorporated Trades* (Aberdeen: J. & J. P. Edmond & Spark, 1887).

Bamford, F., *A Dictionary of Edinburgh Furniture Makers* (London: Furniture History Society, 1983).

Baxter, W. T., 'The Account Charge and Discharge', in *The Accounting Historians Journal*, 7:1 (1980).

Ben-Amos, I. K., 'Failure to Become Freemen: Urban Apprentices in Early Modern England' in *Social History*, 16:2 (1991).

Besonen, N., 'Allen Helps Unearth Treasure Trove in Scotland', in *L'Anse Sentinel*, (L'Anse, Michigan, 16 March 2016).

Black, C. F., *Italian Confraternities in the Sixteenth Century* (Cambridge: Cambridge University Press, 1989).

Borsay, P., *The English Urban Renaissance: Culture and Society in the Provincial Town 1660–1770* (Oxford: Clarendon Press, 1991).

Braudel, F. P. and Spooner, F., 'Prices in Europe from 1450 to 1750', in Rich, E. E. and Wilson, C. H. (eds), *The Cambridge Economic History of Europe from the Decline of the Roman Empire, Volume 4: The Economy of Expanding Europe in the Sixteenth and Seventeenth Centuries* (Cambridge: Cambridge University Press, 1967).

Bridenbaugh, C., *The Colonial Craftsman* (Dover: New York, 1990).

Brown, A., *Civic Ceremony and Religion in Medieval Bruges, c.1300–1520* (Cambridge: Cambridge University Press, 2013).

Burnett, C. J., *Officers of Arms in Scotland, 1290–2016* (Edinburgh: Scottish Record Society, 2016).

Cameron, J., *James V: The Personal Rule, 1528–1542* (East Linton: Tuckwell Press, 1998).

Campbell, I., and Stewart, M., 'The Evolution of the Medieval and Renaissance City', in Edwards, B. and Jenkins, P. (eds), *Edinburgh: The Making of a Capital City* (Edinburgh: Edinburgh University Press, 2005).

Campbell, W., *History of the Incorporation of Cordiners in Glasgow* (Glasgow: Robert Anderson, 1883).

Carnie, R. H., 'Perth Booksellers and Bookbinders in the Records of the Wright Calling, 1538–1864', in *The Bibliotheck*, 1:4 (1958).

Carr, H., *The Mason and the Burgh* (London: Quatuor Coronati Lodge, 1954).

Colston, J., *The Guildry of Edinburgh: Is it an Incorporation?* (Edinburgh: Colston and Company, 1887).

Colston, J., *The Incorporated Trades of Edinburgh* (Edinburgh: Colston & Co., 1891).

Colvin, H., *A Biographical Dictionary of British Architects, 1600–1840* (New Haven: Yale University Press, 1995).

Connor, R. D., Simpson, A. D. C. and Morrison-Low, A. D. (eds), *Weights and Measures in Scotland: A European Perspective* (Edinburgh: NMS Enterprises Ltd & Tuckwell Press, 2004).

Cowan, M., *Death, Life and Religious Change in Scottish Towns, c.1350–1560* (Manchester: Manchester University Press, 2012).

Cruikshank, J., *Sketch of the Incorporation of Masons; and the Lodge of Glasgow St John* (Glasgow: W. M. Ferguson, 1879).

Cullen, K. J., Whatley, C. A., and Young, M., 'King William's Ill Years: New Evidence on the Impact of Scarcity and Harvest Failure during the Crisis of the 1690s on Tayside', in *Scottish Historical Review*, 85:220:2 (2006).

Curtis, R., 'Lead', in Jenkins, M. (ed.), *Building Scotland: Celebrating Scotland's Traditional Building Materials* (Edinburgh: John Donald, 2010).

Dalgleish, G. and Maxwell, S., *The Lovable Craft, 1687–1987* (Edinburgh: Royal Museum of Scotland, 1987).

(Dennison) Torrie, E. P., *The Gild Court Book of Dunfermline, 1433–1597* (Edinburgh: Scottish Record Society, 1986).

(Dennison) Torrie, E. P., 'The Guild in Fifteenth-Century Dunfermline', in Lynch, M., Spearman, M. and Stell, G. (eds) *The Scottish Medieval Town* (Edinburgh: John Donald, 1988).

Dennison, E. P., Ditchburn, D., and Lynch, M., (eds), *Aberdeen Before 1800: A New History* (East Linton: Tuckwell Press, 2002).

Dennison, E. P., 'The Myth of the Medieval Burgh Community', in Harris, B. and MacDonald, A. (eds), *Scotland: The Making and Unmaking of the Nation, c.1100–1707*, Vol. 3 (Dundee: Dundee University Press, 2006).

Dennison, E. P., 'Urban Society and Economy', in Harris, B. and MacDonald, A. R. (eds), *Scotland: The Making and Unmaking of the Nation, c.1100–1707*, vol. 2 (Dundee: Dundee University Press, 2006).

Devine, T. M., 'The Merchant Class of the Larger Scottish Towns in the Later Seventeenth and Early Eighteenth Centuries', in Gordon, G., and Dicks, B. (eds), *Scottish Urban History* (Aberdeen: Aberdeen University Press, 1983).

Devine, T. M., *Clanship to Crofter's War: The Social Transformation of the Scottish Highlands* (Manchester: Manchester University Press, 1994).

Devine, T., 'The Modern Economy: Scotland and the Act of Union', in Devine, T., Lee, C. H., and Peden, G. C. (eds), *The Transformation of Scotland: The Economy Since 1700* (Edinburgh: Edinburgh University Press, 2005).

Dickie, W., 'Scottish Burghal Life in the 16th and 17th Centuries, Illustrated by Extracts from Kirkcudbright Records', in *The Transactions and Journal of Proceedings of the Dumfriesshire and Galloway Natural History and Antiquarian Society*, 17 (1906).

Dingwall, H., 'The Importance of Social Factors in Determining the Composition of the Town Councils in Edinburgh 1550–1650', in *Scottish Historical Review*, 65:1 (1986).

Dingwall, H. M., *Late Seventeenth-Century Edinburgh: A Demographic Study* (Aldershot: Scolar Press, 1994).

Dolan, C., 'The Artisans of Aix-en-Provence in the Sixteenth-Century: A Micro-Analysis of Social Relationships', in Benedict, P. (ed.), *Cities and Social Change in Early Modern France* (Routledge: London, 1992).

Dunbar, J. G., *The Stirling Heads* (Edinburgh: Her Majesty's Stationery Office, 1975).

Durkan, J., 'Notes on Glasgow Cathedral', in *The Innes Review*, 21:1 (1970).

Durkan, J. and Reid-Baxter, J. (eds), *Scottish Schools and Schoolmasters, 1560–1633* (Woodbridge: Scottish History Society, 2013).

Edgren, L., 'Craftsmen in the Political and Symbolic Order: The Case of Eighteenth-Century Malmö', in Crossick, G. (ed.), *The Artisan and the European Town, 1500–1900* (Aldershot: Scolar Press, 1997).

Edwards, B. and Jenkins, P. (eds), *Edinburgh: The Making of a Capital City* (Edinburgh: Edinburgh University Press, 2005).

Epstein, S. A., *Wage Labor and Guilds in Medieval Europe* (Chapel Hill: University of North Carolina Press, 1991).

Ewen, E. and Nugent, J. (eds), *Finding the Family in Medieval and Early Modern Scotland* (Aldershot: Ashgate, 2008).

Falconer, J. R. D., 'A Family Affair: Households, Misbehaving and the Community in Sixteenth-Century Aberdeen', in Ewen, E. and Nugent, J. (eds), *Finding the Family in Medieval and Early Modern Scotland* (Aldershot: Ashgate, 2008).

Farr, J. R., *Hands of Honor: Artisans and Their World in Dijon, 1550–1650* (Ithaca: Cornell University Press, 1988).

Farr, J. R., *Artisans in Europe, 1300–1914* (Cambridge: Cambridge University Press, 2000).

Fischer, D. H., *The Great Wave: Price Revolutions and the Rhythm of History* (Oxford: Oxford University Press, 1996).

Fitch, C., and Davis, D. H., *The History of the Worshipful Company of Pattenmakers of the City of London* (London: Worshipful Company of Pattenmakers, 1962).

Fitzsimmons, M. P., *From Artisan to Worker: Guilds, the French State, and the Organization of Labour, 1776–1821* (Cambridge: Cambridge University Press, 2010).

Flandrin, J., *Families in Former Times: Kinship, Household and Sexuality* (Cambridge: Cambridge University Press, 1979).

Fleet, C., Wilkes, M. & Withers, C., *Scotland: Mapping the Nation* (Edinburgh: Birlinn, 2013).

Fleet, C. and MacCannell, D., *Edinburgh: Mapping the City* (Edinburgh: Birlinn, 2014).

Fothringham, H. S., *Heraldry of the Incorporated Trades of Edinburgh* (Edinburgh: Convenery of the Trades of Edinburgh, 2013).

Fraser, W. H., *Conflict and Class: Scottish Workers, 1700–1838* (Edinburgh: John Donald, 1988).

Fraser, W. H., *A History of British Trade Unionism 1700–1998* (Basingstoke: Macmillan, 1999).

Friedrichs, C. R., *Urban Society in an Age of War: Nördlingen, 1580–1720* (Princeton: Princeton University Press, 1979).

Gemmill, E. and Mayhew, N., *Changing Values in Medieval Scotland: A Study of Prices, Money, and Weights and Measures* (Cambridge: Cambridge University Press, 2006).

Gibson, A. J. S. and Smout, T. C., *Prices, Food and Wages in Scotland, 1550–1780* (Cambridge: Cambridge University Press, 1995).

Gillespie, R., 'Landlords and Merchants: Belfast 1600–1750', in Clarke, H. B., (ed.) *Irish Cities* (Dublin: Mercier Press, 1995).

Gourlay, G., *Anstruther: Or Illustrations of Scottish Burgh Life* (Anstruther: George Gourlay, 1888).

Grant, F. J., *Court of the Lord Lyon: List of His Majesty's Officers of Arms and Other Officials With Genealogical Notes, 1318–1945* (Edinburgh: Scottish Record Society, 1945).

Grant, I. F., *The Social and Economic Development of Scotland Before 1603* (Edinburgh: Oliver and Boyd, 1930).

Gray, I., *A Guide to Dean of Guild Court Records* (Glasgow: University of Glasgow, 1994).

Gray, R. Q., *The Labour Aristocracy in Victorian Edinburgh* (Oxford: Clarendon Press, 1976).

Guidicini, G., 'Municipal Perspective, Royal Expectations, and the Use of Public Space: The Case of the West Port, Edinburgh, 1503–1633', in *Architectural Heritage*, 22 (2011).

Habib, V., 'Eighteenth-Century Upholsterers in the Edinburgh Old Town', in *Scottish Archives: The Journal of the Scottish Records Association*, 11 (2005).

Hanawalt, B. A. (ed.), *Women and Work in Preindustrial Europe* (Bloomington: Indiana University Press, 1986).

Harris, E., *British Architectural Books and Writers, 1556–1785* (Cambridge: Cambridge University Press, 1990).

Hay, G., *History of Arbroath to the Present Time, With Notices of the Civil and Ecclesiastical Affairs* (Arbroath: Thomas Buncle, 1876).

Hay, G., 'The Late Medieval Development of the High Kirk of St Giles, Edinburgh', in *Proceedings of the Society of Antiquaries of Scotland*, 107 (1975–6).

Haythornthwaite, J. A., Wilson, N. C., and Batho, V. A., *Scotland in the Nineteenth Century: An Analytical Bibliography of Material Relating to Scotland in Parliamentary Papers, 1800–1900* (Aldershot: Scolar Press, 1993).

Historischen Museum Regensburg, *Regensburg: Wasser und Stadt* (Regensburg: Museen der Stadt Regensburg, 1997).

Houston, R. A., *Scottish Literacy and the Scottish Identity: Illiteracy and Society in Scotland and Northern England, 1600–1800* (Cambridge: Cambridge University Press, 2002).

Jackson, S., 'Edinburgh Cabinet Makers' Wage Agreements and Wage Disputes, 1805 to 1826', in *Scottish Archives: The Journal of the Scottish Records Association*, 11 (2005).

Jackson, S., 'Kirk Furnishings: The Liturgical Material Culture of the Scottish Reformation', in *Regional Furniture: The Journal of the Regional Furniture Society*, 21 (2007).

Jenkins, M. (ed.), *Building Scotland: Celebrating Scotland's Traditional Building Materials* (Edinburgh: John Donald, 2010).

Johnston, T., *The History of the Working Classes in Scotland* (East Ardsley: EP Publishing Ltd, 1974).

Jupp, E. B., *An Historical Account of the Worshipful Company of Carpenters fo the City of London Compiled Chiefly from Records in their Possession* (London: William Pickering, 1848).

Kirk, J., 'Royal and Lay Patronage in the Jacobean Kirk, 1572–1600', in Macdougall, N. (ed.), *Church, Politics and Society: Scotland, 1408–1929* (Edinburgh: John Donald, 1983).

Knoop, D. and Jones, G. P., *The Scottish Mason and the Mason Word* (Manchester: Manchester University Press, 1939).

Laing, D., 'Note respecting the Royal Exchange, Edinburgh, and the Original List of Subscribers in 1752', in *Proceedings of the Society of Antiquaries of Scotland*, 4 (1860–2).

Lambert, J. M., *Two Thousand Years of Gild Life* (Hull: A. Brown & Sons, 1891).

Lamond, R., 'The Scottish Craft Gild as a Religious Fraternity', in *The Scottish Historical Review*, 16:63 (1919).

Law, A., *Education in Edinburgh in the Eighteenth Century* (London: University of London Press, 1965).

Lewis, A., *The Builders of Edinburgh New Town, 1767–1795* (Reading: Spire Books Ltd, 2014).

Lewis, D., *Edinburgh Water Supply A Sketch of its History Past and Present* (Edinburgh, 1908).

Lillehammer, A., 'The Scottish-Norwegian Timber Trade in the Stavanger Area in the Sixteenth and Seventeenth Centuries', in Smout, T. C. (ed.), *Scotland and Europe, 1200–1850* (Edinburgh: John Donald, 1986).

Lockhart, B. R., *Jinglin' Geordie's Legacy: A History of George Heriot's Hospital and School* (Edinburgh: John Donald, 2009).

Lorvik, M., 'Mutual Intelligibility of Timber Trade Terminology in the North Sea Countries During the Time of the "Scottish Trade"', in *Nordic Journal of English Studies* 2:2 (2003).

Lucas, A. T., 'Making Wooden Sieves', in *The Journal of the Royal Society of Antiquaries of Ireland*, 81:2 (1951).

Lucas, A. T., 'Further Notes on Making Wooden Sieves', in *The Journal of the Royal Society of Antiquaries of Ireland*, 84:1 (1954).

Lynch, M., 'Whatever Happened to the Medieval Burgh? Some Guidelines for Sixteenth and Seventeenth Century Historians', in *Scottish Economic & Social History*, 4:1 (1978).

Lynch, M., *Edinburgh and the Reformation* (Edinburgh: Edinburgh University Press, 1981).

Lynch, M., 'Social and Economic Structure of the Larger Towns, 1450–1600', in Lynch, M., Spearman, M. and Stell, G. (eds), *The Scottish Medieval Town* (Edinburgh: John Donald, 1988).

Lynch, M., 'Towns and Townspeople in Fifteenth-Century Scotland', in Thomson, A. F. (ed.), *Towns and Townspeople in the Fifteenth Century* (Gloucester: Alan Sutton, 1988).

Lynch, M., 'Continuity and Change in Urban Society, 1500–1700', in Houston, R. A., and Whyte, I. D. (eds), *Scottish Society 1500–1800* (Cambridge: Cambridge University Press, 1989).

Lynch, M., *Scotland: A New History* (London: Pimlico, 2000).

Lythe, S. G. E., *The Economy of Scotland in its European Setting, 1550–1625* (Edinburgh: Oliver and Boyd, 1960).

MacCulloch, D., *Reformation: Europe's House Divided, 1490–1700* (London: Penguin, 2004).

MacGibbon, D. and Ross, T., *The Ecclesiastical Architecture of Scotland*, 3 vols (Edinburgh: David Douglas, 1896–7).

Mackenzie, W. M., *The Scottish Burghs* (Edinburgh: Oliver and Boyd, 1949).

Macmillan, D., *Scottish Art, 1460–1990* (Edinburgh: Mainstream Publishing, 1990).

Mair, C., *History of the Incorporation of Coopers of Glasgow* (Glasgow: Angels' Share, 2004).

Marshall, J. S., *Old Leith at Work* (Edinburgh: Edina Press, 1977).

Marshall, R., *Ruin and Restoration: St Mary's Church, Haddington* (Haddington: East Lothian Council Library Service, 2001).

Marwick, J. D., 'The Municipal Institutions of Scotland: A Historical Survey (Concluded)', in *Scottish Historical Review*, 1:3 (1904).

Marwick, J. D., *Edinburgh Guilds and Crafts* (Edinburgh: Scottish Burgh Record Society, 1909).

McNeill, P. G. B. & MacQueen, H. L. (eds.), *Atlas of Scottish History to 1707* (Edinburgh: The Scottish Medievalists, 1996).

McRoberts, D., 'Notes on Scoto-Flemish Artistic Contacts', in *Innes Review*, 10 (1959).

M'Culloch, W. T., 'Note Relating to "Haddo's Hole," in St Giles's Church, Edinburgh', in *Proceedings of the Society of Antiquaries of Scotland*, 4 (1860–2).

Mill, A. J., *Mediaeval Plays in Scotland* (Edinburgh: William Blackwood & Sons Ltd, 1927).

Mill, A. J., 'The Perth Hammermen's Play: A Scottish Garden of Eden', in *The Scottish Historical Review*, 49:148:2 (1970).

Mitchison, R., *The Old Poor Law in Scotland: The Experience of Poverty, 1574–1845* (Edinburgh: Edinburgh University Press, 2000).

Moffat, A., *Kelsae: A History of Kelso from Earliest Times* (Edinburgh: Birlinn, 2006).

Montias, J. M., *Artists and Artisans in Delft: A Socio-Economic Study of the Seventeenth Century* (Princeton: Princeton University Press, 1982).

Mowat, S., *The Port of Leith: Its History and its People* (Edinburgh: John Donald, 1994).

Murdoch, R., 'Glass', in Jenkins, M. (ed.), *Building Scotland: Celebrating Scotland's Traditional Building Materials* (Edinburgh: John Donald, 2010).

Murray, A. L., 'Financing the Royal Household: James V and his Comptrollers, 1513–43', in Cowan, I. B. and Shaw, D. (eds), *The Renaissance and Reformation in Scotland: Essays in Honour of Gordon Donaldson* (Edinburgh: Scottish Academic Press, 1983).

Mylne, R. S., *The Master Masons to the Crown of Scotland and their Works* (Edinburgh: Scott & Ferguson and Burness & Company, 1893).

Nenadic, S., 'Architect Builders in London and Edinburgh, c.1750–1800, and the Market for Expertise', in *Historical Journal*, 55:3 (2012).

Newland, K., 'The Acquisition and Use of Norwegian Timber in Seventeenth-Century Scotland', in *Vernacular Architecture*, 42 (2011).

O'Day, R., *The Professions in Early Modern England, 1450–1800* (Harlow: Longman, 2000).

Perry, D., 'Inverness: An Historical and Archaeological Review', in *The Proceedings of the Society of Antiquaries of Scotland*, 128 (1998).

Peterson, C. E. (ed.), *The Rules of Work of the Carpenters' Company of the City and County of Philadelphia 1786* (Mendham, NJ: Astragal Press, 1992).

Phelps Brown, E. H. and Hopkins, S. V., 'Seven Centuries of Building Wages', reprinted from *Economica* 22:87 (1955) in Carus-Wilson, E. M. (ed.), *Essays in Economic History*, vol. 2 (London: Edward Arnold Ltd, 1966).

Phelps Brown, E. H. and Hopkins, S. V., 'Seven Centuries of the Prices of Consumables, Compared with Builders' Wage-Rates', in Carus-Wilson, E. M. (ed.), *Essays in Economic History*, vol. 2 (London: Edward Arnold Ltd, 1966).

Prak, M., Lis, C., Lucassen, J., and Soly, H. (eds), *Craft Guilds in the Early Modern Low Countries* (Aldershot: Ashgate, 2006).

Price, R., *Masters, Unions and Men: Work Control in Building and the Rise of Labour, 1830–1914* (Cambridge: Cambridge University Press, 1980).

Pryke, S., 'Pattern Furniture and Estate Wrights in Eighteenth-Century Scotland', in *Furniture History*, 30 (1994).

Ritchie, P. E., *Mary of Guise in Scotland, 1548–1560* (East Linton: Tuckwell Press, 2002).

Rappaport, S., *Worlds Within Worlds: Structures of Life in Sixteenth-Century London* (Cambridge: Cambridge University Press, 2002).

Rodger, R., 'The Evolution of Scottish Town Planning', in Gordon, G. and Dicks, B., *Scottish Urban History* (Aberdeen: Aberdeen University Press, 1983).

Rodger, R., 'Structural Instability in the Scottish Building Industry 1820–80', in *Construction History*, 2 (1986).

Rodger, R., *Housing in Urban Britain, 1780–1914* (London: Macmillan, 1989).

Rodger, R., *The Transformation of Edinburgh: Land, Property and Trust in the Nineteenth Century* (Cambridge: Cambridge University Press, 2004).

Rodger, R., *Edinburgh's Colonies: Housing the Workers* (Glendaruel: Argyll Publishing, 2011).

Salzman, L. F., *Building in England Down to 1540: A Documentary History* (Oxford: Clarendon Press, 1997).

Sanderson, M. H. B., *A Kindly Place? Living in Sixteenth-Century Scotland* (East Linton: Tuckwell Press, 2002).

Smith, A. M., *The Three United Trades of Dundee: Masons, Wrights & Slaters* (Dundee: Abertay Historical Society, 1987).

Smith, A. M., *The Nine Trades of Dundee* (Dundee: Abertay Historical Society, 1995).

Smith, J., *The Hammermen of Edinburgh and Their Altar in St Giles Church* (Edinburgh: William J. Hay, 1906).

Smith, T. B., 'Master and Servant', in Lord Normand, et al., *An Introduction to Scottish Legal History* (Edinburgh: The Stair Society, 1958).

Smout, T. C., MacDonald, A. R., and Watson, F., *A History of the Native Woodlands of Scotland, 1500–1920* (Edinburgh: Edinburgh University Press, 2005).

Stevenson, D., *The First Freemasons: Scotland's Early Lodges and their Members* (Aberdeen: Aberdeen University Press, 1989).

Stevenson, D., *The Origins of Freemasonry* (Cambridge: Cambridge University Press, 2005).

Stevenson, D., 'Apprenticeship: Scottish Stonemasons' Indentures, 1573–1740', in *Scottish Archives: The Journal of the Scottish Records Association*, 17 (2011).

Stewart, L. A. M., *Urban Politics and the British Civil Wars: Edinburgh, 1617–53* (Leiden: Brill, 2006).

Stone, L., *The Family, Sex and Marriage in England, 1500–1800* (London: Penguin, 1990).

Sturt, G. *The Wheelwright's Shop* (Cambridge: Cambridge University Press, 1958).

Swanson, H., *Building Craftsmen in Late Medieval York* (York: Borthwick Papers, 1983).

Tarule, R., *The Artisan of Ipswich: Craftsmanship and Community in Colonial New England* (Baltimore: Johns Hopkins University Press, 2004).

Terpstra, N., *The Politics of Ritual Kinship: Confraternities and Social Order in Early Modern Italy* (Cambridge: Cambridge University Press, 2000).

Thomson, D., *The Weavers' Craft: Being a History of the Weavers' Incorporation of Dunfermline* (Paisley: Alexander Gardner, 1903).

Tittler, R., *Portraits, Painters, and Publics in Provincial England, 1540–1640* (Oxford: Oxford University Press, 2012).

Todd, M., *The Culture of Protestantism in Early Modern Scotland* (New Haven: Yale University Press, 2002).

Torrie (Dennison), E. P., *The Gild Court Book of Dunfermline, 1433–1597* (Edinburgh: Scottish Record Society, 1986).

Torrie (Dennison), E. P., 'The Guild in Fifteenth-Century Dunfermline', in Lynch, M., Spearman, M. and Stell, G. (eds) *The Scottish Medieval Town* (Edinburgh: John Donald, 1988).

Towill, E. S., 'The Minutes of the Trades Maiden Hospital', in *The Book of the Old Edinburgh Club*, 28 (1953).

Trout, A., *City of the Seine: Paris in the Time of Richelieu and Louis XLV, 1614–1715* (New York: St Martin's Press, 1996).

Turnbull, J., *The Scottish Glass Industry, 1610–1750: 'To Serve the Whole Nation with Glass'* (Edinburgh: Society of Antiquaries of Scotland, 2001).

Unwin, G., *The Gilds & Companies of London* (London: George Allen & Unwin Ltd, 1938).

Van der Sterre, G., *Four Centuries of Dutch Planes and Planemakers* (Leiden: Primavera Press, 2001).

Wahrman, D., *Mr. Collier's Letter Racks: A Tale of Art & Illusion at the Threshold of the Modern Information Age* (Oxford: Oxford University Press, 2012).

Walton, K. M., 'The Worshipful Company of Upholders of the City of London', in *Furniture History*, 9 (1973).

Warden, A. J., *Burgh Laws of Dundee* (London: Longmans, Green & Co., 1872).

Warrack, J., *Domestic Life in Scotland, 1488–1688: A Sketch of the Development of Furniture and Household Usage (Rhind Lectures in Archaeology, 1919–20)* (New York: E. P. Dutton and Company, 1921).

Watt, D., *The Price of Scotland: Darien, Union and the Wealth of Nations* (Edinburgh: Luath Press Limited, 2007).

Weaver, L., 'Some Architectural Leadwork. Article VII – Scottish Lead Spires', in *The Burlington Magazine for Connoisseurs*, 9:41 (August 1906).

Webb, J. J., *The Guilds of Dublin* (London: Kennikat Press, 1970).

Whitelaw, C. E., *Scottish Arms Makers* (London: Arms and Armour Press, 1977).

Wilson, D., *Memorials of Edinburgh in the Olden Time*, vol. 2 (Edinburgh: Adam and Charles Black, 1891).

Wood, M., 'The Neighbourhood Book', in *The Book of the Old Edinburgh Club*, 23 (1940).

Woodward, D., 'Wage Rates and Living Standards in Pre-Industrial England', in *Past & Present*, 91 (1981).

Woodward, D., *Men at Work: Labourers and Building Craftsmen in the Towns of Northern England, 1450–1750* (Cambridge: Cambridge University Press, 2002).

UNPUBLISHED SECONDARY SOURCES

Allen, A., 'Incorporation of Mary's Chapel Project: Report & Catalogue of Sources Extant' (Unpublished, 2014). Copies held by ECA, NLS and NRS.

Fothringham, H. S., 'The Trades Maiden Hospital of Edinburgh' (Edinburgh: Unpublished Booklet, 2013).

Unpublished PhD Thesis

Pryke, S., 'The Eighteenth Century Furniture Trade in Edinburgh: A Study Based on Documentary Sources' (University of St Andrews PhD thesis, 1995).

Index of Subjects

Index of Places